EARLY PRAISE

"Filled with rich theoretical insights and fascinating on-the-ground stories, this wonderfully-written and absorbing book tells the story of how activists in mainland China, Taiwan, and Hong Kong think and strategize—sometimes opportunistically and at other times with deliberate intent—to advance democracy in their respective societies. The result is a compelling analysis of how and why some efforts have succeeded while others have failed, and the lessons future democracy activists should take away from both."

Elizabeth Economy, C. V. Starr Senior Fellow and Director for Asia Studies at the Council on Foreign Relations and Distinguished Visiting Fellow at Stanford University's Hoover Institution

"Andreas Fulda's book is a powerful longitudinal comparison of three Chinese entities that live under very different political systems, mainland China, Taiwan and Hong Kong, and a convincing advocacy for democratization. Fulda well understands the magnitude of the obstacles that so far have prevented the People's Republic from democratizing: the Chinese Communist Party's Soviet or Leninist culture, the economic privileges accumulated by the Party's Nomenklatura and its inclination to rule by bribery and by fear in order to protect them. Nonetheless, Taiwan and Hong Kong's own trajectories as well as the maturation of mainland China's democratic movement over the years have demonstrated that future political change is possible in the People's Republic as well."

Jean-Pierre Cabestan, Professor of Political Science, Hong Kong Baptist University

"An informed and vivid study that tackles an important political issue of our time: the specter of China's sharp power. Dr. Fulda's monograph presents a comparative and historically grounded analysis of the trends and repercussions of democracy movements in China and its periphery, which does not only enhance our understanding of the nexus between mass protests and authoritarian resilience, but more specifically, offers a heuristic device to unpack the operations of the party-state's united front against dissent."

Edmund Cheng, Deputy Director, Comparative Governance and Public Policy Research Centre, Hong Kong Baptist University

"This is an inspiring and timely book. Andreas Fulda makes a crucial point which cannot be reiterated enough: as researchers, we must give legitimacy to all potential outcomes for China's future. This process starts with acknowledging that the Chinese Communist Party's power is not inevitable. Research on Chinese politics often operates on the assumptions that the CCP will organically change itself and that democracy advocates are somehow not 'normal' people and will not be effective. Fulda suggests otherwise. By applying theories of and for political change to case studies in China, Hong Kong and Taiwan, he offers an innovative way for filling this major gap in existing literature. Fulda sets a standard that breaks the confines of existing analytical approaches. It is a must-read contribution."

Samantha Hoffman, Resident Fellow at the
Australian Strategic Policy Institute

"In this fresh and courageous book, Fulda pulls at the roots of his subject—democracy in China, Hong Kong and Taiwan—like a gardener tackling a by-now gnarly field, and finds hope, even a plan of action: Fill the gap between theory and practice by learning from Chinese democracy practitioners, plant into democracy theory ideas of change drawn from development studies, cultivate a humanizing pedagogy that rejects domination by propaganda and power, and move away from the internalized compliance with Communist Party discourse that is by now widespread in western academia. An inspiring read packed with ideas."

Didi Kirsten Tatlow, former MERICS Visiting Academic Fellow. Didi
reported from China for her hometown newspaper, the South China Morning
Post *of Hong Kong, the* International Herald Tribune *(now the global edition*
of The New York Times*) and* The New York Times*, from 2003 to 2017*

"Most of the recent political science debate on China has been centered on the regime, its governance system and its assumed stability, perfectness, fragility or decay. The results are relevant but necessarily limited as they do not take into account systematically the strategic interaction of the regime with a variety of democratizing movements, which are often hidden because of inherent regime secrecy and information blockades, officially dictated framing and sanctioned taboos. Andreas Fulda, in his role as a social scientist and civil society practitioner, takes a fresh and alternative look from the perspective of the democratizing movements at the comparative political development of Mainland China, Taiwan and Hong Kong.

His actor-centric approach reveals through twelve democratizing episodes as case studies the asynchronous processes of the gradual construction of democracy movements and democracy in the states of Greater China. It makes visible and intelligible that the democracy movements of Mainland China are vitally alive, developing, learning their lessons and preparing—by strategic decentralization, multiplication of arenas and combining different strategies and actors (anti-establishment, trans-establishment and establishment reformers)—the next steps of peaceful democracy advocacy aiming at a gradual democratic transformation.

As a dialogue between theory and practice, external observer assessment and actor perspective, it is a fundamental contribution to the story of political development of Reform China framed by a democratic counter-narrative based on the structural trends and the experiences, learning processes and the horizons of expectation of the democracy movements. The implicit subtext of the actors and the author alike are the urgency, possibility and strategic lessons to be drawn of a social liberalism protecting Chinese citizens from fear of many kinds of political and social injustice. Everybody, social scientist or democratic activist, who is concerned about the shift to sharp authoritarianism in China and its threatening global impact and is interested in democratic alternatives made in China, should read the book. His second decisive contribution is to highlight the relevance of a civic, civil, democratic nationalism and of democratic citizen diplomacy for a sustainable peace settlement between the states of the Greater China region—in contrast to a narrow, ethnic nationalism which is present on all three sides of the Greater China arena which is identified by the author as a threat and a case of pathological learning."

Horst Fabian, Civil Society Ambassador Europe—China and
independent researcher focusing on the linkages between
China / Cuba, democratization and sustainable development

"Andreas Fulda shows that even the democracy movements in the Chinese region are not exempt from the global trend towards nationalism. His critical and judicious study is a plea to combine the struggle for rights and freedom with an effort to build peace in the region."

Mark Siemons, editor of the German newspaper Frankfurter
Allgemeine Zeitung *and author of the book*
Die chinesische Verunsicherung *(Hanser, 2017), in which he*
reflects on his insights as long-term cultural correspondent in Beijing

"This is a highly engaged and engaging consideration of the continuing struggle for democracy in Mainland China, Taiwan and Hong Kong. Dr. Fulda ventures beyond purely scholarly curiosity to offer practitioners fresh and stimulating analysis of past achievements and failures. The book offers some encouragement —and words of warning—to readers looking for a roadmap to democratic change in China."

Nicola Macbean, The Rights Practice

THE STRUGGLE FOR DEMOCRACY IN MAINLAND CHINA, TAIWAN AND HONG KONG

The key question at the heart of this book is to what extent political activists in mainland China, Taiwan and Hong Kong have made progress in their quest to liberalise and democratise their respective polities. Taking a long historical perspective, the book compares and contrasts the political development trajectory in the three regions from the early 1970s—from the election-driven liberalisation in Taiwan from 1969, the Democracy Wall Movement in mainland China in 1978, and the top-down political reforms of Governor Patten in Hong Kong after 1992—until the present day. More specifically, it sets out the different strategies and tactics political activists have taken, assesses the lessons activists have learned from both successes and failures and considers how these experiences have informed their struggles for democracy. Importantly, the book demonstrates that at the same time, throughout the period and earlier, the Chinese Communist Party has been making use of "sharp power"—penetrating the political and information environments in Western democracies to manipulate debate and suppress dissenters living both inside and outside China—in order to strengthen its domestic position. The book discusses the nature of this sharp power, explores the rise of the security state within mainland China and examines the effectiveness of the approach, arguing that in Taiwan and Hong Kong the approach has been counter-productive, with civil society, campaigns for greater democracy and the flourishing of religion in part stimulated by the Chinese Communist Party's sharp power practices.

Andreas Fulda is Assistant Professor in the School of Politics and International Relations, University of Nottingham.

CHINA POLICY SERIES

Series Editor: Zheng Yongnian, East Asian Institute, National University of Singapore

For more information about this series, please visit https://www.routledge.com/China-Policy-Series/book-series/SECPS

THE STRUGGLE FOR DEMOCRACY IN MAINLAND CHINA, TAIWAN AND HONG KONG

Sharp Power and its Discontents

Andreas Fulda

Routledge
Taylor & Francis Group

LONDON AND NEW YORK

First published 2020
by Routledge
2 Park Square, Milton Park, Abingdon, Oxon OX14 4RN

and by Routledge
52 Vanderbilt Avenue, New York, NY 10017

Routledge is an imprint of the Taylor & Francis Group, an informa business

© 2020 Andreas Fulda

British Library Cataloguing in Publication Data
A catalogue record for this book is available from the British Library

Library of Congress Cataloging-in-Publication Data
A catalog record has been requested for this book

ISBN: 978-1-138-32834-1 (hbk)
ISBN: 978-0-367-33490-1 (pbk)
ISBN: 978-0-429-44872-0 (ebk)

Typeset in Times New Roman
by Taylor & Francis Books

CONTENTS

ILLUSTRATIONS

Figures

Tables

PREFACE

This book is the culmination of a long journey, which began 30 years ago in the summer of 1989. After living in Cairo for three years our family had just moved to Geneva. My father, a German career diplomat, was going to work on human rights issues at the Permanent Mission of the Federal Republic of Germany to the Office of the United Nations. Whilst waiting for our shipping containers to arrive from Egypt we stayed in a temporary serviced apartment. Apart from attending secondary school and learning French this left me with plenty of time on my hands. Two past-times helped me transition into my new life in Switzerland. Me and my three brothers would frequently practise tennis by hitting balls against a wall at a nearby courtyard. In the evenings we would listen to French-language news broadcasts, the only time my parents would allow us to watch TV for longer periods of time.

While I struggled to understand French TV commentators, I vividly recall the news broadcast of People's Liberation Army soldiers pouring into Tiananmen square on the night of 4 June 1989. Just a day after the brutal suppression of mainland China's anti-corruption and pro-democracy movement, a very different kind of drama caught my attention, this time playing out on the tennis courts of the French Open. On 5 June 1989, Michael Chang, a 17-year-old American of Taiwanese descent, defeated then number one tennis player Ivan Lendl in the quarter final. These two unrelated events, in such quick succession, gave me a first taste of Asia, a region and people which I previously had not paid any attention to. Seeing the TV images of the military crackdown on student protesters in Beijing was gut-wrenching. Watching the quarter final between Michael Chang and Ivan Lendl, on the other hand, was exhilarating. Against the tall and towering figure of Lendl the much shorter Chang engaged in a proverbial struggle between David and Goliath. Michael Chang managed to pull off one of tennis history's biggest upsets and later went on to win the 1989 French Open finals. When watching these events on TV I picked up two greatly contradictory messages: the military crackdown in mainland China as well as the broad smile of young Michael Chang proudly holding up his French Open trophy. These contrasting images evoked two diametrically opposed emotional reactions: a disgust for the arbitrariness of authoritarian rule and an admiration for the tenacity and fighting spirit of a young Asian-American teenager. Little did I know at the age of 12 that these two opposite ends on a spectrum of emotional reactions would continue to define my later China engagement.

In 1996 I decided to study Mandarin Chinese. I had thought about learning Japanese, but when I asked my brother which Asian language he would suggest he advised me to learn Chinese instead. Although I initially felt intimidated by the complexity of Chinese characters I thought that learning a particularly difficult language would be a good challenge to take on. In my first year of undergraduate studies at the University of Cologne in 1996–7 I also instinctively knew that my understanding of mainland China would be incomplete if I did not develop a firm grasp of how the Chinese Communist Party governs the country. This is why I chose to write my very first essay assignments about Mao Zedong's talks in Yan'an in the 1940s and the radical phase of the Cultural Revolution in the mid-1960s. These early studies confirmed my initial impression of mainland China's authoritarian political system being rather cruel and arbitrary.

My first year of undergraduate studies also coincided with the crisis in the Taiwan Straits. News reports about life-fire missile tests by the People's Liberation Army aimed at intimidating the Taiwanese electorate ahead of the first free and fair presidential election struck a chord with me. A small democratic island state was being bullied by its much bigger neighbour, another David versus Goliath situation. I thus decided to go to Taiwan to improve my Mandarin Chinese skills. From 1998 to 1999 I spent one year in Taipei, which honed my interest in the island's political development. Enthusiastic to further my growing understanding of Taiwan, I became part of the first Taiwan studies cohort at the School of Oriental and African Studies in London, where I pursued an MA in Chinese Studies in 2000–1. Originating out of my postgraduate studies I published my first two peer-reviewed journal articles in 2002, one on Taiwan's democratisation and the second on the politics of factionalism in Taiwan's Democratic Progressive Party.

Upon graduating from the School of Oriental and African Studies I interned at the German Council for Foreign Relations in Berlin for three months. This is where I would meet my later PhD supervisor, Professor Eberhard Sandschneider. I subsequently decided to do two things in parallel: to gain some first-hand experience of mainland China by working for GTZ, Germany's bilateral development agency with operations in mainland China, and to simultaneously write a PhD thesis about the challenge of providing political development aid to China. During my field work I soon realised that in the process of international cooperation, German development agencies had essentially been co-opted by their mainland Chinese counterparts. My PhD thesis thus turned into an insider's critique of a dysfunctional system of Sino-German development cooperation. It was published as a German-language monograph with VS Verlag fuer Sozialwissenschaften (now owned by Springer) in 2009.

Working for German and Chinese development agencies between 2003 and 2007 allowed me to observe a donor-recipient landscape in transition. My practical China engagement offered me first-hand experience in the field of civil society building. In my PhD I had argued for greater civil society inclusion in state-to-state development cooperation. In order to put insight into practice I decided to raise funds for civil society-related projects. I subsequently coordinated the capacity-building project Participatory Urban Governance Programme for Migrant Integration, which was funded by the United States State Department and implemented jointly by the American Bar Association and the China Association for NGO Cooperation (CANGO). From 2004 until 2007 I worked as an integrated expert at CANGO, supported by the German Center for International Migration and Development.

Being embedded in a Chinese government-organised non-governmental organisation for three years was an eye opener. Working with a Chinese line manager and Chinese co-workers allowed me to see the world from a mainland Chinese perspective. During my time at CANGO I also worked closely with its member organisation Shining Stone Community Action (SSCA), a political development non-governmental organisation committed to promoting inclusive and participatory urban governance in mainland China. As an active supporter of SSCA's growth and maturation and with the help of American and European funders we jointly implemented various capacity-building initiatives aimed at enhancing governance innovation at the local level. Between 2005 and 2010 we introduced participatory big group moderation techniques with imaginative titles such as Future Search Conference, Open Space and Appreciative Inquiry, which enabled Chinese environmental and social development non-governmental organisations to develop cooperative relationships with the party-state and to include a wider range of stakeholders in their grassroots work. By organising capacity-building workshops at the national level as well as local pilots at the community level I became a participant observer of political reform processes. During countless meetings with local government officials, civil society practitioners and action-oriented Chinese academics, I observed how reform-minded individuals managed to find common ground. Since I did not want to create problems for these progressive and very open-minded individuals I decided against quoting their often highly thought-provoking statements in my academic work. Yet these wide-ranging conversations, conducted exclusively in Mandarin Chinese and often over lengthy lunch or dinner meetings (affectionately called *chifanhui* by my Chinese colleagues), greatly expanded my knowledge and understanding of mainland China's state and society.

After relocating to Europe in 2007 I continued my practical engagement with China's organised society by frequently returning to mainland China for project work. As a consultant to the American Bar Association I designed and helped implement the Social Policy Advocacy Coalition for Healthy and Sustainable Communities, a capacity-building project funded by the Rockefeller Brothers Fund. This initiative aimed to enhance the policy advocacy capabilities of Chinese environmental organisations. I was a co-author of the resulting *Policy Advocacy Manual on Environment and Health for NPOs*, a Chinese-language monograph which I published together with Huang Haoming and Zhao Daxing in 2013.

I subsequently also raised funds from the European Commission and British Foreign and Commonwealth Office for the European Union-China Civil Society Dialogue on Participatory Public Policy, which I managed from 2011 until 2014. In the context of this programme me and my European and Chinese cooperation partners organised eight civil society dialogues, held in Ningbo, Guangzhou, Beijing and Bonn. From 2011 until 2014 800 participants discussed issues ranging from climate change, environmental health, labour relations, child welfare, social entrepreneurship, information disclosure and government procurement of civil society organisation services to disability rights. In the context of this dialogue series we prototyped the communication and collaboration conference model, which maintains "the strengths and comfort of a speaker-led format while providing an interactive and participatory process that is designed to enhance relationships, deepen understanding of the topics, and create actionable projects".[1] The three-day dialogues enabled Chinese civil society practitioners as well as European academics and practitioners from the United Kingdom, Germany, Belgium, France, Italy, Greece, Estonia, Poland, Romania and Latvia to engage in constructive discussions with Chinese academics and policy makers from the central, provincial and municipal levels. As an outcome of this project I published *Civil Society Contributions to Policy Innovations in the PR China*, an edited volume in 2015 on collective policy entrepreneurship under the conditions of collaborative state–society relations.

From 2014 until 2017 I also worked as an academic advisor to the China Social Sector Pioneer Program, funded by the Legatum Foundation and implemented jointly by the Philadelphia-based Geneva Global and Shanghai-based Social Venture Group. As part of this project I conducted a series of in-depth interviews with foreign and domestic foundation representatives and civil society practitioners,[2] which informed an open access research article about the contested role of foreign and domestic foundations.[3] Following the ascent of the Xi/Li administration in 2012, however, any kind of initiative aimed at strengthening China's civil society became increasingly difficult to implement. In 2013 the Chinese party-state declared civil society a politically sensitive term. The semi-liberal era of Western engagement with China's civil society had come to an abrupt end.

Luckily, after my completion of the PhD at the Free University of Berlin I had a second leg to stand on. In 2007 I was offered a tenured position as Assistant Professor for Contemporary Chinese Studies at the University of Nottingham. My work as a lecturer not only allowed me to share my various insights with undergraduate, postgraduate and PhD students but also offered me an opportunity to compare my practical experiences with the evolving academic discourse about current Chinese affairs, thus engaging in what Donald Schoen has termed continuous "action-in-reflection". Teaching a wide range of modules on contemporary Chinese culture and society, social change and public policy in China's reform era, government and politics, the struggle for democracy in mainland China, Taiwan and Hong Kong, as well as European Union–China relations allowed me to develop a broad knowledge and understanding of all things Chinese. Such extensive teaching over the past 12 years has helped lay the foundation for this monograph.

This book has also benefited from extensive feedback from friends and colleagues, both at the University of Nottingham and beyond. I am particularly indebted to Horst Fabian and Martin Thorley, who have commented in great detail on almost every book chapter. I am also grateful to Katharine Adeney, Oana Burcu, Jean-Pierre Cabestan, Edmund Cheng, Elizabeth Economy, Bernhard Fulda, Samantha Hoffman, Nicola Macbean, Christian and Erik Schicketanz, Mark Siemons, Didi Kirsten Tatlow as well as Mark Pixley and Karen Lim who provided me with most helpful additional feedback and suggestions for revisions. I would also like to thank my friend and colleague Scott Pacey for encouraging me to finally write this monograph. I should not forget to thank Melanie Markin for the many good conversations we have had when she was stopping by my office in the early hours of the day.

This monograph would not have seen the light of day without the support of the following individuals. I have greatly benefited from many conversations I have had with my academic mentor Steve Tsang over the past eight years, whose knowledge and understanding of mainland China, Taiwan and Hong Kong is second to none. I would also like to thank my former University of Nottingham colleague Zheng Yongnian for his unwavering trust in me and his willingness to include this timely and important book in his monograph series. I am also grateful to Peter Sowden, our Asia and Russia and Eastern Europe editor at Routledge who has steadfastly supported this book project from day one. I am also indebted to Dawn Preston for her very thorough editing of the book. All remaining errors are my own.

This monograph is dedicated to all of the anti-establishment muckrakers, the trojan horse reformers and the trans-establishment bridge builders in mainland China, Taiwan and Hong Kong. It is up to them to seek common ground and to chart a democratic future for the region. It is my sincere hope that citizens in all three places will realise that—despite whatever disagreements they may have—they will see that they also have shared ambitions and aspirations: to live a life in peace, prosperity and, most importantly, free from fear.

Notes

1 Pixley, Mark and Lim, Karen (2015), Bridging the Gaps between European and Chinese Civil Societies, in: Andreas Fulda (Ed.), *Civil Society Contributions to Policy Innovation in the PR China*, Palgrave Macmillan, Houndmills and New York, 254.
2 China Development Brief (2015), Thinking Strategically about Civil Society Assistance in China. Available online: www.chinadevelopmentbrief.cn/publications/thin king-strategically-about-civil-society-assistance-in-china/ (accessed 8 January 2019).
3 Fulda, Andreas (2017), The Contested Role of Foreign and Domestic Foundations in the PRC: Policies, Positions, Paradigms, Power, *Journal of the British Association for Chinese Studies*, 7(July). Available online: http://eprints.nottingham.ac.uk/44636/1/JBACS-7-Fulda-p-63-99.pdf (accessed 8 January 2019).

ABBREVIATIONS

CCP	Chinese Communist Party
CDP	China Democracy Party
CHRF	Civil Human Rights Front
Comintern	Communist International
CSO	civil society organisation
DP	Democratic Party
DPP	Democratic Progressive Party
GDP	gross domestic product
HKSAR	Hong Kong's Special Administrative Region
KMT	Nationalist Party
LegCo	Legislative Council
MoCA	Ministry of Civil Affairs
NCM	New Citizen movement
NGO	non-governmental organisation
NT	New Tide
OCLP	Occupy Central with Love and Peace
PLA	People's Liberation Army
PRC	People's Republic of China
ROC	Republic of China
TOC	theory of change
TOPC	theory of and for political change
UM	Umbrella movement

1

INTRODUCTION

On 16 December 2017 the *Economist* published its widely cited cover story "Sharp power. The new shape of Chinese influence".[1] Sharp power in this context is understood as an approach taken by authoritarian regimes such as Russia and China's "that pierces, penetrates, or perforates the political and information environments in the targeted countries".[2] The *Economist*'s editorial critiqued efforts by the Chinese Communist Party (CCP) to manipulate debate in Western democracies such as Australia, New Zealand, Britain or Canada through covert activities coordinated by its United Front Work Department. In this book I argue that while the CCP's sharp power approach has captured the global imagination, the united front approach itself is actually not a new phenomenon. Since the founding of the autocratically governed People's Republic of China (PRC, henceforth mainland China) in 1949, CCP organs and CCP members had close to 70 years to perfect its united front work,[3] which has consistently targeted Chinese opposition groups both at home and abroad.

While the *Economist* has been using the term sharp power to refer to the CCP's international power projection through non-conventional hard power, in this book I argue that the sharp power approach is essentially an extension of the united front methodology, which was formulated as early as December 1935 and was put into practice by 1937. Van Slyke has described it as "an early stage development of a set of policies and techniques for gaining popular support, for isolating opponents, for expressing the communist programme in nationalist terms, and for deferring (but not forsaking) revolutionary objectives".[4] This means that in the context of this book I will extend the meaning of sharp power and apply it to the CCP's governing philosophy at home and abroad. I argue that the CCP has been effective in its application of sharp power tactics to contain political opposition to the party-state in mainland China. The CCP's fine-tuning of Leninist forms of governance over the past decades has also informed united front tactics employed at the periphery of mainland China, most notably the democratic and self-governing Republic of China on Taiwan (henceforth Taiwan) and the semi-democratic Hong Kong Special Administrative Region (henceforth Hong Kong). Law professor Zhang Xuesheng has succinctly pointed out that:

> the concept of communist dictatorship that the CCP adhered to then and now, in principle, stands in fundamental contrast to the constitutional government of a liberal democracy. This means that the continuation of the CCP's rule must be predicated on the elimination of the concepts of freedom, democracy, and the rule of law.[5]

This also means that it is in the CCP's organisational self-interest to undermine the development and consolidation of liberal democratic polities at mainland China's periphery. CCP-led efforts to frustrate democracy in Taiwan and Hong Kong are driven by the fear among top CCP leaders that a successful liberalisation and democratisation in both regions will inspire mainland Chinese citizens to demand the same liberties for themselves. While there is a growing body of literature on China's authoritarian political system, Taiwan's democratisation process and Hong Kong's struggle for greater political autonomy under the "One Country, Two Systems" formula, up-to-date research which offers a critical comparison of political development in all three regions is noticeably absent. The research puzzle at the heart of this book is to what extent political activists in mainland China, Taiwan and Hong Kong have made progress in their quest to liberalise and democratise their respective polities. More specifically, this book addresses the following research questions: What kind of lessons have democracy activists in all three regions drawn from their struggles for democracy? Which kind of lessons learned have arguably advanced their political causes? Are there also cases of pathological learning? And to what extent can critical scholarship advance our analytical understanding of long-term democratisation processes whilst simultaneously enhancing practitioner reflexivity?

It is important to note that Chinese societies in Taiwan and Hong Kong have been at the receiving end of the CCP's sharp power approach for many decades. In the past two decades, however, Taiwanese and Hong Kong citizens have mounted a robust defence of liberal democratic values and practices, primarily in the form of social and political movements but also through the ballot box. This means that attempts by the CCP to influence the political development on mainland China's periphery have been much less successful and, in fact, have accelerated the struggle for democracy in Taiwan and Hong Kong. In this book the struggle for democracy in all three regions is understood as an ongoing and open-ended historical process marked by deliberate attempts by activists to liberalise and democratise political institutions and political culture with the help of reform strategies and tactical approaches. A closer inspection of the different political development trajectories in main-land China, Taiwan and Hong Kong offers new and novel insights on sharp power and its discontents. Findings from this book will not only help inform the global debate about "exporting authoritarianism with Chinese character-istics"[6] but also highlight the in-built limitations and lack of sustainability of sharp power approaches as a means to consolidate authoritarian rule in mainland China.

China as a longitudinal study

This book is informed by a historical perspective which compares and con-trasts the political development trajectory in mainland China, Taiwan and Hong Kong from the early 1970s to the present day. This time frame is chosen as democracy movements in the three regions were kick-started by an election-driven liberalisation in Taiwan in 1969, the Democracy Wall move-ment in mainland China in 1978[7] and the top-down political reforms of Governor Patten in Hong Kong after 1992. In her keynote address to the 2018 Annual Conference of the British Association for Chinese Studies, former BBC China correspondent Carrie Gracie reminded her audience that "China is a longitudinal study and you need to stick with it over the long term."[8] Such a historically grounded approach, Gracie mused, could provide greater historical awareness for the cyclical nature of China's development. In this book I not only concur with Gracie's suggestion but would add that a comparative perspective is vital to a better understanding of China and its periphery. While this book will show that political change in mainland China, Taiwan and Hong Kong has followed different trajectories, the refusal of the CCP to allow democratisation processes to unfold, either in mainland China or at its periphery, has major implications for all three territories. Xi Jinping's decision to declare himself leader for life in 2018 has been widely interpreted as a rejection of international convergence. China's hard authoritarian turn under Xi has thrown into disarray the entire academic discourse about insti-tutionalised leadership succession and authoritarian resilience.

As I will argue in Chapter 2 the strategic decision to block any conceivable pathway to mainland China's liberalisation and democratisation did not occur in 2018 but had already been made by top CCP leaders in June 1989. From an even longer historical perspective it can be argued that since its establishment in Shanghai in 1921 the CCP has been a political organisation whose monistic ideology has been diametrically opposed to liberal democratic thought and practice. He Baogang has pointed out that:

> [according] to the official ideology of China, which is based on Marxism-Leninism and Mao Zedong Thought, the dominant concept of democracy is not that of liberal democracy. Instead, democracy is seen in Mao's terms: the masses keeping watch of the bureaucracy under the monocratic

guidance of a national leader. It is also seen as good government "serving the people" … China has sought to combine democracy with authority, dictatorship and centralism rather than with freedom.[9]

Discussing the struggle for democracy raises the question of political legitimacy of the authoritarian political regimes. While the CCP has ruled mainland China autocratically since 1949, Taiwan was under one-party rule by the Nationalist Party (KMT) from 1945 until 2000 and liberalised and democratised in the late 1980s and early 1990s. Hong Kong was a British Crown Colony from 1843 until 1997. Incremental reforms to the political system were introduced by the last British governor Chris Patten prior to Hong Kong's return under mainland Chinese sovereignty in 1997, leaving the newly established Hong Kong Special Administrative Region in a semi-autocratic and semi-democratic limbo.

The question whether or not an authoritarian political regime such as mainland China's party-state enjoys political legitimacy, and if so, to what extent, helps to illuminate some of the major tensions in the academic field of Chinese studies in general and social and political science research on China's political system in particular. In this book I argue that research on contemporary Chinese politics is dominated by three different camps of researchers, which can be described as normativists, positivists and academic practitioners (see Table 1.1).

Each camp follows different axiomatic systems, understood "as the set of undemonstrated (and indemonstrable) 'basic beliefs' accepted by convention or established by practice as the building blocks of some conceptual or theoretical structure or system".[10] In the following I will use the salient issue of CCP political legitimacy (or lack thereof) as a yardstick to highlight the different axiomatic bases and conceptual roots of each of the three camps. I will also

TABLE 1.1 Key perspectives on the CCP's political legitimacy (or lack thereof)

Camp	Key perspectives on the CCP's political legitimacy
Normativists (Judgement-oriented perspective)	CCP lacks democratic political legitimacy
Positivists (Compartmentalised perspective)	CCP enjoys popular support due to its output capacity (e.g. economic growth)
Practitioners (Improvement-oriented perspective)	CCP lacks political legitimacy, but the latter could be enhanced with the help of social policies

explain what the differences between these camps mean for our discussion about the struggle for democracy in mainland China, Taiwan and Hong Kong.

Normativists

Normativist scholars argue that the CCP does not enjoy democratic political legitimacy. They point to the fact that the CCP gained political power through the barrel of a gun and as the victor in the civil war with the Nationalist Party in 1949. Since constitutional "and other legal acts do not contain any provisions concerning the legal nature of the CCP",[11] normativists would also argue that the CCP lacks a legal foundation. Furthermore, in the absence of free and fair elections on the regional and/or national level, the CCP has not obtained regular and renewed democratic legitimacy since 1949. An example of a normative China scholar is Frank Dikoetter. Such normative critiques of the CCP, however, have not gone uncontested. Critics maintain that normativists engage in "wishful thinking"[12] and measure mainland China's political system against an ideal-type democracy, rather than trying to understand the way it is actually governed. This critique of normative scholarship highlights the problem of mirroring. Seen in this light, normativist scholars stand accused that their scholarship tells us more about their own values, world-views and ideology rather than informing us about the actual functioning of mainland China's political system.

While normativists provide a convincing and compelling critique of China's oppressive system of governance, their judgement-oriented perspective struggles to explain why despite the lack of political legitimacy the CCP so far has remained the "only game in town". Normativists also run the danger of applying a teleological view of China's political development, where liberal democracy is seen as the only possible destination of present and future travel. The problem with teleological views of history, however, is that even if we were to accept the concept of path dependence, the trajectory of China's political development is arguably open ended. There are many possible scenarios as to how it could evolve in the future: the party-state could become ever more hard authoritarian/militaristic (as seems to be the case under Xi Jinping's leadership), or it could revert to emphasising the soft authoritarian side (as under former leader Hu Jintao) or alternatively decide to become more liberal democratic (which has not happened since the founding of the PRC in 1949). Due to their inherently teleological leanings, normativist scholars run the danger of overlooking the open-ended nature of political development.

Positivists

The question of the CCP's political legitimacy is seen rather differently by positivist researchers, the second camp of China analysts. Instead of asking the question whether or not the CCP enjoys *democratic* political legitimacy, the alternative question is raised whether or not it enjoys *popular support*. A prime example is a landmark research article by Gunter Schubert, who argued that the CCP under Jiang Zemin and Hu Jintao's leadership managed to enhance political legitimacy through non-democratic means.[13] While thought provoking, Schubert's focus on output legitimacy of the party-state is highly problematic, as he deliberately excludes other key pathways for enhancing political legitimacy, e.g. constitutional democracy and free and fair elections. Furthermore, his argument could be called ahistorical, since the CCP, as a political organisation, is directly responsible for the death of between 36 million[14] and 45 million[15] Chinese citizens during the Great Leap Forward (1958–62) and the civilisation rupture of the Cultural Revolution (1966–76), which almost completely tore away the social fabric of mainland China's society. This means that while the CCP may enjoy some form of popular support for its ability to generate economic output since 1978, it also has to shoulder the historical responsibility for some of the most heinous crimes against humanity in the 20th century.[16]

Positivists have a tendency to frame their research in apolitical categories. Rather than asking the question of political legitimacy, for example, they discuss China's state capacity or whether or not the CCP has succeeded in civilising and institutionalising its elite politics. While there is value to such specific and rather narrow and technical research approaches, the latter also led to the fragmentation and compartmentalisation of the academic field. Another problem with positivist research is that it tends to be politically conservative, as researchers generally assume a continuation of the status quo rather than foreseeing possible political change. To further complicate matters, positivists may hold fairly critical views of the CCP in private, but in line with their positivist paradigm, in their written scholarship do not explicitly state their value judgements. Such acts of depoliticisation, while understandable from the vantage point of an individual researcher concerned about obtaining research visas and access to the field, actually leads to a highly conformist and politically conservative field of Chinese studies.

Furthermore, while it is perfectly acceptable to *suspend* judgement in intercultural encounters, *withholding* judgement in academic research is problematic, as a reader will rightly want to know what the academic's conclusions are. Last but not least, while the positivist paradigm explicitly calls for scientifically proven predictions of future developments, positivist China scholars tend to stay rather mum about their expectations regarding China's future political trajectory. By not making their expectations explicit positivists give themselves the liberty to swiftly move back and forth between optimistic and pessimistic outlooks on China's political development, without having to provide an explanation for their often rapidly changing assessments.

China practitioners

A third and final group are China practitioners. In the context of mainland China's reform and opening up after 1978 the party-state extended an
olive branch to the outside world and started to welcome the participation
of foreign experts (*waiguo zhuanjia*) to live and work in mainland China.
This opened up the opportunity for non-Chinese to become active participants in Chinese development processes.[17] China practitioners, in contrast to the more theoretically oriented China-watching normativists and
positivists, concern themselves with practical problem solving. They tend
to be developmental in their view of China and have an interculturally
informed improvement-oriented perspective. China practitioners differ from
normativists insofar as they are more willing to engage in what He Baogang has coined "thoughtful wishing".[18] This pragmatic approach is useful
for engaging China under the conditions of authoritarianism, but it also
has its shortcomings.

While the lack of political legitimacy of the CCP is certainly recognised by
most China practitioners, the question is not how to judge this shortcoming
but how to improve and enhance the CCP's political legitimacy with the help
of concrete and specific reform steps.[19] One problem with the approach taken
by China practitioners is that objective hurdles to the development of a more
liberal-democratic political culture and political institutions may be either
overlooked or downplayed for strategic reasons.[20] Additionally, China practitioners at times exaggerate the significance of incremental administrative
reforms. While the latter can be seen as a step towards reformation of the
political system and thus as potential precursors of liberalisation and democratisation, administrative reforms equally can lead to political restoration
and the strengthening of the CCP's grip on the Chinese state, business and
society. Confronted with this contradiction, China practitioners tend to
describe progress with the help of metaphors such as "one step forward, two
steps back" or "two steps forward, one step back". Such caveats underline the
China practitioner's perception of non-linear and cyclical Chinese political
development processes.

Overcoming "mountaintopism"

The increasing specialisation and fragmentation of the field of contemporary
Chinese studies has been critiqued by Alice Miller. In her words,

> the China-watching community suffers from a contemporary variety of
> what Chairman Mao might have described as "mountaintopism" (山头主
> 义): analysts have command over their parochial base area of interest but
> lose track of the overall picture. In many respects, analysts today seem to
> talk past each other because they specialize in narrower fields and draw

on bodies of evidence with which those working in other areas are not familiar.[21]

But is it possible to not only overcome the shortcomings of the three camps but also to build on their respective strengths? While there are limits to combining positivist with post-positivist research approaches,[22] I agree with Miller that a synthesis of competing research approaches is required to advance the field of political science in general and the study of Chinese politics in particular. I contend that a synthesis of the normative, positivist and practitioner perspective can offer a more holistic view of China's multifaceted and open-ended political development. In light of the ongoing debate about censorship and self-censorship in contemporary Chinese studies,[23] I would like to explain in greater detail how I position myself vis-à-vis the previously described three camps. In this book I attempt a synthesis by offering (1) a historically informed *normative critique* of existing political regimes in mainland China, Taiwan and Hong Kong; (2) an *empirical analysis* of the corresponding democracy movements; and (3) *practice-oriented reflections* and policy recommendations towards advancing liberal-democratic reforms in all three regions. As none of these three interrelated positions are self-explanatory I will briefly explain the rationale behind them.

The subtitle of this book—*Sharp Power and Its Discontents*—makes it fairly clear that my scholarship is informed by a *pre-scientific* belief of the desirability of liberal democracy, in mainland China, at its periphery and beyond. When using the term liberal democracy in this book I refer to Robert Dahl's concept of capital D Democracy as polyarchy. In a democracy with a large number of people citizens should have their "preferences weighted equally in conduct of government".[24] The eight requirements are "freedom to form and join organizations, freedom of expression, right to vote, eligibility for public office, right of political leaders to compete for support and votes, alternative sources of information, free and fair elections, and institutions for making government policies depend on votes and other expressions of preference".[25] I also subscribe to Judith Shklar's notion that "(every) adult should be able to make as many effective decisions without fear or favor about as many aspects of her or his life as is compatible with the like freedom of every other adult".[26] As I outlined in the preface to this book, my ethics and values are informed by a variety of influences: the liberal and social-democratic values which my parents instilled in me during my family upbringing; insights I gained during my university studies of contemporary China in the late 1990s and early 2000s; as well as experiential learning during eight years of living and working in Taiwan and mainland China between 1998 and 2011.

In addition to these biographical reasons, part of my professional self-understanding as a scholar is that social and political science cannot be value-free. Here I concur with Andrew Nathan who has argued that:

many historians and social scientists believe that value judgements may legitimately be made in the course of an inquiry, as long as they are clearly expressed as such and are separated from statements of fact. Some argue further that social inquiry is incomplete without an ethical dimension and that reasoned argument about value issues should be a standard part of social science research. Some even hold that ethical judgement constitutes social science's main reason for being and the ultimate source of its meaning. In one way or another, all these views recognise that values play an important role in social science inquiry alongside empirical analysis.[27]

Based on this fact/value distinction I consider my scholarship *emancipatory action research*. In Huttunen and Heikkinen words, "[an] emancipatory action researcher feels inclined to criticise the bureaucratisation of social systems. His or her task is to act as a 'process moderator' who shares responsibility equally with participants."[28] I also agree with Wachman, who has argued that democratisation should be understood as "a *process* rather than a *condition* that inheres once certain conditions are present".[29] Based on such a post-positivist understanding of social and political science I argue that one cannot separate the observer from the observed. This means that China scholars, once they start researching mainland China, Taiwan and/or Hong Kong, inevitably become participants of the respective political processes.

One of the existing realities China scholars face is that under conditions of authoritarianism, the choice of research topics, research partners, as well as research approaches are all politically circumscribed. Censorship and resulting self-censorship, however, ultimately undermine our academic autonomy. As I have argued in my book review of *Doing Field Work in China,*

> [This] excellent volume has one failing: the lack of courage by contributors to address the fundamental question of academic autonomy … By depoliticizing their China engagement, academics try to neutralize the presence of the party-state, solve the issue of access, and overcome the difficulties associated with collaboration. This pragmatic strategy, however understandable from the vantage point of an individual researcher engaging with China, comes at a high cost to the field of contemporary Chinese studies as a whole: it ultimately leads to a tacit acceptance of the official party-state discourse, a strong alignment with party-state controlled research organisations and a collaboration with some of the most conservative academics in the field.[30]

Outlining my value judgments and ethical considerations as part of this introductory chapter thus is an effort to create greater transparency about my pre-scientific value orientations and to highlight my self-understanding as a critical academic with a consciousness.

Research approach

While firmly grounded in the normative camp I am mindful of the danger that normative scholars merely mirror their respective world-views and ideologies in their scholarship. I broadly agree with the positivist camp that social and political science research needs to be grounded in empirical evidence. This is why this book is split into a first theoretical part spanning Chapters 1–4 and a second empirical part including Chapters 5–11. At the heart of my empirical chapters are the contestation of authoritarian state power by individuals, through self-help groups, community-based organisations, informal and formal networks, social and political movements, and where they are allowed to operate—political parties. In the empirical part of this book I subscribe to Migdal, Kohli and Shue's "state-in-society" perspective. Migdal et al. highlight that "states vary in their effectiveness based on their ties to society".[31] Central to their analysis of state–society relations is the insight that "states must be disaggregated".[32] The three authors argue that the boundaries between state and society cannot be neatly separated but overlap. They further argue that "social forces, like states, are contingent on specific empirical conditions".[33] They also highlight that state–society relations are not only marked by political contestation, but can also include elements of cooperation.[34]

In this book I examine state–society relations by offering a thick description[35] of 12 closely viewed critical incidents,[36] where political activists in mainland China, Taiwan and Hong Kong have come into direct conflict with representatives of their respective state. Rather than simply focusing on a single event, in my thick description of the episodes I will follow Sidney Tarrow's approach of investigating "longer and more complicated episodes and trajectories of collective action, reaction, and regime change".[37] A focus on episodes helps to highlight the cyclical nature of struggles for democracy, which are marked by progress and setbacks, but also hold the promise of quantum leaps in political development processes. By examining four episodes per region I will not only shed light on contested state–society relations. Seen from a longitudinal and comparative perspective the 12 episodes as empirical case studies will also reveal fascinating insights into the development trajectories of the respective democracy movements in all three regions.

This book is also informed by the future orientation of China practitioners. As part of the action orientation of my scholarship, I assert that social and political science should not be limited to the discussion of problems and challenges but also offer tentative solutions, be it in the form of policy recommendations or as practice-oriented reflections. This means that our discussion of the struggle for democracy should not be limited to post facto rationalisations of political history but also include *ex ante* assumptions about the future. This particular position is informed by the scholarship of German historian Reinhart Koselleck. Reflecting on the semantics of historical time, Koselleck has argued that any attempt to interpret history requires scholars to familiarise themselves with their studied protagonists' "spaces of experience" as well as "horizons of expectation".[38] His key argument is that individuals make decisions based both on rationalisations of their past personal experiences as well as assumptions about the efficacy of their actions in the future. Koselleck's distinction between spaces of experience and horizons of expectation inform my critique of the predominantly post facto orientation of democratisation studies in Chapter 3. In the context of this introductory chapter, however, Koselleck's differentiation between spaces of experience and horizons of expectation also informs my position on the need to offer practice-oriented reflections.

When we concern ourselves with the study of the *political history* of mainland China, Taiwan and Hong Kong we also need to make explicit our *expectations towards the three regions' political future*. While we do not have a crystal ball which can be used to look into the future, we nevertheless have to be transparent about our assumptions regarding potential future political change. Scholars should be more open about their deeply held assumptions and convictions when developing their arguments. Do we consider structure or agency to be of greater importance in political reform processes? If it is the former, what are the implications for political reform? And if scholars consider agency to be of greater importance, which kind of actors do they consider to be the most important in such change processes? And how do we derive our key assumptions about future developments? Being more explicit about our horizons of expectation not only makes our arguments more transparent, but also deflects criticism of our China scholarship being supposedly ahistorical or historically static. I argue that when describing a political transition process, our description of any given development trajectory cannot be confined to the past and present, but in order for us to sketch the trajectory we need to include the future as well.

In this book I draw on a very wide range of secondary sources, ranging from tweets, documentaries, newspaper articles, United States embassy cables revealed by Wikileaks, op-eds, think tank reports, journal articles and monographs, to primary sources such as speeches and policy documents. My inclusive approach to sources is inspired by the approach of the curatorial journalism of Seth Abramson, who has suggested that:

> the ongoing federal investigation into collusion between the Kremlin and Donald Trump's presidential campaign is the most complex, far-ranging criminal investigation of our lifetimes. The story of Trump–Russia collusion crosses so many continents, decades and areas of expertise—and has swept into its net so many hundreds of public officials and private citizens from nations around the world—that it can be difficult to understand any one piece of reporting on the scandal without having access to the context provided by several dozen others.[39]

Since information about the 12 struggles for democracy in mainland China, Taiwan and Hong Kong is similarly scattered across the fields of media, academia and diplomacy, I see it as my task to connect the dots between far-flung pieces of information. My research approach thus is both constructivist and curatorial.

What follows is a brief overview of the following chapters of this book. In Chapter 2 I argue that the case of mainland China shows the limits of conventional modernisation theory, as economic modernisation does not necessarily lead to political liberalisation and democratisation. While in the case of Taiwan and Hong Kong there is a stronger degree of correlation between socio-economic modernisation and political change, even at China's periphery the main driving force for political reform was not simply the outcome of economic transformation. Whereas in Taiwan the Japanese colonial era and the subsequent formation of rival ethnic groups played an important formative role in Taiwan's democratisation during the KMT era post-1947,[40] in the case of Hong Kong the British colonial government's instrumentalisation of religion in the fight against communism had a lasting effect on Hong Kong's post-1997 democracy movement.[41] I explain why the military crackdown on peaceful protesters in the year 1989 was a pivotal movement in the PRC's political history. It consolidated CCP rule, entrenched its crony capitalist system and inhibited the development of democracy, social equality, transparency as well as accountability in mainland China. Drawing on the case of mainland China I explain why economic modernisation since 1978 did not bring about political liberalisation and democratisation.

The underlying critique of modernisation theory also informs Chapter 3, in which I outline how democratisation studies as a sub-field of political science can be invigorated by overcoming the artificial distinction between theory and practice, by combining *emic* and *etic* perspectives and by borrowing from the theory of change discourse in development studies. In Chapter 4 I outline the novel heuristic devices of theories of and for political change (TOPC). The scholarship by Gene Sharp, Saul Alinsky and Paulo Freire are presented as TOPC which help analyse the country-specific case studies of political regimes in mainland China, Taiwan and Hong Kong in Chapters 5, 7 and 9, respectively, and which help reveal hidden patterns in the democracy movements in all three regions in the corresponding Chapters 6, 8 and 10. I conclude the book with a critical discussion of sharp power and its discontents in Chapter 11.

Notes

1 *Economist* (2017), Sharp Power: The New Shape of Chinese Influence, 16 December.
2 National Endowment for Democracy (2017), Sharp Power: Rising Authoritarian Influence. Available online: www.ned.org/wp-content/uploads/2017/12/Introduction-Sharp-Power-Rising-Authoritarian-Influence.pdf (accessed 10 January 2018).

3 As pointed out by Ann-Marie Brady in a tweet on 6 October 2018. Brady, Ann-Marie (2018), "[it] cannot be emphasized enough: United front work is a task of ALL CCP agencies, as well as a basic task of EVERY CCP member. All CCP agencies, from the International Liaison Dept to Central Propaganda Dept are involved in it. It is NOT solely targeted at Overseas Chinese." 6 October. Tweet. Available online: https://twitter.com/Anne_MarieBrady/status/1048540389265854465 (accessed 8 October 2018).

4 Van Slyke, L. (1970), The United Front in China, *Journal of Contemporary History*, 5(3), 126.

5 Zhang, Xuezhong (2019), Bid Farewell to Reform and Opening Up—On China's Perilous Situation and Its Future Options, translated by Andrea Worden. Available online: https://chinachange.org/2019/01/07/bid-farewell-to-reform-and-opening-up-on-chinas-perilous-situation-and-its-future-options/ (accessed 8 January 2019).

6 Congressional-Executive Commission on China 2017, The Long Arm of China: Exporting Authoritarianism with Chinese Characteristics. Available online: www.cecc.gov/events/hearings/the-long-arm-of-chinaexporting-authoritarianism-with-chinese-characteristics (accessed 10 January 2018).

7 Spence, Jonathan (1999), *The Search for Modern China*, Norton, New York, 624–30.

8 Dauncey, Sarah (2018), "China is a longitudinal story and you need to stick with it over the long term', but the depth and consistency nowadays in journalistic and diplomatic knowledge is no longer there ... @BBCCarrie @bacs_china." 12 September. Tweet. Available online: https://twitter.com/chinesesarah/status/1039891868132274185 (accessed 8 October 2018).

9 He, Baogang (1996), *The Democratization of China*, Routledge, London, 43–4.

10 Lincoln, Yvonne S. and Guba, Egon G. (1985), *Naturalistic Inquiry*, Sage, London, 33–6.

11 Heuser, Robert (1987), The Legal Status of the Chinese Communist Party, Occasional Papers/Reprints Series in Contemporary Asian Studies. Available online: https://digitalcommons.law.umaryland.edu/cgi/viewcontent.cgi?article=1080&context=mscas (accessed 9 October 2018).

12 He, Baogang (1996), *The Democratization of China*, Routledge, London, 7.

13 Schubert, Gunter (2014), Political Legitimacy in Contemporary China Revisited: Theoretical Refinement and Empirical Operationalization, *Journal of Contemporary China*, 23(88), 1–19.

14 Yang, J., Guo, J. and Mosher, S. (2012), *Tombstone: The Untold Story of Mao's Great Famine*, translated by Stacy Mosher and Guo Jian, edited by Edward Friedman, Gou Jian and Stacy Mosher, introduction by Edward Friedman and Roderick MacFarquhar, Penguin, London.

15 Dikoetter, Frank (2010), *Mao's Great Famine*, Bloomsbury, London.

16 Other positivist scholars who have followed a similar line of thought have tried to assess popular support for the CCP by conducting empirical survey research. While I would concede that the CCP enjoys a certain amount of popular support despite the lack of democratic institutions, in my view positivist researchers have been rightly critiqued for their refusal to engage with the normative dimensions of their work. Furthermore, it is debatable whether it is possible to conduct survey-based empirical research in a politically highly circumscribed environment and still claim objective validity of empirical research findings. Arguably, public opinion surveys measure first and foremost the efficacy of CCP propaganda.

17 Fulda, Andreas (2019), The Emergence of Citizen Diplomacy in EU–China Relations: Principles, Pillars, Pioneers, Paradoxes, *Diplomacy and Statecraft*, Spring.

18 He, Baogang (1996), *The Democratization of China*, Routledge, London, 7.

19 Fulda, Andreas (Ed.) (2015), *Civil Society Contributions to Policy Innovation in the PR China*, Palgrave Macmillan, Basingstoke.

20 During my capacity-building work as a practitioner in mainland China from 2004 to 2014 I never addressed the proverbial elephant in the room, the CCP. When

referring to the party-state, I spoke of an ideal-type good government which should be addressing human needs. Such a pragmatic strategy worked well to steer clear of political censorship and allowed me to engage with Chinese civil society organisations. During times of severe political repression, e.g. the hard-authoritarian turn under Xi Jinping since 2012, where the party-state has become much more visible and commanding, such a pragmatic strategy is no longer feasible.

21 Miller, Alice (2018), Valedictory: Analyzing the Chinese Leadership in an Era of Sex, Money, and Power, *China Leadership Monitor*, Autumn. Available online: www.hoover.org/sites/default/files/research/docs/clm57-am-final.pdf (accessed 9 October 2018).
22 Lincoln, Y., & Guba, E. (1985). *Naturalistic Inquiry*, Sage, Newbury Park, CA.
23 Inside Higher Ed (2018), Gauging China's "Influence and Interference" in US Higher Ed. Available online: www.insidehighered.com/news/2018/09/12/wilson-center-releases-study-chinas-influence-and-interference-us-higher-ed (accessed 9 October 2018).
24 Dahl, R. (1971), *Polyarchy: Participation and Opposition*, Yale University Press, New Haven, CT, 3.
25 Ibid.
26 Shklar, Judith (1989), The Liberalism of Fear, in: Nancy Rosenblum (Ed.), *Liberalism and the Moral Life*, Harvard University Press, Cambridge, MA, 21.
27 Nathan, Andrew (1997), *China's Transition*, Columbia University Press, New York, 198.
28 Huttunen, Rauno and Heikkinen, Hannu L.T. (1998) Between Facts and Norms: Action Research in the Light of Jürgen Habermas's Theory of Communicative Action and Discourse Theory of Justice, *Curriculum Studies*, 6(3), 309.
29 Wachman, Alan M. (1994), *Taiwan: National Identity and Democratization*, M.E. Sharpe, Armonk, NY, 37.
30 *Nias Press* (2011), Not an Issue Going away Soon. Available online: www.niaspress.dk/blogs/gerald/blog/2011-june/not-issue-going-away-soon (accessed 11 October 2018).
31 Migdal, Joel, Kohli, Atul and Shue, Vivienne (1994) Introduction, in: Joel Migdal, Atul Kohli and Vivienne Shue (Eds), *State Power and Social Forces: Domination and Transformation in the Third World*, Cambridge University Press, Cambridge, 2.
32 Ibid., 3.
33 Ibid.
34 Ibid., 4.
35 Geertz, C. (1973), *The Interpretation of Cultures: Selected Essays*, Basic Books, New York.
36 Edvardsson, Bo (1992), Service Breakdowns: A Study of Critical Incidents in an Airline, *International Journal of Service Industry Management* 3(4), 17.
37 Tarrow, Sidney (2012), *Strangers at the Gates: Movements and States in Contentious Politics*, Cambridge University Press, Cambridge, 3.
38 Koselleck, R. (2004), *Futures Past: On the Semantics of Historical Time*, translated by Keith Tribe, Columbia University Press, New York.
39 *Guardian* (2018), Trump-Russia Is Too Complex to Report: We Need a New Kind of Journalism. Available online: www.theguardian.com/commentisfree/2018/nov/22/trump-russia-too-complex-to-report-we-must-turn-curatorial-journalism (accessed 14 December 2018).
40 Fulda, A. (2002). Reevaluating the Taiwanese Democracy Movement: A Comparative Analysis of Opposition Organizations under Japanese and KMT Rule, *Critical Asian Studies*, 34(3), 357–94.
41 Ng, Nancy and Fulda, Andreas (2018), The Religious Dimension of Hong Kong's Umbrella Movement, *Journal of Church and State*, 60(3), 1 August, 377–97.

2

MAINLAND CHINA'S INCOMPLETE MODERNISATION

On 11 March 2018, China's National People's Congress—the CCP's rubber-stamp legislature—approved changes to mainland China's party constitution to allow the abolition of term limits for incumbent CCP chairman Xi Jinping 2,958 to 2.[1] The journalists Chris Buckley and Adam Wu were quick to point out the historical significance of this decision, which in theory will allow Xi to rule for life.[2] China experts took to Twitter to comment on this new development. Zeng Jinghan, author of a recently published monograph on the CCP,[3] offered a critical self-reflection, musing "(as) a scholar who had faith in the institutionalisation of China's power succession, I need to sit down and study its limits now".[4] Christian Goebel, a political scientist and sinologist whose research similarly focuses on the adaptability of the Chinese party-state to social, economic and political challenges, fired off a series of tweets the same day, stating that the move confirmed his previously expressed concerns of "China becoming a personalized dictatorship".[5] In another tweet Goebel also erected a virtual "new tombstone on the graveyard of political science concepts. R.I.P. Authoritarian Resilience (01/2003–02/2018)".[6] The lifting of term limits for China's president has unravelled previous attempts by the CCP to civilise faction politics at the political elite level. This development has been widely interpreted as a further entrenchment of one-party rule under the new strongman Xi Jinping.[7]

In stark contrast, the French political scientist François Godement has critiqued mainstream commentary to Xi's decision to firmly install himself as the new paramount leader of a top-down Leninist party. According to Godement, "the real question is, why are we still so surprised and shocked?"[8] Godement argues that Xi's tenure for life "has more to do with us than with Xi Jinping or China".[9] According to Godement, [post-modern] thought has dominated since the end of the Cold War. The end of ideology, the great convergence that globalization was supposed to bring about, and the gradual disappearance of armed conflict have led Europe and to some extent the United States to believe in "the end of history": a benign Jurgen Habermas-Barack Obama project supported by a gaggle of economists. True, some nails stuck out, notably Vladimir Putin. But he could be seen as a hold-out on the road to decline of a second-rate power. The return of personality politics in many democracies is already raising question marks about that worldview. But with Xi Jinping acquiring life-long authority over the world's rising superpower (if he so wishes) we can no longer blind ourselves to the fact that history has returned.[10]

In this book I concur with Godement's assessment that history has indeed returned. I argue that the strategic decision against the introduction of even the most incremental forms of liberal democratic thought and practice proceeded the developments in 2018 by more than 30 years, and can be located in the fateful months leading up to the 4 June massacre in 1989, when the CCP's top leadership authorised the People's Liberation Army (PLA) to suppress mainland China's nation-wide anti-corruption and pro-democracy movement. The year 1989, rather than the year 2018, should be seen as the key pivotal moment in mainland China's political development, which firmly set the country on its current development trajectory.

Limits of modernisation theory

In this chapter I argue that mainland China should be seen as a key case study which illustrates the limits of conventional modernisation theory. The latter postulates that sustained economic development is positively correlated with the gradual emergence of more liberal-democratic forms of governance. Carothers distilled its key argument as follows:

> Reduced to bare essentials, modernization theory conceived of development as a linear process ending up in an American-style social, economic and political system—and held that the various elements of the development process would be mutually reinforcing. In particular, economic development would generate democracy by helping countries achieve a middle class, a high literacy rate, and other socioeconomic features then considered preconditions for democracy.[11]

Modernisation theory was initially developed by Lipset, Almond and Coleman, and Rustow from the early 1960s onwards.[12] While empirical studies have time and again questioned the overly simplistic causal relationship between economic growth and political liberalisation,[13] modernisation theory remains popular to this day,[14] particularly among elites working in the field of development aid and diplomacy.[15] In this book I argue that in the case of mainland China, economic reforms have neither led to liberal democracy or social equality, nor have they enhanced transparency and accountability. This arguably *incomplete* modernisation in mainland China holds the key to our understanding of the struggle for democracy in mainland China and its periphery, most noticeably Taiwan and Hong Kong.

Modernisation without democracy

On 17 May 1989, at the height of mainland China's nation-wide anti-corruption and pro-democracy movement, Deng Xiaoping made the fateful decision not to allow piecemeal liberalisation and democratisation of its autocratic political system. Deng's power as China's paramount leader (*zui gao lingdao ren*) grew out of the barrel of a gun: as the chairman of the CCP's Central Military Commission and as a member of the first generation of communist revolutionaries his authority was only checked by an amorphous group of party elders.[16] Following a split decision of the highest organ of the CCP, the Politburo Standing Committee, which pitted the conservative hardliners Li Peng and Yao Yilin against the moderate reformers Zhao Ziyang and Hu Qili,[17] Deng's casting vote in favour of the hardliners meant that China's largest pro-democracy movement after 1949 was doomed to fail.[18] Deng's decision to impose martial law ended a decade of relative political liberalisation during the 1980s and closed the door to political reform from 1989 onwards.

When the Politburo Standing Committee made its fateful decision to employ the PLA against its own people the hardliners were 61 (Li Peng), 72 (Yao Yilin) and 84 (Deng Xiaoping) years old. Geremie Barmé and John Crowley described the mindset of these gerontocrats in the documentary *The Gate of Heavenly Peace* as follows:

> Deng Xiaoping's greatest fear would be *dongluan*: turmoil, chaos, upheaval. When the students of 1989 took to the streets, they too were branded as stirring up *dongluan*. Many leaders in the government saw them in the light of the past; they were a throwback to the horrors of the Cultural Revolution that had nearly destroyed China.[19]

It was inconceivable for them that mainland China could one day be governed in less autocratic and non-Leninist ways. This misperception of millions of Chinese citizens as troublemakers without a good cause to rebel stood in great contrast with the lived experiences and political demands of participants of the 1989 movement.

Throughout the weeks and months of the 1989 movement protesters in Beijing and more than 300 cities nation-wide made "abstract demands for 'freedom and democracy'"[20] and called for political dialogue between the party-state and "voluntary groups arising spontaneously to represent the various social sectors".[21] Movement participants requested a re-evaluation of the role of former CCP general secretary Hu Yaobang, who was ousted in 1987 and whose death in spring 1989 triggered the movement. Demonstrators also opposed the party-state's relentless campaign against supposedly "bourgeois liberalisation" and asked for the rehabilitation of the campaigns' victims.[22] More specifically, movement leaders demanded freedom of speech,[23] freedom of press[24] and freedom of association.[25] In *The Gate of Heavenly Peace* Geremie Barmé and John Crowley highlighted the inability of movement leaders to agree on their goals, strategies and tactics.

Reflecting on the occasional chaos and confusion that marked collective decision making among student leaders Barmé and Crowley raised the question, "(but) if real democracy was to be implemented, how were the people to take charge?".[26] Jonathan Unger, on the other hand, has pointed out that students, intellectuals, workers and ordinary citizens *"did* project a vague vision of what they wanted, and it was summed up in the word 'Democracy'".[27] Democracy was meant to bring about "an independent judiciary, beyond the reach of a Party leader's sway".[28] They also wanted more "freedom from the petty constraints imposed upon them at their place of work".[29] According to Unger, "(what) the urban populace of China was demanding, in short, was no less and no more than 'civil society'".[30] As the latter project of independent civic groups undermined Leninist organising principles, the CCP was steadfastly opposed to such political demands.

Yet China's 1989 movement was as much a call for greater political liberalisation as it was a critique of the hasty introduction of capitalist modes of production into China. Slavoj Žižek has argued that

> [instead] of treating contemporary China as an oriental-despotic distortion of capitalism one should see in it the repetition of the development of capitalism in Europe itself. In early modernity, most European states were far from democratic—if they were (as was the case in Holland), they were so only for the liberal elite, not for the popular classes. The conditions for capitalism were created and sustained by a brutal state dictatorship, very much like today's China: the state legalized violent expropriations of the common people which turned them into proletarians and disciplined them in their new roles. There is thus nothing exotic about China: what is happening there merely repeats our own forgotten past.[31]

Žižek's insight is important since it questions the idea that economic modernisation will inevitably lead to political liberalisation and democratisation. But why did a nominally communist government consent on reforming its planned economy? The CCP's embrace of capitalism after 1978 was born out of desperation after the catastrophe of China's Cultural Revolution (1966–76). Tony Saich aptly summarised that what China's "lost decade" "did result in was a shattered social fabric with students required to turn on their teachers, children encouraged to denounce their parents, and authority in all its forms held up to ridicule".[32] According to Frederick C. Teiwes, "Mao Zedong left a difficult legacy for the post-Mao state: a fractured and grievance-riddled society, a party-state with reduced legitimacy and weakened dominance over society, faction-infested institutions, ambiguous official norms and a divided top leadership".[33]

In order to rebuild the authority of the party-state the CCP adopted the "Four Modernizations" at its Third Plenary Session of the Eleventh Central Committee in December 1978, which prioritised agriculture, light industry, national defence and science and technology. The Third Plenum marked one of the rare moments in CCP history, where the party's Marxist-Leninist ideology was significantly altered and introduced capitalist modes of production into mainland China.[34] For some Chinese citizens, however, the four modernisations did not go far enough. A former red guard and electrician from Beijing with the name of Wei Jingsheng had the courage to challenge Deng's reform agenda. Disillusioned by decades of political manipulation during the Maoist era,[35] Wei bemoaned that Chinese citizens had "been tempered in the Cultural Revolution and cannot be that ignorant now. Let us find out for ourselves what should be done."[36] The solution to China's political, economic and social ills, according to Wei, was to be found in a "fifth modernization", the introduction of liberal democracy.

Rather than an outcome of a development process, Wei saw liberal democratic thought and practice as a pre-condition for social development:

> If the Chinese people want modernization, they must first put democracy into practice and modernize China's social system. Democracy is not merely an inevitable stage of social development, as Lenin claimed. In addition to being the result of productive forces and productive relations that have developed to a certain stage, democracy is also the very condition that allows for such development to reach beyond this stage.[37]

Wei also reminded his fellow Chinese citizens that political change would not come easy and called on others to join the struggle for democracy: "Does democracy come about naturally when society reaches a certain stage? Absolutely not. An enormous price is paid for every tiny victory, so much so that even coming to a recognition of this fact requires sacrifices."[38] Wei Jingsheng's critique of Maoist totalitarianism and Deng's hard authoritarianism thus was based on the assumption that without individual freedom, citizens become pawns by political elites with illiberal and anti-democratic agendas.

While Wei's essay about China's fifth modernisation was steeped in the theory and language of Marxist-Leninist-Mao Zedong thought, his key ideas and insights closely resemble those of Indian economist Amartya Sen. Just like Wei, Sen has argued that human beings require opportunities to fulfil their human capabilities, regardless of the current development status of the society they inhabit.[39] In a particularly striking example, Sen argued that "in terms of the actual functioning of being well-nourished, the fasting Gandhi did not differ from a starving famine victim, but the freedoms and opportunities they respectively had were quite different".[40] He points out that:

> (t)he fact that many of the terrible deprivations in the world seem to arise from a lack of freedom to avoid those deprivations (rather than from choice, including choosing to be "indolent": a classic issue in the historical literature on poverty) is an important motivational reason to emphasize the role of freedom.[41]

In his publication *Development as Freedom* Sen pointed out that "the working of democracy and of political rights can even help to prevent famines and other economic disasters. Authoritarian rulers, who are themselves rarely affected by famines (or other such economic calamities), tend to lack the incentive to take timely preventive measures".[42] Sen's insight is particularly noteworthy with reference to mainland China, as Mao's economic policy of the Great Leap Forward in the late 1950s and 1960s led to a famine which would cost between 36 million[43] and 45 million[44] Chinese citizens their lives. While Wemheuer has argued that "Mao and the CCP learnt from 1961, and the regime has since been able to prevent the outbreak of a serious deadly famine",[45] the CCP as a political organisation bears the historical responsibility for the death of millions of Chinese citizens. As I argue in Chapter 5, the historical errors of the CCP are a major disincentive for the party-state to liberalise and democratise. Such obstacles to the development of more liberal-democratic political institutions, however, do not feature in conventional modernisation theory.

Modernisation without social equality

Wei's "Fifth Modernization" essay from 1978 landed him a lengthy prison sentence, which lasted from 1979 until 1993. He thus could not participate in China's 1989 movement. Wuer Kaixi, a young student leader of 1989, reflected on the motivation of his generation to join the struggle for democracy:

> Cui Jian is China's most famous singer. His song "Nothing to my name" expresses our feelings. Does our generation have anything? We don't have the goals our parents have. We don't have the fanatical idealism our older brothers and sisters once had. So what do we want? [pauses] Nike shoes. Lots of free time to take our girlfriends to a bar. The freedom to discuss an issue with someone. And to get a little respect from society.[46]

With the benefit of hindsight it is clear that both Wei Jingsheng in the late 1970s and Wuer Kaixi in the late 1980s erred in their assessment that China would require a more liberal political system in order to develop. Yet their political instincts were not entirely wrong.

While China has modernised economically over the past 30 years, this development has not led to greater social equality. China's gini coefficient, which measures inequality in a given country based on a spectrum ranging from 0 representing perfect equality and 1 denoting perfect inequality,[47] has continuously risen since mainland China's reform and its opening-up period (1978: 0.2124; 1989: 0.3185; 2001: 0.3603).[48] Since China's World Trade Organization accession in 2001 the coefficient has been consistently above the 0.4 threshold (2003: 0.479; 2013: 0.473),[49] which is widely regarded as a highly unequal society with high risk of social unrest. In a 2013 United Nations report DESA Economic Affairs Officer Sergio Vieira reported that "(the) Gini coefficient increased by 24 per cent in China, 16 per cent in India, and 4.5 per cent in South Africa, compared to 5.5 per cent in OECD countries on average, between early 1990s and late 2000s".[50] The paradox of a rapidly developing economy and widening social inequality can be explained by the way China's political economy developed post-1989.

While initially successful in kick-starting China's rural economy in the early 1980s, the gradual transition away from a planned to a more market-oriented economy throughout the 1980s and 1990s created both winners and losers. Chinese economist He Qinglian described three generations of immediate beneficiaries of China's early economic reforms. During a process of "marketisation of power", a first generation of individuals who formally belonged to the "five black categories" of landowners, rich famers, etc. as well as released prisoners could only make a living as small privately owned businesses (so-called *getihu*, which could range from working as a street peddler to more complex businesses such as barber shops or factories). A second generation belonged to qualified workers who were made redundant in the wake of the restructuring of China's state-owned enterprises. And yet a third generation of beneficiaries was to become the most influential group of nouveaux riche during the early period of China's reform era. This third generation included self-employed people who remained close contacts of party-state officials. This latter group initially exploited the "dual-track price system" whereby they procured goods produced under the planned economy cheaply and sold it at much higher prices on the private market.[51]

In her monograph *The Pitfalls of Modernization*, He Qinglian describes how partial public property reforms subsequently granted state officials the capacity and the means to plunder state assets in collusion with a range of other actors.[52] She illustrates that since 1991 this third generation of CCP cadres and their cronies exploited China's incremental economic reforms at every step of the way, thus accumulating historically unprecedented wealth in a very short period of time.[53] During the transformation of thousands of state-owned enterprises into stock-listed private companies, for example, local regulators and company managers engaged in rampant rent seeking, stripping close to 46 billion yuan of state assets.[54] A second example relates to China's property market. As a nominally communist state, the PRC's land is owned by the party-state and leased for development. During China's early reform period in the 1990s and 2000s this state monopoly on land provided local government officials and developers with ample opportunities to benefit from land resource allocation, including the destruction and reallocation of existing rural and urban neighbourhoods.[55] In this process, many CCP cadres and colluding property developers became multi-millionaires. The corruption and collusion between regulators and developers also impacted on the ability of the state to collect taxes: An investigation of 88 property companies in Nanjing in the year 2002 revealed that 87 companies had evaded taxes to the tune of 50 million yuan.[56]

He Qinglian argues that by no later than 1999 the Chinese party-state was captured by rent-seeking elites, who started to concentrate power, occupy the levers of system transformation, undermine control systems, hinder the introduction of the rule of law and which showed an insatiable appetite for resources ranging from people, finances, to materials.[57] Against the backdrop of state capture it becomes clearer that the suppression of China's nation-wide anti-corruption and pro-democracy movement in 1989 was also the birth date of China's crony-capitalist system, as outlined by Pei Minxin.[58] Pei defines China's "rapacious crony capitalism"[59] by quoting Xi Jinping:

> Corruption in regions and sectors are interwoven; cases of corruption through collusion are increasing; abuse of personnel authority and abuse of executive authority overlap; the exchange of power for power, power for money, and power for sex is frequent; collusion between officials and businessmen and collusion between superiors and subordinates have become intertwined; the methods of transferring benefits to each other are concealed and various.[60]

The concentration of the nation's wealth in the hands of a couple of hundred politically well-connected Chinese families has also severely skewed the trajectory of mainland China's social stratification.

In modernisation theory, a burgeoning middle class is widely seen as a prerequisite for political liberalisation and democratisation. Alpermann summarises this perspective as follows: "In the classical view, the rising expectations of middle class individuals regarding political representation and protection against arbitrary state actions create political tensions and generate demands for democratization and the rule of law respectively."[61] Among social scientists the idea that an olive-shaped society—with few rich people at the top, a vast middle class and few poor people at the bottom—is more conducive to social and political stability than a society shaped like a pyramid (Figure 2.1).[62] According to Chen Dongdong, a

> middle class is seen as the core component of society of modest prosperity and should, therefore, be allowed to grow as much as possible in order that "an olive-shaped social strata model can develop out of the current pyramid structure". This is seen as the only way to avoid conflict between rich and poor and to ensure long-term stability.[63]

A persistent problem in middle-class studies, however, is the lack of a generally accepted definition of middle class and how it should be measured. Chen and Goodman have argued that consumerism, modern lifestyles and privileged access to health and education should be seen as key characteristics of members of the middle class.[64] In the Chinese context, Lu Xueyi has identified six elements that identify members of the middle class, ranging from the type of work (intellectual labour in a safe and clean environment); rights and duties at the workplace (including responsibilities, the right to speak up, make suggestions and exercise some form of control); income, including all perks, patrimonial assets and other benefits directly or indirectly deriving from employment; skills (especially education higher than high school, training and experience); lifestyle and consumption habits; as well as moral and civic consciousness.[65] Lu's conceptualisation, however, did not only serve academic purposes, as his monograph coincided with CCP chairman Jiang Zemin's Three Represents theory and supported the notions of a "civilised" and "advanced" middle strata. This indicates that China's social stratification and the shape of China's society is relevant both when discussing the potential for democratic reform as well as when analysing the resilience of a given authoritarian system. While no consensus exists as to how to define and measure China's middle class,[66] it can be safely argued that urban mainland Chinese citizens have materially benefited from China's economic modernisation.

China's nascent middle class, which developed as an outcome of China's economic development, so far has not played the role designated by modernisation theory. According to Hefele and Dittrich,

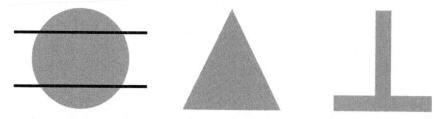

FIGURE 2.1 Ideal types of social stratification: an olive-, pyramid- or T-shaped society?

(the) main difference between the Western and Chinese concept of a middle class lies in the unique role played by party functionaries as a result of their having access to power and resources. Working in the state sector is seen as a key factor in becoming part of the middle class, and having a close relationship with the political elite can have a significant impact on financial success.[67]

Mindful of the potential for China's middle class to demand greater social and political reform,[68] the CCP has been actively courting key groups to ensure their loyalty to the party-state, e.g. by providing Chinese scholars working for universities with higher salaries or by selling flats to "state-sector employees at highly subsidized prices, sometimes at as little as one-fifth of the original construction cost (Unger 2006)".[69] Such preferential policies mean that especially urban Chinese have benefited from the property boom in the late 1990s and early 2000s. Rapidly rising property prices in cities such as Beijing, Shanghai, Guangzhou and Shenzhen have produced wealth in a very short period of time. The caveat is that in the absence of a functioning rule of law, such material gains remain under constant threat from possible land and house expropriation for the sake of redevelopment, thus leaving these new members of China's middle class in a rather precarious situation.[70] Christopher Balding, a former associate professor at the HSBC School of Business at Peking University, has called the precarious nature of property rights the biggest danger to stability in China.[71]

The strategic co-optation of potential opponents to CCP rule has also extended to China's growing class of private entrepreneurs. According to Hendrischke, the CCP has granted private entrepreneurs a slew of privileges, which range from policy support for private enterprises, access to CCP organs such as the National People's Congress or Chinese People's Political Consultative Conference, to facilitated business deals and expedited access to credit.[72] In the words of Christopher Buckley "getting ahead and getting rich in contemporary urban China requires a combination of skills, entrepreneurial ability and access to bureaucratic power, and those who do best should be the people who have the largest quantities of these resources".[73] China's post-1989 political economy thus has provided economic opportunities for the politically well connected, while leaving the majority of Chinese citizens behind.

Consequentially, Chinese society neither stratified into an olive shape nor a pyramid, but instead has turned into an inverted T structure.[74] In a widely discussed essay, Chinese sociologist Li Qiang argued on the basis of his analysis of census data:

> Chinese society has several characteristics: the income gap between the poor and the rich is expanding; social wealth is controlled by a few people; the disparity between town and countryside and between different

regions is becoming serious increasingly and the disparity problem also exists in both urban and rural areas; the low-income earners are marginalized from the mainstream society and the phenomenon of people gathering wealth by illegal means is quite common.[75]

While Li has primarily blamed China's Maoist institution, the household registration system (*hukou*),[76] for this structural imbalance, I would argue that the lack of social mobility is all but guaranteed when the country's wealth is controlled by a small elite.

But how serious is the problem of lack of upward mobility in contemporary China? How widespread is the feeling of relative deprivation within mainland Chinese society?[77] In his book *Age of Ambition: Chasing Fortune, Truth, and Faith in the New China*, long-time China watcher Evan Osnos has vividly described how ordinary Chinese citizens are increasingly aware of the lack of upward mobility. Osnos recounts how his interlocutors have experienced the increasing lack of development opportunities under the conditions of crony capitalism. In Osnos' words:

> [one] of the things that you feel very acutely if you've been to China in the past ten years is this rising sense of possibility and then this declining sense of possibility. I very much felt a need to convey this in the writing. Some of this is structural: I start off with cases of meeting people in China when they were defined above all by this sense of soaring aspiration and possibility. But as the years ticked by—and this was not an arc I anticipated or set out to describe— people felt that the space in which they might actualize what they wanted to do was narrowing. People at the bottom of the income scale no longer felt that previous sense of economic possibility and opportunity, and likewise for people at the upper end of the income scale who were beginning to dabble in what it meant to be politically active. Whether it was Ai Weiwei or Wang Gongquan, guys who had decided to try out the experience of being politically active, they also felt that their bandwidth for available action was narrowing. My hope is that the reader comes away at the end of this book with a sense of that arc, because that's very much a part of how I experienced it.[78]

Osnos' anecdotal evidence was collected during his nine-year stay as a foreign journalist in mainland China (2005–13).[79] It resembles the rising discontent among ordinary Chinese citizens in 1989, who were upset about the increasing corruption and collusion between CCP cadres and their cronies during the first phase of China's economic reforms in the early 1980s.

Osnos' findings are also mirrored in the academic literature about relative deprivation in China.

In a landmark article Zheng Yongnian provided an analysis of the winners and losers of economic reforms. Zheng includes the social group of party and government cadres, who benefited most from the infusion of market principles into China's formerly planned economy. Further beneficiaries included private enterprise bosses, acting personnel, the urban and rural self-employed, state-owned enterprise managers and professionals.[80] In Zheng's words, "farmers and state-owned enterprise workers were the biggest losers in this process".[81] Arguing that weaker elements of Chinese society need to be defended, Zheng comes to the sobering conclusion that in contemporary China,

> (both) economic and political transformations mean that "money" and "power" are now the two key players in China's development. Both players occupy strategic positions within the country's hierarchical system. That implies that while both play an important role in promoting development, they will continue to dominate the course of China's development. Meanwhile, these two players can exchange their resources, be it money for power or power for money, for their own benefit.[82]

Modernisation without transparency and accountability

State capture by rent-seeking elites has meant that the post-1989 Chinese party-state has started to erratically move back and forth between the role of a developmental and predatory state.[83] Mancur Olson has described the problem of predation as follows: "the consensus would probably be that when there is a stronger incentive to take than to make—more gain from predation than from productive and mutually advantageous activities—societies fall to the bottom".[84] In its developmental role, the party-state resembles what Olson has called a "stationary bandit", a mafia-like organisation which has a self-interest to:

> monopolize crime in the neighborhood, [as] it will gain from promoting business profitability and safe residential life there. Thus, the secure Mafia family will maximize its take by selling protection—both against the crime it would commit itself (if not paid) as well as that which would be committed by others (if it did not keep out other criminals). Other things being equal, the better the community is as an environment for business and living, the more the protection racket will bring in.[85]

During predation, however, the Chinese party-state resembles what Olson refers to as a "roving banditry". The latter can be described as plundering bandits who disregard the ability of their victims to recover from their losses, thus having no means to be productive in the future. Large-scale and systemic corruption can thus be considered as the predatory practice of plundering.

The widely publicised milk scandal of 2008 in mainland China is a prime example of the CCP simultaneously engaging in developmental and predatory practices. State capture in this context meant that the party-state forfeited its role as regulator and agreed to the Chinese dairy industry's demand to set a very low standard for milk nutrition levels. In the words of Zhu Hongjun this allowed "China's backward dairy sector"[86] with its "disparate livestock-rearing standards and issues of milk quality",[87] a "laggard industry ... to dictate standards".[88] In order to deal with low levels of food nutrition, the party-state commissioned scientific research to explore ways to boost protein levels:

> China's top scientific body—the Chinese Academy of Sciences (CAS)—'discovered' as early as 1999 that adding melamine to food could boost its protein levels. In turn, the reports allege that rogue biologists cashed in on their chemical invention by promoting the sale of products containing melamine—even charging for training in how to use them—for years.[89]

Melamine, however, turned out to be unsuitable for human consumption. Consequently, six Chinese babies who were fed mainland Chinese milk formula died and more than 300,000 got ill, with many of the babies developing kidney stones.[90] When the scandal broke the party-state mobilised its propaganda machine to silence victims, thus sweeping the combined state and market failure under the proverbial carpet. In light of the persistent regulatory failures of the Chinese party-state, Zheng Yongnian has made the case for China's government to either

> regulate or die. This is the lesson one can draw from the current financial crisis in the United States. The issue is who regulates who. While the government can regulate the market, the two sides can also share mutual benefits. If this is the case, then there will be no morality and social justice. No one can regulate money, and no one can regulate power.[91]

Other high-profile corruption cases in China temporarily shed light on the predatory nature of the party-state. In 2011 China's former minister for railways, Liu Zhijun, was arrested for corruption and sentenced to death in 2013. In 2015 his death sentence was commuted to life imprisonment. Prior to his downfall, Liu enjoyed a lavish lifestyle: "The Beijing Times reported that investigations into Liu recovered 16 cars and more than 350 flats. He had 18 mistresses 'including actresses, nurses and train stewards'."[92] In 2014, Liu's partner in crime Zhang Shuguang, the former deputy chief engineer of the now defunct Ministry of Railways, also received a suspended death sentence. Zhang had personally benefited from the rapid expansion of China's high-speed railway system in even more egregious ways:

China Central Television, the state broadcaster, appeared to confirm rumours about the enormous sums that had been stolen. In a report on the Sina Weibo website, that was quickly deleted by censors, CCTV said Mr Zhang had $2.8 billion in his overseas accounts and that Mr Liu had taken up to 1 billion yuan (£95 million) in bribes.[93]

To put this corruption scandal into perspective, it is worth comparing it to the biggest corruption scandal in post-World War Europe. During the 1980s and 1990s the French oil company Elf Aquitaine illegally spent about £300 million for commissions to facilitate oil deals and property investments. Among the most notable cases of corruption was a £30 million commission to acquire the East German Leuna oil refinery in 1992. Elf Aquitaine also lent Thomson, a French state-owned defence company, a helping hand by funnelling £250 million to secure a £1.6 billion sale of six Lafayette war ships from France to Taiwan. As part of these illegal transactions, former French foreign minister Roland Dumas' ex-mistress Christine Deviers-Joncour received 65 million francs (US$9.3 million) from Elf Aquitaine between 1989 and 1993.[94] Jon Henley, a *Guardian* journalist, has considered the Elf Aquitaine corruption case "perhaps the biggest financial scandal in a western democracy since the end of the second world war".[95] If one compares and contrasts the alleged bribe of US$9.3 million for former French minister Roland Dumas with the graft of former Railway Ministry's deputy chief engineer Zhang Shuguang it becomes evident that the former bribe is dwarfed by the supposed extraction of US$2.8 billion by Zhang Shuguang. Zhang's corruption, however, is by no means an outlier but indicative of the extent of systemic and endemic corruption in mainland China.

When Wikileaks dumped 250,000 United States diplomatic cables into the public domain in 2010, one of the cables revealed the extent of corruption among Chinese top political leaders from the vantage point of a senior American diplomat. The cable revealed that the Chinese Politburo should be better understood as business empires, in which individual Politburo members wield control over vast industries. The United States Embassy had been briefed by Chen Jieren, a "nephew of He Guoqiang, of China's nine most senior Politburo members".[96] He

told American diplomats in 2009 that the Communist party has carved up the country's economic "pie" among its leaders. "It was well known," Chen stated in a cable since released by Wikileaks, "that former premier Li Peng and his family controlled all electric power interests; Politburo Standing Committee member and security czar Zhou Yongkang and associates controlled the oil interests; the late former top leader Chen Yun's family controlled most of the banking sector; Politburo Standing Committee member Jia Qinglin was the main interest behind major

Beijing real estate developments; Hu Jintao's son-in-law ran Sina.com; and Wen Jiabao's wife controlled China's precious gems sector."[97]

The stratospheric proportions of plundering of mainland China's assets was also revealed in 2011, when

> the People's Bank of China published a report that looked at corruption monitoring and how corrupt officials transfer assets overseas. The report quotes statistics based on research by the Chinese Academy of Social Sciences: 18,000 Communist Party and government officials, public-security members, judicial cadres, agents of state institutions and senior-management individuals of state-owned enterprises have fled China since 1990. Also missing is about $120 billion.[98]

Yukon Huang has pointed out that the "chance of going to jail for corruption, according to one study, is only 3 percent in China – making corruption a low risk, high return gamble".[99] Wedeman's seminal study of corruption in mainland China revealed that "rapid increases in the number of senior cadres and officials charged with misconduct and the monies linked to corruption, reveal a pattern of intensifying corruption wherein growth in high-level corruption has outstripped growth in other forms of malfeasance and, perhaps more critically, growth in 'ordinary' corruption".[100] The CCP has thus not only been complicit in the plundering of state assets but according to Pei its predatory practices have led to "the erosion of government's ability to provide essential public services, such as public safety, education, health, environmental protection, and enforcement of laws and rules".[101]

This is particularly evident when reviewing official statistics on public expenditure for China's health and education. In 2015, the global average health expenditure as a percentage of gross domestic product (GDP) was 9.9 percent. When comparing the statistics for war-torn Sudan with those of the PRC, the Sudanese government spent 6.3 percent of its GDP on healthcare in comparison to the PRC's 5.3 percent.[102] In terms of education, the situation is even more dire. The Chinese government stopped reporting its overall expenditure on education in 1999, which flatlined at a mere 1.88 percent of the country's GDP. The extremely low expenditure stands in stark contrast to Sudan's 2.21 percent in 2009 and the world's average of 4.74 percent.[103] The very low levels of public expenditure for health and education raise doubts about the CCP's willingness to address social inequality in China with the help of social policy. When comparing the CCP's approach to stability preservation between the German Empire (1862–90) and the PRC (1949–) I explained CCP's approach to social management in post-Maoist China with reference to Bismarck's political statesmanship in the late 19th century. A major finding of this study was that whereas "Bismarck's social policy can be described as too little, too late, the post-Maoist dismantling of the traditional welfare state and the accompanying privatisation could equally be described as too much, too soon. In both instances, the resulting welfare states were rudimentary at best, providing only limited safety nets for vulnerable groups."[104]

Corruption of an entire people?

In the absence of a free media, independent judiciary, labour unions and other forms of an independent and assertive civil society which could act as a check on the power of the party-state, corruption, collusion and nepotism have spread from the elite to the mass level. Reflecting on the pervasiveness of corruption, collusion and nepotism both in China's state and society Ci Jiwei has argued that

> (it) is no longer remotely alarmist to speak of the corruption of an entire people (quanmin fubai), although this is no doubt an exaggeration if taken literally to cover all individual members of society … the norms that are violated by so many in every walk of life are very elementary one indeed (dixian lunli, as they are called in Chinese) not ones that require altruism or the adoption of perfectionist conceptions of the good.[105]

Rent seeking, understood as "all largely unproductive, expropriate activities, which bring positive return to the individual but not to society",[106] has become normalised and is now a defining feature in every industry and sector of Chinese society. This is evident from the plethora of ethical transgressions and illegal practices in the food industry, education system, healthcare system and journalism.

In terms of food safety, almost no day passes without another report about transgressions in China's food-processing industry. The use of carcinogenic gutter oil in Chinese restaurants[107] is just as common as scandals about adultered food, such as fake mutton made out of "rat, mink and fox meat".[108] Chinese scientists working in partnership with the food-processing industry have advised agro-businesses how to mask unsafe food additives in the government screenings of pig meat.[109] China's primary and secondary education sector provides another example of deteriorating professional ethics. While Chinese parents already pay relatively high fees for the education of their children, it is commonplace that school administrators charge fees of up to US$16,000 for a place in a Beijing middle school. Furthermore, in order to pay attention to children, secondary school teachers expect "gifts" which range from organic rice and iPads to short overseas trips.[110] Corrupt practices also abound in China's higher education. They range from fraud such as "fabricating or tampering with data",[111] pervasive plagiarism and "corruption in academic appointments and evaluation"[112] such as "bribery, favouritism, abuse of power, and monopoly of academic resources in academic appointments, publication, awards and funding applications".[113] In China's healthcare sector it is a commonplace phenomenon for patients to be overtreated and overcharged for their prescribed medication and medical procedures. Low pay for surgeons and nurses means that patients are expected to bribe them.[114] Corrupt practices have also made inroads into the profession of journalism. Chinese journalists routinely expect to be paid "transportation fees" of up to £30 for attending public events. To ensure media coverage, they are often provided with so-called "red envelopes" with up to £300.[115] Civilian anti-corruption websites, modelled after their Indian counterparts, emerged in 2011[116] but were soon shut down by the authorities. Ci explains the scale of the problem as follows:

> Once a crisis of justice and social order is under way, whatever its causes, it has a tendency to sustain and even aggravate itself. This is because noncompliance with norms of justice by some members of society, unless corrected in an effective and timely fashion, tends to weaken the motive of compliance on the part of others, thus leading to progressively worse overall noncompliance.[117]

Ci's sobering assessment reveals the crux of mainland China's incomplete modernisation.

In this chapter I have used the example of mainland China during the post-1978 reform and opening-up period to critique basic tenets of modernisation theory. While mainland China's economy has grown in leaps and bounds, due to the nature of its post-1989 political economy fruits of economic growth have been distributed in a very unequal way and benefited CCP cadres and their cronies in disproportionate ways. Economic modernisation has also led to the formation of a Chinese middle class, but as I have argued in this chapter, it remains heavily dependent on the patronage of party-state gatekeepers. Modernisation in mainland China has led to a vicious circle, where an autocratic crony-capitalist CCP has shown little concern for the establishment of a liberal democracy and invested few of its resources to strive for social equality. Systemic and endemic corruption and collusion have also spread from the party-state and infected large swathes of mainland Chinese society, thus undermining transparency and accountability in public and private affairs.

The struggle for democracy in mainland China, therefore, is not just a fight to reform the political institutions of an autocratic regime but also an effort to enhance social equality and enhance transparency and accountability in mainland China's state and society. For Taiwanese and Hong Kong citizens living at the periphery of mainland China, this scenario does not bode well. Given the challenges that mainland Chinese democrats face, the journey to outgrow the CCP dictatorship will take decades rather than years. This means that in the meantime, citizens in a liberal democratic Taiwan and a semi-democratic Hong Kong need to guard themselves against CCP-led "sharp power" intrusions aimed at undermining their young democratic institutions. Whether they accept it or not, both Taiwanese and Hong Kong citizens thus have a stake in the outcome of the struggle for democracy in mainland China. In Chapter 3 I will provide an analytical framework which helps to identify the different stakeholder groups involved in this struggle and how to make sense of their respective strategies and tactics.

Notes

1 *New York Times* (2018), China's Legislature Blesses Xi's Indefinite Rule. It Was 2,958 to 2, 11 March. Available online: www.nytimes.com/2018/03/11/world/asia/china-xi-constitution-term-limits.html (accessed 13 August 2018).
2 *New York Times* (2018), Ending Term Limits for China's Xi Is a Big Deal. Here's Why, 10 March. Available online: www.nytimes.com/2018/03/10/world/asia/china-xi-jinping-term-limit-explainer.html (accessed 13 August 2018).
3 Zeng, Jinghan (2015), *The Chinese Communist Party's Capacity to Rule: Ideology, Legitimacy and Party Cohesion*, Palgrave Macmillan, New York.
4 Zeng, Jinghan (2018), "Sorry that I have to turn down all media enquiries and op-ed invitation on the constitution amendments. *As a scholar who had faith in the institutionalisation of China's power succession, I need to sit down and study its limits now.*" 25 February. Tweet. Available online: https://twitter.com/Jinghan_Zeng/status/968027811834458114 (accessed 13 August 2018).
5 Goebel, Christian (2018), "This is what I wrote for the @bti_project in 02/15: 'China would be the first autocracy to reform itself successfully from within … There is a significant risk of *China becoming a personalized dictatorship.*' I seldom make predictions, but this definitely was on the horizon." 25 February. Tweet. Available online: https://twitter.com/Chri5tianGoebel/status/967710887715975168 (accessed 13 August 2018).
6 Goebel, Christian (2018), "A new tombstone on the graveyard of political science concepts. R.I.P. Authoritarian Resilience (01/2003–02/2018)." 25 February. Tweet. Available online: https://twitter.com/Chri5tianGoebel/status/967765683001090054 (accessed 13 August 2018).
7 *Reuters* (2018), China Says Lifting Term Limits Is about Protecting Authority of Party. Available online: www.reuters.com/article/us-china-parliament-politics/china-says-lifting-term-limits-is-about-protecting-authority-of-party-idUSKBN1GG0CR (accessed 13 August 2018).
8 Godement, Francois (2018), Xi's Rule for Life: What Does Our Anxiety Reveal?, European Council on Foreign Relations. Available online: www.ecfr.eu/article/commentary_xis_rule_for_life_what_does_our_anxiety_reveal (accessed 13 August 2018).
9 Ibid.
10 Ibid.
11 Carothers, Thomas (1999), *Aiding Democracy Abroad: The Learning Curve*, Carnegie Endowment for International Peace, Washington, DC, 20.
12 Lipset, S. (1959), Some Social Requisites of Democracy: Economic Development and Political Legitimacy, *American Political Science Review*, 53(1), 69–105; Almond, G., Coleman, J. and Woodrow Wilson School of Public International Affairs, Center of International Studies (1960), *The Politics of the Developing Areas*, Princeton University Press, Princeton, NJ; Rustow, D. (1970), Transitions to Democracy: Toward a Dynamic Model, *Comparative Politics*, 2(3), 337–63.

13 Loewenthal, R. (1963), Staatsfunktion und Staatsform in Entwicklungslaendern, in: R. Loewenthal (Ed.), *Die Demokratie im Wandel der Gesellschaft*, Verlag, Berlin, 164–92; O'Donnell, G.A. (1973), *Modernization and Bureaucratic-Authoritarianism*, University of California Press, Berkeley, CA; Huntington, S. (2006), *Political Order in Changing Societies*, Yale University Press, New Haven, CT.

14 Erdmann, G. (1996), *Demokratie und Demokratiefoerderung in der Dritten Welt. Ein Literaturbericht und eine Erhebung der Konzepte und Instrumente*, Zentralstelle Weltkirche der Deutschen Bischofskonferenz, Bonn, 3.

15 Faria, H., Montesinos-Yufa, H. and Morales, D. (2014), Should the Modernization Hypothesis Survive Acemoglu, Johnson, Robinson, and Yared? Some More Evidence, *Econ Journal Watch*, 11(1), 17–36.

16 Nathan, Andrew and Link, Perry (2001), *The Tiananmen Papers*, Public Affairs, New York.

17 Ibid., 223–96.

18 Fewsmith, Joseph (n.d.), What Zhao Ziyang Tells Us about Elite Politics in the 1980s. Available online: www.democracy.uci.edu/files/docs/conferences/fewsmith. pdf (accessed 5 March 2018).

19 天安门 The Film (1995), *The Gate of Heavenly Peace*. Available online: www. tsquare.tv/film/transcript.html (accessed 5 March 2018).

20 Béja, Jean-Philippe and Goldman, Merle (2011), The Impact of the June 4th Massacre on the Pro-Democracy Movement, in: Jean-Philippe Béja (Ed.), *The Impact of China's 1989 Tiananmen Massacre*, Routledge, New York, 8.

21 Ibid., 35.

22 Ibid., 41.

23 Wang, Dan (1990), II: Wang Dan, On Freedom of Speech for the Opposition, in: Mok Chiu Yu and Frank Harrison (Eds), *Voices from Tiananmen Square*, Black Rose Books, New York, 38–41.

24 XXX, Teacher at People's University (1990), Why Does China Need Democracy?, in: Han Minzhu, *Cries for Democracy: Writings and Speeches from the 1989 Chinese Democracy Movement*, Princeton University Press, Princeton, NJ, 151–63.

25 Wanding, Ren (1990), III: Ren Wanding: Why Did the Rally in Memory of Hu Yaobang Turn into a Democracy Movement?, in: Mok Chiu Yu and Frank Harrison (Eds), *Voices from Tiananmen Square*, Black Rose Books, New York, 42–7.

26 天安门 The Film (1995), *The Gate of Heavenly Peace*. Available online: www. tsquare.tv/film/transcript.html (accessed 5 March 2018).

27 Unger, Jonathan (1991), Introduction, in Jonathan Unger (Ed.), *The Pro-Democracy Protests in China: Reports from the Provinces*, M.E. Sharpe, New York, 4.

28 Ibid.

29 Ibid.

30 Ibid., 5.

31 Žižek, Slavoj (2011), *Living in the End Times*, Verso, London, 154.

32 Saich, Tony (2001), *Governance and Politics of China*, Palgrave, New York, 42.

33 Teiwes, Frederick C. (2000), The Maoist State, in: David Shambaugh (Ed.), *The Modern Chinese State*, Cambridge University Press, Cambridge, 159.

34 *China Quarterly* (1979),Quarterly Documentation, *China Quarterly*, 77, 168.

35 Lin, Weirong (1996), An Abortive Chinese Enlightenment: The Cultural Revolution and Class Theory. PhD diss., University of Wisconsin-Madison.

36 Wei, Jingsheng (1978), The Fifth Modernization: Democracy, in: Wm. Theodore de Bary and Richard Lufrano (Eds), *Sources of Chinese Tradition: From 1600 through the Twentieth Century*, 2nd ed., Vol. 2, Columbia University Press, New

York, 2000, 497–500. Available online: http://afe.easia.columbia.edu/ps/cup/wei_jingsheng_fifth_modernization.pdf (accessed 20 August 2018).

37 Ibid.

38 Ibid.

39 Sen, Amartya (2004), Elements of a Theory of Human Rights, *Philosophy and Public Affairs*, 32, 334.

40 Ibid.

41 Ibid.

42 Sen, Amartya (2000), *Development as Freedom*, Knopf, Borzoi Books, New York, 16.

43 Yang, J., Guo, J. and Mosher, S. (2012). *Tombstone: The Untold Story of Mao's Great Famine*, translated by Stacy Mosher and Guo Jian; edited by Edward Friedman, Gou Jian and Stacy Mosher; introduction by Edward Friedman and Roderick MacFarquhar, Penguin, London.

44 Dikoetter, Frank (2010), *Mao's Great Famine*, Bloomsbury, London.

45 Wemheuer, Felix (2011), Review: SITES OF HORROR: MAO'S GREAT FAMINE (with Response), *China Journal*, 66(July), 162.

46 天安门 The Film (1995), *The Gate of Heavenly Peace*. Available online: www.tsquare.tv/film/transcript.html (accessed 5 March 2018).

47 Ceriani, L. and Verme, P. (2012), The Origins of the Gini Index: Extracts from Variabilità e Mutabilità (1912) by Corrado Gini, *Journal of Economic Inequality*, 10(3), 421–43.

48 Chen, J., Dai, D., Pu, M., Hou, W. and Feng, Q. (2010), The Trend of the Gini Coefficient of China. *IDEAS Working Paper Series from RePEc*, 20.

49 Yang, Yaowu and Yang, Chengyu (2015), China's Gini Coefficient *: Myths and Realities, *China Economist*, 10(6), 78.

50 Vieira, Sergio (2012), Inequality on the Rise? An Assessment of Current Available Data on Income Inequality, at Global, International and National Levels. Background document for the WESS 2013. Available online: www.un.org/en/development/desa/policy/wess/wess_bg_papers/bp_wess2013_svieira1.pdf (accessed 20 August 2018).

51 Qinglian, He (2006), China in the Modernisierungsfalle, *Bundeszentrale für politische Bildung*, 48–9.

52 Her monograph was initially published in Chinese under the title *Xiandaihua de xianjing* in 1998 in Beijing by the publishing house Jinri Zhongguo chubanshe. It was soon thereafter banned and He Qinglian had to flee China in 2001.

53 Ibid., 49–50.

54 Ibid., 58.

55 Ibid., 83–90.

56 Ibid., 90.

57 Ibid., 150–1.

58 Pei, Minxin (2016), *China's Crony Capitalism: The Dynamics of Regime Decay*, Harvard University Press, Cambridge, MA.

59 Ibid., 2.

60 Ibid., 1.

61 Alpermann, Bjoern (2016), Fukuyama and the Chinese Middle Class: Modernization Theory 1.5, *Journal of Chinese Governance*, 1(3), 445.

62 Lu, Xueyi (2004), *Dangdai Zhongguo Shehui Liudong* (Social Mobility in Contemporary China), Shehui kexue wenxian chubanshe, Beijing; Peilin, Li and Di, Zhu (2016), Make Efforts to Develop an Olive-Shaped Distribution Pattern: An Analysis Based on Data from the Chinese Social Survey for 2006–2013, *Social Sciences in China*, 37(1), 5–24; China.org.cn (2010), China Needs to Change from a Pyramid into an Olive. Available online: www.china.org.cn/opinion/2010-04/21/content_19875821.htm (accessed 13 August 2018).

63   As quoted by Hefele, Peter and Dittrich, Andreas (2011), China's Middle Class. A Driving Force for Democratic Change or Guarantor of the Status Quo?, 12. Available online: www.kas.de/wf/doc/kas_29625-544-2-30.pdf?111205133611 (accessed 13 August 2018).

64   Chen, Minglu and Goodman, David S.G. (2013), Introduction: Middle Class China—Discourse, Structure and Practice, in: Minglu Chen and David S.G. Goodman (Eds), *Middle Class China: Identity and Behaviour*, Cheltenham, Edward Elgar, 3.

65   Lu, Xueyi (2002), *Dangdai zhongguo shehui jieceng yanjiu baogao* (Research Report on Contemporary China's Social Stratification), Shehui kexue wenxian chubanshe, Beijing.

66   I concur with Alpermann who argues "that the middle class is an essentially contested concept, including the idealistic associations this evokes. Thus it will remain elusive, no matter how hard scholars try to establish a common understanding about its meaning." Alpermann, Bjoern (2016), Fukuyama and the Chinese Middle Class: Modernization Theory 1.5, *Journal of Chinese Governance*, 1(3), 450.

67   Ibid.

68   This view is supported by findings from a comprehensive public opinion survey conducted by Pan and Xu. The two authors found that "(those) who are relatively better off in China's era of market reform tend to welcome additional market liberalization as well as political reform toward democratic institutions and tend not to endorse traditional social norms." Pan, Jennifer and Xu, Yiqing (2018), China's Ideological Spectrum, *Journal of Politics*, 80(1), 271.

69   Elfick, Jacqueline (2011), Class Formation and Consumption among Middle-Class Professionals in Shenzhen, *Journal of Current Chinese Affairs*, 40(1), 195.

70   For a very graphic illustration of the problem of house expropriation see *Guardian* (2014), China's Nail Houses: The Homeowners Who Refuse to Make Way—in Pictures. Available online: www.theguardian.com/cities/gallery/2014/apr/15/china-nail-houses-in-pictures-property-development (accessed 14 August 2018). For a discussion of the challenge of land expropriation see Chen, L. (2014), Legal and Institutional Analysis of Land Expropriation in China, in: H. Fu and J. Gillespie (Eds), *Resolving Land Disputes in East Asia: Exploring the Limits of Law*, Cambridge University Press, Cambridge, 59–85.

71   Balding, Christopher (2018), "People ask me: what is the greatest threat to social stability in China? They expect to hear debt, human rights, environment, or political crackdown. I always say and it isn't even close: real estate prices." 6 October. Tweet. Available online: https://twitter.com/BaldingsWorld/status/1048475296603824128 (accessed 8 October 2018).

72   Hendrischke, H. (2013), Institutional Determinants of the Political Consciousness of Private Entrepreneurs, in: Minglu Chen and David S.G. Goodman, *Middle Class China: Identity and Behaviour*, Edward Elgar, Cheltenham, 139.

73   Buckley, Christopher (1999), How a Revolution Becomes a Dinner Party: Stratification, Mobility and the New Rich in Urban China, in: Michael Pinches (Ed.), *Cultural and Privilege in Capitalist Asia*, Routledge, London, 210.

74   Li, Qiang (2005), "Ding Zi Xing" Shehui Jiegou Yu "Jiegou Jinzhang" ("Inverted T-Shaped" Social Structure and "Structural Tension"), *Shehuixue Yanjiu*, 2, 55–73.

75   *China Daily* (2006), Society in a Reversed T-shape—Expert. Available online: www.chinadaily.com.cn/china/2006-08/08/content_659260.htm (accessed 14 August 2018).

76   *Independent* (2017), Outdated "Urban Passports" Still Rule the Lives of China's Rural Citizens China's Hukou System Is a Relic of the Mao Era—and It's Holding the Nation's Rural Population Back, 13 January. Available online: www.independent.co.uk/news/world/politics/outdated-urban-passports-still-rule-the-lives-of-china-s-rural-citizens-a7517181.html (accessed 14 August 2018).

77 Relative deprivation is understood as the phenomena of people comparing themselves "to other people, groups, or even themselves at different points in time [which] lead people to believe that they do not have what they deserve, [and thus] they will be angry and resentful". Smith, H., Pettigrew, T., Pippin, G. and Bialosiewicz, S. (2012), Relative Deprivation: A Theoretical and Meta-Analytic Review, *Personality and Social Psychology Review*, 16(3), 203.

78 *Guernica* (2014), The Arc of Possibility. Available online: www.guernicamag. com/the-arc-of-possibility/ (accessed 13 August 2018).

79 Osnos, Evan (2014), China, Up Close. Available online: https://theamerica nscholar.org/china-up-close/#.W3pv_y3MxDV (accessed 20 August 2018).

80 Zheng, Yongnian (2010), Society Must Be Defended: Reform, Openness, and Social Policy in China, *Journal of Contemporary China*, 19(67), 807.

81 Ibid., 806.

82 Ibid., 816.

83 Pei, Minxin (2006), *China's Trapped Transition: The Limits of Developmental Autocracy*, Harvard University Press, Cambridge, MA, 132–66.

84 Olson, Mancur (2000), *Power and Prosperity: Outgrowing Communist and Capitalist Dictatorships*, Basic Books, New York, 1.

85 Ibid., 5

86 Zhu, Hongjun (2012), How Milk Standards Triggered Uproar in China. Available online: www.chinadialogue.net/article/show/single/en/5141-How-milk-standa rds-triggered-uproar-in-China (accessed 22 August 2018).

87 Ibid.

88 Ibid.

89 *Asia Times Online* (2008), Greed, Mad Science and Melamine. Available online: www.atimes.com/atimes/China/JK14Ad01.html (accessed 6 June 2012).

90 BBC (2010), China Dairy Products Found Tainted with Melamine. Available online: www.bbc.com/news/10565838 (accessed 22 August 2018).

91 Zheng, Yongnian (2010), Society Must Be Defended: Reform, Openness, and Social Policy in China, *Journal of Contemporary China*, 19(67), 818.

92 *Guardian* (2013), Liu Zhijun, China's Ex-Railway Minister, Sentenced to Death for Corruption, 8 July. Available online: www.theguardian.com/world/2013/jul/ 08/liu-zhijun-sentenced-death-corruption (accessed 1 November 2017).

93 *Telegraph* (2011), Chinese Rail Crash Scandal: "Official Steals $2.8 billion", 1 August. Available online: www.telegraph.co.uk/news/worldnews/asia/china/ 8674824/Chinese-rail-crash-scandal-official-steals-2.8-billion.html (accessed 1 November 2017).

94 *New York Times* (1999), A Seamy French Tale of Sex, Politics and an Oil Company's Lost Millions. Available online: www.nytimes.com/1999/02/11/ world/a-seamy-french-tale-of-sex-politics-and-an-oil-company-s-lost-millions.htm l (accessed 21 August 2018).

95 *Guardian* (2001), France Pursues Bigger Picture in Elf Scandal, 2 June. Available online: www.theguardian.com/world/2001/jun/02/jonhenley (accessed 1 Novem- ber 2017).

96 *Telegraph* (2012), Chinese Leader Wen Jiabao's Family "Accumulate Billions" during His Time in Office. Available online: www.telegraph.co.uk/news/world news/asia/china/9634920/Chinese-leader-Wen-Jiabaos-family-accumulate-billions- during-his-time-in-office.html (accessed 21 August 2018).

97 Ibid.

98 *Time* (2011), China's Great Swindle: How Public Officials Stole $120 Billion and Fled the Country, 26 June. Available online: http://content.time.com/time/world/a rticle/0,8599,2079756,00.html#ixzz1e3ayab9l (accessed 1 November 2017).

99 Huang, Yukon (2015), The Truth about Chinese Corruption, Carnegie Endow- ment for International Peace. Available online: https://carnegieendowment.org/ 2015/05/29/truth-about-chinese-corruption-pub-60265 (accessed 21 August 2018).

100 Wedeman, Andrew (2004), The Intensification of Corruption in China, *China Quarterly*, 180, 920.
101 Pei, Minxin (2006), *China's Trapped Transition: The Limits of Developmental Autocracy*, Harvard University Press, Cambridge, MA, 169.
102 World Bank (2018), Current Health Expenditure (% of GDP). Available online: https://data.worldbank.org/indicator/SH.XPD.CHEX.GD.ZS?locations=SD-CN-1W (accessed 21 August 2018).
103 World Bank (2018), Government Expenditure on Education, Total (% of GDP). Available online: https://data.worldbank.org/indicator/SE.XPD.TOTL.GD.ZS?locations=SD-CN-1W (accessed 21 August 2018).
104 Fulda, Andreas (2016), Learning from Bismarck? A Comparative Study of Stability Preservation Approaches in the German Empire (1862–90) and the People's Republic of China (PRC) during the Mao (1949–1976) and Post-Mao Period (1976–), CPI Working Paper Series. Available online: www.nottingham.ac.uk/iaps/documents/cpi/working-papers/wp-no-19-fulda.pdf (accessed 21 August 2018).
105 Ci, Jiwei (2014), *Moral China in the Age of Reform*, Cambridge University Press, Cambridge, 15.
106 Krueger, A. (1974), as quoted in footnote 2 in: Dabla-Norris, E. and Wade, P. (2001), Rent Seeking and Endogenous Income Inequality, IMF Working Paper. Available online: www.imf.org/external/pubs/ft/wp/2001/wp0115.pdf (accessed 14 April 2017).
107 *Washington Post* (2013), You May Never Eat Street Food in China Again after Watching This Video. Available online: www.washingtonpost.com/news/world views/wp/2013/10/28/you-may-never-eat-street-food-in-china-again-after-wa tching-this-video/?noredirect=on&utm_term=.dc27b1f9b3a6 (accessed 21 August 2018).
108 *Guardian* (2013), China Fake Meat Scandal: Telling Your Rat from Your Mutton. Available online: www.theguardian.com/world/2013/may/03/china-fa ke-meat-rat-mutton (accessed 21 August 2018).
109 *Times Higher Education* (2009), Toxic Result of Corrosion of Ethics. Available online: http:// www.timeshighereducation.co.uk/406589.article (accessed 16 May 2013).
110 *Business Insider* (2013), Chinese Parents Are Spending up to $16,000 Just in Bribes to Get Their Kids into Good Schools, 8 October. Available online: www.busi nessinsider.com/china-corruption-begins-at-schools-2013-10?IR=T (accessed 1 November 2017).
111 Ren, Kai (2012), Fighting against Academic Corruption: A Critique of Recent Policy Developments in China, *Higher Education Policy*, 25, 19–38, 24.
112 Ibid.
113 Ibid.
114 *Business Insider* (2014), Healthcare Is So Corrupt in China that Patients Have to Bribe Doctors for Proper Care, 23 May. Available online: www.businessinsider. com/healthcare-is-so-corrupt-in-china-that-patients-have-to-bribe-doctors-2014-5?IR=T (accessed 1 November 2017).
115 AdAge (2015), It's Time for Brands and PR Agencies to Stop Paying Off the Chinese Media, 23 November. Available online: http://adage.com/article/guest-columnists/time-brands-pr-agencies-stop-paying-chinese-media/301432/ (accessed 1 November 2017).
116 CNN (2011), Anti-Corruption Websites Pop Up in China. Available online: http://edition.cnn.com/2011/WORLD/asiapcf/06/26/china.corruption/index.html (accessed 21 August 2018).
117 Ci, Jiwei (2014), *Moral China in the Age of Reform*, Cambridge University Press, Cambridge, 19.

3

DISSECTING THE DYNAMICS OF THE STRUGGLE FOR DEMOCRACY

In Chapter 2 I outlined mainland China's lack of progress towards more liberal-democratic forms of governance during the past three decades. Mainland China's slide towards regime decay[1] raises doubts about the validity and applicability of conventional modernisation theory in the case of countries with hard authoritarian political systems. This finding is highly significant, as modernisation theory remains a dominant strand of the academic discipline of democratisation studies, a sub-field of political science.[2] In this chapter I will make the case that in order to stay relevant, democratisation studies needs to overcome its theoretical stasis by linking theory and practice, by borrowing from the anthropological concept of *emic* and *etic* approaches, and by embracing the "theory of change" discourse pioneered in the field of development studies. Based on this critique of conventional democratisation studies I will make the case in Chapter 4 that "theories of and for political change" (TOPC) can be useful both for *post facto* analysis of political history as well as for *ex ante* strategic planning in the struggle for democracy. These TOPC will also form the vignettes for my analysis of the trajectory of the democracy movements in the three respective regions in Chapters 6, 8 and 10.

Erdmann has defined democratisation studies as follows: "The object of research on transitions is not changes in government but changes in political systems, of political regimes, the dissolution and displacement of old (authoritarian) and the building of a new (democratic) political rule".[3] According to Merkel, democratisation studies has developed four strands of theory, promoted by *system-oriented modernisation theorists; structuralists* who have focused on the interplay between state and social classes; *culturalists* who have honed in on religion and culture and the resulting forms of social interactions; as well as *actor theoretians* who concentrate on the explicitly political sphere.[4] While all four of the aforementioned theoretical strands have helped shed light on different aspects of democratisation processes around the world, to date democratisation studies *as a whole* has failed to develop theoretical frameworks which can be used to both analyse *and* anticipate political change in hard authoritarian environments such as mainland China's.

In the words of Whitehead, given

> the prominence and extensiveness of democratization processes in the real world, a political science discipline which offered no systematic or well-grounded approaches to the interpretation of this reality would be abdicating from an essential task. But our chances of producing a strong predictive theory are slight. Despite a decade of work on transitions from authoritarian capitalist rule, our discipline was not well-placed to predict ... or even anticipate the wave of democratizations which swept the ex-Soviet bloc after 1989; nor can we now offer high probability predictions about whether or how the remaining Communist Party ruled countries (China, Cuba, Korea, Vietnam) will fall into line. Even the core terminology we use—"breakdown", "liberalization", "transition", "consolidation" and "democracy" itself—is inherently somewhat fuzzy.[5]

Erdmann has similarly critiqued democratisation studies for the academic field's inability to develop generalisable rules for democratic transitions. At the heart of his critique is the realisation that democratisation studies are inherently *post facto* rationalisations of historical political processes.[6]

Dearth of studies on China's democratisation

In the case of a hard authoritarian political system such as mainland China's, democratisation studies has consequently struggled to discern the seeds for future political change. The same could be said about area studies approaches to the subject matter. A noticeable exception has been He Baogang's seminal study *The Democratization of China*, which offers insights about "different conceptions of democracy [in the Chinese discourse], and, in particular, about their implications for different types of political developments".[7] His study, however, is primarily a historical analysis of Chinese democracy discourses and aims to offer an intellectual justification for liberal democracy. He is also rather light on prescriptive recommendations beyond a call for the promotion of liberal political principles and practices in mainland China.[8] Another outlier in the academic literature about China's democratisation is Bruce Gilley's admittedly speculative monograph *China's Democratic Future*, in which he writes how a democratic China may look in the future and how it could come about.[9] Gilley has mused about the lack of academic discussion about democratic reform in China:

The lack of serious treatment of regime change in China is puzzling given the importance of the country and the evidence of such change elsewhere. One reason is that many scholars and observers simply believe that this scenario is unlikely, that China will be one of the great exceptions to the global trend of democratization. They favor predictions of a maintenance of the present system or a slow transition to some new form of political system. Those who share my belief in the likelihood of a bounded and decisive democratic transition, meanwhile, are understandably reluctant to engage in a detailed prediction. For some, it is because transitions are among the most contingent and therefore unpredictable events in politics. For others, self-censorship may play a role.[10]

The problem of censorship and self-censorship is particularly acute when it comes to mainland Chinese scholarship on the subject matters. While mainland Chinese scholars such as Yu Keping[11] and Li Fan[12] have theorised about democracy in the Chinese context, they stay clear of the study of contentious politics when broaching the topic. In this regard they echo the tendency among non-Chinese scholars to separate theory from practice. Given that activist scholar and Nobel Peace Prize laureate Liu Xiaobo went to prison and ultimately had to pay with his life for drafting pro-democratisation articles, Yu and Li's caution should not come to anyone's surprise. In their published works both Yu and Li effectively substantiate democracy with good government and political reform with administrative reform. While such creative discursive strategies allow them to publish their monographs in mainland China, such political compromises to avoid censorship dilute their contribution to global democratisation studies. Administrative reform under hard authoritarian conditions, after all, can be just as useful for political reformation (as it could pave the way to liberalisation and democratisation) as it can foster political restoration (and contribute to authoritarian resilience and/or regime decay). As such, their scholarship could be more accurately described as contributing to the field of public administration studies. Consequently, there is a dearth of either theoretically informed or empirically grounded area studies research on the subject matter. But if neither democratisation studies nor the field of contemporary Chinese studies have produced theories which can be used to explain the trajectory of political development in mainland China, Taiwan and Hong Kong's past, present and future, are there any other suitable alternative ways to dissect the dynamics of the struggle for democracy in the three regions?

Bridging theory and practice

In this book I aim to solve this riddle by bridging the gap between theories about democratisation processes and the day-to-day practice of activists struggling for democracy. This novel approach is informed by American educator John Dewey's insight that good theory is derived from practice, and that good practice should be informed by theory.[13] One persistent problem in democratisation studies is its exclusively theoretical orientation and lack of concern for the practicalities of political struggle. While some social and political scientists have dedicated their entire academic careers to studying democratisation processes, democracy activists do not necessarily have the time and resources to extensively study their respective political systems. While in theory *post facto* rationalisations of the political development trajectory up to the present day could indeed help inform an activist's political position and choice of strategies and tactics in the struggle for democracy, in practical terms, and especially during fast-moving political events, democracy activists rely on *ex ante* assumptions about how their agency is going to impact on ongoing political change processes. One of my central arguments therefore is that there is a need to overcome the gap between the academic field of democratisation studies and the lived experiences of democracy activists.

While a certain gap between theory and practice in political science may be unavoidable, we should try harder to overcome largely self-referential academic discourses by injecting a healthy dose of realism gained from the frontline of the struggle for democracy. Here I concur with Crosina and Bartunek's assessment that since

> academia and practice share so much common ground, neither ultimately makes much sense without the other—whether academics and practitioners are aware of it or not. We have also shown how this awareness does not prevent us from putting ourselves at the center of our own universe, but does certainly increase the tension on those who find themselves playing bridging roles between academia and practice. In other words, the notion that academics and practitioners are separate is full of contradictions. If we really believe in clear academic–practitioner distinctions the paradoxical joke is on us.[14]

Seen in this light, democracy activists should be active participants in the academic conversation, rather than treated as supposedly passive objects of academic inquiry. This requires us as democratisation scholars to familiarise ourselves with the political thought and practice of democracy activists in different parts of the world. The need to incorporate the practitioners' perspective becomes clearer when reviewing critical reflections by participants in China's nation-wide anti-corruption and pro-democracy movement in 1989. The following overview of uncertainties and ambivalent feelings that mainland Chinese political activists experience when struggling for democracy are indicative of the plethora of paradoxes they face.

Uncertainties, ambivalences and paradoxes of political activism

Liu Xiaobo, the former literary critic, activist and Nobel Peace Prize laureate who died of cancer as a political prisoner on 13 July 2017, had this to say about his role during the 1989 movement:

After the May 27th decision to leave [Tiananmen square] was overturned by people like Chai Ling, the students were in a predicament: they couldn't leave, yet by simply hanging on, the movement was losing its appeal, and the number of people coming to the Square was dwindling. In our joint meetings the discussions focused on how to straighten things out in the Square. The students should either take the initiative to leave or stay on but improve their image—they couldn't afford just to sit there passively. But none of us could come up with anything practical. So I thought I might as well go on a hunger strike … There's no way for me to know whether our hunger strike had affected the government's decision to launch the bloody crackdown. If it did, I would feel guilty for the rest of my life. From the moment I walked out of the Square, my heart has been heavy, after all that bloodshed on June 4th. I've never gotten over this.[15]

Another 1989 student activist, Wang Dan, reflected on how he and other members of the movement were unaware of the very real dangers of their political activism to their lives and well-being:

We hoped we could have freedom—not necessarily the right to vote, but a free life. That was our understanding … It was the first time when the government told people not to go on the streets and they went anyway. We were making history … I don't think we were brave. We didn't have the experience to feel fear.[16]

Such levels of ambivalence and uncertainty about the success of their activism arguably also extend beyond fast-moving political events. I vividly recall a conversation with a prominent mainland Chinese civil society practitioner which took place about ten years ago in her Beijing office. When explaining to her the dangers of Chinese non-governmental organisations (NGOs) becoming co-opted and absorbed by a highly corporatist party-state, she replied to me as follows: "If I had known what you are telling me right now from the outset, I probably would not have founded my NGO".

Another example about the unpredictability of the efficacy of political activism is the Chinese artist and activist Ai Weiwei. After concluding my video-recorded interview with him in his Beijing studio on 24 June 2010,[17] I asked Ai why he would not consider seeking political change in China through a cooperative approach towards the CCP. I asked him this question since I was aware of the extremely high personal risks Ai was willing to take with his political activism.[18] I remember that in his answer he expressed deep scepticism about the viability of cooperative approaches to advance political change in mainland China. My worry about his personal well-being, however, was not unfounded. On 3 April 2011, just ten months after I interviewed him, Ai was abducted by Chinese security forces at Beijing Airport. His extraordinary ordeal only came to an end after 81 days and thanks to an international campaign to release him.[19]

The described predicaments by mainland Chinese political activists suggest that during their struggle for democracy they may neither have a complete picture of all the political obstacles and political opportunity structures,[20] nor do they necessarily fully appreciate the extent of risks to their personal well-being. These findings should caution any student of democratisation processes to assume that individual actors struggling for democracy have the capacity to make highly rational and long-term strategic decisions. Instead, it should be assumed that the rationality and agency of democracy activists are bound by a variety of contextual factors, which are shaped by time- and situation-contingent political challenges, opportunities as well as risks.

This insight raises doubts about the utility of highly theoretical actor-oriented analytical frameworks in democratisation studies such as Schubert, Tetzlaff and Vennewald's concept of strategic and conflict-capable groups (SCOG). This group of German political scientists distinguish between actors such as the military, private entrepreneurs, state officials, professionals, land-owners, workers, employees, religious specialists and marginal groups. Whereas strategic groups are defending the autocratic status quo, conflict-capable groups are in opposition to the existing regime. Schubert et al. ana-lyse strategic and conflict-capable groups based on their class status, social structure, culture and ethnicity, and availability of resources and threat potential. In order to operationalise the SCOG concept, strategic and con-flict-capable groups are supposed to be analysed in three steps, which measure the social structure and stratification on the societal level, the profile of elites within the groups and the resources and strategies available to the groups. Erdman rightly points out that the SCOG concept is a useful heuristic device for historical studies of democratisation processes, yet is less useful for ven-turing a prognosis and has little relevance to policy-oriented analysis.[21]

Generalisable insights from democratisation studies

But are there possibilities to build on the insights gained from largely *post facto* democratisation studies to inform theories which are useful for *ex ante* political analysis by democracy activists? The specific examples above about the ambivalence and paradoxes that mainland Chinese democracy activists experience are indicative as to how experiences from practitioners can enrich the academic discourse about democratisation processes. Likewise, and despite its aforementioned shortcomings, democratisation studies has already generated numerous generalisable insights which are highly relevant for democracy activists, in the Greater China region and elsewhere. Erdmann highlights the following key findings from the literature:

(1) *Open-ended nature of political development processes.* Democratisation studies scholars by and large agree that political development processes are

path dependent. Merkel has pointed out that the direction of political development pathways can be influenced by political and social actors.[22] In such change processes, however, there is no silver bullet to successful democratisation. The nature of the existing authoritarian regime neither determines the trajectory of liberalisation and democratisation, nor does it determine whether the latter political change processes will be successful. Furthermore, the type of transition, whether it is directed by elites from the top down or supported by the masses from the bottom up, does not result in predictable results.[23]

(2) *Process character and periodisation of transition.* Democratisation studies distinguishes between different periods in political transformation processes: liberalisation, democratisation and consolidation. Such sequencing helps to underscore the procedural nature of political development and the need to think about transition in periods of time. Seen in this light, liberal democracy is not a state which can be achieved when a given country meets certain criteria, but should be seen as an ongoing historical process. This insight is relevant to appreciate that political transition processes will seldom lead to "neat" outcomes, e.g. a perfect liberal democracy. Instead, transition processes are more likely to produce a great variety of "in-between" states ranging from liberalising autocracies to defective democracies.[24]

(3) *Volatility of the transition process.* Democratisation studies scholars also agree that political transition processes are characterised by high political uncertainty. In the words of German political scientist and China expert Sandschneider, "instability as such is not a bad thing—to the contrary: it can be an essential precondition for reforms and the resulting political progress".[25] Compared with periods of "routine politics", during times of political contestation political and social actors in fact enjoy a high degree of autonomy.[26] In times of political conflict and turmoil, political and social actors can form new types of coalitions that would not be available otherwise. During times of political mobilisation, e.g. at the advent of social and political movements such as 1989, new political opportunity structures arise which allow for the trying and testing of novel reform strategies and tactics.

The three generalisations are highly significant for democracy activists, as they run counter to culturally deterministic arguments against liberalisation and democratisation[27] and emphasise the importance of agency and autonomy of political and social actors in times of rapid political change. They show that just as practice can inform theory, good theory can also help inform practice. The three generalisations also support the finding by Crosina and Barunket that the

> central dichotomy in which we, academics, think we and practitioners are embedded, to which great quantities of scholarly attention have been devoted, is not much of a dichotomy at all in the larger scheme of things. It may not even be the major issue that divides us. Paying so much

attention to it might decrease our ability to see the bigger world, and the steps we might be able to take to benefit its common welfare.[28]

Advantage of combining *etic* and *emic* perspectives

In the following I argue that any new theory in democratisation studies which fails to bridge the gap between a globally applicable theory and the practicalities and particularities of the struggle for democracy in a given regional context is unlikely to advance the knowledge and understanding of our field. In Chapter 1 I outlined how three different camps of researchers study Chinese politics. They can be described as normativists, positivists and academic practitioners. While normativists and positivists fall in the category of China watchers, academic practitioners belong to the group of China practitioners. This overview suggests that there are academic practitioners who are already combining critical academic inquiry with practical-political activism. But to what extent is it possible to bridge the gap between a global discourse about democratisation and practices of the local struggles for democracy in mainland China, Taiwan and Hong Kong? How relevant are views of outsiders for the reform discourse within the Greater China region?

In order to answer these questions, democratisation scholars need to be mindful of the anthropological distinction of *etic* and *emic*. Whereas *etic* signifies the views and concepts of outsiders observing and analysing a relatively distant place, culture, society or political system, an *emic* perspective comes from within the social group under observation.[29] In a recent online discussion hosted by ChinaFile on the topic of *How to Fight China's Sharp Power*, Kristin Shi-Kupfer, director of the Research Area on Politics, Society and Media at the Mercator Institute for China Studies, has argued that

> (as) non-Chinese China observers, we can start right where we are, in the midst of our professional and private circles, by how we talk to and interact with Chinese people: 1) Follow and analyze debates among Chinese people. Being knowledgeable about current debates can help to strike up a conversation signaling informed interest. Knowing the spectrum of opinions allowed to be voiced in Chinese media, online platforms, or academic journals can be used to build questions and arguments during a more focused or official meeting. Doubts and questions expressed by Chinese themselves about a topic, such as the Belt and Road Initiative, can be used by Western scholars to counter the C.C.P. claim that only "Westerners" criticize China because they apply their own "Western" values.[30]

Shi-Kupfer makes a compelling case for non-Chinese China observers wedded to their *etic* concepts and understandings to pay more attention to *emic* Chinese reform discourses. Yet endeavours to bridge theories of democratisation studies with practices of the struggle for democracy should not be seen as a one-way street. Arguably, *etic* views and concepts of outsiders can be extremely valuable to participants in the indigenous Chinese language discourse, too. In the following I argue that bridging theory and practice in democratisation studies requires us to combine *etic* and *emic* perspectives in intelligent ways. A good starting point, as Shi-Kupfer reminds us, is to better understand *emic* discourses about political reform in the Greater China region.

Reform within or outside the system?

The Chinese-language discourse about political reform reveals a rather peculiar dichotomy. When speaking with political activists in mainland China, Taiwan and Hong Kong during the past 20 years, my interlocutors have regularly invoked the terms of *tizhiwai* ("outside the system") and *tizhinei* ("inside the system") to frame their discussion about reform camps and reform strategies. Eva Pils outlines that the

> "system" (*tizhi*) as rights lawyers, academic critics and others discuss it, is that of the Party-State with its interconnected institutions. It includes the formal political-legal institutions of the Party-State; but also those other political actors that are under the Party-State's control. Thus, "the system" as a concept is quite open; but talking about the system means clearly to include the Party and its various agencies.[31]

This primarily oral Chinese-language discourse occasionally also finds its way into published English-language academic works. One example is the United States-based Chinese political scientist He Li, who defines *tizhi wai* in rather disparaging terms. He suggests that this political camp primarily includes disgruntled members of the 1989 generation "who gave up hope of transforming 'the untransformable' and decided to search for better and more feasible alternatives or took up residence overseas. Without a domestic presence, the influence of the exiled intellectuals is limited, and they have become increasingly irrelevant to politics back in China."[32]

In stark contrast, He suggests that the *tizhi nei* camp includes "professors, economists, journalists, lawyers, think tank policy analysts, government officials, and members of management. [This] group believes that the existing party-state can be transformed from within, and that the development of civil society depends to some extent on the tacit consent of the party in power."[33] The way He frames the two camps is indicative of the highly polarised *emic* discourse about political reform, which is not only highly reductionist but also morally charged. In personal discussions I have time and again experienced that my mainland Chinese interlocutors, especially those who have chosen to work within the confines of the party-state, tend to become rather defensive when *tizhi nei* and *tizhi wai* categories are invoked. He's description of the *tizhi wai* camp is a case in point. His critique of their supposed "irrelevance"—although primarily aimed at Chinese political dissidents who have relocated to the United States—is a thinly veiled attack on Chinese citizens in and outside mainland China, who dare to break free from ideological constraints imposed by the CCP. Seen from this vantage point, any effort to change mainland China's political system from the outside is doomed to fail. He describes the *tizhi nei* camp in strikingly different terms, as attracting highly skilled Chinese citizens who aim to "reform the political system from within". This perspective rests on the assumption that despite the numerous limitations that the CCP puts upon the freedom of speech of Chinese citizens, *tizhi nei* proponents supposedly have sufficient space to advocate for meaningful political reform.

Yet such polemical and rather one-sided views of the opposing reform camp is not only a hallmark of *tizhi nei* proponents. In my communications with mainland Chinese democracy activists over the past 20 years, I time and again experienced that those who position themselves outside the system tend to use the term *tizhi nei* as a way to denigrate and disparage individuals close to the Chinese party-state. The latter are seen as beneficiaries of CCP one-party rule. From a vantage point of supposed moral superiority, such *tizhi wai* proponents also have a tendency to ridicule *tizhi nei* supporters for being naive in thinking that they can bring about political change from within.

Why ascribed categories matter

Jean-Louis Rocca has highlighted that the two *emic* categories of *tizhi wai* and *tizhi nei* in fact are linked to socio-economic status and access to resources. According to Rocca:

> Chinese sociologists make a parallel distinction between people "in" and "out" of the system (*tizhinei, tizhiwai*). Zhou Xiaohong distinguished between the rearguard middle stratum (*zhongjian jieceng houwei*), characterized by a high degree of connection with the political apparatus (for example, SOE leaders), and the vanguard middle stream (*zhongjian jieceng qianwei*, composed of high professionals, etc.) that would show more independence. More recently, Li Lulu systematized the distinction between those "outside the system" relying on their labor force, their properties and the market for a living, and those "inside the system" depending upon power and relations.[34]

Pils argues that "(the) use of expressions such as 'inside' or 'outside the system' (*tizhi nei/tizhi wai*) captures, albeit in an imprecise way, a person's or organisation's attitude toward or position vis-à-vis the system".[35] *Tizhi nei* and *tizhi wai* categories are thus ascribed categories, understood as statuses "which are assigned to individuals without reference to their innate differences or abilities".[36] The anthropologist Ralph Linton has argued that the "bulk of the ascribed statuses in all social systems are parcelled out to individuals on the basis of sex, age, and family relationships. However, there are many societies in which purely social factors are also used as a basis of ascription."[37] In the case of mainland China, a person's ascribed proximity to the party-state is such a decisive factor. Jean-Philippe Béja has argued that in the case of mainland China, the CCP has actively pushed Chinese citizens "outside the system by the refusal of authorities, acting on lessons drawn from June 4, to let them find or keep employment in a state-owned unit (danwei), media outlet or university. Therefore, ironically, it is the Party that appoints the members of the opposition."[38]

Uneasy about the polarisation between the anti- and pro-establishment camps and the resulting pressures to declare one's political position, Chinese discourse participants have argued that it should be possible to neither belong to the *tizhi wai* nor to the *tizhi nei* camp. One proponent of carving out and occupying a third space is the Chinese writer Hu Fayun. When asked by the *New York Times* journalist Ian Johnson which of the two camps he belonged to, Hu suggested that he was:

[somewhere] in between. Before Tiananmen in 1989 I was quite hopeful. A lot of people hoped. But a lot of this hope was destroyed by the tanks and machine guns. Since then I've become more critical and my works have a harder time getting published. And yet I am not *tizhi-wai*. I still get a pension but except for that don't have any relation to the system. I don't attend the association's study session or writing competitions and don't follow their value system for writing. I feel I am a free and independent person. I basically separated myself from the system after 1989. After that I basically didn't attend their meetings. It's been almost thirty years now ... I do not take as much direct action as some. If you think of Ai Xiaoming. If she sees that rights are being violated, she grabs a camera and goes to record it. Perhaps it has something to do with my personality or way of life. Ever since being a sent-down youth in the Cultural Revolution, I've feared hardship and fatigue. I like to be at home. But in some important questions, for example Charter 08, I was among the first signers. In important actions, if I feel I should express myself, then I try to pick up my courage. I don't want to give up my freedom to express myself because of this dread. So when a lot of people reject interviews with the foreign media, I feel I should talk. I try to be as candid as possible and frankly say my views.[39]

The review of the primarily oral Chinese-language *emic* discourse reveals at least three distinctive reform camps: (1) critics of CCP rule, who lack access

to party-state resources and who are at risk of political persecution (*tizhi wai*);
(2) individuals supportive of the CCP, who benefit from party-state patronage
but sacrifice individual autonomy as part of their political proximity to power
(*tizhi nei*); and (3) a third group of people, who may be ideationally or materially linked to either of the two camps, but who prefer to carve out and
occupy an intermediate political space. The latter group have not been deno-
ted a label or categorisation in the *emic* discourse, but if a Chinese-language
term existed, it would be something along the lines of "a position between the
inside and the outside of the system" (*tizhi nei wai zhijian*). As I will show in
Chapters 8 and 10, the *emic* discourse extends to Taiwan and Hong Kong as
well.

Similarities between *emic* and *etic* discourses

As the Chinese-language *emic* discourse does not provide much further
clarification about the defining features of either of the three camps, a
suitable alternative approach would be to identify an equivalent *etic* discourse which can help shed light on these *emic* categories. One such
equivalent *etic* discourse has been developed by the Institute of Cultural
Affairs International (ICAI), an international non-profit organisation
based in Canada.[40] ICAI describes itself as "a global community of non-
profit organisations *advancing human development worldwide*".[41] While
initially rooted in the "predecessor organisations, the Faith & Life Community and the Ecumenical Institute, of the United States in the 1950s &
1960s", ICAI swiftly evolved into a secular globally operating non-profit
organisation.[42] In his book *The Courage to Lead: Transform Self,
Transform Society*, the Australian community organiser, educator and
former director of publications of ICAI Canada Brian Stanfield reflected
on more than 50 years of ICAI activism. He consequentially distilled the
categories of a pro-establishment, disestablishment (henceforth anti-
establishment) and trans-establishment to describe three distinctive and
yet inter-related reform camps which ICAI practitioners engage with.[43]

In Stanfield's words, the "pro-establishment refers to those parts of society
that guard the status quo. They work to preserve what is, guided by what has
been. The pro-establishment is dedicated to maintaining familiar standards,
while resisting their disruption. They are the bankers, lawyers, elected representatives, bishops, business leaders—the leaders and 'pillars of civilization'."[44] The anti-establishment is defined as standing "in opposition to the
commonly accepted social structures and traditions of society. Consequently,
it is in tension with the pro-establishment. The disestablishment demands that
the pro-establishment be accountable, and that it makes care structures
inclusive."[45] The third category of the trans-establishment, on the other hand,
is defined in contrast to the first two categories:

While the disestablishment and pro-establishment argue over the shape of the present or the past, the transestablishment asks the futuristic questions on behalf of everyone else, and dares to imagine something different ... The intent of the transestablishment is to model and create the new, while holding the tension between the pro-establishment and the disestablishment, honouring the gifts and wisdom of each. It beckons people to a new way of operating, seeking to build on the gifts of the past, while overcoming the past's limitations.[46]

It is rather striking how much the *etic* categories—used in the day-to-day work of globally operating ICAI practitioners and summarised by Stanfield—overlap with the previously described *emic* ones developed by politically active citizens in the Chinese-language discourse. Whereas the category of the pro-establishment corresponds with *tizhi nei*, the anti-establishment is the equivalent of the *tizhi wai* category. The trans-establishment, on the other hand, is a new category which is not commonly used in the Chinese-language *emic* reform discourse, yet which corresponds to the intermediate position *tizhi nei wei zhijian*, as expressed by Chinese writer Hu Fayun.

One of the major differences between Stanfield's *etic* categories and the *emic* Chinese-language discourse is that Stanfield uses the categories in a rather non-judgemental way. He argues that in

a broad picture, society needs all three of these dynamics. Without the pro-establishment, there would be chaos and no structures for the transestablishment to re-create, and nothing to engage the passion of the disestablishment. Without the disestablishment, the pro-establishment would never be held accountable to the forces of change. Without the transestablishment or the disestablishment, society would stagnate and grow repressive.[47]

The willingness to engage with both pro-establishment and anti-establishment is rooted in the ICAI mission "to build a just and equitable society in harmony with Planet Earth".[48] Stanfield's rather charitable view of the pro-establishment requires clarification, especially in the context of the struggle for democracy. A more conventional view of a given country's establishment would be to critique it along the lines of British journalist and political activist Owen Jones. Writing about the British establishment, he outlines that "(today's) Establishment, in my view, is bound together by common economic interests and a shared set of mentalities: in particular a mentality that holds that those at the top deserve ever greater power and wealth".[49] Jones' description of the British establishment would not be out of place if uttered word for word by anti-establishment Chinese democracy activists critical of mainland China's pro-establishment camp.

Are ascribed categories reversible?

In the following I argue that in the struggle for democracy such rather antagonistic views of the opposing political camps can be self-defeating. This rather counterintuitive insight becomes more evident when recognising that ascribed membership in one of the three camps should not be seen as permanent and irreversible, but as reversible.[50] Politically active citizens can and do move in and out of the three reform camps. The American community organiser Saul Alinsky has argued that history "is a relay of revolutions; the torch of idealism is carried by the revolutionary group until this group becomes an establishment, and then quietly the torch is put down to wait until a new revolutionary group picks it up for the next leg of the run. Thus the revolutionary cycle goes on."[51]

Alinsky reminds us that those who started off in the anti-establishment camp can over time become the new establishment. In the case of Taiwan, former public interest lawyer Chen Shui-bian, an anti-establishment figure who defended political activists from the *dangwai* movement (literally "outside the party", the party in question was the ruling KMT) in the late 1970s, later became the first democratically elected president from the independence-leaning Democratic Progressive Party (DPP), thus entering the ranks of a new DPP-dominated Taiwanese political establishment post-2000. The reverse, however, can also be true. In the case of mainland China, the former general secretary of the CCP, Zhao Ziyang, occupied one of the most prestigious high-level posts of the CCP throughout the mid-1980s. During the 1989 movement his reformist camp was defeated by CCP hardliners, thus effectively turning him into a political dissident and persona non grata. Zhao died under house arrest in 2005. The reversible nature of group membership is important, as it suggests that intercamp coalitions are both possible and, under certain conditions, desirable.

In democratisation studies, academics such as Burton, Gunther and Higley have pointed out the importance of "elite settlements" and "elite convergence" in political transformation processes.[52] Their scholarship suggests that democratic transitions will in part hinge upon the strategic interactions between the three reform camps of anti-establishment, pro-establishment and trans-establishment. This means that while the pro-establishment camp *in its entirety* may indeed be a major obstacle to democratisation processes, *some of its liberal and pro-democracy leaning proponents—at least potentially*—could become strategic allies of anti-establishment and trans-establishment actors. Burton and Higley have suggested that a "consensually unified elite structure created by a settlement constitutes the primary basis for subsequent political stability [and] is a necessary condition for the emergence and sustained practice of representative democratic politics".[53] Yet as Chapters 6, 8 and 10 will show, such elite settlements should be considered an exception rather than a rule in democratisation processes. I will argue that only in the case of Taiwan can we discern an informal elite pact in the early 1980s.

Stanfield's *etic* categories thus describe three political camps which are both distinctive and yet inter-related. Stanfield suggests that in political change processes the trans-establishment camp plays a significant bridging role. He argues that a

> person or group operating out of a transestablishment approach will work with anyone to create new responses, often quietly behind the scenes. When we act as the transestablishment, we abandon the dualism of good people and bad people, or of friends and enemies. As the trans-establishment, we assume that all players are potential allies. We seek collaboration, partnership, and cooperation at every point. As Abraham Lincoln declared, "I destroy my enemies when I make them my friends".[54]

Stanfield's description of the trans-establishment approach mirrors Chinese historian Xu Jilin's call for Chinese intellectuals to "create a 'public' by devising a language of translations—*a discourse*—among increasingly differentiated social groups, not to mention factionalized intellectual groups".[55] A key similarity between Stanfield and Xu's conceptualisation lies in the desire of political reformers trying to bridge and link up opposing forces, rather than to take sides in a highly partisan political struggle.

Ideal-type reform approaches as analytical vignettes

But is it possible to associate a distinctive reform approach with any of the three camps, in the way Brian Stanfield or Xu Jilin imagine their ideal-type trans-establishment approach? Do distinctively anti-establishment or pro-establishment reform approaches exist, which explain the behaviour of ascribed members in the respective political camps? If our ambition was to develop theory which empirically *proves* that individuals in the three political camps *possess the same "orientations to action"*, [56] the answer would be no. From an analytical point of view, one should not assume that individuals—who are either ascribed to the anti-establishment, pro-establishment or trans-establishment camp—hold on to highly uniform attitudes. This does not mean, however, that there are no ideal-type reform approaches, which are commensurate with the ascribed positions of the three reform camps. As I will show in the following, such ideal-type reform approaches not only exist but can also be applied as analytical vignettes in empirical case studies with the objective of dissecting the dynamics of the struggle for democracy as well as furthering practitioner reflexivity.

How theories of change can help capture "horizons of expectations"

In the following I argue that democratisation studies should venture beyond disciplinary boundaries and engage in theoretical borrowing from the field of development studies. Development practitioners concerned with the efficiency and effectiveness of development assistance have for many years discussed the question of how their aid projects can be better designed to bring about meaningful socio-economic change. At the heart of this debate are so-called 'theories of change' (TOC). The latter are used to describe how development practitioners think that aid projects and programmes bring about changes in the real world. Cathy James has defined a TOC as "an ongoing process of reflection to explore change and how it happens—and what that means for the part we play in a particular context, sector and/or group of people".[57] Craig Valters has argued that TOC fulfil a number of interrelated objectives:

> Taking a Theory of Change approach will likely include use of a tool in some form, but is broader, reflecting a desire to embed a critical and adaptive approach to development thinking and practice in organisational practice (Stein and Valters, 2012).
>
> As Stein and Valters (2012) detail more extensively, "Theories of Change fulfil a number of different purposes, including strategic planning, communication, accountability and learning. For example, an organisation may use Theories of Change as a way to communicate their goals to funders, but also to promote internal learning on programme strategy. They can also be completed at a number of different levels, including macro, sectoral, organisational and project/programme (James, 2011). While the basic idea of making explicit and critically assessing assumptions of change processes remains on each level, it is a very different task to develop an overarching organisational Theory of Change (perhaps more simply understood as a vision statement) than it is to develop implementation Theories of Change that speak closely to diverging realities at the local level.[58]

While TOC have primarily gained currency among social development practitioners working in the global aid industry, their utility is not confined to the project or organisational level. As the discussion of Wei Jingsheng and Amartya Sen's political philosophy in Chapter 2 has shown, their macro-level TOC are fundamentally at odds with the state-led development model of the CCP. The main point of divergence is the key question whether political freedom should be considered the precondition for human development or a consequence of socio-economic modernisation. Here the importance of any given TOC becomes apparent. While Wei and Sen have faith in people's innate capabilities to take over responsibility for their own well-being, the

CCP considers paternalistic, elite-led tutelage as the precondition for state-led development of society. Identifying an actor's TOC is thus of key importance to better understand their respective agency in democratisation processes.

In Chapter 1 I referred to the scholarship of German historian Reinhart Koselleck. Koselleck argues that any attempt to interpret history requires scholars to familiarise themselves with their studied protagonists' "spaces of experience" as well as "horizons of expectation".[59] In the context of this study this leads to the realisation that political activists make decisions based both on rationalisations of their past personal experiences as well as assumptions about the efficacy of their actions in the future. Without theories of change, however, we cannot capture their respective horizons of expectation. When discussing critical incidents we need to ask what political activists hoped to achieve. What were their assumptions about the future from the vantage point of the historical moment of time they found themselves in?

Depending on the available political opportunity structures at any given moment democracy activists can take their struggle for democracy to different kinds of what Cheng Tun-Jen has called "bargaining arenas". When ruling elites emphasise hard authoritarian means such arenas may be limited to reform efforts within the given political system. In the aftermath of 1989, for example, Chinese democracy activists had almost no meaningful venue to pursue their agenda other than working within the system. This gradually changed after the 1995 Fourth World Conference on Women in Beijing, which provided cover for more semi-autonomous civic groups dealing with poverty alleviation, child welfare and women's issues. During the early years of the Hu Jintao era (2002–12) soft authoritarian modes of governance were emphasised over hard authoritarian approaches. This allowed public interest lawyers such as Xu Zhiyong to emerge and experiment with more daring forms of political participation, e.g. in the forms of his advocacy-oriented NGO Open Constitution Initiative, which lobbied for the rule of law and constitutionalism. With the ascent of Xi Jinping since 2012, tacitly approved bargaining arenas have been dismantled one by one, leaving activists no other choice but to explore non-sanctioned arenas such as street protests and human rights litigation in mainland China's party-state-controlled court system. Bargaining arenas, however, are not only limited to the domestic realm but can include the international sphere as well. In May 2018, German chancellor Merkel met with Li Wenzhu in Beijing, the wife of jailed public interest lawyer Wang Quanzhang.[60] This suggests that participants of mainland China's civil rights movement have at times managed to internationalise their cause by directly addressing high-ranking Western politicians.[61]

In this chapter I critiqued democratisation studies as an academic field for its inability to predict democratic changes in countries with hard authoritarian regimes such as mainland China. In order to further theoretical innovation, I made the case to bridge theory and practice, and combine *emic* and *etic* discourses about political change in creative ways. I also made the case that in order to overcome the theoretical stagnation of democratisation studies, scholars with an interest in democratic political reform should borrow from the TOC discourse in development studies. In Chapter 4 I will outline how ideal-type TOPC can help inform our understanding of the struggle for democracy in mainland China, Taiwan and Hong Kong.

Notes

1 Pei, Minxin (2016), *China's Crony Capitalism: The Dynamics of Regime Decay*, Harvard University Press, Cambridge, MA.
2 Merkel, Wolfgang (2003), *Demokratie in Asien. Ein Kontinent zwischen Diktatur und Demokratie*, Dietz, Bonn, 32–5.
3 Erdmann, G. (1996), *Demokratie und Demokratiefoerderung in der Dritten Welt. Ein Literaturbericht und eine Erhebung der Konzepte und Instrumente*, Zentralstelle Weltkirche der Deutschen Bischofskonferenz, Bonn, 19, author's translation.
4 Merkel, Wolfgang (1999), *Systemtransformationen*, Leske + Budrich, Opladen, 78.
5 Whitehead, L. (1998), Comparative Politics: Democratization Studies, in: Robert Goodin and Hans-Dieter Klingemann (Eds), *A New Handbook of Political Science*, Oxford University Press, Oxford, 2.
6 Erdmann, G. (1996), *Demokratie und Demokratiefoerderung in der Dritten Welt*, Zentralstelle Weltkirche der Deutschen Bischofskonferenz, Bonn, 19.
7 He, Baogang (1996), *The Democratization of China*, Routledge, London, 3.
8 Ibid., 215–31.
9 Gilley, Bruce (2004), *China's Democratic Future*, Columbia University Press, New York.
10 Ibid., xiii.
11 Yu, K. and ProQuest. (2009), *Democracy Is a Good Thing: Essays on Politics, Society, and Culture in Contemporary China*, Brookings, Washington, DC.
12 Li, Fan (2008), *Zhongguo minzhu de qianyan tansuo*, Shijie yu zhongguo yanjiusuo.
13 Dewey, J. (1997), *Experience and Education*, First Touchstone, New York.
14 Crosina, Eliana and Bartunek, Jean M. (2017), The Paradoxical Mystery of the Missing Differences between Academics and Practitioners, in: Wendy K. Smith, Marianne W. Lewis, Paula Jarzabkowski and Ann Langley (Eds), *The Oxford Handbook of Organizational Paradox*, Oxford University Press, Oxford, 15.
15 天安门 The Film (1995), *The Gate of Heavenly Peace*. Available online: www.tsquare.tv/film/transcript.html (accessed 5 March 2018).
16 *Guardian* (2009), Tiananmen: The Flame Burns On. Available online: www.theguardian.com/world/2009/may/03/tiananmen-square-anniversary-china-protest (accessed 28 August 2018).
17 Fulda, Andreas (2010), Ai Weiwei on Contemporary Art and Civil Society in China. Available online: https://vimeo.com/15172939 (accessed 28 August 2018).
18 Nine months prior to the interview Ai had undergone an emergency operation resulting from a police beating in Sichuan province, see *Spiegel Online* (2009), Chinese Artist Accuses Government for Injury. Available online: www.spiegel.de/international/germany/operation-in-munich-chinese-artist-accuses-government-for-injury-a-649346.html (accessed 28 August 2018).
19 Fulda, Andreas (2012), The Case of Ai Weiwei: A Seismograph of Political Fault Lines in China and Beyond, ECRAN Short Paper, Europe China Research and Advice Network.
20 Giugni cites Tarrow's definition of political opportunity structures as "consistent but not necessarily formal, permanent, or national signals to social or political actors which either encourage or discourage them to use their internal resources to form social movements (Tarrow 1996: 54, emphasis in original)". Giugni, M.

(2009), Political Opportunities: From Tilly to Tilly, *Swiss Political Science Review*, 15(2), 361. The *emic* equivalent to the *etic* concept of political opportunity structures is the Chinese expression *"tianshi, dili, renhe"*.

21 Erdmann, G. (1996), *Demokratie und Demokratiefoerderung in der Dritten Welt*, Zentralstelle Weltkirche der Deutschen Bischofskonferenz, Bonn, 55–64.

22 Merkel, Wolfgang (2003), *Demokratie in Asien. Ein Kontinent zwischen Diktatur und Demokratie*, Dietz, Bonn, 156–7.

23 Erdmann, G. (1996), *Demokratie und Demokratiefoerderung in der Dritten Welt*, Zentralstelle Weltkirche der Deutschen Bischofskonferenz, Bonn, 66.

24 Ibid., 68.

25 Sandschneider, Eberhard (2003), Chinas Zukunft. Projektion und Wirklichkeit, *Internationale Politik*, 2. Available online: https://zeitschrift-ip.dgap.org/de/article/getFullPDF/9334 (accessed 24 August 2018), author's translation.

26 Ibid.

27 For a critique of culturally deterministic arguments against liberalisation and democratisation, see Merkel, Wolfgang (1999), *Systemtransformationen*, Leske + Budrich, Opladen, 95–100.

28 Crosina, Eliana and Bartunek, Jean M. (2017), The Paradoxical Mystery of the Missing Differences between Academics and Practitioners, in: Wendy K. Smith, Marianne W. Lewis, Paula Jarzabkowski and Ann Langley (Eds), *The Oxford Handbook of Organizational Paradox*, Oxford University Press, Oxford, 16.

29 For a discussion about the difference between *etic* and *emic* perspectives see Punnett, B., Ford, D., Galperin, B. and Lituchy, T. (2017), The Emic-Etic-Emic Research Cycle, *AIB Insights*, 17(1), 3–6.

30 ChinaFile (2018), How to Fight China's Sharp Power: A ChinaFile Conversation. Available online: www.chinafile.com/conversation/how-fight-chinas-sharp-power (accessed 24 August 2018).

31 Pils, Eva (2014), *China's Human Rights Lawyers: Advocacy and Resistance*, Routledge, London, 64. In Taiwan, "the system" was a reference to the KMT, which governed the island-state uninterrupted from 1949 until 2000 (see also Chapter 5). In Hong Kong, "the system" refers to an amalgam of representatives of the Hong Kong SAR government in cahoots with self-serving tycoons who do the CCP's bidding (see also Chapter 7).

32 Li, H. (2015), *Political Thought and China's Transformation: Ideas Shaping Reform in Post-Mao China*, Palgrave Macmillan, Basingstoke, 18.

33 Ibid.

34 Rocca, Jean-Louis (2017), *The Making of the Chinese Middle Class: Small Comfort and Great Expectations*, Basingstoke, Palgrave Macmillan, 93.

35 Ibid., 65.

36 Linton, Ralph (1936), *The Study of Man: An Introduction*, D. Appleton-Century, New York, 115.

37 Ibid., 126.

38 Béja, Jean-Philippe (2009), China since Tiananmen: The Massacre's Long Shadow, *Journal of Democracy*, 20(3), 12.

39 *New York Review of Books* (2016), Inside and Outside the System: Chinese Writer Hu Fayun. Available online: www.nybooks.com/daily/2016/11/28/china-inside-and-outside-system-hu-fayun/ (accessed 24 August 2018).

40 I would like to thank Shenzhen-based organisational developer Mark Pixley for bringing ICAI's work to my attention.

41 ICA International (2018), Our History. Available online: www.ica-international.org/about-us/our-history/ (accessed 28 August 2018).

42 Ibid.

43 Stanfield, Brian (2012), *The Courage to Lead: Transform Self, Transform Society*, Canadian Institute of Cultural Affairs, Bloomington, 169.

44 Ibid.

45 Ibid.
46 Ibid.
47 Ibid.
48 ICA International (2018), Our Mission and Values. Available online: www.ica -international.org/about-us/our-mission-and-values/ (accessed 28 August 2018).
49 Jones, Owen (2015), *The Establishment. And How They Get Away with It*, Penguin, London, xii.
50 See also Foladore's discussion of Ralph Linton's concept of "ascribed status", Foladare, I. (1969). A Clarification of "Ascribed Status" and "Achieved Status", *Sociological Quarterly*, 10(1), 53–61.
51 Alinsky, Saul (1971), *Rules for Radicals: A Pragmatic Primer for Realistic Radicals*, Vintage Books, New York, 22.
52 Burton, Michael G., Gunther, Richard and Higley, John (1992), Introduction: Elite Transformations and Democratic Regimes, in: John Higley and Richard Gunther (Eds), *Elites and Democratic Consolidation in Latin America and Southern Europe*, Cambridge University Press, Cambridge, 1–38.
53 Burton, Michael G. and Higley, John (1987), Elite Settlements, *American Sociological Review*, 52(3), 304.
54 Stanfield, Brian (2012), *The Courage to Lead: Transform Self, Transform Society*, New Society Publishers, Gabriola Island, 170.
55 Cheek, T. (2006). Xu Jilin and the Thought Work of China's Public Intellectuals, *China Quarterly*, 186, 414.
56 Diamond, L. (Ed.) (1994), *Political Culture and Democracy in Developing Countries*, Lynne Rienner, Boulder, 8.
57 James, C. (2011), Theory of Change Review: A Report Commissioned by Comic Relief, Comic Relief, London, as quoted by Valters, Craig (2015), Theories of Change: Time for a Radical Approach to Learning in Development, *Overseas Development Institute*. Available online: www.odi.org/sites/odi.org.uk/files/odi-a ssets/publications-opinion-files/9835.pdf (accessed 29 August 2018).
58 Valters, Craig (2015), Theories of Change: Time for a Radical Approach to Learning in Development, Overseas Development Institute. Available online: www. odi.org/sites/odi.org.uk/files/odi-assets/publications-opinion-files/9835.pdf (accessed 29 August 2018).
59 Koselleck, Reinhart (2004), *Futures Past: On the Semantics of Historical Time*, translated by Keith Tribe, Columbia University Press, New York.
60 *South China Morning Post* (2018), German Chancellor Angela Merkel Met Wives of Jailed Lawyers during China Visit. Available online: www.scmp.com/news/ china/policies-politics/article/2148156/german-chancellor-angela-merkel-met-wi ves-jailed (accessed 11 January 2019).
61 For a comprehensive discussion of political arenas see Jasper, James and Duyvendak, Jan Willem (Eds) (2015), *Players and Arenas: The Interactive Dynamics of Protest*, Amsterdam University Press, Amsterdam.

4

THEORIES *OF* AND *FOR* POLITICAL CHANGE

In this chapter I argue that the TOC discourse from the field of development aid can also be instructive for a better understanding of the dynamics of the struggle for democracy. Arguably, both scholars engaging in democratisation studies as well as political activists involved in the struggle for democracy have to make their assumptions about political development explicit, so that they can be critically assessed. Such TOPC can serve the same purposes as TOC in the neighbouring academic discipline of development studies. The TOPC can help enrich the academic discourse of democratisation studies just as much as they can enhance practitioner reflexivity among democracy activists. Such TOPC, however, do not have to be developed from scratch, as the existing scholarship of the American political theorist and peace activist Gene Sharp[1], American community organiser Saul Alinsky[2] and Brazilian educator Paulo Freire[3] can be considered extensions of the espoused dispositions towards political reform within the three reform camps of anti-establishment, pro-establishment[4] and trans-establishment, respectively.

Since I discuss political developments in mainland China, Taiwan and Hong Kong, *etic* TOPC are useful as an analytical framework which can be applied to all three regions. If I were to choose an *emic* TOPC originating from mainland China, Taiwanese and Hong Kong scholars and activists could argue that it does not apply to them. If I were to apply an *emic* TOPC from Taiwan, the same counterargument could be made by mainland Chinese and Hong Kong scholars and activists. This is why an *etic* framework is in order, not to claim that this is how mainland Chinese, Taiwanese and Hong Kong democracy activists think and act, but to interpret their actions from the standpoint of an outside observer.

The TOPC by Gene Sharp, Saul Alinsky and Paulo Freire

Gene Sharp spent his lifetime developing a theory of non-violent struggle, a decisively *anti-establishment approach* to bringing about political change.[5] In the preface of his seminal study *From Dictatorship to Democracy* he begins with the assertion that "(one) of my major concerns for many years has been how people could prevent and destroy dictatorships".[6] First published in Bangkok in 1993 his monograph has been translated into 34 languages.[7] The British journalist Louise Gray has pointed out that "(the) writings of 83-year-old political scientist Dr Gene Sharp are credited with providing the blueprint for the overthrow of governments in Serbia, Ukraine, Guatemala and Indonesia and, most recently, with revving up the activists who launched the Arab Spring".[8] Sharp's scholarship thus is of particular relevance to *tizhi wai* proponents with an interest in regime change in mainland China.

Saul Alinsky's key study *Rules for Radicals: A Pragmatic Primer for Realistic Radicals*, finalised just a year before his death in 1972, develops 13 rules which political activists can use when contesting the power held by pro-establishment actors. Alinsky's work has informed the political thought and practice of countless American community organisers. Prominent politicians from the United States Democratic Party were strongly influenced by his teachings. Hillary Clinton wrote her undergraduate thesis about Alinsky.[9] Two-term president Barack Obama, on the other hand, taught Alinsky at workshops during his time as a community organiser in Chicago.[10] Alinsky describes the purpose of his contribution in particularly poignant ways: "*The Prince* was written by Machiavelli for the Haves on how to hold power. *Rules for Radicals* is written for the Have Nots on how to take it away."[11] For this endeavour to succeed, Alinsky argues that political activists have to work *within* the system. One of his key arguments is that "it is most important for those of us who want revolutionary change to understand that revolution must be proceeded by reformation. To assume that a political revolution can survive without the supporting base of a popular reformation is to ask for the impossible in politics."[12] Alinsky's TOPC thus is particularly relevant to the *tizhi nei* proponents in the Chinese-language discourse about political reform, not least since they *proclaim* to work towards reform of the autocratic system *from within the system*.

The third TOPC was developed by the Brazilian educator Paulo Freire. In *Pedagogy of the Oppressed* he describes the primary objective of his book to

> present some aspects of what the writer has termed the pedagogy of the oppressed, a pedagogy which must be forged *with*, not *for*, the oppressed (whether individuals or peoples) in the incessant struggle to regain their humanity. This pedagogy makes oppression and its causes objects of reflection by the oppressed, and from that reflection will come their necessary engagement in the struggle for their liberation.[13]

Freire's work has greatly influenced educators worldwide.[14] His liberation theology[15] also informed the thinking of Benny Tai, a university professor and initiator of Occupy Central with Love and Peace in 2014, Hong Kong's biggest political movement since the British handover of the former crown colony under PRC sovereignty in 1997, which later morphed into the 79-day Umbrella movement.[16] What qualifies Freire's TOPC as a distinctively *trans-establishment approach* is his insistence that "the oppressed must not, in seeking to regain their humanity (which is a way to create it), become in turn oppressors of the oppressors, but rather restorers of the humanity of both. This, then, is the great humanistic and historical task of the oppressed: to liberate themselves and their oppressors as well." Freire's work is particularly relevant for trans-establishment reformers who seek to position themselves between the competing camps of the anti- and pro-establishment, the *tizhi nei wai zhijian* position.

Shared convictions of Sharp, Alinsky and Freire

While dissimilar in terms of their reform approaches, Gene Sharp, Saul Alinsky and Paulo Freire actually share a number of pre-scientific value orientations and world-views. They all profoundly dislike the cruelty, arbitrariness and violence of authoritarianism. They also agree that autocratic forms of governance have inherent vulnerabilities. While critical of the autocratic elites' abuse of power, Sharp, Alinsky and Freire do not hold back in their critique of politically like-minded activists. Sharp criticises the tendency among democracy activists for using only a few select methods,[17] relying too much on chance[18] and for being overly reactive to initiatives by the dictatorship.[19] Alinsky, on the other hand, is critical of practitioners acting without thinking about the specific issue at hand and activists who blindly follow predetermined ideas which have little bearing on the actual situation in which they find themselves.[20] Freire is critical of the fear of freedom among the oppressed. In his words:

> [one] of the gravest obstacles to the achievement of liberation is that oppressive reality absorbs those within it and thereby acts to submerge human beings' consciousness. Functionally, oppression is domesticating. To no longer be prey to its force, one must emerge from it and turn upon it. This can be done only by means of the praxis: reflection and action upon the world in order to transform it.[21]

While all three are in favour of political defiance, they also firmly reject political violence. Sharp rejects it since "*by placing confidence in violent means, one has chosen the very type of struggle with which the oppressors nearly always have superiority*".[22] Alinsky considers political violence a form of psychosis.[23] Freire is highly critical of sectarianism, "fed by fanaticism".[24]

Their works are to varying degrees descriptive, prescriptive and reflexive. Some of the key differences between the three can be explained in relation to their biographies. Whereas Sharp was a political theorist and peace activist, Alinsky and Freire can be more accurately described in the Gramscian category of "organic intellectuals". The latter two paid a high personal price for their political advocacy. Alinsky went in and out of jail for his political activism in the United States, a time he considered useful for developing his TOPC.[25] Freire's work "was once considered such a threat to the established order that he was forced to leave Brazil for some twenty years before returning to São Paulo".[26] While Sharp, Alinsky and Freire agree on a wide range of key principles, they nevertheless developed fairly distinctive TOPC. In the following I will briefly outline the key differences between the ideal-type reform approaches espoused by Sharp, Alinsky and Freire. I will begin with Gene Sharp's decisively *anti-establishment approach* and his concept of non-violent struggle.

Gene Sharp's advocacy of non-violent struggle: an anti-establishment approach

According to Sharp,

> [non-violent] struggle is a much more complex and varied means of struggle than is violence. Instead, the struggle is fought by psychological, social, economic, and political weapons applied by the population and the institutions of the society. These have been known under various names of protests, strikes, noncooperation, boycotts, disaffection, and people power. As noted earlier, all governments can rule only as long as they receive replenishment of the needed sources of their power from the cooperation, submission, and obedience of the population and the institutions of the society. Political defiance, unlike violence, is uniquely suited to severing those sources of power.[27]

In the appendix of *From Dictatorship to Democracy* Sharp provides a list of 198 methods of non-violent action, ranging from methods of non-violent protest and persuasion, social non-cooperation, economic non-cooperation, political non-cooperation and non-violent intervention.[28] According to Sharp non-violent struggle undermines any given autocratic regime and helps empower society.[29] Non-violent struggle also helps to speed up the democratisation of society, as it raises the population's self-confidence, provides means to resist undemocratic control, allows for freedom of speech and freedom of assembly and the rejuvenation of a previously politically neutralised civil society.[30] It can lead to conversion of autocratic elites to the democratic cause, accommodation, non-violent coercion and disintegration of the autocratic regime.[31]

Sharp holds a rather antagonistic position towards the pro-establishment. He advises democracy activists

> to plan carefully how the democratic forces can weaken the support that people and groups have previously offered to the dictatorship. Will their support be weakened by revelations of the brutalities perpetrated by the regime, by exposure of the disastrous economic consequences of the dictators' policies, or by a new understanding that the dictatorship can be ended? The dictators' supporters should at least be induced to become "neutral" in their activities ("fence sitters") or preferably to become active supporters of the movement for democracy.[32]

Similarly, he advises against negotiation with autocratic elites, as the

> call for negotiations when basic issues of political liberties are involved may be an effort by the dictators to induce the democrats to surrender peacefully while the violence of the dictatorship continues. In those types of conflicts the only proper role of negotiations may occur at the end of a decisive struggle in which the power of the dictators has been effectively destroyed and they seek personal safe passage to an international airport.[33]

In the key prescriptive parts of his book, Sharp's specific advice to democracy activists is as follows:

> When one wants to bring down a dictatorship most effectively and with the least cost then one has four immediate tasks:
>
> - One must strengthen the oppressed population themselves in their determination, self-confidence, and resistance skills;
> - One must strengthen the independent social groups and institutions of the oppressed people;
> - One must create a powerful internal resistance force; and
> - One must develop a wise grand strategic plan for liberation and implement it skilfully.[34]

Gene Sharp calls on democracy activists to recognise their own power: "Democrats cannot hope to bring down a dictatorship and establish political freedom without the ability to apply their own power effectively."[35] According to Sharp, "the conflict in which political defiance is applied is a constantly changing field of struggle with continuing interplay of moves and counter-moves. Nothing is static. Power relationships, both absolute and relative, are subject to constant and rapid changes. This is made possible by the resisters continuing their nonviolent persistence despite repression."[36] For this struggle to succeed, strategic planning is key.[37] According to Sharp, democracy activists need to develop a grand strategy, strategies for implementation of the grand strategy in campaign form, tactics and methods.[38] Without a grand strategy, democracy movements are likely to fail.[39] For the latter, no blueprints exist but have to be developed according to the characteristics of the given political regime.[40] In order to enhance practitioner reflexivity, Sharp provides lists of fundamental questions to ask when designing a grand strategy, which include questions about the strengths and weaknesses of the regime.[41] When devising the grand strategy, planners need to discard political actions which are counterproductive to the cause.[42]

Sharp's concern about "the most effective ways in which dictatorships could be successfully disintegrated with the least possible cost in suffering and lives"[43] is central to Sharp's TOPC. Asked by a BBC journalist whether Sharp's suggested non-violent resistance puts democracy activists at risk, he replied as follows: "Any defiance of a dictatorship is risky. They won't like it."[44] When asked about his personal responsibility for democracy activists being jailed for possessing his book *From Dictatorship to Democracy*, he provided the following answer: "They are already in personal trouble, simply by living under the extreme dictatorship. This is a tool by which they can not make their situation worse, but a tool by which they can eventually bring their country to liberation."[45] The latter quote by Sharp summarises the focus of his TOPC. Sharp's analysis centres around the macro and meso levels of authoritarian political regimes. He provides advice at the micro level with the hope that democracy activists will feel empowered to continue their struggle. In the following I will contrast Sharp's TOPC with Saul Alinsky's *trojan horse approach* aimed at the political reformation of the establishment. As the following overview will show, the Alinsky TOPC reveals a number of key dissimilarities.

Saul Alinsky's principle and practice of realistic radicalism: a trojan horse approach

At the heart of Saul Alinsky's scholarship and political advocacy is the understanding that one has to work within the system in order to be able to pave the way for reformation and subsequent radical democratic change. In the preface of his book *Rules for Radicals* he maintains:

> [as] an organizer I start from where the world is, as it is, not as I would like it to be. That we accept the world as it is does not in any sense weaken our desire to change it into what we believe it should be—it is necessary to begin where the world is if we are going to change it to what we think it should be. That means working in the system.[46]

Alinsky points out that he is not interested in dogma, but in continued questioning. He sees great value in "the free, open, questing, and creative mind of man".[47] Working within the system means that organisers need to infiltrate the pro-establishment and weaken it from within through reformation work.

This is done with the intention to support what Alinsky refers to as the "Have-nots" and the "Have-a-Little, Want Mores" in society. With these categories Alinsky refers to disenfranchised social groups and the precarious middle class, respectively. In Alinsky's words, a "revolutionary organizer must shake up the prevailing patterns of their lives—agitate, create disenchantment and discontent with the current values, to produce, if not a passion for change, at least a passive, affirmative, non-challenging climate".[48] Yet in stark contrast to Sharp's view on negotiations with autocratic elites, Alinsky argues that tactical engagement with autocratic elites is necessary and that compromises can be made. Alinsky's highly pragmatic orientation to political activism is most evident when he discusses the virtues of compromise:

> Compromise is another word that carries shades of weakness, vacillation, betrayal of ideals, surrender of moral principles. In the old culture, when virginity was a virtue, one referred to a woman's being "compromised". The word is generally regarded as ethically unsavoury and ugly. But to the organizer, compromise is a key and beautiful word. It is always present in the pragmatics of operation. It is making the deal, getting that vital breather, usually the victory. If you start with nothing, demand 100 per cent, then compromise for 30 per cent, you're 30 per cent ahead.[49]

Less prescriptive than Sharp, Alinsky calls on activists to work within the system, embrace an ideology of change, where contradictions are accepted, a duality of all phenomena is recognised, and that rather than thinking in terms of cause and consequence, activists should think in terms of probabilities.[50]

Alinsky considers the following key qualities that organisers must possess: curiosity, irreverence, imagination, a sense of humour, a bit of a blurred vision of a better world, an organised personality, a well-integrated political schizoid, ego, a free and open mind and political relativity.[51] The goal of the organiser is to create "the new out of the old".[52] He distinguishes these qualities of organisers with those of conventional political leaders. According to Alinsky there is a "basic difference between the leader and the organizer. The leader goes on to build power to fulfil his desires, to hold and wield the power for purposes both social and personal. He wants power himself. The organizer finds his goal in creation of power for others to use."[53] Alinsky's concept of power differs from Sharp's, as he is less interested in wielding power over his opponents. Instead, he believes in the power of self-organisation: "once you organize people around something as commonly agreed upon as pollution, then an organized people is on the move. From there it's a short and natural step to political pollution, to Pentagon pollution."[54] At the heart of Alinsky's TOPC is the understanding that activists have to develop powerful organisations if they want to succeed.[55] In marked contrast to Sharp's TOPC,

Alinsky is sceptical about grand strategies. This is evident when offering reflections on training he conducted in the United States. Alinsky frowns at overly prescriptive attempts to impose a political agenda on people.[56] This, however, does not prevent him from formulating 13 rules which a skilled organiser can employ in the political struggle. The rules are not formulated as dogma, but are supposed to be used by organisers mindful of the need to employ the right kind of tactics considering the specific situation in which they find themselves:

- Rule 1. "Power is not only what you have but what the enemy thinks you have."[57]
- Rule 2. "Never go outside the experience of your people."[58]
- Rule 3. "Wherever possible go outside of the experience of the enemy."[59]
- Rule 4. "Make the enemy live up to their own book of rules."[60]
- Rule 5. "Ridicule is man's most potent weapon."[61]
- Rule 6. "A good tactic is one that your people enjoy."[62]
- Rule 7. "A tactic that drags on too long becomes a drag."[63]
- Rule 8. "Keep the pressure on, with different tactics and actions, and utilize all events of the period for your purpose."[64]
- Rule 9. "The threat is usually more terrifying than the thing itself."[65]
- Rule 10. "The major premise for tactics is the development of operations that will maintain a constant pressure upon the opposition."[66]
- Rule 11. "If you push a negative hard and deep enough it will break through into its counterside."[67]
- Rule 12. "The price of a successful attack is a constructive alternative."[68]
- Rule 13. "Pick the target, freeze it, personalize it, and polarize it."[69]

In *Rules for Radicals* Alinsky devotes considerable time to justify his trojan horse approach against critics who he refers to as "means-and-ends moralists and non-doers".[70] Drawing on specific examples in world history Alinsky makes the case that *particular ends* justify *particular means*. In the second chapter he painstakingly lays out his reasoning and develops 11 rules relating to the ethics of means and ends.[71] His political-pragmatic credentials again shine through when Alinsky states that the

> man of action views the issue of means and ends in pragmatic and stra-tegic terms. He has no other problem; he thinks only of his actual resources and the possibilities of various choices of action. He asks of ends only whether they are achievable and worth the cost; of means, only whether they will work. To say that corrupt means corrupt the ends is to believe in the immaculate conception of ends and principles. The real arena is corrupt and bloody. Life is a corrupting process from the time a child learns to play his mother off against his father in the politics of when to go to bed; he who fears corruption fears life.[72]

Alinsky's TOPC is thus mostly concerned with the analysis of the meso level of systems, which can be an organisation or network of individuals which acts in transparent and accountable ways. Addressing such systems, Alinsky shares critical reflections on tactics that help activists "to organize for power: how to get it and to use it".[73] In the following I will contrast both Sharp's and Alinsky's TOPC with Paulo Freire's pedagogy of the oppressed, a distinctively *trans-establishment approach.*

Paulo Freire's pedagogy of the oppressed: a trans-establishment approach

The discussion of the previous two TOPC has revealed that while Sharp aims to prevent and destroy dictatorships through non-violent struggle, Alinsky strives for a reformation within the system in order to pave the way for radical democratic change of the system itself. Whereas the former two TOPC could be considered *state-centric* (in a sense of primarily addressing the abuse of power by pro-establishment elites), Brazilian educator Freire pursues a more *society-centric* objective. At the heart of *Pedagogy of the Oppressed* is the perennial question of how

> the oppressed, as divided, unauthentic beings, participate in developing the pedagogy of their liberation? Only as they discover themselves to be "hosts" of the oppressor can they contribute to the midwifery of their liberating pedagogy. As long as they live in the duality in which *to be* is to *be like*, and to *be like* is to *be like the oppressor*, this contribution is impossible. The pedagogy of the oppressed is an instrument for their critical discovery that both they and their oppressors are manifestations of dehumanization.[74]

What distinguishes Freire's TOPC from Sharp and Alinsky is that according to Freire only genuine dialogue between the oppressed and oppressors can lead to a liberation of both the anti- and the pro-establishment. According to Freire the danger is that as a result of a successful political struggle, the former oppressed become the new oppressors of the old oppressors.[75] For Freire, "the authentic solution of the oppressor-oppressed contradiction does not lie in a mere reversal of position, in moving from one pole to the other. Nor does it lie in the replacement of the former oppressors with new ones who continue to subjugate the oppressed—all in the name of their liberation."[76]

In contrast to Sharp, Freire is not opposed to negotiating with autocratic elites. At the same time he certainly would not agree with many of Alinsky's trojan horse tactics when engaging with the pro-establishment. While Freire is highly critical of the use of violence by oppressors,[77] he acknowledges the importance of former oppressors joining the struggle of the oppressed. But he also provides a warning not to expect too much from these actors, as "they almost always bring with them the marks of their origin: their prejudices and their deformations, which include a lack of confidence in the people's ability to think, to want, and to know".[78] Instead he calls upon educators to live *with* others in solidarity;[79] engage in problem-posing education as humanist and liberating praxis;[80] enable and engage in genuine dialogue grounded in faith in people, humility, love and critical thinking;[81] and to counter what Freire calls anti-dialogical matrices such as conquest, divide and rule, manipulation, and cultural invasion with dialogical matrices such as coop- eration, unity for liberation, organisation and cultural synthesis.[82] In Freire's words, a

> revolution is made neither by the leaders for the people, nor by the people for the leaders, but by both acting together in unshakable solidarity. This solidarity is born only when the leaders witness to it by their humble, loving, and courageous encounter with the people. Not all men and women have sufficient courage for this encounter—but when they avoid encounter they become inflexible and treat others as mere objects; instead of nurturing life, they kill life; instead of searching for life, they flee from it. And these are oppressor characteristics.[83]

The active participation of the oppressed throughout the entirety of the poli- tical struggle is of critical importance, since otherwise "they may participate in that process with a spirit more revanchist than revolutionary. They may aspire to revolution as a means of domination, rather than as a road to liberation."[84]

A grand strategy for democratisation, as envisaged by Sharp, devised by democracy activists for the masses, thus isn't Freire's key approach to bring- ing about political change. He is sceptical of revolutionary leaders bestowing liberation as a gift to their people. Freire makes the case that

> leaders do bear the responsibility for coordination and, at times, direction—but leaders who deny praxis to the oppressed thereby inva- lidate their own praxis. By imposing their word on others, they falsify that word and establish a contradiction between their methods and their objectives. If they are truly committed to liberation, their action and reflection cannot proceed without the action and reflection of others. Revolutionary praxis must stand opposed to the praxis of the dominant elites, for they are by nature antithetical. Revolutionary praxis cannot tolerate an absurd dichotomy in which the praxis of the people is merely that of following the leaders decisions—a dichotomy reflecting the prescriptive methods of the dominant elites. Revolu- tionary praxis is a unity, and the leaders cannot treat the oppressed as their possession.[85]

Here, Freire's scepticism vis-à-vis overly pragmatic means–ends combinations becomes apparent. He is highly critical of the former oppressed using the strategies of their former oppressors.[86] He is sceptical of manipulative strategies like the "banking model" of education[87] as well as other anti-dialogical methods based on conquest, divide and rule, manipulation and cultural invasion.[88] In Freire's words, propaganda, "management, manipulation—all arms of domination—cannot be the instruments of their rehumanization. The only effective instrument is a humanizing pedagogy in which the revolutionary leadership establishes a permanent relationship of dialogue with the oppressed."[89] In stark contrast to Sharp's and Alinsky's TOPC, Freire thus is primarily concerned with the question as to how the oppressed can break the vicious circle of oppression. While Freire touches on the macro and meso levels in terms of his analysis, he primarily offers critical reflections aimed at the micro level of individuals and groups.

In the following I argue that Sharp's, Alinsky's and Freire's TOPC provide democratisation scholars with analytical vignettes which can shed light on the dynamics of the struggle for democracy. In this book I will be using these three *etic* TOPC as analytical vignettes in order to critique the evolution of the political regimes in mainland China, Taiwan and Hong Kong in Chapters 5, 7 and 9. The TOPC will also guide my analysis of 12 case studies as closely viewed critical incidents in the struggle for democracy in the Greater China region in Chapters 6, 8 and 10. The three TOPC, as analytical vignettes, provide a robust analytical framework which allows for intra-regional and inter-regional comparisons in Chapter 11. Seen in their entirety, the gained insights are not only relevant for democratisation scholars with an interest in mainland China and its periphery but also for democracy activists in all three regions.

In the second part of this book I will apply my theoretical insights from Chapters 1 to 4 to the empirical study of the struggle for democracy in mainland China, Taiwan and Hong Kong in Chapters 5 to 10. In Chapters 5, 7 and 9 I will describe how the respective authoritarian regimes evolved in mainland China, Taiwan and Hong Kong throughout the 20th century. For each country case study I will answer the following leading questions:

1. What is/was the power base of the regime?
2. What are the regime's key instruments of cooperation and coercion?
3. What are the fundamental vulnerabilities of the regime?

In Chapters 6, 8 and 10 I will identify the key stakeholders belonging to the three reform camps of anti-establishment, pro-establishment and trans-establishment. In my discussion of 12 selected episodes I will apply the TOPC by Sharp, Alinsky and Freire to assess the trajectory of the democracy movements in mainland China, Taiwan and Hong Kong. The following leading questions will structure the twelve episodes:

1. What antecedents informed the struggle for democracy and what were the perceived political opportunities by participants at the time?
2. Which reform camp initiated the specific struggle for democracy?
3. Which strategic reform approach was taken?
4. What were the key lessons learned?

Notes

1 Sharp, Gene (2012), *From Dictatorship to Democracy*, Serpent's Tail, London.
2 Alinsky, Saul (1989 [1971]), *Rules for Radicals: A Pragmatic Primer for Realistic Radicals*, Vintage Books, New York.
3 Freire, Paolo (2014), *Pedagogy of the Oppressed*, Bloomsbury Academic, New York.
4 With the caveat that Alinsky's TOPC is not a pro-establishment approach but a *trojan-horse approach* aimed at the political reformation of the establishment.
5 *Guardian* (2018), Gene Sharp Obituary, 12 February. Available online: www.theguardian.com/world/2018/feb/12/gene-sharp-obituary (accessed 3 September 2018).
6 Sharp (2012), *From Dictatorship to Democracy*, xviii.
7 BBC (2015), Gene Sharp: Hardtalk. Available online: www.youtube.com/watch?v=4wZESH4D1ik (accessed 3 September 2018). At 1:49 Gene Sharp provides this number in response to the presenter's assertion that his book was translated into dozens of languages.
8 *Telegraph* (2011), Gene Sharp: How to Start a Revolution. Available online: www.telegraph.co.uk/culture/film/filmmakersonfilm/8841546/Gene-Sharp-How-to-Start-a-Revolution.html (accessed 3 September 2018).
9 *Washington Post* (2016), Hillary Clinton, Saul Alinsky and Lucifer, Explained. Available online: www.washingtonpost.com/news/the-fix/wp/2016/07/20/hillary-clinton-saul-alinsky-and-lucifer-explained/?utm_term=.bf8fbcb10dbf (accessed 3 September 2018).
10 *New Republic* (2007), The Agitator. Available online: https://newrepublic.com/article/61068/the-agitator-barack-obamas-unlikely-political-education (accessed 3 September 2018).
11 Alinsky (1989), *Rules for Radicals*, 3.
12 Ibid., xxi.
13 Freire (2014), *Pedagogy of the Oppressed*, 48.
14 Mayo, P. and ProQuest (2013), *Echoes from Freire for a Critically Engaged Pedagogy*, Peter Mayo, New York.
15 Kirylo, J.D. and Boyd, D. (2017), A Freirean Imprint on Liberation Theology, in: Asoke Bhattacharya (Ed.), *Paulo Freire*, Sense Publishers, Rotterdam.
16 Tse, Justin K.H. (2016), Epilogue: Conscientization in the Aftermath of Occupying Hong Kong, in: Justin K.H. Tse and Jonathan Y. Tan (Eds), *Theological Reflections on the Hong Kong Umbrella Movement*, Palgrave Macmillan, New York.
17 Sharp (2012), *From Dictatorship to Democracy*, 46.
18 Ibid., 60.
19 Ibid., 64.
20 Alinsky (1989), *Rules for Radicals*, 67.
21 Freire (2014), *Pedagogy of the Oppressed*, 33.
22 Sharp (2012), *From Dictatorship to Democracy*, 6, italics in original.
23 Alinsky (1989), *Rules for Radicals*, xxii–xx.
24 Freire (2014), *Pedagogy of the Oppressed*, 19.
25 Alinsky (1989), *Rules for Radicals*, 155–8.
26 Freire (2014), *Pedagogy of the Oppressed*, 9.

27 Sharp (2012), *From Dictatorship to Democracy*, 45.
28 Ibid., 124–35.
29 Ibid., 46–50.
30 Ibid., 58.
31 Ibid., 54.
32 Ibid., 98–9.
33 Ibid., 19.
34 Ibid., 12.
35 Ibid., 26.
36 Ibid., 52.
37 Ibid., 62–3.
38 Ibid., 72.
39 Ibid., 59.
40 Ibid., 81.
41 Ibid., 75 and 80–1.
42 Ibid., 76.
43 Ibid., xx.
44 BBC (2015), BBC (2015), Gene Sharp: Hardtalk. Available online: www.youtube.com/watch?v=4wZESH4D1ik (accessed 3 September 2018).
45 Ibid.
46 Alinsky (1989), *Rules for Radicals*, xix.
47 Ibid., 4.
48 Ibid., xxi–xxii.
49 Ibid., 59.
50 Ibid., xxii–18.
51 Ibid., 72–80.
52 Ibid., 80.
53 Ibid.
54 Ibid., xxiii.
55 Ibid., xx.
56 Ibid., 63–80. See the chapter The Education of an Organizer.
57 Ibid., 127.
58 Ibid.
59 Ibid.
60 Ibid., 128.
61 Ibid.
62 Ibid.
63 Ibid.
64 Ibid.
65 Ibid., 129.
66 Ibid.
67 Ibid.
68 Ibid., 130.
69 Ibid.
70 Ibid., 25.
71 Ibid., 26–45.
72 Ibid., 24–5.
73 Ibid., 10.
74 Freire (2014), *Pedagogy of the Oppressed*, 30.
75 Ibid., 29.
76 Ibid., 39.
77 Ibid., 40–1.
78 Ibid., 42.
79 Ibid., 57.
80 Ibid., 67.

81 Ibid., 69–73.
82 Ibid., 106–64.
83 Ibid., 110.
84 Ibid., 108.
85 Ibid., 125–6.
86 Ibid., 27.
87 Ibid., 53.
88 Ibid., 119–48.
89 Ibid., 50.

5

THE CALAMITY OF CHINESE COMMUNIST PARTY RULE IN MAINLAND CHINA

Commenting on the state of political affairs in mainland China under Xi Jinping, Stein Ringen has argued that one should consider the PRC's political regime a "state that is totalitarian at home and imperialistic abroad".[1] In his monograph *The Perfect Dictatorship: China in the 21st Century*, Ringen argues that what

> is emerging is a new brand of totalitarianism which looks less totalitarian than it is. This is not totalitarianism light, meaning less totalitarian than it could be. It is a totalitarianism with all the tools of the trade ready to be deployed but also a kind in which those tools are not put to use when not needed. Not exactly soft totalitarianism but rather sophisticated totalitarianism.[2]

Samantha Hoffman has critiqued such tendencies among China scholars to assess the CCP in overly binary terms. She argues that the CCP "has developed a form of authoritarianism that cannot be measured through traditional political scales like reform versus retrenchment. This version of authoritarianism involves both 'hard' and 'soft' authoritarian methods that constantly act together."[3] Hoffman points out that the "CCP has always been explicit that it does not intend to liberalise politically"[4] and that coercion "is not turned off to allow for co-optation, instead the two operate together in unison".[5] In Chapter 2 I described this two-pronged approach to governing China. The party-state did not simply suppress China's anti-corruption and pro-democracy movement of 1989 but consequently also started coopting proponents of China's nascent middle class and the rising private entrepreneurs throughout the 1990s and early 2000s.

In this chapter I trace how the CCP gained power during the Republican period (1911–49). I argue that the CCP's formative years as revolutionary political party launched by Lenin's Communist International (Comintern) hold the key to our understanding of the CCP's illiberal party ideology. I will show how during the civil war with the KMT Mao Zedong managed to firmly weave his world-view into the fabric of the CCP. In this chapter I will also outline how the CCP, following the defeat of the KMT and the founding of the PRC in 1949, has attempted to mould China's economy and society in its Marxist-Leninst-Maoist image. Assessing the CCP from a longitudinal perspective—from its inception in the early 1920s, its rise to power in 1949 and its various policy failures from the early 1950s until the late 1980s—I will argue that throughout its reign over mainland China the CCP has employed a united front method involving hard and soft authoritarian strategies and tactics. In this chapter I will not discuss the post-Tiananmen development of the CCP from a communist revolutionary party to a crony-capitalist regime, which I already covered in my critique of modernisation theory in Chapter 2. Instead, I will conclude this chapter with reflections on the vulnerabilities of mainland China's party-state, as exemplified by the CCP's Document No. 9 from 2013.

Mainland China's "winner-takes-all" conception of politics

When discussing political conflicts in mainland China over the past 20 years, my interlocutors have often invoked the formulation "你死我活" to describe Chinese political culture. This expression can be crudely translated into "you die, I live". It can also be interpreted along the lines of zero-sum thinking, such as "I get 100 points and you get zero".[6] Thomas Gold has described Chinese political culture "as revealed in centuries of practice, [which] takes a zero-sum, moralistic view of political disagreements, in which the ultimate objective is the elimination of rivals as well as their followers, families, and even names".[7] Joseph Fewsmith argues that the tendency to solve political matters by domination in mainland China was originally a consequence of the emperor system. According to Fewsmith this approach to politics was greatly strengthened by the end of the dynastic system in 1911, the humiliation China suffered at the hands of foreigners, the ravages of internal conflict, the revolutionary ideologies (with their privileged claims to truth) of the KMT and the CCP and the struggle for power between those two political parties during the civil war.[8] Fewsmith suggests that a "winner-take-all conception of politics has been a hallmark of CCP politics".[9] To understand how this narrow conception of the political process came about, we need to reflect on the revolutionary history of the CCP.

The CCP's rise to power

The CCP was founded with the help of Soviet Comintern agents in Shanghai in 1921.[10] The Comintern was sceptical, however, that the nascent CCP would be able to survive on its own. It subsequently sent Mikhail Borodin, a "professional revolutionary" and Bolshevik who grew up in a Russian-Jewish family in Latvia, to China to facilitate the organisational growth of the CCP. In line with Comintern instructions, Borodin played a key role in forging a strategic alliance between the young CCP and the KMT. Borodin orchestrated a first united front between the competing political parties, which lasted from 1923 until 1927. From the outset, Borodin was attempting to square a political circle. In Spence's words,

> Borodin's task was delicate and complex. He had to develop the Kuomintang to the point where it could become strong enough to reunite China and rout the Imperialist powers. At the same time (and the irony of this was to grow apparent later) he had to strengthen the Communist Party so that it might eventually transform a successful Kuomintang nationalist revolution into a socialist revolution. He had enemies on two flanks: certain Chinese Communists saw the dangers implicit in an alliance with a party dominated by the bourgeoisie; and conservative members of the Kuomintang felt that the Communists were dangerous allies, and should be crushed before they grew too strong.[11]

Following a general strike which helped Shanghai workers wrestle the city back from warlord control, KMT leader Chiang Kai-shek took advantage of their willingness to follow Comintern orders to "bury their arms and disband their pickets".[12] On 12 April 1927, Chiang ordered his troops to round "up the Communists and labor leaders in the city and had them shot".[13] After Chiang outmanoeuvred the CCP following the Shanghai massacre, "executions of radicals took place daily".[14]

Following the failure of the first united front (1923–7), the conflict between the CCP and KMT morphed into a civil war. While fighting against the insurgent CCP, the KMT also had to deal with the Japanese invasion in 1931. In under two years Japan defeated the KMT in the north-east of China and established the puppet state of Manchukuo.[15] In 1937, occasional skirmishes with the Japanese army became a full-scale war against Japan.[16] Following the Xi'an incident, where Chiang Kai-shek was kidnapped by warlord-turned-KMT general Zhang Xueliang, Chiang agreed to form a second united front between the CCP and KMT, which lasted between 1936 and 1941. It led to the formation of a National Revolutionary Army of CCP and KMT troops. In Myers' words,

> Japan's invasion resulted in the Nanjing state's scorched-earth policy and a retreat to the southwest provinces of Yunnan, Guizhou and Sichuan, with the new capital located in Chongqing, Sichuan province ... the Chongqing state opted for maximum conventional warfare, intensified its extraction of physical and human resources to support its large

bureaucracy and military, and failed to win the strong support of the local elites and ordinary people for its goals.[17]

After relocating to Nanjing, "the Nanjing state became engaged in a full-blown civil war with the Chinese Communist Party and its Red Army".[18] According to Myers, the KMT lost the civil war for three reasons: it overestimated its military capabilities, it failed to control inflation and lost military and economic support from the United States.[19]

The CCP, on the other hand, had not only managed to recover from KMT suppression following the first united front. During the early 1930s it also established the Jiangxi Soviet in central China, which served as a testing ground for its nascent party policies.[20] When the KMT threatened to destroy the CCP stronghold the PLA retreated to Shaanxi province in a series of marches which have come to be known as the so-called "long march". Van Slyke reminds us about the formative nature of these experiences, as the

> party has always looked back on these years, "the Yenan period", as a time of trial and triumph over enormous obstacles, a time of purity, idealism, and commitment, a time when the unity between the party and the people was forged. During the Yenan period the party gained confidence in its ability to lead and inspire all but the most "reactionary" groups in Chinese society. This confidence hardened into conviction, and from this conviction the party has drawn much of its sense of legitimacy. In a broad sense, this leadership of a genuinely responsive populace was what Mao meant by the united front.[21]

It was in the Shaanxi town of Yenan (also spelled Yan'an in the academic literature) where Mao Zedong developed his idea to add the "mass line" to the Leninist concept of "democratic centralism"[22] and started advocating "rectification" among rank-and-file party members.[23] Mao popularised his doctrines through a series of speeches which came to be known as the "Yan'an talks". In Mao's world-view, independent voices needed to be subjugated to CCP control. Cheek argues that "Mao held that only the rectification doctrine operating through a Leninist Party structure could succeed—the intellectual must be subordinated to the organisational process of the group".[24] The Yenan period is significant for us to understand the illiberal and anti-democratic roots of the CCP. According to Cheek, the "fading of wild lilies, the demise of the left-wing writers in Yan'an, marks the end of the cosmopolitanism and individualism—epitomised by Lu Xun—of the May Fourth tradition. That cosmopolitanism and individualism became 'Trotskyism' and 'absolute egalitarianism' in the rectification movement."[25] It is during the Yenan period that CCP ideology morphed into ideocracy, understood as a "political system whose activities are pursued in reference to the tenets of a monistic ideology. More specifically, the legitimacy of the political system is derived from the monistic ideology, which establishes a universal frame of reference for the participants of the system."[26]

The ideocracy of the CCP in the 1940s was not limited to overt hostility vis-à-vis independent-minded Chinese intellectuals. All means were permissible to achieve the ends of the communist utopia. A case in point are the war crimes committed by the PLA against unarmed civilians during the final years of the civil war. In *White Snow, Red Blood*, a Chinese-language first-hand account by Zhang Zhenglong, a former PLA officer involved in the CCP's battles in north-east China, "describes in chilling detail how, in 1948, the PLA laid siege to Changchun, the provincial capital of Jilin, and starved it into submission. An estimated 150,000 civilians are said to have died in this stand-off between the Communist and Nationalist forces that was previously described as a 'bloodless victory'."[27] According to Zhang, "Changchun was like Hiroshima ... [the] casualties were about the same. Hiroshima took nine seconds; Changchun took five months."[28] Taiwanese writer Lung Ying-tai, who interviewed numerous PLA soldiers for her study of the siege of Changchun for her Chinese-language book *Big River, Big Sea: Untold Stories of 1949*, has similarly suggested that between 100,000 and 650,000 people may have perished during the PLA's blockade of the city.[29]

For Mao Zedong practically any means were acceptable to achieve his ultimate end, which was to help the CCP win the civil war against the KMT. If this required subjugating China's intelligentsia to the whims of an ever changing party doctrine, this could be justified with reference to the CCP as the nation's Avant Garde. If war crimes against the Chinese population would accelerate the victory against the KMT, this was a price Mao was willing to pay. When the CCP emerged victorious in 1949, it had survived close to three decades of trials and tribulations as a revolutionary party. In this process it had emancipated itself from Comintern control. During the Yenan period in the early 1940s, Mao had sinicised its party ideology. During the second united front with the KMT the PLA also mastered guerrilla warfare, initially against the Japanese and later against the troops of the KMT. Gaining power at any cost, however, reinforced the pre-modern Chinese political culture of winner takes all. By interpreting the political process entirely as a zero-sum game, the CCP succumbed to what Nobel Peace Prize laureate Liu Xiaobo has called an "enemy mentality". Liu has critiqued enemy mentality for its tendency "to poison the spirit of a nation, incite cruel mortal struggles, destroy a society's tolerance and humanity, and hinder a nation's progress toward freedom and democracy".[30] Fitzgerald has similarly critiqued enemy mentality as the preferred means by which

> China's Communist Party secures its mandate to rule, and how senior party leaders secure their mandate to lead. By mounting ferocious campaigns against imaginary enemies in the world beyond the party—class enemies in the past, foreign enemies today—party leaders can conduct

the purges they need if they are to overcome their rivals and place their own people in positions throughout the system ... The enemy mentality that drives China's Communist Party is an existential requirement of a Leninist vanguard party.[31]

A trinity of party, government and military

With the founding of the PRC in 1949 the CCP began to mould mainland China in its own Marxist-Leninist-Maoist image. The new political system that emerged after 1949 can be described as a trinity of party, government and military (*dang zheng jun*). From the outset, party structures and state structures were designed to be inseparable. Behind every state organ a corresponding party organ was hard-wired into mainland China's political system.[32] In order to protect its authority, the party-state also had to control the army. The PLA's loyalty to the CCP not only allowed the party-state to cement its authority domestically, but also to project its power beyond mainland China's borders.[33] Commenting on the state of the history of CCP–PLA relations at the turn of the millennium, Shambaugh has argued that the

> army would certainly follow orders from the party leadership to use force against external threats and most likely against internal ones as well. The army does remain loyal to the party. There is no danger of a military coup d'état of the army against the party, as is often the case in other one-party authoritarian states.[34]

Despite ongoing debates throughout the 1980s about the need to separate the party from the state (*dang zheng fenkei*)[35] and to turn the army into a national military subject to state control (*dang jun fenkai*),[36] the trinity of party, government and military has remained unchanged since 1949.

A wide range of regulatory policies were implemented in the early 1950s to ensure the CCP's top-down control of the economy and society. Brown and Pickowitz have argued that "China's rulers had consolidated power through a mixture of popular enthusiasm for change plus terror and indoctrination".[37] The two authors argue that in the early years of the PRC the CCP in many aspects aped the approach taken by the Nationalists before:

> In such areas as urban policy, public security, industrial development, education, labor relations, ethnic minorities, and rural health care, the Communists behaved in the early 1950s much like the Nationalists had in the 1930s and 1940s. Like the Nationalists, the Communists were committed to the formation of a strong state, even if accelerated state-building weakened the ability of social groups to express their own will. Hence, even though the Communists were the self-proclaimed party of the urban proletariat, they moved quickly after spring 1949 to impose tight state

control of the labor movement, just as the Nationalists had done in the past.[38]

The CCP's first Five-Year Plan in 1953 marked a first clear break from the KMT's approach to governing mainland China.[39] Private enterprises were successively shut down and replaced by State-Owned Enterprises. Mainland China's economy was geared towards heavy industries such as coal and steel. Changes to the economic structure included agrarian reforms. Clarke highlights that when

> the Chinese Communist Party assumed control over mainland China in 1949, it did not follow Russia's Bolsheviks in immediately abolishing the private ownership of land. In the countryside, a violent land reform movement brought a change in owners, but not in the ownership regime itself; full collectivization did not occur until the late 1950s.[40]

Bramall highlights the intended and unintended consequences of land reform in the 1950s:

> [in] so far as land reform eliminated semi-feudal relations of production in the Chinese countryside, its effects were beneficial. But in those parts of the People's Republic where land reform was driven by naive egalitarianism and an almost millenarian faith in the poor peasantry, the process of capital accumulation was disrupted and slow growth was the inevitable consequence.[41]

He describes the CCP's approach to land reform as only partially successful, as breaking

> up rich peasant farms reduced land productivity and increased the collective action problems associated with organising irrigation. Just as Meiji Japan's cultivating landlords were agents of rural progress, so too China's rich peasants. In other words, the notion that a poor peasantry could preside over the modernisation of the Chinese countryside was little more than a dream in the context of the 1950s. The preservation of the rich peasant economy was not ideal, not least because it facilitated neither the development of irrigation networks nor mechanisation; considerations such as these lay behind the drive towards collectivisation after 1955.[42]

Directly linked to land collectivisation and the introduction of a planned economy along Soviet lines was the CCP's establishment of the household registration system (*hukou zhidu*). The *hukou* can be described as a "kind of passport system, which limits access to public services, based on the birthplace of the holder".[43] By distinguishing between Chinese citizens with a rural or an urban *hukou*, the

> promulgation of this legislation in January 1958 took away one major basic right of the Chinese citizen, the freedom of internal migration and residence, a right encoded in China's constitution for the first 26 years of the People's Republic (Zhu, 2003). The freedom of mobility is a fundamental one, for it not only gives an individual the opportunity to enhance his/her well-being by moving to a better place or a better job (or joining family), but also increases the individual's political power to rein in the tyranny of a rogue state by threat of exit (Tiebout, 1956; Moses, 2006).[44]

According to Chan, the

> gradual development of a new, more encompassing version of hukou during the 1950s was an inevitable outcome of the establishment of a command economic system, which required meticulous planning and control of all macro and micro facets of society, and pursuit of a Stalinist-type, Big Push industrialization strategy premised on the unequal exchange of industry and agriculture. Implementing such a strategy, the state siphoned off resources in the rural sector for capital accumulation in industry through the well-known process of "scissors prices".[45]

As part of the *hukou* system, urban Chinese were organised "according to the local units in which they worked (*danwei*) so as to increase the efficiency of social control and indoctrination".[46] While the CCP defeated the KMT in the civil war, it was far less effective as a ruling party after 1949. The period 1959–76 was marked by two major party policy failures, which have become known as the Great Leap Forward (1958–62) and the Cultural Revolution (1966–76). Seen in their entirety, these two decades of CCP-induced political turmoil and chaos should be considered a mainland China variant of what Dan Diner has called a "rupture in civilisation" (*Zivilisationsbruch*).[47]

The calamity of the Great Leap Forward, 1958–62

In the case of the Great Leap Forward, Mao's ill-advised economic policies and an overly rigid political system relying almost entirely on command and control created a perfect storm. Mao had the fantastical idea of overtaking Britain in steel production in only a matter of years. Teiwes and Sun argue that whereas in "1956 Mao was willing to listen to others, and he demonstrated considerable respect for the CCP's economic specialists. In 1958 he concluded running the economy was 'no big deal' and took control himself."[48] Frank Dikötter describes how the peasant masses were mobilised to transform both agriculture and industry at the same time, converting a backward economy into a modern communist society of plenty for all. In the pursuit of a utopian paradise, everything was collectivised, as villagers were herded together in giant communes which heralded the advent of communism. People in the countryside were robbed of their work, their homes, their land, their belongings and their livelihood.[49]

Dikötter estimates that "at least 45 million died unnecessarily between 1958 and 1962".[50] Not all of the victims starved to death due to Mao's neglect for crop production. Drawing on party records Dikötter suggests that

by a rough approximation 6 to 8 percent of the victims were tortured to death or summarily killed—amounting to at least 2.5 million people. Other victims were deliberately deprived of food and starved to death. Many more vanished because they were too old, weak or sick to work— and hence unable to earn their keep. People were killed selectively because they were rich, because they dragged their feet, because they spoke out or simply because they were not liked, for whatever reason, by the man who wielded the ladle in the canteen.[51]

Macfarquhar and Schoenhals argue that despite the enormous hardships endured by Chinese people CCP

cadres held the country together and enabled the CCP to weather the calamity (of the Great Leap Forward). By 1966, the Chinese economy had recovered sufficiently for a Soviet-style third Five-Year Plan ... to be scheduled. But the Cultural Revolution overwhelmed careful plans and policies. For a decade, the Chinese political system was first thrown into chaos and then paralyzed.[52]

The ten lost years of the Cultural Revolution, 1966–76

According to Teiwes, the

Cultural Revolution, notwithstanding the very real social tensions it tapped, was the individual creation of Mao Zedong ... Whatever Mao's motives, which surely involved some combination of distress at the real loss of a revolutionary idealism in society, fears of a "Soviet revisionist" future for China, anger at official institutions that he believed to be bureaucracies aloof from the people and unresponsive to his wishes, and warped accumulated resentment at various leaders for imagined slights and disloyalty, he had no strategic plan for the Cultural Revolution.[53]

Mao, with the help of his wife Jiang Qing, unleashed an unprecedented attack on the party bureaucracy by encouraging young Chinese to become Red Guards. According to Wang Ban, the Cultural Revolution allowed "power elites [to engage in] ... corruption, usurpation, and personal vendettas".[54] The enemy mentality which informed such personal vendettas, however, was not just the privilege of the elite few but came to affect the entire party-state apparatus. In Lin Weiran's words,

> ordinary people ... found that the seemingly spontaneous mass move-ment was actually tightly controlled by the power holders. The ordinary people were shocked not only by the double-faced behaviour of the party officials, but also by their carelessness in making political decisions, which often had dire consequences for innocent people. They learned that their leaders had concerns of their own; they either were following the orders of their superiors, acting to attack objects of their personal dis-pleasure, or some combination thereof.[55]

During the radical period of the Cultural Revolution (1966–9), mainland China veered on the brink of another civil war. Red Guards became so mili-tant that by 1968 the PLA was mobilised to fight out-of-control units in south-west China.[56] Meisner has highlighted that "nowhere was the blood-shed greater than it was in Kwangsi [Guangxi], where Wei Kuo-ch'ing [Wei Guoqing], political commissar of the provincial military district and future ally of Teng Hsiao-p'ing [Deng Xiaoping], carried out massacres and mass executions of radical Red Guards that were shocking even by the bloody standards at the time".[57] Saich argues that once "the People's Liberation Army ... put the students back in their place, many became cynical towards the party and authority and alienated from the political process, a legacy that has persisted to this day".[58]

Bottom-up impulses for "reform and opening up" in the early 1980s

The policy failures of the Great Leap Forward and the Cultural Revolution meant that beginning "in 1978, the Chinese government undertook a program of economic reform largely because it had no other choice. Politically, the Cultural Revolution had undermined Maoist ideology by driving it to the extremes; economically, the country was on the 'brink of collapse'."[59] The CCP under Deng Xiaoping's leadership was forced to reverse course on a number of early Maoist policies, ranging from the decollectivisation of rural communes and the relaxing of overly stringent regulations governing work units in urban China. The early socio-economic reforms of the 1980s, how-ever, were not a result of top-down CCP initiatives, as Barry Naughton has suggested,[60] but originated by rural Chinese challenging the orthodoxy of party ideology from below. It is important to remember that throughout the 1980s the introduction of market mechanisms into China's economy remained hotly contested within the party.[61] The highly effective use of a new household responsibility system "which restores the individual household and replaces the production team system as the unit of production and accounting in rural area[s]"[62] was in fact piloted by rural Chinese in Xiaogang village, Fengyang county, Anhui province.

A report in the *People's Daily Online* describes the risks that the villagers took to defy official CCP policies: "In 1978, 18 villagers at Xiaogang risked their lives to sign a secret agreement that divided the then People's Commune-owned farmland into pieces for each family to cultivate. They promised that each household would deliver a full quota of grain to the state and to the commune, and keep whatever remained."[63] When the household responsibility system proved to be an effective way to increase the yield of crops this farming method was first legalised and later applied all across China. While it has been claimed that "China" lifted hundreds of millions out of poverty as a result of the party-state's economic reforms,[64] it probably would be more accurate to say that starting from the early 1980s Chinese farmers lifted themselves out of poverty despite the efforts of the CCP to keep them in their place.

Protecting the party-state's authority: the united front method

The CCP in part survived the party policy failures of the Great Leap Forward and the Cultural Revolution thanks to the reluctant introduction of market mechanisms to jumpstart its struggling economy. There is a tendency in the academic literature to see a marked difference between the Maoist and post-Maoist periods. While the former is described as a phase of totalitarianism, the latter is portrayed as authoritarian rule. David Shambaugh's scholarship is a case in point. Shambaugh has argued that

> Mao bequeathed to Deng a "totalistic" state characterized by highly personalized and concentrated power; and expansive and intrusive Leninist organizational apparatus that employed commandist, coercive and mobilizational techniques of rule; with autarkic approaches to development and foreign affairs. The Chinese state under Mao was all-inclusive, playing multiple roles normally left to the private sector in many countries: employer, saver, investor, manager, economic planner, price settler, social provider and redistributor of social and economic sources. All of these formally totalistic functions performed by the Maoist state changed fundamentally under Deng.[65]

He further argues that "Deng's [reform] program changed the nature of the state from being a proactive agent of social-political change to being a more passive facilitator of economic change and reactive arbiter of social-political tensions. The Chinese state 'withdrew' from its former all-intrusive and hegemonic roles in the life of the nation."[66] In the following I argue that such narratives of a transition of totalitarian to authoritarian forms of CCP governance are only partially correct, since Deng Xiaoping had no qualms in using both soft and hard authoritarian modes of political control to consolidate CCP rule.

We have to remember that on the political front the CCP has never given up protecting its authority with the help of the united front method. The latter originated out of the CCP's struggle during the civil war and underwent various iterations during the first and second united front with the KMT.[67] Van Slyke has described the united front method as follows:

> Functionally, the united front approach divides society into three strata, not on the basis of class theory, but with reference to a specific goal. The first group is always the party itself, together with those willing to give enthusiastic support to its leadership in the achievement of this goal. The middle group, numerically the largest, is made up of waverers—those ambivalent or unconcerned about the outcome, and who could go either way. The third group is the enemy, who will strenuously and actively oppose the party's efforts. Since the party and its supporters are a minority, goals and policies must be selected so as to limit the size of the enemy and minimize the number of waverers siding with the enemy. This can be done by winning over some of the uncommitted so that their strength is added to that of the revolutionary core, and by neutralizing others so that they do not participate on either side. All those except the enemy are thought of as falling within the scope of the united front.[68]

The united front approach has been applied by the CCP since its inception as a revolutionary party in 1921. After the founding of the PRC it led to the formation of a United Front Work Department and the establishment of the Chinese People's Political Consultative Conference.[69] The CCP's united front method cannot be explained without recourse to Mao's concept of contradictions in society. According to Mao,

> at any moment there exist many contradictions in society, not just a simple thesis and antithesis. But there is always a principal contradiction, not only more important but also different in kind from other contradictions. This principal contradiction cannot be resolved without struggle; sooner or later, therefore, it becomes "antagonistic", in contrast to "non-antagonistic" contradictions that can be either peacefully resolved or temporarily suspended. After one principal contradiction has been resolved, another arises to take its place.[70]

In her seminal study *Democracy Challenged: The Rise of Semi-Authoritarianism*, Marina Ottaway has described the games that authoritarian regimes play to protect their authority. The following paragraph encapsulates the essence of the CCP's united front method particularly well. She highlights that since

> their real goal is to prevent competition that might threaten their hold on power, they devote considerable effort to issues that are not normal parts of the political process of democratic countries. In particular, they seek to prevent the emergence of competing political organizations, rather than just to defeat them in elections; they do their best to control the flow of information to the citizens, hoping to sway public opinion; they manipulate institutions and constitutions to their own advantage with remarkable frequency and thus undermine and distort them; and, in a growing number of cases, they seek to maintain political stability over the long run not by allowing institutions to consolidate but by manipulating the succession process in ways that are usually associated with monarchies rather than republics.[71]

The instrumentalisation of ethnic and cultural nationalism to shore up popular support for an illiberal and anti-democratic CCP, for example, is a prime example of a highly manipulative game the CCP has been playing since the founding of the PRC. Yahuda has argued that CCP nationalists have used patriotism to unite disparate ethnic groups, thus closing the political room available for the exercise of self-determination or for different ethnic groups to develop their own accounts of their history. The CCP's continuous emphasis on the supposed superiority of the Han has also evoked a kind of racial or ethnic patriotism that transcends state boundaries.[72]

Rule by bribery

In the following I will outline how the CCP has governed mainland China during the Maoist and post-Maoist eras with the help of the united front method, a two-pronged process of simultaneous co-optation and coercion, where proverbial carrots and sticks are applied to suppress opposition to party-state rule. In Chapter 3 I outlined how individuals who are supportive of CCP rule can benefit from party-state patronage. While political proximity to power (*tizhi nei*) requires them to sacrifice individual autonomy, the privileges that come with this position are considerable. In a scathing critique of the political status quo in Xi's China Tsinghua law professor Xu Zhangrun lambasted the "inclusive retirement-to-grave care for high-level cadres according to a standard that is far and away above that allowed to the average citizen. These cadres retain the privileges they enjoyed during their working lives, including premium health care and special access to luxury resorts for recreation and holidays."[73] This suggests that joining the CCP and climbing the greasy pole as a CCP cadre opens up avenues to resources that otherwise cannot be accessed.

For those unwilling or unable to become CCP cadres, maintaining a close relationship with representatives of the party-state can be considered a necessity for upward mobility. He Qinglian explains the drive towards a close alignment with the party-state as follows:

> The fact is that what has emerged in China is a system for distributing resources that is rooted in neither a purely planned nor a market-based economy. Instead, rent-seeking activities that lead to acquisition of capital and other forms of wealth rely on a highly elaborate and informal network or web of social connections ... Informal networks of social relationships are, in short, a major resource, in that they are the key mechanism for mobilizing and directing the flow of wealth, making them not just of great economic significance, but also critical to the way in which China goes about handling its raw materials and other such social resources.[74]

In Chapter 2 I outlined how this highly intransparent and exclusive approach to resource distribution has accelerated the co-optation of middle-class and private entrepreneurs. Osburg has outlined why the co-optation of the latter group is particularly problematic:

> The new rich businessmen I studied operated in tightly-bound social networks governed by an ethos of mutual aid and brotherhood. This ethos benefits the well-connected members of these networks, who have insider access to deals, capital, and opportunities. From the perspective of those on the outside of elite networks, however, these relationships are the basis of corruption. As I say in my book, "the moral economy of elite guanxi networks results in very immoral consequences for the public good".[75]

In Chapter 2 I also outlined that the gradual transition away from a planned to a more market-oriented economy throughout the 1980s and 1990s created both winners and losers. I showed that CCP economic policies disproportionally benefited cadres, state-owned enterprise managers and their cronies. To a lesser extent, economic growth nurtured a nascent middle class in mainland China which remains highly dependent on party-state patronage. In the absence of a functioning rule of law losers of mainland China's modernisation process have time and again opted for direct action to air their grievances. In order to prevent mass incidents (*qunti shijian*) spiralling out of control and thus threatening the survival of the party-state, the CCP has also used financial offers to pacify conflict-capable groups in Chinese society. The

CCP's elaborate stability-preservation system (*weiwen tizhi*) includes funds to buy off disgruntled citizens.[76] Chen Xi describes how the

> weiwen system's final drawback is its perverse tendency to encourage unruly behavior. When the CCP's fondness for the "mass line" meets the instrumentalist attitude toward legality that is common within both officialdom and society at large, the result is contempt for rules and forms. Courts and agencies will bend the law to keep boisterous petitioners quiet, so ordinary Chinese citizens (provided they calculate that repression is not a major risk) have learned to "act out" in order to guard their interests or boost their bargaining power. Compensation for houses demolished under eminent domain is often minimal, but a few homeowners with the nerve to "make trouble" have received excessive payouts. Similarly, judges have received orders from on high to keep working with unhappy litigants even after their cases have been formally decided when the litigants resorted to "troublemaking" petitions. Following the principle of "the squeaky wheel gets the grease" in order to keep the peace certainly holds the danger of teaching people that disruptive tactics are a shortcut to special treatment.[77]

Rule by bribery thus encourages Chinese citizens either to become part of the system or to manipulate the system to their own advantage.

Rule by fear

While the CCP has shown a remarkable willingness to "rule by bribery", it has also combined this seemingly benign governing approach with the far more draconian "rule by fear". The CCP's re-engineering of China's society in the 1950s included highly pervasive methods of political control. In order to ensure the political loyalty and obedience of Chinese citizens, the CCP introduced the notorious personal file system (*dang'an zhidu*). *New York Times* journalist Andrew Jacobs describes how the system has systematically undermined individual autonomy: "The dossiers start with a citizen's middle-school grades, whether they play well with others and, as they become adults, list their religious affiliations, psychological problems and perceived political liabilities."[78] As Chinese citizens cannot normally access their dossier, the personal file system is supposed to induce fear and lead to self-censorship, as negative comments on file can jeopardise a person's job prospects and lead to other forms of discrimination. In 2014 mainland Chinese film-maker Zhu Rikun directed the documentary *The Dossier*, in which he portrays public intellectual and pro-Tibetan activist Tsering Woeser. In the documentary Woeser reads "excerpts from her secret government 'dossier'", a dossier which she got hold of by chance.[79] The personal file system was designed to ensure that individuals internalise and compartmentalise their discontent, thus ensuring that from the CCP's point of view contradictions in society remain non-antagonist. When Chinese citizens overcome their fear and stand up to authority, as they have done time and time again, the CCP has shown few qualms in employing the entire spectrum of highly oppressive techniques. In this chapter I discussed how the PLA committed war crimes against the Chinese people during the final years of the civil war. In Chapter 2 I also described how the CCP leadership ordered the PLA to shoot at unarmed protesters during the 1989 anti-corruption and pro-democracy movement. During the chaos of the Great Leap Forward and the Cultural Revolution, political disobedience could lead to summary executions.

A constant of CCP rule in mainland China has been the pervasive use of labour camps (*laogai*),[80] re-education camps (*laojiao*)[81] and other extra-judicial correction facilities such as "black jails"[82] to imprison critics of one-party rule. While the mass terror of Maoist political campaigns came to an end in the late 1970s, from 1983 until 1986 Deng Xiaoping authorised so-called "strike hard" campaigns, which ostensibly were directed against organised crime in mainland China, but which in fact often also caught political opponents to CCP rule in its dragnet. According to Wang and Minzner, "it was characterized by mass arrests, rapid sentencing procedures and high execution rates—with perhaps as many as 10,000 persons executed in a three-year period".[83] A more recent example of an ongoing "strike hard" campaign is Xinjiang, where since 2014 the CCP has unleashed an unprecedented assault on ethnic minorities.[84] By 2018 it is estimated that more than 1 million Uyghurs and Kazakhs were being held in extra-judicial detention facilities.[85]

Stability preservation at all costs?

Chinese scholar Yu Jianrong has criticised the CCP's reliance on what he terms "rigid stability". He defines this term with reference to three key characteristics:

> First, it is a form of political stability founded upon the exclusive and closed nature of political power; Second, "rigid stability" seeks absolute social tranquility as a goal of governance, viewing all forms of protest— be they marches, demonstrations and strikes by workers, retailers and the transport sector—as a form of disorder and chaos that begs suppression by any means; and, Third, with state violence as its foundation, "rigid stability" relies upon the quasi-legal control of social ideology and social organizations.[86]

Yu is particularly critical of the CCP's tendency to pursue stability at all costs. His critique is mirrored in Feng Chongyi's observation that "stability preservation in China today relies predominantly on extralegal measures and methods, which has the effect of undermining social stability and existing legal institutions. Under the guise of preserving stability, the state bureaucracy has been given a free hand, more coercive power and more resources to crush dissent."[87] In 2010 a report from Tsinghua University researchers claimed that "this year's [Chinese] budget for internal security has reached 514 billion yuan". The report went on to note that public safety expenditure "increased by 16 per cent last year and will be augmented by a further 8.9 per cent this year. This increase has put expenditure on internal security in the same league as national defence spending."[88]

In his landmark publication *China's Trapped Transition*, Minxin Pei has described how corrupt local governments have entered into alliances with organised crime and formed local mafia states.[89] Peng Wang has described this process as "red–black collusion between police officers and local gang-sters".[90] In Chapter 7 I will compare and contrast these emerging local mafia states in mainland China with the phenomenon of "black gold" (*hei jin*) in Taiwan politics under the Kuomintang since the early 1950s. Such alliances have allowed CCP cadres to externalise the costs of repression by hiring thugs to intimidate petitioners or beat up protestors.[91] Lynette Ong notes how "thugs-for-hire":

> augments the state's coercive capacity to induce acquiescence in addition to its traditional repressive capacity, such as the military, the police, and the intelligence agencies. However, it diverges in a few dimensions from the traditional coercive institutions undergirding illiberal states. First, a private agent as the actor is distinct from state agents such as the military and police connected with political elites. Second, in contrast to the formal coercive apparatus that forms part of the state's permanent coercive capacity, "thugs-for-hire" (while serving useful functions under certain conditions), are dispensable at other times. The third-party nature of [thugs-for-hire] allows the state to shed and disengage it when it is not in use. This is strategic from the perspectives of costs and evasion of responsibility.[92]

Endemic and systemic nature of human rights abuses

While the CCP has signed but not ratified a number of international human rights covenants,[93] in the absence of an independent media and judiciary, human rights abuses in mainland China remain endemic and systemic. According to Andrew Nathan, the CCP bears the responsibility for a litany of human rights violations which range from imprisonment, arbitrary detention or forced exile, religious repression, violations related to criminal procedure, torture and abuse of inmates of prisons and labour camps, forced resettlement, forced abortion and sterilisation, denial of the right to strike, denial of freedom of the Chinese and foreign press, mistreatment of homosexuals, eugenic practices, wide use of the death penalty without inadequate safeguards, the harvesting of organs from condemned prisoners for transplantation, kidnapping, trafficking and abuse of women and girls, to export of prison labour products.[94]

A particular insidious means of oppression has been the use of mainland China's psychiatric system to lock up critics.[95] A joint report by Human Rights Watch and the Geneva Initiative on Psychiatry found that "in many cases since the late 1950s … detained dissidents, non-conformists, 'whistle-blowers', and other dissenters have additionally been subjected to forensic psychiatric evaluation by the legal authorities, found to be criminally insane and then forcibly committed to various types of psychiatric institutions".[96] Such immoral and unethical practices remain part and parcel of the CCP's toolkit of political repression. In 2018 Dong Yaoqiong, a female Chinese student live-streamed her anti-CCP protest by pouring ink on a Xi poster.[97] In violation of Article 30 of China's Mental Health Law[98] she was subsequently sent to a Hunan psychiatric institution to undergo compulsory "treatment".[99] This shows that the CCP still applies the Maoist practice of involuntary psychiatric treatment to punish dissidents.

How vulnerable is mainland China's party-state?

In this chapter I have portrayed the Chinese party-state as a political regime which time and again has shown its willingness to use both hard and soft authoritarian means to protect its authority by either suppressing public discontent or coopting conflict-capable groups in society. While the exact number of mainland China's "mass incidents" is disputed,[100] anecdotal

> evidence over the last five years suggests a rise in "anger-venting" mass incidents—large scale, often violent, riots that erupt from seemingly minor incidents and reflect general discontent rather than specific rights violations. In June 2008, over 10,000 rioters set fire to a police station in Guizhou province when police allegedly covered up a murder perpetrated by relatives of local government officials—the latest in a string of alleged misdemeanors.[101]

A more recent and particular gruesome example of a mass incident leading to vigilante justice is the murder of four construction workers in a land dispute in Yunnan province in 2014.[102] Disgruntled citizens first hand-cuffed the migrant workers and then set them on fire. It is the rise of such extreme political violence which informs the concluding part of this chapter, in which I will offer reflections on the vulnerabilities of mainland China's party-state.

In April 2013 the General Office of the CCP distributed Document No. 9, an internal communiqué which urged the CCP leadership to guard against seven political "perils", including constitutionalism, civil society, "nihilistic" views of history, "universal values", and the promotion of "the West's view of media". It also called on Party members to strengthen their resistance to "infiltration" by outside ideas, renew their commitment to work "in the ideological sphere", and to handle with renewed vigilance all ideas, institutions, and people deemed threatening to unilateral Party rule.[103]

Document No. 9 is a key document to understand how the CCP perceives its own vulnerabilities at the beginning of the 21st century. What transpires from this internal communiqué is a party-state that sees itself under siege, encircled by enemies both within and outside China. The CCP's continued enemy mentality is evident from the text's terminology of struggle. External and internal CCP enemies are labelled as "capitalist class", "western anti-China forces", "anti-government forces" as well as "people with ulterior motives within China".[104] A monolithic "West" is given ontological status and blamed for pursuing regime change at all costs.

Document No. 9 reveals an anxiety that internal and/or external actors may engage in what is termed "historical nihilism" and "distort Party history and the history of New China".[105] The communiqué's authors provide a long litany of how such supposed historical nihilism is expressed, e.g. by rejecting

the revolution; claiming that the revolution led by the Chinese Communist Party resulted only in destruction; denying the historical inevitability in China's choice of the Socialist road, calling it the wrong path, and the Party's and new China's history a "continuous series of mistakes"; rejecting the accepted conclusions on historical events and figures, disparaging our Revolutionary precursors, and vilifying the Party's leaders ... By rejecting CCP history and the history of New China, historical nihilism seeks to fundamentally undermine the CCP's historical purpose, which is tantamount to denying the legitimacy of the CCP's long-term political dominance.[106]

In the context of this chapter this accusation is particularly noteworthy, as it reveals a deep-seated fear that independent scholarship and journalism may fundamentally question the CCP's own rather one-sided historiography and thus undermine the party-state's political legitimacy.

The CCP's need to control the official historical narrative is also evident from the directive "Seven Don't Speaks" (*qi bu jiang*), which was orally communicated to Chinese university administrators in 2013. One of the taboo topics not to be raised in Chinese classrooms are "the historical errors of the CCP".[107] The "Seven Don't Speaks" directive is one of the rare instances of the CCP acknowledging that it has made mistakes in the past. Ian Johnson has pointed out that it is hard to overstate history's role in a Chinese society run by a communist party. Communism itself is based on historical determinism: one of Marx's points was that the world was moving inexorably towards communism, an argument that regime-builders such as Lenin and Mao used to justify their violent rises to power. In China, Marxism is layered on top of much older ideas about the role of history. Each succeeding dynasty wrote its predecessor's history, and the dominant political ideology—what is now generically called Confucianism—was based on the concept that ideals for ruling were to be found in the past, with the virtuous ruler emulating them. Performance mattered, but mainly as proof of history's judgment. That means history is best kept on a tight leash.[108]

While Dahl has argued that autocratic regimes are more likely to tolerate a political opposition when the expected costs of toleration decrease, the expected costs of suppression increase and/or the costs of suppression exceed the costs of toleration,[109] in the case of mainland China these axiomatic assumptions are unlikely to apply. From the CCP's perspective the cost of oppression will always be seen as lower than the cost of liberalisation. The combination of the historical crimes committed by the CCP together with the fear of what would happen to leading CCP cadres during a democratic transition explains why the CCP has been willing to invest rather extraordinary resources to protect its authority. A report by mainland Chinese researchers at Tsinghua University revealed that by 2010 the expenditure for domestic stability preservation had become as big as the CCP's spending on national defence.[110] The securitisation of mainland China under Xi Jinping since 2012[111] thus should be seen as a sign of profound weakness of an embattled regime, not as a sign of strength. The sheer magnitude of the combined historical errors of the CCP—including but not limited to the war crimes committed during the civil war, the reign of terror during the Great Leap Forward and Cultural Revolution, and the suppression of the peaceful anti-corruption and pro-democracy movement—can be considered key disincentives for the party-state to liberalise and democratise. It is not an exaggeration to surmise that throughout the 20th century every family in mainland China has been victimised by the CCP in one way or another. During a possible liberalisation and democratisation of mainland China's political systems calls would be made for financial compensation. Paying adequate reparations to so many former victims and their families, however, will not be possible. The public anger at the CCP's crimes against humanity would also inevitably lead to the CCP's fall from power. Political persecution and a loss of the wide array of privileges that both low- and high-ranking CCP cadres and their cronies currently enjoy would follow. While a Truth and Reconciliation process modelled on the South African example could be an alternative way to come to terms with historical crimes committed by the CCP, under the conditions of autocratic one-party rule this will not be possible.

While the CCP as a political organisation has certainly learned from its failures, it has never allowed a public discussion about the traumata it has inflicted on mainland Chinese society. To a certain extent, however, Chinese people themselves have been complicit in the CCP's cover up. In the afterword of *The People's Republic of Amnesia* Louisa Lim argued that the

> "forgetting" that has engulfed China is not just enforced from above; the people themselves have colluded in this amnesia and embraced it. Forgetting is a survival mechanism, almost second nature. China's people have learned to avert their eyes and minds from anything unpleasant, allowing their brains to be imprinted with false memories—or allowing the real memories to be erased—for the sake of convenience ... China's Communist Party constantly alludes to the nation's 5,000 years of history while omitting its more recent acts of shame. In a country that has done more to alleviate poverty than any other country in the world, does it really matter? The answer is that it does. It matters because the national identity of this new world power is based on lies. When those lies are taught in schools, passed unchallenged from one generation to the next, and truth-telling is punished, a moral vacuum gapes ever larger, the debt grows greater, and the cost paid is the dearest of all: a loss of humanity.[112]

But as with any generalisation, there are exceptions. In Chapter 6 I will discuss four closely viewed episodes during the past 30 years where conscientious mainland Chinese citizens have challenged party-state authority and attempted to liberalise and democratise political institutions and political culture with the help of reform strategies and tactical approaches. While mainland China's democracy movement has so far been unable to outgrow the CCP's authoritarianism, they reveal that democracy activists have come a long way since 1989.

Notes

1   ChinaFile (2018), Stein Ringen: "The Truth about China". Available online: www.chinafile.com/reporting-opinion/viewpoint/stein-ringen-truth-about-china (accessed 22 October 2018).
2   Ringen, Stein (2016), *The Perfect Dictatorship: China in the 21st Century*, Hong Kong University Press, Hong Kong, 143.
3   Hoffman, Samantha (2017), Programming China: The Communist Party's Autonomic Approach to Managing State Security, *Merics China Monitor*, 12 December. Available online: www.merics.org/sites/default/files/2017-12/171212_China_Monitor_44_Programming_China_EN_.pdf (accessed 22 October 2018).
4   Hoffman, Samantha (2017), *Programming China: The Communist Party's Autonomic Approach to Managing State Security*, PhD thesis, University of Nottingham, September, 14.
5   Ibid.

6 Cohen, Jonathan R. (2016), A Genesis of Conflict: The Zero-Sum Mindset, *Cardozo Journal of Conflict Resolution*, 17, 427. Available online: https://scholarship.law.ufl. edu/cgi/viewcontent.cgi?referer=https://www.google.com/&httpsredir=1&article= 1759&context=facultypub (accessed 23 October 2018).

7 Gold, Thomas (1997), Taiwan: Still Defying the Odds, in: Larry Diamond, Marc Plattner, Yun-han Chu and Hung-mao Tien (Eds), *Consolidating the Third Wave Democracies*. John Hopkins University Press, Baltimore, CO, 167.

8 Fewsmith, Joseph (1999), Elite Politics, in: Merle Goldman and Roderick Mac-Farquhar (Eds), *The Paradox of China's Post-Mao Reforms*, Harvard University Press, Cambridge, MA, 49.

9 Ibid.

10 Spence, Jonathan (1980), *To Change China: Western Advisors in China*, Penguin, Harmondsworth.

11 Ibid., 187.

12 Ibid., 198.

13 Ibid.

14 Ibid., 199.

15 Spence, Jonathan (1990), *The Search for Modern China*, W.W. Norton & Company, New York, 392.

16 Ibid., 437.

17 Myers, Ramon H. (2000), The Nationalist State, in: David Shambaugh (Ed.), *The Modern Chinese State*, Cambridge University Press, Cambridge, 65.

18 Ibid., 68.

19 Ibid., 69–70.

20 Heilmann, Sebastian (2008), From Local Experiments to National Policy: The Origins of China's Distinctive Policy Process, *China Journal*, 59(January).

21 Van Slyke, L. (1970), The United Front in China, *Journal of Contemporary History*, 5(3), 127–8.

22 Dirlik, Arif (2014), Mao Zedong Thought and the Third World/Global South, *Interventions*, 16(2), 250.

23 Van Slyke, L. (1970), The United Front in China, *Journal of Contemporary History*, 5(3), 119–35.

24 Cheek, Timothy (1984), The Fading of Wild Lilies: Wang Shiwei and Mao Zedong's Yan'an Talks in the First CPC Rectification Movement, *Australian Journal of Chinese Affairs*, 11(January), 26.

25 Ibid.

26 Piekalkiewicz, Jaroslaw and Penn, Alfred Wayne (1995), *Politics of Ideocracy*, State University of New York Press, New York, 25.

27 Barmé, Geremie R. (1991), A Small Matter of Truth, *China Supplement*. Available online: https://ro.uow.edu.au/cgi/viewcontent.cgi?referer=https://www.google. com/&httpsredir=1&article=2634&context=alr (accessed 23 October 2018).

28 *New York Times* (2009), China Is Wordless on Traumas of Communists' Rise. Available online: www.nytimes.com/2009/10/02/world/asia/02anniversary.html (accessed 23 October 2018).

29 *South China Morning Post* (2009), 1949: The Untold Story. Available online: www.scmp.com/article/693063/1949-untold-story (accessed 23 October 2018).

30 Nobel Prize (2010), Liu Xiaobo Nobel Lecture. I Have No Enemies: My Final Statement. Available online: www.nobelprize.org/prizes/peace/2010/xiaobo/lec ture/ (accessed 23 October 2018).

31 Fitzgerald, John (2017), Liu Xiaobo's Message from Prison to the West. Available online: https://researchbank.swinburne.edu.au/file/659fea08-bf25-42ca-905a -d23d51a8f8eb/1/2017-fitzgerald-human_dignity_and.pdf (accessed 23 October 2018).

32 Liu, M. (2001), *Administrative Reform in China and Its Impact on the Policy-Making Process and Economic Development after Mao: Reinventing Chinese*

Government/Meiru Liu, Lampeter, Lewiston, NY. The duality of this organisational structure is the reason why the Chinese government is commonly referred to as a party-state.

33 Shambaugh, David (2002), Civil-Military Relations in China: Party-Army or National Military?, *Copenhagen Journal of Asian Studies*, 16. Available online: https://rauli.cbs.dk/index.php/cjas/article/viewFile/3/3 (accessed 23 October 2018).

34 Ibid., 11.

35 Yan, Jiaqi (1989), *Toward a Democratic China: The Intellectual Autobiography of Yan Jiaqi*, University of Hawaii, Honolulu, 108–18.

36 Shambaugh, David (2002), *Modernizing China's Military: Progress, Problems, and Prospects*, University of California Press, Berkeley, CA, 26.

37 Brown, Jeremy and Pickowicz, Paul G. (2007), The Early Years of the People's Republic of China: An Introduction, in: Jeremy Brown and Paul G. Pickowicz (Eds), *Dilemmas of Victory: The Early Years of the People's Republic of China*, Harvard University Press, Cambridge, MA, 4.

38 Ibid., 6–7.

39 Shabad, Theodore (1955), Communist China's Five Year Plan, *Far Eastern Survey*, 24(12), 189–91.

40 Foreign Affairs (2017), Has China Restored Private Land Ownership? The Implications of Beijing's New Policy. Available online: www.foreignaffairs.com/a rticles/china/2017-05-16/has-china-restored-private-land-ownership (accessed 23 October 2018).

41 Bramall, Chris (2000) Inequality, Land Reform and Agricultural Growth in China, 1952–55: A Preliminary Treatment. *Journal of Peasant Studies*, 27(3), 51.

42 Ibid., 50.

43 *Independent* (2017), Outdated "Urban Passports" Still Rule the Lives of China's Rural Citizens:
China's Hukou System Is a Relic of the Mao Era—and It's Holding the Nation's Rural Population Back, 13 January 2018. Available online: www.indep endent.co.uk/news/world/politics/outdated-urban-passports-still-rule-the-lives-of-china-s-rural-citizens-a7517181.html (accessed 14 August 2018).

44 Chan, Kam Wing (2009), The Chinese Hukou System at 50, *Eurasian Geography and Economics*, 50(2). Available online: http://citeseerx.ist.psu.edu/viewdoc/down load?doi=10.1.1.526.182&rep=rep1&type=pdf (accessed 23 October 2018), 198.

45 Ibid., 199.

46 Spence, Jonathan (1990), *The Search for Modern China*, W.W. Norton & Company, New York, 541–2.

47 Diner, Dan (2006), Rupture in Civilization: On the Genesis and Meaning of a Concept in Understanding, in: Moshe Zimmermann (Ed.), *On Germans and Jews under the Nazi Regime: Essays by Three Generations of Historians*, Magnes Press, Jerusalem, 33–48.

48 Teiwes, Frederick C. with Sun, Warren (1999), *China's Road to Disaster: Mao, Central Politicians, and Provincial Leaders in the Unfolding of the Great Leap Forward, 1955–1959*, M.E. Sharpe, New York, 81.

49 Dikötter, Frank (2011), *Mao's Great Famine: The History of China's Most Devastating Catastrophe, 1958–62*, Bloomsbury, London, 6.

50 Ibid., 7.

51 Ibid., 7–8.

52 MacFarquhar, Roderick and Schoenhals, Michael (2006), *Mao's Last Revolution*, Harvard University Press, Cambridge, MA, 2.

53 Teiwes, Frederick C. (2000), The Maoist State, in: David Shambaugh (Ed.), *The Modern Chinese State*, Cambridge University Press, Cambridge, 143–4.

54 Wang Ban quoting Cao Zhenglu in Wang, Ban (2014), Conclusion: In the Beginning Is the Word: Popular Democracy and Mao's Little Red Book, in

Alexander Cook (Ed.), *Mao's Little Red Book: A Global History*, Cambridge University Press, Cambridge, 275.

55 Weiran, Lin (1996), *An Abortive Chinese Enlightenment: The Cultural Revolution and Class Theory*, PhD dissertation, University of Wisconsin-Madison, 234–5.

56 Meisner, Maurice Jerome (1986), *Mao's China and After: A History of the People's Republic*, Free Press, New York, 361.

57 Ibid.

58 Saich, Tony (2001), *Governance and Politics of China*, Palgrave, Houndmills, 42.

59 Fewsmith, Joseph (2001), *Elite Politics in Contemporary China*, M.E. Sharpe, Armonk, NY, 64.

60 Naughton, Barry (1999), The Pattern and Logic of China's Economic Reform, in: Orville Schell and David Shambaugh (Eds), *The China Reader: The Reform Era*, Vintage Books, New York, 302.

61 Spence, Jonathan (1990), *The Search for Modern China*, W.W. Norton & Company, New York, 712–47.

62 Lin, Justin Yifu (1987), The Household Responsibility System Reform in China: A Peasant's Institutional Choice, *American Journal of Agricultural Economics*, 69 (2, May), 410.

63 *People's Daily Online* (2008), The Xiaogang Village Story. Available online: http://en.people.cn/90002/95607/6531490.html (accessed 24 October 2018).

64 *Business Standard* (2017), China Lifting 800 Million People Out of Poverty Is Historic: World Bank. Available online: www.business-standard.com/article/international/china-lifting-800-million-people-out-of-poverty-is-historic-world-bank-117101300027_1.html (accessed 24 October 2018).

65 Shambaugh, David (2000), The Chinese State in the Post-Mao Era, in: David Shambaugh (Ed.), *The Modern Chinese State*, Cambridge University Press, Cambridge, 161.

66 Ibid., 163.

67 Cole, Allan B. (1951), The United Front in the New China, *Annals of the American Academy of Political and Social Science*, 277(September), 35–45.

68 Van Slyke, L. (1970), The United Front in China, *Journal of Contemporary History*, 5(3), 128.

69 Wang, R., & Groot, G. (2018). Who Represents? Xi Jinping's Grand United Front Work, Legitimation, Participation and Consultative Democracy, *Journal of Contemporary China*, 27(112), 1–15.

70 Van Slyke, L. (1970), The United Front in China, *Journal of Contemporary History*, 5(3), 134.

71 Ottaway, Marina (2003), *Democracy Challenged: The Rise of Semi-Authoritarianism*, Carnegie Endowment for International Peace, Washington DC, 138.

72 Yahuda, Michael (2000), The Changing Faces of Chinese Nationalism: The Dimensions of Statehood, in: Michael Leifer (Ed.), *Asian Nationalism*, Routledge, London, 34–5; Carrico, Kevin (2017), *The Great Han: Race, Nationalism, and Tradition in China Today*, University of California Press, Oakland, CA.

73 China Heritage (2018), Imminent Fears, Immediate Hopes—a Beijing Jeremiad. Available online: http://chinaheritage.net/journal/imminent-fears-immediate-hopes-a-beijing-jeremiad/ (accessed 25 October 2018).

74 Qinglian, He (2001), as quoted by Osburg, John (2013), *Anxious Wealth: Money and Morality among China's New Rich*, Stanford University Press, Stanford, CA, 78–9.

75 *Economic Times* (2013), Rich Are Widely Hated in China: John Osburg, Professor, Rochester University, 5 May. Available online: http://articles.economictimes.indiatimes.com/2013-05-05/news/39042565_1_chengdu-china-chinese-journalists (accessed 21 November 2013).

76 Feng, Chongyi (2013), The Dilemma of Stability Preservation in China, *Journal of Current Chinese Affairs*, 42(2), 3–19.

77 Chen, Xi (2013), The Rising Cost of Instability, *Journal of Democracy*, 24(1, January), 63.

78 *New York Times* (2015), A Rare Look into One's Life on File in China, 15 March. Available online: https://sinosphere.blogs.nytimes.com/2015/03/15/a-ra re-look-into-ones-life-on-file-in-china/?mcubz=0 (accessed 28 April 2018). The importance of the dang'an system cannot be overstated. In the 21st century, the CCP is now trying to augment this analogue system into the digital era by introducing its highly contested social credit system.

79 Cinema on the Edge (2018), *The Dossier*. 档案 Dang'an. Available online: http:// cinemaontheedge.com/the-dossier/ (accessed 23 October 2018).

80 Wu, Harry (1992), *Laogai: The Chinese Gulag*, translated by Ted Slingerland; foreword by Fang Lizhi, Lynne Rienner, Boulder, CO.

81 Jiang, Su (2016). Punishment without Trial: The Past, Present and Future of Reeducation through Labor in China. *Peking University Law Journal*, 4(1), 45– 78.

82 Human Rights Watch (2009), "An Alleyway in Hell": China's Abusive "Black Jails". Available online: www.gbv.de/dms/spk/sbb/recht/toc/61753697X.pdf (accessed 25 October 2018).

83 Wang, Yuhua and Minzner, Carl (2015), The Rise of the Chinese Security State, *China Quarterly*, 222, 347–8.

84 Radio Free Asia (2014), China Steps Up "Strike Hard" Campaign in Xinjiang. Available online: www.rfa.org/english/news/uyghur/strike-hard-01092014172927. html (accessed 26 October 2018).

85 ChinaFile (2018), How Should the World Respond to Intensifying Repression in Xinjiang? Available online: www.chinafile.com/conversation/how-should-worl d-respond-intensifying-repression-xinjiang (accessed 26 October 2018).

86 *China Story* (2013), China's Rigid Stability—Yu Jianrong 于建嵘 Analyses a Predicament. Available online: www.thechinastory.org/2013/01/chinas-rigid-sta bility-an-analysis-of-a-predicament-by-yu-jianrong-于建嵘/ (accessed 25 October 2018).

87 Feng, Chongyi (2013), The Dilemma of Stability Preservation in China, *Journal of Current Chinese Affairs*, 42(2), 7.

88 Kelly, David (2010), Costs of Maintaining Stability in China. Available online: www.eastasiaforum.org/2010/05/23/costs-of-maintaining-stability-in-china/ (accessed 14 December 2018).

89 Pei, Minxin (2006), *China's Trapped Transition: The Limits of Developmental Autocracy*, Harvard University Press, Cambridge, MA, 159–66.

90 Wang, Peng (2017), *The Chinese Mafia: Organized Crime, Corruption, and Extra-Legal Protection*, Oxford University Press, Oxford.

91 *New Yorker* (2014), The Thugs of Mainland China. Available online: www.new yorker.com/news/news-desk/thugs-mainland-china-hong-kong-protests (accessed 25 October 2018).

92 Ong, Lynette (2018), "Thugs-for-Hire": Subcontracting of State Coercion and State Capacity in China, *Perspectives on Politics*, 16(3), 680–95.

93 Sceats, Sonya, with Breslin, Shaun (2012), China and the International Human Rights System, Chatham House. Available online: www.chathamhouse.org/sites/ default/files/public/Research/International%20Law/r1012_sceatsbreslin.pdf (accessed 25 October 2018).

94 Nathan, Andrew (1997), *China's Transition*, Columbia University Press, New York, 249–51.

95 *Psychology Today* (2010), China's Psychiatric Mistreatment of Political Dis-sidents. Available online: www.psychologytoday.com/gb/blog/side-effects/201011/ chinas-psychiatric-mistreatment-political-dissidents (accessed 25 October 2018).

96 Human Rights Watch and Geneva Initiative on Psychiatry (2002), Dangerous Minds: Political Psychiatry in China Today and Its Origins in the Mao Era.

Available online: www.hrw.org/reports/2002/china02/china0802.pdf (accessed 25 October 2018).

97   *Independent* (2018), Chinese Woman Disappears after Spraying Ink on Poster of Xi Jinping. Available online: www.independent.co.uk/news/world/asia/china -woman-dong-yaoqiong-disappears-spraying-ink-xi-jinping-a8455166.html (accessed 25 October 2018).

98   NCBI (2012), Mental Health Law of the People's Republic of China. Available online: www.ncbi.nlm.nih.gov/pmc/articles/PMC4198897/ (accessed 25 October 2018).

99   Radio Free Asia (2018), Woman Who Splashed Xi Jinping Poster Sent to Psychiatric Hospital. Available online: www.rfa.org/english/news/china/hospita lized-07232018105734.html (accessed 25 October 2018).

100 *Financial Times* (2010), The Accuracy of China's "Mass Incidents". Available online: www.ft.com/content/9ee6fa64-25b5-11df-9bd3-00144feab49a (accessed 26 October 2018).

101 Ibid.

102 *Guardian* (2014), Villagers Burn Four Construction Workers to Death in China Land Dispute. Available online: www.theguardian.com/world/2014/oct/16/china -construction-workers-burn-to-death-land-dispute (accessed 26 October 2018).

103 ChinaFile (2013), Document 9: A ChinaFile Translation. How Much Is a Hardline Party Directive Shaping China's Current Political Climate? Available online: www.chinafile.com/document-9-chinafile-translation (accessed 26 October 2018). This internal document was allegedly leaked by Chinese journalist Gao Yu, who was subsequently punished with a seven-year prison sentence. After serving one and a half years of her prison sentence, Gao was released on medical parole in 2015.

104 Ibid.

105 Ibid.

106 Ibid.

107 China Media Project (2013), Control, on the Shores of China's Dream. Available online: http://chinamediaproject.org/2013/05/22/positive-energy-for-press-control/ (accessed 26 October 2018).

108 *Guardian* (2016), China's Memory Manipulators. Available online: www.thegua rdian.com/world/2016/jun/08/chinas-memory-manipulators (accessed 27 October 2018).

109 Dahl, Robert (1971), *Polyarchy: Participation and Opposition*, Yale University Press, New Haven, CT, 15.

110 East Asia Forum (2010), Costs of Maintaining Stability in China. Available online: www.eastasiaforum.org/2010/05/23/costs-of-maintaining-stability-in-china/ (accessed 27 October 2018).

111 Wang, Yuhua and Minzner, Carl (2015), The Rise of the Chinese Security State, *China Quarterly*, 222, 339–59.

112 Lim, Louisa (2014), *The People's Republic of Amnesia: Tiananmen Revisited*, Oxford University Press, New York, 211.

6

THE TRIALS AND TRIBULATIONS OF MAINLAND CHINA'S DEMOCRACY MOVEMENT

Commenting on the plethora of often localised and disconnected opposition groups that have emerged both inside and outside mainland China after 1989, Jean-Philippe Béja has argued that convenient "shorthand terms such as 'the dissident community' or 'the opposition' should not obscure the reality that we are dealing with a loose, unstructured movement that lacks a unified strategy and program".[1] While I do not disagree with Béja's overall assessment, this chapter will reveal that from 1989 until the present day mainland China's democracy movement has in fact developed by leaps and bounds. In the theoretical part of this book I argued that in order to discern continuity and change within a country's given democracy movement, we need to conduct longitudinal studies. In this chapter I will draw on my critique of democratisation studies in Chapter 3, use the three TOPC by Gene Sharp, Saul Alinksy and Paulo Freire developed in Chapter 4 as my analytical vignettes and analyse four closely viewed episodes that can help shed light on the trials and tribulations of mainland China's democracy movement. In this chapter I have chosen to focus on the most important struggles for democracy in mainland China since the 1978 Democracy Wall movement. The first episode will focus on the anti-corruption and pro-democracy movement of 1989. The second episode will discuss the failed attempt to establish the China Democracy Party (CDP) in 1998. The third episode analyses mainland China's Charter 08 from 2008. The fourth episode dissects the dynamics of the New Citizen movement (NCM) between 2009 and 2014. In all four episodes I will answer the following leading questions:

1. What antecedents informed the struggle for democracy and what were the perceived political opportunities by participants at the time?
2. Which reform camp initiated the specific struggle for democracy?

3. Which strategic reform approach was taken?
4. What were the key lessons learned?

Episode 1: Mainland China's nation-wide anti-corruption and pro-democracy movement of 1989

Antecedents and political opportunities

Mainland China's nation-wide anti-corruption and pro-democracy movement of 1989 was fuelled by various sources of public discontent. Naughton has pointed out that before "1989, China was pursuing an incremental transition to a market economy under the tutelage of the Communist Party"[2] and that the "1980s reform has been characterised as de-centralizing, dual track, and making extensive use of particularistic bargains and contracting".[3] The intransparent and unaccountable nature of incremental economic reforms allowed CCP cadres and their cronies to exploit regulatory loopholes and enrich themselves. Spence points out that petty

> peculations had no doubt often been practiced in the past by CCP members, but by 1985 it was becoming corruption on an enormous scale. The newly affluent Chinese who were able to benefit from the economic reforms were thirsting for consumer goods, and the temptation to reroute scarce imports their way in black-market deals was hard to resist.[4]

Public anger at widespread corruption and collusion was compounded by a general dissatisfaction with the way the CCP governed mainland China's economy. While the early 1980s were marked by an economic upswing, by the late 1980s inflation was threatening the moderately improved living standards of both rural and urban Chinese.[5]

Economic grievances, however, had existed in mainland China before. So, why was it that in spring 1989 public discontent exploded on a nation-wide level and according to Nathan and Link spread to "almost every major Chinese city"?[6] In Sharp's words, political "defiance campaigns against dictatorships may begin in a variety of ways. In the past these struggles have almost always been unplanned and essentially accidental."[7] This was also the case with mainland China's 1989 movement. Protests were initially triggered by the death of former CCP general secretary Hu Yaobang. As a scapegoat for mainland China's economic woes of the late 1980s Hu had been removed from office in 1987. His death in spring 1989 provided cover for protesters to congregate in public. While mourning Hu protesters could also air their various other pent-up frustrations. They may not have had a clear vision of the destination of their journey, but according to Unger students, intellectuals, workers and ordinary citizens, they "*did* project a vague vision of what they wanted, and it was summed up in the word 'Democracy'".[8] Specific demands related to an independent judiciary[9] and more freedoms at their workplace.[10] During the 1989 movement activists also demanded freedom of speech,[11] freedom of press[12] and freedom of association.[13] In Chapter 4 I outlined Sharp's critique of democracy activists relying too much on chance to advance their cause. In Sharp's words, while "spontaneity has some positive qualities, it has often had disadvantages. Frequently, the democratic resisters have not anticipated the brutalities of the dictatorship, so that they suffered gravely and the resistance has collapsed. At times the lack of planning by democrats has left crucial decisions to chance, with disastrous results."[14]

Labour leader Han Dongfang, one of the key protagonists of 1989, acknowledged this weakness of the movement when reflecting on conversations he had during his 22 months in prison:

> When I was in jail I debated with my interrogators. They insisted that the movement was premeditated and well-planned. I told them it wasn't. I said that if conditions existed in our country for people to premeditate and plan such a huge movement, then the Communist Party would have been long gone, vanished without a trace.[15]

Han has compared

> the 1989 Democracy Movement to an unripe fruit. People were so hungry that they were desperate. When they suddenly discovered a fruit, they pounced on it, and swallowed it whole. Then they got a stomach ache and a bitter taste in the mouth. So should they have eaten the fruit? You can say they shouldn't have, but they were hungry. And if you say that they should have, what they ate was still green, inedible.[16]

Key actors

The 1989 movement initially was almost entirely student-led. Elizabeth Perry has critiqued the "emperor-worship mentality"[17] among student leaders, whereby students submitted "to a familiar pattern of ceremonial politics".[18] Perry describes

> this recycling of tradition ... on April 22, 1989, a day of government-scheduled memorial services for former Party general secretary Hu Yaobang ... students managed to convert an official ceremony into a counterhegemonic performance ... Yet a striking feature of the April 22 counterceremony was its adherence to traditionally sanctioned modes of behavior. Three student representatives attempted—in the age-old

manner of Chinese scholarly remonstrance—to present a petition demanding an explanation for the ouster of Hu Yaobang and a meeting with the current premier, Li Peng. Denied entrance to the Great Hall of the People, the young emissaries suddenly fell to their knees and began to kowtow. Embarrassed at being implicitly likened to the imperial court, officials eventually opened the doors, allowing the students to present their petition to a low-ranking functionary who summarily rejected their demands.[19]

Perry's description of student leaders as inherently wedded to the imperial concepts of Confucian scholars is useful as it prevents us from classifying them as anti-establishment actors. While they were indeed highly critical of the party-state they could also be considered aspiring members of mainland China's pro-establishment. This internal contradiction limited the student leaders' choices and prevented them from adopting far more militant (and perhaps more successful) anti-establishment strategies.

Once under way the 1989 movement attracted a wide range of other social actors joining the struggle for democracy. When witnessing the polarisation between student protestors and the government, 12 writers and scholars aimed to bridge the gap between the opposing camps. The way they positioned themselves suggests that they belonged to what I referred to as the trans-establishment camp in Chapter 3. A lack of acceptance from protesters and the party-state, however, meant that their attempts at mediation were futile. One of the trans-establishment scholars, the journalist and writer Dai Qing, was subsequently jailed for 10 months for her involvement in the 1989 movement.[20] While initially keeping a distance from the labour movement, in the final weeks before the crack-down on 4 June 1989, a student–labour alliance emerged. The establishment of the independent Beijing Workers' Autonomous Federation at Tiananmen Square was significant, as it received

> considerable material and moral support from the city's workers, and was able to marshal significant resources within a relatively short period of time. The workers' movement grew most rapidly after the declaration of martial law— precisely at the time that the student movement began to melt away and play a less decisive role in events.[21]

This development supports Sharp's observation that non-violent struggle speeds up the democratisation of society, as it raises the population's self-confidence, provides means to resist undemocratic control, allows for freedom of speech and freedom of assembly and the rejuvenation of a previously politically neutralised civil society.[22] It also shows that 1989 was essentially led by two reform camps: student leaders, who critiqued the party-state but at the same time aspired to become future members of mainland China's establishment, and more anti-establishment-minded labour leaders with an interest in an independent labour movement.

Strategic reform approach

Despite the internal contradictions and lack of a commonly agreed strategy the 1989 movement exhibited a number of strengths. Sharp and Jenkins have identified eleven accomplishments: 1) the movement's ability to openly challenge the party-state, 2) the conduct of perhaps the largest hunger strike in history, 3) the defiance of martial law over a two-week period, 4) the mobilisation of students at 350 colleges and universities nation-wide, 5) demonstrations against corruption and for freedom in almost all major Chinese cities, 6) garnering the support of Chinese urbanites, 7) temporarily splitting the party-state's leadership, 8) winning over support from serving and retired army leaders unwilling to crack down on the protestors, 9) the successful blocking of the 38th Army trying to enter Beijing, 10) the delegitimisation of the Chinese party-state before the crackdown, and 11) pioneering non-violent struggle as a central means to oppose authoritarianism in mainland China.[23]

Yet at the same time, the 1989 movement also had a number of inherent weaknesses. Elizabeth Perry has pointed out that while the movement indeed managed to entice millions of Chinese people to take to the streets, the corporatist nature of the party-state also meant that work units could not only be mobilised but also demobilised rather quickly.[24] She has also critiqued the student's eagerness to engage in a political dialogue, which she considers an "admission of the hold that the state continued to exert; protesters wanted a role in the official political pageant, which for them remained the only real show in town".[25] Perry is scathing in her critique of the self-understanding of student leaders: "Perhaps the most distressing aspect of the demand for dialogue was the limited cast of characters included in the request. Perpetuating a Confucian mentality that assigned to intellectuals the role of spokesmen for the masses, students assumed that they were the only segment of society whose voice deserved to be heard."[26]

Geremie Barmé and John Crowley, on the other hand, have critiqued student leaders for their apparent inability to engage in a *constructive* dialogue with government. In the documentary *The Gate of Heavenly Peace* Barmé and Crowley argue "(*duihua*), dialogue, was a key part of the reformers' strategy to open up the political system. It was aimed at making officials at all levels more responsive to popular opinion."[27] While critical of the government's unwillingness to engage in a meaningful dialogue with student representatives, much of the documentary hones in on internal disagreements among students on whether or not and how to engage in a meaningful dialogue with the party-state.

Perry's critique of the student leaders as the self-elevated dialogue participants fails to convince since it was students who initiated the movement. This means that they had every right to represent themselves. Also Barmé and Crowley's critique of the nature of the dialogue misses the point. The problem was not how the dialogue was conducted, but that students thought they could actually achieve a negotiated settlement with the party-state in the first place. While during times of routine politics—and even under the conditions of authoritarianism—one can make a legitimate case in favour of a transformative Freirean dialogue between oppressors and oppressed, during a highly polarised confrontation such as the 1989 movement there can and should only be one winner, which is the insurgent democracy movement.

Sharp has convincingly argued that democrats should not engage in negotiations with dictators. He reminds us that the "offer by a dictatorship of 'peace' through negotiations with the democratic opposition is, of course, rather disingenuous. The violence could be ended immediately by the dictators themselves."[28] In the case of the anti-corruption and pro-democracy movement of 1989 the CCP leadership could have taken the step to overturn the *People's Daily* editorial of 26 April, which denounced the protesters as "an extremely small number of people with ulterior purposes ... [who] sow dissension among the people, plunge the whole country into chaos and sabotage the political situation of stability and unity".[29] Chris Buckley has pointed out that "a warning meant to deter protest instead inflamed it".[30] This supports Sharp's contention that "'negotiations' does not mean that the two sides sit down together on a basis of equality and talk through and resolve the differences that produced the conflict between them".[31] He warns that a "dictator's peace is often no more than the peace of the prison or of the grave".[32]

Lessons learned

As the 1989 movement did not achieve any of its self-declared goals the question arises what key lessons can be learned from this unsuccessful struggle for democracy. Gene Sharp and Bruce Jenkins observed the 1989 movement in Beijing from May 28 until June 6. When interviewing student leaders and participating protesters they realised that while the movement stuck to non-violent struggle as a matter of principle, they "were unable to uncover any evidence of more formal understanding of the nature of nonviolent struggle. None of the students we spoke with knew of any books, pamphlets, or audio-visual materials (in any language) dealing with nonviolent struggle."[33] Sharp and Jenkins also noted that those "interviewed often stated that the lack of a 'universally recognised organisation' was the weakest aspect of their movement".[34] They also pointed out that "it was difficult to ascertain any significant degree of strategic thinking in the pro-democracy movement ... Much of the planning of actions appears to have been more tactical than strategic. We found no evidence of coordinated plans which encompassed a range of mutually supporting actions over specified periods of time."[35] Whereas workers subscribed to an anti-establishment strategy, students effectively pursued a trojan horse approach. The 12 writers and scholars who tried to mediate between movement leaders and the government on the other hand subscribed to a trans-establishment tactic.

Sharp and Jenkins have pointed out two strategic errors of the entire movement. They found that protesters accepted a very high risk by occupying "a physical spot of whatever symbolic value" and suggest that a retreat from Tiananmen Square prior to 4 June would have made better tactical sense. They write that in "retrospect, a very good moment for withdrawal would have been after the people of Beijing had repeatedly halted and turned away the 38th Army. The students could then have claimed victory and gone out to thank the people, spreading their message of anti-corruption and democracy throughout Beijing and eventually the countryside."[36] Their second critique relates to

> the failure to mobilise on a large-scale massive non-cooperation with the system by the very people whose work made its continuation possible. This included especially the civil service, the military forces, the police and the operators of communications and transportation. The methods of non-cooperation, especially in this case political non-cooperation (as well as strikes and economic boycotts), usually constitute the most powerful of the many methods of nonviolent struggle.[37]

Episode 2: The failed attempt to establish the China Democracy Party in 1998

Antecedents and political opportunities

One of the key lessons of 1989 was that a political opposition movement without a functioning organisation was unlikely to succeed. To remedy this shortcoming, in 1998 democracy activists attempted to establish an opposition party which they named the China Democracy Party. I recall a conversation about the CDP with a German diplomat in Beijing in 2001, who was genuinely perplexed that during the late 1990s Chinese democracy activists had tried to establish an opposition party. He was puzzled: Why would anyone attempt to challenge the authority of the CCP head on, just nine years after the bloody crackdown on protesters on Tiananmen Square as well as in other parts of the country? To answer this question we need to understand how in the years 1997 and 1998 China's domestic and international situation was closely intertwined and how this created political opportunities for critics of CCP rule. Teresa Wright has pointed out that beginning

> in 1997 ... a renewed political thaw began, partly related to the uncertainty surrounding Deng Xiaoping's death in January, but also deriving

from China's desire to participate as an equal in the international community. Significantly, US President Bill Clinton planned a visit in June 1998, and UN High Commissioner for Human Rights Mary Robinson was expected in September 1998. The first inklings of a political opening occurred in March 1997, when the National People's Congress amended the Criminal Law such that political crimes of "counter-revolution" would be repealed; they were replaced by a less political designation of offences regarding "national security". Next, in September, the 15th Party Congress stressed the need to govern the country by law, and for the first time made reference to human rights. In October, Chinese leaders signed the UN Covenant on Economic, Social and Cultural Rights and intimated that, after years of resistance, they would soon sign the Covenant on Civil and Political Rights as well. The following month, Wei Jingsheng was released on medical parole and exiled to the United States. In March 1998, Foreign Minister Qian Qichen formally announced that the regime had indeed decided to sign the latter covenant.[38]

These developments gave Chinese democracy activists hope of a political opening.

Key actors

The CDP was the brainchild of Wang Youcai, a former student leader in the 1989 movement. He helped draft the CDP constitution and came up with the idea to legally register CDP branches on the provincial level.[39] In its founding document, the "Open Declaration of the Establishment of the CDP Zhejiang Preparatory Committee", the CDP founders asserted that "a government is the servant of the public and not the one which controls it",[40] criticised the CCP for not allowing opposition parties to exist, condemned its use of torture and reform through labour and admonished the CCP for using "violence and violent intimidation"[41] to protect its authority.

When analysing the membership structure of the CDP, Wright found that the short-lived proto-opposition party "includes individuals of widely ranging age, educational background and protest experiences".[42] The majority of its activists were between 30 and 60 years of age. While many had actively participated in the 1989 movement, others had previously been involved in mainland China's Democracy Wall movement of 1978–80. A smaller group of CDP activists were involved in labour activism.[43] Merle Goldman has pointed out that a "multiclass membership—of marginalized or disestablished intellectuals, owners of small businesses, and ordinary workers—was typical of most [CDP] branches".[44] Goldman suggests that although

at any one time the CDP never numbered more than about two hundred activists and it did not appear to attract a mass following, the multiclass makeup of its membership, its nationwide organizational reach, its participation in local elections, its efforts to help laid-off workers publicize their plight, and particularly its attempts through legal procedures to establish an alternative party, were regarded by the CCP as a direct threat to its legitimacy and authority.[45]

Strategic reform approach

Despite being critical of continued CCP rule in mainland China, CDP initiator Wang Youcai was wary of overly militant anti-establishment approaches. Another activist with the family name Wang—Wang Bingzhang—had suggested in early 1998 that the CDP should work to overthrow the CCP in a revolution. In retrospect, the CCP's extremely harsh treatment of Wang Bingzhang—he was expelled from China in 1998 and later abducted from Vietnam by Chinese security agents in 2002[46]—suggests that Wang Youcai's much more cautious approach emphasising the legal character of the CDP may have saved his life.[47]

Wright has pointed out that "although the demands of the CDP were couched in moderate, loyalist terms, the very goal of establishing an opposition party demonstrates a clear break from earlier emphases on reforming the Communist Party".[48] But while pursuing an essentially anti-establishment objective, Wang Youcai in fact opted for a trojan horse strategy of working within the system. This was particularly evident when he and other CDP activists emphasised the preparatory nature of their opposition party. To further cushion the blow against the CCP, Wang Youcai and his supporters also opted for a trans-establishment reform approach by trying to register CDP preparatory committees with mainland China's Ministry of Civil Affairs (MoCA), first on the provincial and later at the central level. If this strategy had been successful, CDP branches would have become formally recognised civil society organisations (CSOs) and thus directly contributed to the NGOisation of mainland China's democracy movement.[49] Not surprisingly, however, MoCA refused to register the preparatory CDP branches as CSOs. Shortly thereafter the CCP started to arrest CDP activists and gave them lengthy prison sentences. Upon release in the early 2000s former CDP activists reported that they had been tortured while in custody.[50]

The failed attempt to establish the CDP in 1998 not only revealed the continued determination of the CCP to nip any opposition to its rule in the bud. On the side of the mainland Chinese democracy activists it also exposed rather stark internal divisions around the question of strategy and leadership, e.g. who to represent the proto-opposition party as party spokesperson.[51] The CDP also had to compete with an overseas offshoot established by Wang Bingzhang in New York, the Chinese Democracy and Justice Party. Wright has mused that competition among mainland Chinese exiles for financial support in their anti-CCP work has further weakened the mainland Chinese democracy movement.[52] She has further suggested that the CCP's "tradition of glorifying radicalism and intolerance"[53] may have left a lasting impact on the opposition movement, as it discourages compromise and cooperation with people one does not fully agree with.

Lessons learned

The lack of a grand strategy and unity within the CDP—which according to Sharp's TOPC is a key precondition for the success of any democracy movement—is particularly evident when we assess more critically what the CDP initiators tried to achieve. While Wang Youcai's idea to legally register an opposition party with MoCA—a state organ under direct CCP control—made tactical sense, from a strategic perspective his approach lacked coherence. In Chapter 1 I argued that as a political organisation the CCP does not have a legal foundation. From the perspective of political self-preservation the CCP therefore lacks any incentive to tolerate an opposition party which aims to further undermine its already weak political legitimacy. And also from the party-state's understanding of Chinese law, Wang Youcai's approach was based on a misreading of MoCA's CSO regulations. Even if CDP branches had been successfully registered in one or more Chinese provinces, his ultimate plan to link up preparatory CDP branches across provincial boundaries[54] would have violated MoCA rules for CSOs at the time, thus swiftly leading to a partial or complete ban of registered CDP preparatory branches. One does not have to agree with Wang Bingzhang's revolutionary approach to understand that under the conditions of mainland China's one-party-state any opposition party can only exist if it initially operates as an underground organisation, not unlike the CCP did in its early years. The problem with the latter approach, however, is not only that the required secrecy for such an endeavour breeds mistrust. Wright describes in great detail how CDP activists struggled to keep its membership list secret. The far more consequential risk of establishing an illegal underground opposition party is that any failed attempt would likely lead to summary executions of activists instead of lengthy prison sentences. Rather understandably, very few democracy activists in mainland China are willing to take such extraordinary risks.

While Wang Youcai did opt for a trojan horse approach, the CDP did not make any significant inroads into the party-state apparatus. An alternative strategic approach for the CDP could have been to co-opt one of the various CCP factions and work towards a split of the CCP, thus paving the way towards multiparty competition. But this approach would have required extremely high levels of interpersonal trust between political patrons in the CCP and democracy activists, which need to be build up over years if not decades. In their landmark article about elite settlements Burton and Higley have argued that

(1) elite settlements are the result of relatively autonomous elite choices and thus cannot be predicted or explained in terms of social, economic, and cultural forces; (2) the consensually unified elite structure created by a settlement constitutes the primary basis for subsequent political stability; which (3) is a necessary condition for the emergence and sustained practice of representative democratic politics.[55]

Given the high level of polarisation between the anti- and pro-establishment, described in detail in Chapter 3, such elite settlements are unlikely to materialise in mainland China any time soon. As the fate of the CDP suggests, there was no appetite among sufficient numbers of disenfranchised CCP cadres to legitimise a new political party with a view of joining the opposition camp in the future. This can be considered one of the key lessons from the failed attempt to establish the CDP in 1998.

Episode 3: Charter 08: the "grand strategy" of mainland China's democracy movement?

Antecedents and political opportunities

The failed struggles for democracy in 1989 and 1998 left mainland China's democracy movement in a tough spot. In the early 2000s it lacked a coherent strategic vision and was highly fragmented. In order to address both shortcomings three leading political activists with direct experiences in the 1989 movement—poet and writer Liu Xiaobo, former party official-turned-university professor Zhang Zhuhua and writer and former physicist Jiang Qisheng—drafted a political declaration which they called Charter 08.[56] It was published on the 60th anniversary of the Universal Declaration of Human Rights. The authors modelled their document on Charter 77,[57] which in the late 1970s played a pivotal role in uniting a highly factionalised dissident movement in Eastern Europe against their communist regimes. Feng Chongyi has pointed out that

> Charter 08 was not a bolt from the blue but the result of careful deliberation and theoretical debate, especially the discourse on liberalism since the late 1990s. In its timing, Charter 08 anticipated that major political change would take place in China in 2009 in light of a number of important anniversaries. These included the 20th anniversary of the June 4th crackdown, the 50th anniversary of the exile of the Dalai Lama, the 60th anniversary of the founding of the People's Republic of China, and the 90th anniversary of the May 4th Movement.[58]

Key actors

In five waves almost the entirety of mainland China's dissident community, both at home and abroad, signed Charter 08. Signatories included prominent anti-establishment figures and critics of one-party rule ranging from Ai Weiwei, Bao Tong, Cui Weiping, Ding Zilin, He Weifang, Liao Yiwu, Liu Xiaobo, Mao Yushi, Pu Zhiqiang, Tsering Woeser, Wang Dan to Yao Lifa.[59] Yet in marked contrast from 1989 and even 1998, Charter 08 managed to gain the support of a very wide range of liberal-minded mainland Chinese citizens, which also included less well-known pro-establishment and trans-establishment figures. Feng describes the depth and breadth of the broad coalition of the 303 initial signatories of Charter 08: "In term of professional and social diversity, the 303 original signatories of Charter identified themselves as scholars of all disciplines, lawyers, writers, journalists, editors, teachers, artists, officials, public servants, engineers, businessmen, workers, peasants, democracy activists and rights activists".[60] Perry Link has argued that subsequently about "10,000 people have now signed, and were there not widespread fear about the consequences, no doubt hundreds of thousands of others who know about the Charter would sign as well. Even if the crypto-Chartists number as many as a million, however, that is less than 0.1 percent of China's population."[61]

Strategic reform approach

With the drafting of Charter 08 its authors "put civic spirit into practice" and encouraged "fellow citizens who feel a similar sense of crisis, responsibility, and mission, whether they are inside the government or not, and regardless of their social status, [to] set aside small differences [and] embrace the broad goals of this citizens' movement".[62] The authors structured their text into three parts. Following a fairly lengthy foreword, which put Charter 08 in a historical context, the second part lists the charter's six key principles of freedom, human rights, equality, republicanism, democracy and constitutional rule. The latter two principles very closely mirror Robert Dahl's concept of capital D Democracy as polyarchy, as outlined in Chapter 1. [63] The subsequent 19 specific "recommendations on national governance, citizens' rights, and social development"[64] reimagine mainland China along liberal-democratic lines. Charter 08 specifically calls for 1) a new constitution, 2) separation of powers, 3) legislative democracy, 4) an independent judiciary, 5) public control of public servants, 6) guarantee of human rights, 7) election of public officials, 8) rural–urban equality, 9) freedom to form groups, 10) freedom to assemble, 11) freedom of expression, 12) freedom of religion, 13) civic education, 14) protection of private property, 15) financial and tax reform, 16) social security, 17) protection of the environment, 18) a federated republic and 19) truth in reconciliation.[65]

Charter 08 differs from the previous struggles for democracy in 1989 and 1998 insofar as it is unambiguous in its anti-establishment objective and desire to overcome one-party rule in mainland China. It more closely resembles Wei Jingsheng's call for a fifth modernisation[66] from 1978, as it considers freedom "the core of universal human values".[67] In marked contrast to Wei's more aspirational concept of freedom, however, the drafters of Charter 08 convey a sense of great urgency. They write

> as the ruling elite continues with impunity to crush and to strip away the rights of citizens to freedom, to property, and to the pursuit of happiness, we see the powerless in our society—the vulnerable groups, the people who have been suppressed and monitored, who have suffered cruelty and even torture, and who have had no adequate avenues for their protests, no courts to hear their pleas—becoming more militant and raising the possibility of a violent conflict of disastrous proportions. The decline of the current system has reached the point where change is no longer optional.[68]

Perry Link has pointed out that the party-state's subsequent harassment of Charter 08 signatories "only serve to underscore China's failure to uphold the very principles that the charter advances".[69] According to Amnesty International chartists in mainland China have been imprisoned, sent to re-education through labour camps, put under house arrest or have been subject to surveillance and/or soft detention.[70] Amnesty International further identified wide-ranging reprisals for signatories "such as disappearance, travel bans, detention, torture, and loss of jobs". Singled out for his role as Charter 08's key editor, Liu Xiaobo was arrested in 2009 and indicted on charges of subverting the Chinese party-state.[71] His conviction rested on six of Liu's texts and on "writing seven sentences, a total of 224 Chinese characters".[72] While serving his prison sentence Liu was awarded the Nobel Peace Prize in 2010.[73] During Liu's time in custody, however, the party-state did nothing to ensure his medical well-being and failed to detect Liu's liver cancer until it had reached terminal phase. Hu Jia, a prominent mainland Chinese critic of one-party rule and HIV/AIDS activist, has suggested that "Beijing has neglected care for Liu on purpose".[74] By allowing Liu to die from liver cancer in prison the CCP violated Article 6 of the International Covenant on Civil and Political Rights, which states that every "human being has the inherent right to life. This right shall be protected by law. No one shall be arbitrarily deprived of his life."[75] Liu Xiaobo shared the same fate of another Nobel Peace Prize laureate in Nazi Germany, the pacifist Carl von Ossietzky, who died from tuberculosis in 1938 in a Berlin hospital under police custody.[76] Liu Xiaobo thus paid an extremely high personal price for helping draft Charter 08. And despite not having been charged and convicted for any wrong-doings, his wife Liu Xia also had to endure eight years of house arrest and only received permission to leave China for exile in Germany in July 2018.[77]

Lessons learned

While the party-state has been partially successful in slowing the spread of liberal thought and practice as embodied and encouraged in Charter 08, I argue that with its promulgation the authors have passed a major milestone in the development of mainland China's democracy movement. One of the persistent critiques of previous struggles for democracy had been the lack of a strategic vision among mainland Chinese activists. Charter 08 has remedied this shortcoming and can now be considered a "grand strategy", as understood in the terms of Gene Sharp's TOPC. And rather than trying to establish an opposition party like the CDP ten years earlier, Charter 08 is more closely modelled on the example of Charter 77. Charter 77 attempted to transcend the need for an organisation and organisational membership was not supposed to lead to oppositional political activity. Instead, as Jonathan Bolton has pointed out, its neutral language and non-confrontational attitude helped "bring together such a diverse grouping of people".[78]

Since its promulgation, Charter 08 has served as a cognitive map for any subsequent political declarations and open letters originating out of mainland China. Frederic Jameson has described the utility of a cognitive map "to enable a situational representation on the part of the individual subject to that vaster and properly unpresentable totality which is the ensemble of society's structures as a whole".[79] It can be safely assumed that a vast majority of politically active mainland Chinese citizens will be aware of its existence. This means that regardless of whether activists belong to the anti-establishment, pro-establishment or trans-establishment they need to position themselves vis-à-vis Charter 08. Potter and Woodman have argued that it "opens a window of opportunity for a possible alliance between the Chartists outside the political system and reformers within the political system".[80] A case in point is the ten-year plan for social and political reform developed by Chinese pro-establishment scholar Yu Jianrong in 2012. When comparing Yu's 10-year plan with Charter 08 I found that while "Yu Jianrong has not signed the Charter 08 sixteen of its nineteen key demands can be identified in one form or another in his ten-year plan".[81] Reflecting on the similarities and differences between the two political reform proposals, I concluded that "Yu Jianrong adopts the reformist goals of the Charter 08 and re-packages it into a more procedural and watered down reform agenda".[82] The probability of Yu not being aware or not having read Charter 08 can be considered zero.

This does not mean, however, that Charter 08 should be considered the logical end point of mainland China's democracy movement. While it now provides a strategic umbrella for mainland China's anti-establishment, pro-establishment and trans-establishment to act upon, its particular genesis has also arguably impeded its reach within mainland China's society. Earlier drafts of Charter 08 were most likely read and commented upon by more than the official three drafters, but the number of active participants in the drafting process will have been in the low double digits. This means that only a handful of people were actively involved in the formulation of Charter 08. While limiting the number of co-authors in formulating such a highly political and sensitive document will have made practical sense at the time, from the perspective of Paulo Freire's TOPC it thus can also be considered a gift by active political elites for the masses.[83] According to Freire, however, strategies and solutions to political problems need to be developed in dialogue with the oppressed people, not by political activists on their behalf. The continued need to involve the wider public in the political reform discourse thus is a key lesson to be learned from the promulgation of Charter 08.

Episode 4: China's New Citizen movement: a Freirean approach to liberation?

Antecedents and political opportunities

Charter 08 can be considered a milestone as it developed a coherent strategic vision for mainland China's highly fragmented democracy movement. And yet it could have been perhaps more impactful if its drafting process had been less of a top-down affair. As the NCM from 2009 onwards[84] will show, a bottom-up approach which includes the widest possible range of societal actors in the formulation of political reform strategies and tactics is not only possible, but the associated constituency building can arguably also be life saving for the democracy activists facilitating such efforts. The contours of the NCM were greatly shaped by Xu Zhiyong, a public-interest lawyer of Christian faith.[85] While Xu did not sign Charter 08,[86] the NCM can clearly be considered an extension of the former. Whereas the drafters of Charter 08 concluded their political declaration by calling upon mainland Chinese to "actively participate in the citizen movement" (*jiji canyu dao gongmin yundong zhong lai*),[87] Xu begins his landmark essay *The New Citizens Movement in China* with the statement "China needs a new citizen movement" (*zhongguo xuyao xin gongmin yundong*).[88] Xu's essay was published during a time of political uncertainty. In July 2012 Xi Jinping had not yet shown his true colours as a political hardliner, which only became more apparent in January 2013.[89] American journalist John Pomfret has furthermore suggested that Xi enjoyed a brief honeymoon with China's liberals in the years preceding his rise to the top.[90]

Key actors

According to Xu the NCM can be considered a political, social, cultural and peaceful progressive movement. In Xu's words, this

> movement is a political movement in which this ancient nation bids utter farewell to authoritarianism and completes the civilized transformation to constitutional governance; it is a social movement to completely destroy the privileges of corruption, the abuse of power, the gap between rich and poor, and to construct a new order of fairness and justice; it is a cultural movement to bid farewell to the culture of autocrats and subjects and instead create a new nationalist spirit; it is the peaceful progressive movement to herald humanity's process of civilizing.[91]

While declaring the "goal of the New Citizens' Movement is a free China ruled by democracy and law, a just and happy civil society with 'freedom, righteousness, love' as the new national spirit",[92] Xu did not call for an immediate overthrow of the CCP.

With his 2012 essay Xu Zhiyong provided an intellectual justification to the NCM. At the time of the publication of his essay the underlying ideas and practices, however, were already spreading throughout the country both online and offline without the help of any centralised organisational structure. Michael Caster has pointed out that the "New Citizens Movement is based on the principal of organizing without organization, a loose network for mobilizing civil resistance and rights defense in response to a history of repressing formal civil organization".[93] The decentralised nature of the NCM differentiates this struggle for democracy from its antecedents. NCM was neither calling for mass mobilisation like the anti-corruption and pro-democracy movement of 1989, nor did it attempt to establish an opposition party like the CDP in 1998. It also went beyond the declaratory nature of the Charter 08 from 2008 by calling for the inclusion of Chinese citizens from all walks of life in the fight against corruption and collusion and in the search for liberal democracy in mainland China.

Strategic reform approach

The NCM signifies a major shift in the organising principles of mainland China's democracy movement. While Xu Zhiyong deserves credit for framing and contextualising the NCM's existence, due to its almost completely decentralised organisational structure it was never owned or controlled by any particular opposition group. Between 2009 and 2014 Chinese citizens from all walks of life filled the movement with life. In China's cybersphere supporters started using NCM insignia such as adding the Chinese characters 公民 (gongmin) to their social media profiles. Offline, NCM supporters across

China would meet for luncheons or dinners to discuss current social, cultural and political affairs. Other offline NCM activities included "an education rights campaign to abolish the household registration (hukou) requirement for children to take national university entrance examination (gaokao) by 2012".[94] A related petition managed to garner 100,000 signatures. NCM activists also formulated a citizen's pledge in 2010, launched an asset transparency campaign in 2012 and published an open letter to Xi Jinping in 2013 "calling for 205 senior officials to publicly disclose their assets".[95] Seen from a holistic perspective, NCM's TOPC cannot be reduced to one reform approach but creatively combines Gene Sharp's anti-establishment with Saul Alinsky's trojan horse and Paulo Freire's trans-establishment approach. Xu Zhiyong's 2012 essay offers a glimpse into the highly sophisticated strategic thinking which informs the NCM.

Xu's essay resembles Paulo Freire's TOPC when he calls for the self-empowerment of the oppressed Chinese people. Xu argues that the "citizen is not a subject—the citizen is an independent and free entity, and he or she obeys a rule of law that is commonly agreed upon. He or she does not have to kneel down to any given person. The citizen is not a layman—the citizen is the master of the country."[96] The influence of his Christian faith becomes apparent when Xu declares his preference for a peaceful resolution of political differences. Xu emphasises that "the New Citizens' Movement's discourse is not 'overthrow', but 'establish'. It is not one social class taking the place of another social class, but letting righteousness take its place in the Chinese nation. It is not hostility and hate, but universal love."[97] Throughout his essay Xu includes a wide range of specific recommendations on how Chinese citizens should avoid corruption and collusion and how they can act ethically.

With his focus on self-organisation, community building and social movements, Xu's advocacy also closely resembles Saul Alinsky's TOPC. Alinsky had argued that "once you organize people around something as commonly agreed upon as pollution, then an organized people is on the move. From there it's a short and natural step to political pollution, to Pentagon pollution."[98] Informed by his experience as civil society practitioner and co-founder of the now defunct CSO Open Constitution Initiative, Xu is aware of the need to link up a wide range of social movements, ranging from

> the "Grass Mud Horse" campaign, the displaced residents campaign, the campaign to oppose the household registration stratification, the campaign to remember June Fourth, the freedom of belief campaign, the blogging campaign, the environmental protection campaign, the food and health safety campaign, the campaign to elect deputies to people's congresses, the microblog-based campaign attacking human trafficking, the campaign to oppose monopolies, [to] the campaign to oppose corruption.[99]

At the same time Xu Zhiyong's political thinking also resembles Gene Sharp's TOPC, especially when he lauds "the lawful defense of citizens' rights, citizens' non-violent non-cooperation, and peaceful democracy movements".[100] Xu's public support for non-violent non-cooperation is remarkable since during the early 2000s many mainland Chinese democracy and human rights activists considered him overly moderate. When he and his CSO Open Constitution Initiative was shut down by authorities in 2009, however, Sharon Hom, executive-director of Human Rights in China, issued a warning: "By suppressing Xu Zhiyong, who is a moderate voice for social change and has dedicated his career to helping forge a society with genuine rule of law, the authorities are running the risk of radicalizing the forces for reform and change in China."[101] As we will see from the subsequent discussion of the lessons learned from the NCM, Hom's words were prophetic.

Lessons learned

Starting from April 2013, NCM advocates were being detained and/or put under house arrest. While some activists were released after short periods of time, a number of leading NCM protagonists were subsequently given prison sentences ranging between two and four years.[102] Based on the charge of "gathering a crowd to disrupt public order", Xu Zhiyong was sentenced to four years in jail in January 2014. Gerda Wielander expressed concern that whenever "he is released, we can assume that his health will have significantly deteriorated".[103] Quoting from Xu's memoir *To Build a Free China: A Citizen's Journey*, Wielander argues that "the weakening of inmates through torture and other cruel practices is part and parcel of China's systematic suppression of 'progressives ... [who] work together to see China through the transition to civilized politics' (Xu, 2017: 277)".[104] Xu Zhiyong was released on 15 July 2017, only two days after Liu Xiaobo had died in prison.[105] Whereas the CCP allowed Liu Xiaobo to die, Xu Zhiyong was released from jail unharmed. What explains the difference in treatment by the Chinese authorities? Whereas Hu Jia has suggested that "given [Liu's] influence and his massive following, it's possible that Beijing does not want him to return to society healthy, physically capable and energetic",[106] it is also possible that despite the more than 10,000 signatories of Charter 08 Liu Xiaobo did not have a big enough constituency to protect him from harm in prison. Xu Zhiyong, on the other hand, had become a household name among petitioners, university students, civil society practitioners and citizen activists all across China. The party-state may have concluded that wilful negligence of the personal well-being of Xu Zhiyong, too, would have been too dangerous, as it would have further mobilised a decentralised NCM.

In September 2016, Xu Zhiyong published an essay[107] on his prison years and recorded a short video message.[108] In his reflections on the trial and subsequent imprisonment Xu recalls how party-state representatives, ranging from judges, prosecutors, interrogators to prison wardens, apologised to him for having to play roles in what they seemed to have perceived as a CCP stitch-up.[109] In a remarkable paragraph towards the end of his prison reflections Xu states that

> I've become a determined revolutionary. It's not that I have changed my mind. It's just that previously I always had illusions about others. It wasn't that I put my faith in someone; what it was is that I was tempted by life and didn't want to shoulder responsibility for this ancient people. But having watched CCTV "Evening News" for three years, a voice said: Stop evading your destiny.[110]

Ending his text with the statement "I am back, China",[111] Xu has signalled that the NCM's struggle for democracy is anything but over.

Reflections on the four episodes from a longitudinal perspective

In this chapter I chose to hone in on four closely viewed critical incidents from 1989 onwards. For each episode I analysed the antecedents which informed the struggle for democracy as well as the perceived political opportunities by participants at the time. I discussed which reform camp initiated the specific struggle for democracy, which strategic reform approach was taken and which kind of key lessons were learned. While none of the struggles for democracy in and of themselves have been effective in overcoming CCP rule, a longitudinal perspective now allows us to see how far mainland China's democracy movement has progressed towards this goal. In this chapter I have argued that the failure of each struggle informed the subsequent struggles. The formulation of Charter 08 signified a turning point in the democracy movement, as for the first time it provided a "grand strategy" for the anti-establishment, pro-establishment and trans-establishment camps to come together to work towards a common objective. The subsequent NCM, on the other hand, signifies a major paradigmatic change in mainland China's democracy movement, as it draws on a comprehensive combination of anti-establishment, trojan horse and trans-establishment strategies, as discussed in the context of Gene Sharp's, Saul Alinsky's and Paulo Freire's TOPC in Chapter 4. Combined with its decentralised approach to organising we are thus witnessing a diversification of actors, arenas, strategies and methods in mainland China's democracy movement. What separates the NCM from previous struggles for democracy is that it is an ongoing movement, which in the way Xu Zhiyong has conceptualised it, cannot be suppressed infinitely. Xu reminds his fellow compatriots that "when every Chinese has taken on the role of a real citizen, our country will have already changed".[112]

It is worth noting that the four episodes I presented in this chapter are heavily dominated by male protagonists. Since 2018 the global "Me too" movement is also spreading across mainland China.[113] Highly committed Chinese university students have also started expressing solidarity with striking factory workers in southern China and are willing to pay a considerable price for their political activism.[114] Such impulses from young Chinese activists, and in particular female activists, are likely to further rejuvenate and embolden mainland China's democracy movement.

In Chapters 7 and 8 I will portray the rise and demise of another Leninist party-state, in the case of Taiwan and the KMT. It will show that it took Taiwanese citizens more than 50 years—if one includes the Japanese colonial period as well, perhaps more than 100 years—to overcome authoritarianism. The key difference to the case of mainland China is that from 1949 onwards, Taiwanese democracy activists had to combat two authoritarian regimes at the same time: the KMT, which constrained their freedom and liberties in Taiwan and among the Taiwanese diaspora living abroad, and the CCP, which has cast an additional shadow on the Taiwanese democracy movement.

Notes

1   Béja, Jean-Philippe (2009), China since Tiananmen: The Massacre's Long Shadow, *Journal of Democracy*, 20(3, July), 12.
2   Naughton, Barry (2009), China: Economic Transformation before and after 1989. Available online: https://pdfs.semanticscholar.org/02e5/b77c98d6afef55a 5cc1b7f0cf0425a1c44a0.pdf (accessed 29 October 2018).
3   Ibid.
4   Spence, Jonathan (1990), *The Search for Modern China*, W.W. Norton & Company, New York, 623.
5   Nathan, Andrew and Link, Perry (Eds), compiled by Liang, Zhang (2001), *The Tiananmen Papers*, Abacus, London, 3.
6   Ibid., xii.
7   Sharp, Gene (2012), *From Dictatorship to Democracy*, Serpent's Tail, London, 80.
8   Unger, Jonathan (1991), Introduction, in: Jonathan Unger (Ed.), *The Pro-Democracy Protests in China: Reports from the Provinces*, M.E. Sharpe, New York, 4.
9   Ibid.
10 Ibid.
11 Wang, Dan (1990), II: Wang Dan, On Freedom of Speech for the Opposition, in: Mok Chiu Yu and Frank Harrison (Eds), *Voices from Tiananmen Square*, Black Rose Books, New York, 38–41.
12 XXX, Teacher at People's University (1990), Why Does China Need Democracy?, in: Han Minzhu (Ed.), *Cries for Democracy: Writings and Speeches from the 1989 Chinese Democracy Movement*, Princeton University Press, Princeton, 151–63.
13 Wanding, Ren (1990), III: Ren Wanding: Why Did the Rally in Memory of Hu Yaobang Turn into a Democracy Movement?, in: Mok Chiu Yu and Frank Harrison (Eds), *Voices from Tiananmen Square*, Black Rose Books, New York, 42–47.
14 Sharp (2012), *From Dictatorship to Democracy*, 61.

15 天安门 The Film (1995), *The Gate of Heavenly Peace*. Available online: www. tsquare.tv/film/transcript.html (accessed 5 March 2018).
16 Ibid.
17 Perry, E. (2015), *Challenging the Mandate of Heaven: Social Protest and State Power in China*, Asia and the Pacific, Armonk, NY, 312.
18 Ibid.
19 Ibid., 312–13.
20 *New York Review of Books* (2005), The Case of Dai Qing. Available online: www.nybooks.com/articles/2005/10/06/china-the-uses-of-fear/ (accessed 29 October 2018).
21 Walder, Andrew G. and Xiaoxia, Gong (1993), Workers in the Tiananmen Protests: The Politics of the Beijing Workers' Autonomous Federation, *Australian Journal of Chinese Affairs*, 29 (January), 27.
22 Sharp (2012), *From Dictatorship to Democracy*, 58.
23 Albert Einstein Institute (1989), Nonviolent Struggle in China: An Eyewitness Account. Available online: www.bmartin.cc/pubs/90sa/90sa_Sharp.pdf (accessed 29 October 2018).
24 Perry, E. (2015), *Challenging the Mandate of Heaven: Social Protest and State Power in China*, Asia and the Pacific, Armonk, NY, 314.
25 Ibid., 315.
26 Ibid.
27 天安门 The Film (1995), *The Gate of Heavenly Peace*. Available online: www. tsquare.tv/film/transcript.html (accessed 5 March 2018).
28 Sharp (2012), *From Dictatorship to Democracy*, 18.
29 天安门 Chronology (1995), It Is Necessary to Take a Clear-Cut Stand against Disturbances, Renmin ribao, People's daily, editorial, printed 26 April 1989. Available online: www.history.ubc.ca/sites/default/files/courses/documents/Tim%20Cheek/April%2026%20Editorial%20in%20People%27s%20Daily.pdf (accessed 29 October 2018).
30 *New York Times* (2014), People's Daily Editorial Fanned Flames of 1989 Protest, Sinosphere. Dispatches from China. Available online: https://sinosphere.blogs.nytimes.com/2014/04/25/peoples-daily-editorial-fanned-flames-of-1989-protest/ (accessed 29 October 2018).
31 Sharp (2012), *From Dictatorship to Democracy*, 19.
32 Ibid., 21.
33 Albert Einstein Institute (1989), Nonviolent Struggle in China: An Eyewitness Account. Available online: www.bmartin.cc/pubs/90sa/90sa_Sharp.pdf (accessed 29 October 2018).
34 Ibid.
35 Ibid.
36 Ibid.
37 Ibid.
38 Wright, Teresa (2002), The China Democracy Party and the Politics of Protest in the 1980s–1990s. *China Quarterly*, 172(December), 908.
39 Duihua (2011), Statement on the Medical Parole of Wang Youcai. Available online: https://duihua.org/wp/?p=1761 (accessed 30 October 2018).
40 Human Rights Watch (2000), China: Nipped in the Bud: The Suppression of the China Democracy Party. Available online: www.hrw.org/report/2000/09/01/china-nipped-bud/suppression-china-democracy-party (accessed 30 October 2018).
41 Ibid.
42 Wright, Teresa (2002), The China Democracy Party and the Politics of Protest in the 1980s–1990s, *China Quarterly*, 172(December), 921.
43 Ibid.
44 Goldman, Merle (2005), *From Comrade to Citizen: The Struggle for Political Rights in China*, Harvard University Press, Cambridge, 172.

45 Ibid., 182.

46 He is currently still serving a lengthy prison sentence in mainland China.

47 In 1998 Wang Youcai was sentenced to 11 years in prison. He was released on medical parole in 2004 and went to the United States.

48 Wright, Teresa (2002), The China Democracy Party and the Politics of Protest in the 1980s–1990s, *China Quarterly*, 172(December), 926.

49 According to Choudry and Kapoor, the "term 'NGOization' is commonly used among many social movements, activist networks and academics to refer to the institutionalisation, professionalisation, depoliticisation and demobilisation of movements for social and environmental change", see Choudry, Aziz and Kapoor, Dip (2013), Introduction: NGOization: Complicity, Contradictions and Prospects, in: Aziz Choudry and Dip Kapoor (Eds), *NGOization: Complicity, Contradictions and Prospects*, Zed Books, London, 1.

50 CDP founding member Hu Depu claims to have been tortured repeatedly while in jail. See Radio Free Asia (2011), Activist Beaten on Release. Available online: www.rfa.org/english/news/china/beating-01242011180518.html (accessed 30 October 2018). Many less well-known CDP members appear to have also been mistreated in jail. See Refworld (2013), China: China Democracy Party (CDP) in Guangdong, Including Structure and Activities; Treatment of CDP Members by Authorities (2012–December 2013). Available online: www.refworld.org/docid/543ba4894.html (accessed 30 October 2018).

51 Wright, Teresa (2002), The China Democracy Party and the Politics of Protest in the 1980s-1990s, *China Quarterly*, 172(December), 916–17.

52 Ibid., 919.

53 Ibid., 918.

54 Chongyi, Feng (2002), Political Parties and the Prospects for Democracy: Perspectives from Provincial China, *Provincial China*, 7(1), April, 81.

55 Burton, Michael G. and Higley, John (1987), Elite Settlements. *American Sociological Review*, 52(3, June), 304.

56 *Guardian* (2008), Charter 08: A Bold Call for Change, Available online: www.theguardian.com/commentisfree/2008/dec/12/china-humanrights (accessed 2 November 2018).

57 Foreign Policy (2017), In Charter 77, Czech Dissidents Charted New Territory. Available online: https://foreignpolicy.com/2017/02/03/in-charter-77-czech-dissidents-charted-new-territory/ (accessed 2 November 2018).

58 Feng, Chongyi (2010), Charter 08, the Troubled History and Future of Chinese Liberalism, *Asia-Pacific Journal*, 2(10, 11 January). Available online: https://opus.lib.uts.edu.au/bitstream/10453/10577/1/2009000459OK.pdf (accessed 31 October 2018).

59 *China Digital Times* (2018), 《零八宪章》签名人员名单汇总（共五批）, Available online: https://chinadigitaltimes.net/space/《零八宪章》签名人员名单汇总(共五批) (accessed 31 October 2018).

60 Feng, Chongyi (2010), Charter 08, the Troubled History and Future of Chinese Liberalism, *Asia-Pacific Journal*, 2(10, 11 January). Available online: https://opus.lib.uts.edu.au/bitstream/10453/10577/1/2009000459OK.pdf (accessed 31 October 2018).

61 Link, Perry (2010), What Beijing Fears Most. Available online: www.nybooks.com/daily/2010/01/27/what-beijing-fears-most/ (accessed 31 October 2018).

62 Link, Perry (2009), China's Charter 08, *New York Review of Books*, 15 January. Available online: www.nybooks.com/articles/2009/01/15/chinas-charter-08/ (accessed 31 October 2018).

63 Dahl, R. (1971), *Polyarchy: Participation and Opposition*, Yale University Press, New Haven, CT, 3.

64 Link, Perry (2009), China's Charter 08, *New York Review of Books*, 15 January. Available online: www.nybooks.com/articles/2009/01/15/chinas-charter-08/ (accessed 31 October 2018).

65 Ibid.

66 Wei, Jingsheng (1978), The Fifth Modernization: Democracy, in: Wm. Theodore de Bary and Richard Lufrano (Eds) (2000), *Sources of Chinese Tradition: From 1600 through the Twentieth Century*, 2nd ed., Vol. 2, Columbia University Press, New York, 497–500. Available online: http://afe.easia.columbia.edu/ps/cup/wei_jingsheng_fifth_modernization.pdf (accessed 20 August 2018).

67 Link, Perry (2009), China's Charter 08, *New York Review of Books*, 15 January. Available online: www.nybooks.com/articles/2009/01/15/chinas-charter-08/ (accessed 31 October 2018).

68 Ibid.

69 Ibid.

70 Amnesty International UK (2013), Charter 08's Legacy and China's Failure to Honor Human Rights Obligations. Available online: www.amnesty.org.uk/blogs/countdown-china/charter-08s-legacy-china's-failure-honor-human-rights-obligations (accessed 2 November 2018).

71 Human Rights in China (2010), Concerning the Incitement to Subvert State Power Case of Liu Xiaobo. Available online: www.hrichina.org/en/content/3206 (accessed 31 October 2018).

72 Quartz (2017), Nobel Prize Winner Liu Xiaobo: A Timeline of a Life Dedicated to the Protesters of Tiananmen Square. Available online: https://qz.com/1023459/nobel-peace-prize-winner-liu-xiaobo-imprisoned-by-china-for-writing-seven-sentences-has-died-in-custody/ (accessed 31 October 2018).

73 Nobel Prize (2010), The Nobel Peace Prize for 2010. Available online: www.nobelprize.org/prizes/peace/2010/press-release/ (accessed 31 October 2018).

74 *Globe and the Mail* (2017), Questions Surround Nobel Laureate Liu Xiaobo's Prison Medical Treatment. Available online: www.theglobeandmail.com/news/world/questions-surround-nobel-laureate-liu-xiaobos-prison-medical-treatment/article35474485/ (accessed 2 November 2018).

75 United Nations Human Rights Office of the High Commissioner (2018), International Covenant on Civil and Political Rights. Available online: www.ohchr.org/en/professionalinterest/pages/ccpr.aspx (accessed 31 October 2018).

76 Windows to World History (2018), Carl von Ossietzky Wins a Nobel Prize While in a Nazi Prison Camp. Available online: https://windowstoworldhistory.weebly.com/carl-von-ossietzky-wins-the-nobel-prize-while-in-a-nazi-prison-camp.html (accessed 2 November 2018).

77 *Guardian* (2018), Liu Xia: Widow of Nobel Laureate Arrives in Berlin after Release from China. Available online: www.theguardian.com/world/2018/jul/10/liu-xia-nobel-laureates-widow-allowed-to-leave-china-for-europe (accessed 31 October 2018).

78 Bolton, Jonathan (2012), *Worlds of Dissent: Charter 77, The Plastic People of the Universe, and Czech Culture under Communism*, Harvard University Press, Cambridge, MA, 153–4.

79 Jameson, Frederic (1991), *Postmodernism, or, The Cultural Logic of Late Capitalism*, Duke University Press, Durham, NC, 51.

80 Béja, Jean-Philippe, Hualing, Fu and Pils, Eva (2012), Introduction, in: Jean-Philippe Béja, Fu Hualing and Eva Pils (Eds), *Liu Xiaobo, Charter 08, and the Challenges of Political Reform in China*, Hong Kong University Press, Hong Kong, 7.

81 Fulda, Andreas (2012), A Convergence of China's Political Reform Agendas, China Policy Institute Policy Paper: No. 3. Available online: www.nottingham.ac.uk/iaps/documents/cpi/policy-papers/policy-paper-2012-03.pdf (accessed 31 October 2018).

82 Fulda, Andreas (2012), Yu Jianrong's Ten Year Plan: A Watered Down Version of the Charter 08?, *Asia Dialogue*, 22 November. Available online: http://theasia

dialogue.com/2012/11/22/yu-jianrongs-ten-year-plan-a-watered-down-version-of-the-charter-08/ (accessed 31 October 2018).

83 Freire, Paolo (2014), *Pedagogy of the Oppressed*, Bloomsbury Academic, New York, 125–6.

84 Human Rights in China (2014), New Citizens Movement Briefing Note. Available online: www.hrichina.org/sites/default/files/new_citizens_movement_brief ing_note_2014.pdf (accessed 2 November 2018).

85 *Telegraph* (2014), The China Manifesto: Detained Activist Xu Zhiyong Calls for End to "Barbaric" One Party Rule. Available online: www.telegraph.co.uk/news/ worldnews/asia/china/10591993/The-China-Manifesto-detained-acti vist-Xu-Zhiyong-calls-for-end-to-barbaric-one-party-rule.html   (accessed   1 November 2018).

86 Independent Chinese PEN Centre (2016), 赵常青：《零八宪章》是中国公民运动的动员令和集合令！. Available online: www.chinesepen.org/blog/archives/ 75427 (accessed 1 November 2018).

87 Radio Free Asia (2016), 零八宪章全文（刘晓波等）. Available online: www.rfa. org/mandarin/pinglun/liuxiaobopinglunzhuanji/lxb-07132017104422.html (accessed 1 November 2018).

88 Wenji, Xu Zhiyong (2012), 中国新公民运动. Available online: http://xuz hiyong2012.blogspot.com/2012/11/blog-post_9281.html (accessed 1 November 2018).

89 SCMP (2013), Xi Jinping's Opposition to Political Reforms Laid out in Leaked Internal Speech. Available online: www.scmp.com/comment/blogs/article/ 1137727/xi-jinpings-opposition-political-reforms-laid-out-leaked-internal (accessed 1 November 2018).

90 Ibid.

91 ChinaChange (2012), The New Citizens Movement in China. Available online: https://chinachange.org/2012/07/11/china-needs-a-new-citizens-movement-xu-z hiyongs-许志永-controversial-essay/ (accessed 1 November 2018).

92 Ibid.

93 Open Democracy (2014), The Contentious Politics of China's New Citizens Movement. Available online: www.opendemocracy.net/civilresistance/michael-ca ster/contentious-politics-of-china's-new-citizens-movement (accessed 1 November 2018).

94 Human Rights in China (2014), New Citizens Movement Briefing Note. Available online: www.hrichina.org/sites/default/files/new_citizens_movement_brief ing_note_2014.pdf (accessed 2 November 2018).

95 Ibid.

96 ChinaChange (2012), The New Citizens Movement in China. Available online: https://chinachange.org/2012/07/11/china-needs-a-new-citizens-movement-xu-z hiyongs-许志永-controversial-essay/ (accessed 1 November 2018).

97 Ibid.

98 Alinsky, Saul (1989 [1971]), *Rules for Radicals: A Pragmatic Primer for Realistic Radicals*, Vintage Books, New York, xxiii.

99 ChinaChange (2012), The New Citizens Movement in China. Available online: https://chinachange.org/2012/07/11/china-needs-a-new-citizens-movement-xu-z hiyongs-许志永-controversial-essay/ (accessed 1 November 2018).

100 Ibid.

101 RConversation (2009), Dark Days for China's Liberals. Available online: https:// rconversation.blogs.com/rconversation/law/ (accessed 2 November 2018).

102 Human Rights in China (2014), New Citizens Movement Briefing Note. Available online: www.hrichina.org/sites/default/files/new_citizens_movement_brief ing_note_2014.pdf (accessed 2 November 2018).

103 Wielander, Gerda (2017), The Dangers of Taking Responsibility and Acting on One's Conscience in 21st Century China: A Review Essay of Xu Zhiyong's To

Build a Free China: A Citizen's Journey, *Journal of the British Association for Chinese Studies*, 7(July), 119.

104 Ibid.

105 *Reuters* (2017), Prominent Rights Activist Xu Zhiyong Freed from Chinese Jail. Available online: https://uk.reuters.com/article/uk-china-rights-corruption/prominent-rights-activist-xu-zhiyong-freed-from-chinese-jail-idUKKBN1A006A (accessed 2 November 2018).

106 *Globe and the Mail* (2017), Questions Surround Nobel Laureate Liu Xiaobo's Prison Medical Treatment. Available online: www.theglobeandmail.com/news/world/questions-surround-nobel-laureate-liu-xiaobos-prison-medical-treatment/article35474485/ (accessed 2 November 2018).

107 China Change (2018), Four Years Afar. Available online: https://chinachange.org/tag/new-citizens-movement/ (accessed 2 November 2018).

108 China Change (2018), Xu Zhiyong (许志永): We Represent the Future of China. Available online: www.youtube.com/watch?v=T2NcfseMIIE (accessed 2 November 2018).

109 China Change (2018), Four Years Afar. Available online: https://chinachange.org/tag/new-citizens-movement/ (accessed 2 November 2018).

110 Ibid.

111 Ibid.

112 China Change (2018), Xu Zhiyong (许志永): We represent the future of China. Xu Zhiyong (许志永): Available online: www.youtube.com/watch?v=T2NcfseMIIE (accessed 2 November 2018).

113 *Guardian* (2018), #MeToo in China: Movement Gathers Pace amid Wave of Accusations. Available online: www.theguardian.com/world/2018/jul/31/metoo-in-china-movement-gathers-pace-amid-wave-of-accusations (accessed 2 November 2018).

114 *Reuters* (2018), China's Student Activists Cast Rare Light on Brewing Labor Unrest. www.reuters.com/article/us-china-labour-protests-insight/chinas-student-activists-cast-rare-light-on-brewing-labor-unrest-idUSKBN1L0060 (accessed 2 November 2018).

7

THE RISE AND DEMISE OF THE KMT PARTY-STATE IN TAIWAN

The Chinese Nationalist Party—or as it is better known under its transcribed Chinese name Kuomintang (KMT)—has for a long time been considered one of the world's richest parties.[1] Yet in November 2016 something remarkable happened: the KMT was unable to pay its staff and had to lay off more than half of its 738 employees.[2] After winning both the presidency and gaining a majority in Taiwan's parliament in January 2016, the Democratic Progressive Party (DPP) had

> passed a law that assumes that all the KMT's property is ill-gotten, bar membership fees, donations and the funding political parties receive from the government. The law allows the government to freeze the KMT's assets while a committee assesses whether the party is the rightful owner, and to seize them if it judges otherwise. The KMT will only be able to reclaim assets it can prove it obtained legitimately.[3]

The DPP's law stripping the KMT of its assets is significant, as it previously ruled the island-state for more than six decades: from 1945 until the narrow election victory of DPP president Chen Shui-bian in 2000, and then again during the KMT presidency of Ma Ying-jeou from 2008 until 2016.

The demise of the KMT's party-state in 2016 also means that it took Taiwan's democracy movement more than 100 years—beginning with the establishment of Taiwan's first opposition organisation, the short-lived Assimilation Society (*Dokakai*) from 1914 to 1915, which lobbied for the rights of Taiwanese under Japanese rule[4]—to overcome authoritarianism by peaceful means. November 2016 marks a turning point in the island's political history, since a financially broken KMT, which Cheng Tun-Jen in 2006 already described as "an anachronistic nation-building party and a catch-all party",[5] will not be able to re-emerge as an autocratic party-state in Taiwan's future. The case of Taiwan shows that it is possible to defeat Leninist parties through social and political movements as well as through the ballot box.

In this chapter I discuss the trajectory of Taiwan's political development from 1945 until 1979, when opposition politicians under the banner of the *dangwai* movement (literally outside the KMT) unsuccessfully challenged the KMT during a human rights rally in the southern city of Kaohsiung (*Gaoxiong*). In the first part of this chapter I argue that the KMT's approach to governing Taiwan in many ways resembled Japanese colonial rule. Soon after relocating to Taiwan, the KMT party-state quickly expanded its control over the island's economy and society. Chiang Kai-shek expropriated the land-owning Taiwanese elites during land reforms in the 1950s and ordered the killing of close to 30,000 islanders during the period of the White Terror (*baise kongbu shidai*), which lasted until the lifting of martial law in 1987. The KMT established an ethnically exclusive regime, which similarly to the CCP's reign in mainland China, applied both soft and hard authoritarian modes of political control to discipline and punish its population.

Due to the inherent contradictions in its party ideology—in marked contrast to the CCP the KMT *did* aspire to democratic norms under Sun Yat-sen's "Three Principles of the People" (*San min zhuyi*)[6]—this high-handed approach to governing Taiwan did not last. In order to grow political roots in Taiwan the KMT had to allow limited electoral contestation in the form of local elections from the 1950s onwards. To rejuvenate its rank-and-file members in the Legislative Yuan—Taiwan's parliament—the KMT also started holding supplementary parliamentary elections in the late 1960s and early 1970s. Such elections created political opportunities for young and more liberal-leaning Taiwanese pro-establishment figures to join the KMT, contest elections and help reform the party-state from within. Unable to absorb all aspiring Taiwanese politicians into its ranks, the KMT unwittingly created conditions for a nascent political opposition, the *dangwai* movement, to take shape from the mid-1970s onwards. In the concluding part of this chapter I argue that Taiwan's democratisation should not be viewed as a top-down process initiated by Chiang Kai-shek's son and successor Chiang Ching-kuo's decision to lift Martial Law in 1987. I argue that rather than seeing Taiwan's lurch into democratisation merely as a transformation of the KMT, it was the result of a combination of internal and external factors as well as both top-down and bottom-up reform initiatives, which cumulatively led to the opening up of Taiwan's political system in the mid-1980s.

Taiwan's troubled return under Republic of China sovereignty

In 1943 Roosevelt, Chiang Kai-Shek and Churchill agreed in Cairo that Formosa—as Taiwan was referred to—should be returned under the sovereignty of the Republic of China (ROC).[7] When Japan surrendered in August 1945

Chiang Kai-Shek sent a highly controversial figure, governor-general Chen Yi, to administer the island's incorporation into the ROC. Chen Yi was suspicious of Taiwanese elites who had emerged during colonial rule, as he suspected them of having collaborated with the Japanese between 1895 and 1945.[8] Chen Yi consequently staffed his administration almost exclusively with mainland Chinese officials. Chen Yi turned a blind eye when KMT cadres and their cronies began asset stripping the island. Denny Roy describes how whole

> plants were dismantled and sent back to the mainland, along with pieces of the island's infrastructure that might be transplanted or sold as scrap: telephone wires, pipes, metal roofing, fire hydrants, railroad switches, and so on. Goods and items of nearly every kind could be sold at inflated prices in Shanghai's voracious markets. By November 1945 Chinese officials had commandeered all of Taipei's garbage trucks for hauling confiscated property to the docks, while uncollected garbage piled up in the streets throughout the city.[9]

To make matters worse, the Chen Yi administration "placed all major Taiwanese industries and enterprises under the supervision of state commissions, which were inevitably staffed by Mainlanders".[10] Dafydd Fell has argued that corruption "and inefficiency were key characteristics of the KMT regime. In contrast to the Japanese era, public order deteriorated seriously. This was exacerbated by an inefficient and corrupt police service and influx of mainland gangsters."[11] Local Taiwanese—referred to as "people from within the province" (*benshengren*) as opposed to mainlanders who were commonly referred to as "people from outside the province" (*waishengren*)—were taken aback by the lack of political representation, economic exclusion, dwindling agricultural output and price inflation during these early years of Chen Yi's mismanagement of the island's economy and society.

On 28 February 1947 a policeman hit a woman selling cigarettes without a licence. This enraged passers-by so much that violence broke out. When a bystander was killed by an officer this local conflict became known as the 2-28 incident, which morphed into an island-wide uprising which included between 50,000 and 60,000 people.[12] This put the Chen Yi administration under considerable pressure to accommodate Taiwanese demands for greater representation. Chen Yi, however, was unwilling to cave into demands for a more inclusive administration and economy, which would provide greater opportunities for local Taiwanese to participate in political and economic life. When faced with the demands for greater self-government in Taiwan he requested Chiang Kai-shek to reinforce his troops. Army units arrived in Keelong (*Jilong*) in the north and Kaohsiung (*Gaoxiong*) in the south in March 1947 and immediately "reasserted the government's control by indiscriminately shooting anyone on the streets. Ch'en declared martial law throughout the island and announced that the [February 28 Incident Settlement] committee was illegal, stating that it had become part of a revolt".[13] Philipps has pointed out that "most islanders never sought a pitched battle with mainland forces because their goals were essentially reformist, not revolutionary"[14] and that nevertheless "the state targeted prominent Taiwanese for arrest or execution".[15] Ketty Chen describes the viciousness of KMT suppression: "Not only did the KMT conduct public executions, many of the arrests and subsequent killings were done in the middle of the night or on the countryside. The disappearances of family members or neighbors further reinforced the fear of the Taiwanese and warned against attempts to revolt against the sovereign."[16] In the aftermath of the 2-28 incident more than 28,000 islanders were killed.[17] During martial law, which lasted from 1947 until 1987, more than 140,000 individuals were tried in military courts, leading to 3,000 to 8,000 executions.[18]

KMT rule in Taiwan after 1945: a neocolonial regime?

Keith Maguire has argued that while "the KMT ran the island as a one party state, the mainlander elite excluded the Taiwanese majority from the decision-making process".[19] When the KMT lost the civil war and Chiang Kai-shek, together with 2 million refugees from mainland China, fled to Taiwan in 1949, the relationship between the mainlander-dominated KMT and the local Taiwanese population had already hit rock bottom.[20] A colloquial saying in Taiwan at the time compared the transition from the Japanese to the KMT: "the dog left, and the pig took over".[21] For the next 40 years, a minority of outsiders with family roots on the mainland thus ruled over a majority of islanders. Simon Long has argued that "most estimates in the late 1980s assumed that 'mainlanders' made up 10–15 per cent of the population of about 20 million".[22] Such continuous rule by outsiders has led to accusations that the KMT party-state on Taiwan can be likened to a quasi-colonial regime. A particularly outspoken critic has been Bruce Jacobs. Based on the definition that "a colonial regime is rule by outsiders for the benefit of the outsiders"[23] he has argued

> that from the establishment of the Dutch colony in 1624 until the death of Chiang Ching-kuo in 1988, Taiwan was ruled by six colonial regimes: (1) the Dutch (1624–1662); (2) the Spanish (1626–1642), who ruled in north Taiwan simultaneously with the Dutch; (3) the Cheng family (1662–1683); (4) the Manchu Qing empire (1683–1895); (5) the Japanese (1895–1945); and (6) the authoritarian Chinese Nationalist regime (1945–1988).[24]

Ketty Chen has echoed Jacob's assessment by arguing that the KMT regime adopted "strategies of infiltration, reorganization and their own variant of colonization of Taiwan".[25] Leo Ching has emphasised that while "considering itself to be the legitimate government of China, and with American assistance, the Nationalist embarked on a neocolonial policy toward the very people they claimed as their citizenry".[26] Similarly, Taiwanese historian Li Yung-chih has described KMT rule on Taiwan since 1945 a case of "political colonialism".[27]

Taiwanese sociologist Michael Hsiao, on the other hand, has dismissed the idea that Taiwan had to endure a KMT variant of colonialism throughout the 20th century. Instead, he has described Taiwan's political trajectory since the Japanese handover as "decolonization [which] did not bring about the independence of Taiwan. It rather became a 'localization'."[28] Steven Phillips has similarly called this transition from Japanese colonial rule to KMT control over Taiwan "a troubled decolonization with an abortive reintegration into China".[29] On balance I contend that in many ways KMT rule after 1945 resembled Japanese colonial rule. Whereas the Japanese military crushed local resistance between 1895 and 1915, the KMT unleashed its White Terror from 1947 until 1987. While an imperialistic Japan considered Taiwan a stepping stone for military expansion into South-East Asia, for a very long time Chiang Kai-shek considered Taiwan merely a base for the military recovery of the Chinese mainland. Whereas the Japanese discriminated against the colonised Taiwanese (*hontojin*), the KMT politically and economically excluded the majority Taiwanese (*benshengren*). Highly draconian laws were meant to discipline the population. Under the Japanese the notorious "Bandit Punishment Ordinance" meted out collective punishment to Taiwanese breaking the colonial laws and regulations. The KMT, on the other hand, used the "Temporary Provisions" under martial law to limit citizens' rights. Both essentially colonial regimes also used language assimilation, and in the case of the KMT, a variant of Capital C Confucianism to indoctrinate the Taiwanese. Last but not least, in both cases Taiwanese elites were strategically co-opted to protect the authority of the highly exclusive and exploitative political regimes.[30]

Language and cultural policies

The KMT's neocolonial approach to its subjects is particularly evident when reviewing the party-state's language and cultural policies of the 1950s. Ann Heylen has pointed out that towards the final years of Japanese colonial rule in Taiwan, "Japanese was largely spoken up through all levels of the social hierarchy; Taiwanese was spoken down the social hierarchy among equals, friends and family".[31] According to Heylen,

> KMT nationalist language policy embarked on an island-wide movement for the promotion of Mandarin only combining the objectives of functional and cultural literacy together (see Cheng, 1994; Wilson, 1970). Unlike the Japanese authorities, the KMT could wrap its language ideology in the shared commonality of Chinese culture and heritage.

Cultural and linguistic markers were presented as the same, and the Taiwanese had little to argue against. There was no point in denying that they did not originate from China, nor that the Chinese-character system was not part of their cultural heritage. Yet, Taiwan's decolonisation process concurred with the implementation of martial law (1947–87) and an official ban, with sanctions of imprisonment for any utterances and expressions that referred to taking pride in the collective Taiwanese memory, including its history, language and cultural practices (i.e. Cohen, 1989; Edmondson, 2002; Wachman, 1994).[32]

The imposition of Mandarin Chinese as the new lingua franca and the suppression of the use of Japanese and Taiwanese (*minanhua*) from 1947 onwards led to widespread resentment of the KMT regime among local Taiwanese. The exclusive use of Mandarin Chinese as Taiwan's official language, however, also served another purpose. According to the leading Taiwan independence advocate and DPP candidate during the first free and fair presidential elections in 1996, Peng Ming-min, the KMT language and cultural policies were designed in a way to deliberately confuse the islanders' "political, ethnic and cultural identity".[33] Peng claims that the KMT politicised ethnicity deliberately in order to "make Taiwanese 'feel that it is a betrayal to our ancestors to be split off from China'".[34] The KMT, however, did not limit its attempts to socially re-engineer the Taiwanese population to the ideational realm. In parallel, land reforms were implemented which would considerably alter the social stratification and political loyalties of Taiwanese society.

Land reform

Simon Long has argued that ruefully "surveying their history on the mainland, the KMT on Taiwan would come to the conclusion that their failure to institute a proper land reform had been a prime cause of their loss of power".[35] One of the reasons the KMT had failed to implement land reforms on the mainland had been the influence of landowning elites in its rank and file.[36] Comparing and contrasting land reform in Taiwan with the collectivisation of land in the mainland during the 1950s Walker has argued that the KMT's "land-to-the-tiller" programme supposedly "was peaceful and orderly".[37] Ketty Chan, on the other hand, has pointed out that the "land reform policy implemented by the KMT has proven to be extremely fruitful for the Party's quest for control. By taking the land away from the Taiwanese land owners, the Party inadvertently dismantled influences the land owners had on the local communities, peasants and farmers."[38] Central to land reform was the decision to rewrite "the deeds to the land. The KMT government then redistributed most of the land amongst the Mainland Chinese, Taiwanese farmers and landowners."[39] While the KMT did not collectivise land as the CCP did in the mainland in the 1950s, it "made profits by charging the tenants rent and then from the selling of the land; and secondly, the land reform also meant the relocation of the 2 million Chinese populations to virtually all areas in Taiwan".[40] This furthered the KMT's grip over an essentially agrarian Taiwanese society and secured the political loyalty of farmers who benefited from the KMT's land reform. Dickson points out that "the elimination of the gentry also created a political vacuum which was immediately filled by local factions, who were quickly coopted into the KMT".[41]

Similarities between the KMT and CCP

Richard McGregor, author of the landmark book on the CCP, *The Party: The Secret World of China's Communist Rulers*, has highlighted the similarities between the KMT and the CCP. In McGregor's words like

> the Party in China, the KMT had been established on Leninist lines. It had its own organizational department for doling out jobs in the state sector. The KMT directly owned some of the largest businesses in the country when it governed Taiwan, rather than just controlling them behind the scenes like the Party in China. The KMT also directly controlled the armed forces.[42]

Just like the CCP, the KMT regime consisted of a trinity of party, government and military (*dang zheng jun*). Following the defeat in the civil war Chiang Kai-shek purposefully copied the organisational structure of the CCP. He instructed party members to learn from the CCP's rectification campaign during the Yenan period, adopted the practice of criticism and self-criticism meetings, embraced the mass line approach and endorsed democratic centralism.[43] In order to distinguish itself from the Leninist CCP party-state, the KMT claimed to be a "revolutionary-democratic party".[44] In his seminal study *The Great Transition: Political and Social Change in the Republic of China*, former minister of foreign affairs (2000–2) Hung Mao-Tien rather charitably described the KMT party-state as a "modernizing authoritarian regime with strong characteristics of a one-party pluralistic system in transition toward a dominant-party system".[45] While Tien has argued that the KMT only used a "minimum use of coercion to achieve consensus",[46] I argue in the following that just like the CCP's rule in mainland China, the KMT's rule in Taiwan included both soft and hard authoritarian approaches. Both carrots and sticks were used to discipline and punish its population.

Corporatism and co-optation

Robert P. Weller has described

> Taiwan's system up to the democratic reforms of the late 1980s as corporatist, where interest groups are created by the state (or at least licensed

by it) as the sole representative for their sector (farmers, workers, youth, and so on). In return for their monopoly, these groups are expected to act in concert with the state. In Taiwan's authoritarian version of this system before martial law was lifted the government maintained strong control over officials of these organizations, who thus acted more as agents of the state than lobbyists for their constituents.[47]

Similarly to the CCP's approach of "rule by bribary"—described in detail in Chapter 5—to be incorporated into the KMT party-state enabled Taiwanese to access resources which otherwise would be out of reach.

Michael Hsiao has stressed that as a consequence of KMT corporatism, no "recognition was granted to any indigenous social forces. Taiwanese civil society fell under the complete control of the Mainlander-dominated central state apparatus."[48] Corporatist control also extended to the religious sphere and affected the lives of Daoist, Buddhist, Confucian and Catholic believers. Cheng-tian Kuo has specified that under "corporatist law, only one national umbrella religious organisation was allowed to exist for each religion to represent the interests of its clergy and believers".[49] A remarkable exception were the wide range of protestant Christian denominations. Kuo has mused that "probably due to the decentralized nature of Protestantism and the foreign connections of most Taiwanese denominations ... [the] KMT government probably did not want to upset these Western Christian denominations, whose missionaries were powerful lobbying groups in the United States, by imposing a state-controlled umbrella organization on them".[50]

In addition to party-state corporatism the KMT also used the strategy of co-optation to pacify Taiwan's society. On the grassroots level, the KMT institutionalised the role of neighbourhood wardens (*lizhang*), which were provided with office space and financial resources. Benjamin Read explains that the "network of wardens and their chosen block captains (*linzhang*) was ... intended to mobilize and incorporate the local citizenry under the externally imposed rule of Chiang Kai-shek's Nationalist Party".[51] Cheng Tun-Jen has furthermore pointed out that by "institutionalizing subnational elections (the provincial assembly, and elections for county and township executives and councils) in the early 1950s, the KMT recruited and manipulated local elites on its own terms".[52] Local factions, on the other hand, expected "material goods and prestige"[53] in return for supporting the party-state during local elections. They ranged from local monopolies in the financial and transport sectors, loans, government procurement of local companies' services, preferential treatment regarding land-use rights as well as tacit approval of illegal activities of local factions, e.g. turning a blind eye to casinos and brothels.[54] Fell has highlighted that a "major component of local-level corruption has been the involvement of gangsters in politics, a phenomenon known as 'black gold'".[55]

In Chapter 2 I described the deterioration of the Chinese party-state from a developmental to a predatory state. In Chapter 5 I described the emergence of alliances between corrupt local governments with organised crime and the formation of local mafia states in the PRC since the early 1990s. In marked contrast this deliberate strategy of the KMT to manipulate grassroots-level politics through local mafia was a defining feature of the KMT party-state from the early 1950s onwards. Local elections thus were not intended to lead to bottom-up democratisation of the political regime. Cheng Tun-Jen and Gang Lin make the case that the "hypothetical red line was that political opposition would not be tolerated if via electoral competition it captures key executive offices with high national status".[56] Cheng and Chou have furthermore argued that at "least three unwritten rules prevented faction politics from subverting the authority of the KMT regime in postwar Taiwan".[57] Local factions were not supposed to engage in central politics; national-level factions were not supposed to merge; and interfactional competition was limited to the Legislative Yuan, Taiwan's parliament.[58]

An unexpected political opening occurred in the early 1970s, when the KMT started to co-opt young, aspirational Taiwanese by providing scholarships to study in the United States and made them "promises of elected office".[59] According to Dickson there were two underlying motivations, one, to improve the reputation of the KMT as an outsider regime, and two, to "improve the effectiveness of the ruling party by attracting young people of talent rather than simply those with political connections".[60] This coincided with a party-ideological shift from retaking "the mainland in favor of the social and economic development of Taiwan to reinforce the legitimacy of its rule".[61] To its credit, the KMT had been relatively successful in developing Taiwan's economy. Thomas Gold has chronicled its economic achievements: In the three decades between 1952 and 1982, Taiwan's gross national product averaged 8.7 percent; its economy underwent massive structural changes from agriculture to industry; Taiwan's export-oriented industries led to major trade surpluses; inflation was effectively controlled; Taiwan accumulated major foreign currency reserves; and the party-state accumulated cumulative budget surpluses between the 1960s and early 1980s.[62] Such rapid economic modernisation also had a knock-on effect on social change. According to Gold the modernising party-state lowered the island's gini co-efficient; created manufacturing jobs; achieved high levels of literacy; and improved living standards of Taiwanese citizens in terms of low infant mortality and increasing life expectancy.[63] Clough has argued that a combination of skilful economic planning by government officials coupled with the "industriousness of its people: workers, farmers and businessmen" led to continued economic growth.[64]

Gunter Schubert has argued that under KMT rule a "new" middle class emerged, which was a direct result and beneficiary of one-party rule. State-sector officials and employees were among the KMT's most loyal supporters.

Old party officials and former military personnel also benefited from the KMT's patronage. In addition, from the early 1970s onwards the KMT attracted liberal-minded professionals and entrepreneurs.[65] Given the KMT's proven ability to engineer Taiwan's economy and society it should not come to anyone's surprise that young Taiwanese would be willing to join the party. The unintended consequence of co-opting a new generation of Taiwanese pro-establishment figures into the KMT apparatus, however, was that this enabled the latter to use trojan horse reform strategies to gradually reform and open up the KMT party-state. Cheng Tun-Jen has argued that the "large number of political activists and the limited scope of political reform led in the end to the formation of a counterelite that challenged the foundations of the KMT regime".[66] This view is supported by Bruce Jacobs finding that "Chiang Ching-kuo had 'liberal' or reformist elements in his leadership. Beginning in 1972, when he became premier and the clear successor to his father, Chiang pushed hard for more Taiwanese as well as for younger, more educated persons among his top leadership."[67] The infusion of young and more open-minded Taiwanese politicians into the mainlander-dominated KMT party apparatus should prove to be of crucial importance during the early to mid-1980s, when the KMT started entering a dialogue with the *dangwai* movement.

Surveillance and the KMT's secret police

The KMT's approach to governing Taiwan during the martial law era, however, was anything but light touch. When the carrots of corporatism and co-optation did not work, the regime had a wide range of proverbial sticks at its disposal. According to Cao Liqun, "Chiang Kai-shek saw the police as an extension of the military ... The main goal of the police was to guard the GMD's regime and to be ready to recover mainland at the earliest possible time."[68] During the White Terror, the KMT's secret police under the Taiwan Garrison Command (*Taiwan jingbei zongsilingbu*)—a domestic military/security organ tasked with enforcing martial law—disappeared political opposition figures who were considered a threat to the regime. Many political prisoners ended up being incarcerated on Green Island, which was located about 33 kilometres off Taiwan's east coast. Prominent inmates include the writer Bo Yang and former dangwai activist and DPP politician Shih Ming-teh. Ketty Chen recounts that on "the Green Island prison, the political prisoners were routinely being subjected to psychological therapies, re-education, and forced composition of confessional letters".[69] She argues that "mysterious disappearances of citizens continued to generate the fear necessary to keep the population in line to prevent uprisings against the regime"[70] and served the goal of turning "the island of Taiwan into the Party's Panopticon, where the individuals living on the island felt the gawking eye of the big brother and the surveillance of his neighbors".[71]

Such accounts for a highly intrusive surveillance of Taiwan's society have not gone unchallenged. In her seminal book *Dictators and Their Secret Police* Sheena Chestnut Greitens found that

> Chiang believed that his legitimacy to power was threatened by popular protest. He designed his coercive, policing institution accordingly (centralized and more inclusive), thus allowing state violence to gradually decrease as the centralized coercive institutions had better communication within. In Greitens' theory, the coercive institution that Chiang had set out to repress popular protests, paradoxically, turned out to "contribute" to the gradual democratization of Taiwan, and the curtailment of Kuomintang political power.[72]

She highlights that following the rather extreme violence of the early years of the White Terror, both the number of individuals sentenced for political crimes and the number of executions in Taiwan dropped dramatically since the early 1960s.[73]

International environment in the 1970s and 1980s

Whereas the KMT party-state succeeded in suppressing political dissent and moulding Taiwan's economy and society in its image in the 1950s and 1960s, it was less successful on the international front. The 1970s ushered in a decade of highly consequential diplomatic set-backs. The KMT had underestimated public anger at its hapless posture during the sovereignty conflict over the Senkako (*diaoyu*) islands, which were claimed by Japan, the ROC on Taiwan as well as the PRC. When the PRC was given United Nations membership in 1971 Chiang Kai-shek decided to leave the United Nations instead of lobbying for dual-seat representation. In 1972, the United States began its rapprochement with the PRC. In the same year Japan recognised the PRC and established diplomatic relations.[74] At the end of the decade, the United States also established diplomatic relations with the PRC and terminated the 1954 Mutual Defence Agreement with the ROC.[75] Congress cushioned this blow to Taiwan by passing the Taiwan Relations Act on 10 April 1979.

These set-backs mattered, since the KMT regime was technically still at war with the PRC. Between 1954 and 1958 military conflict erupted in the Taiwan Straits when the PLA bombed Quemoy (*Jinmen*) off the Fujian coast. Chiang Kai-shek retaliated in kind by bombarding the mainland.[76] The crisis only ended when the United States declared its strategic interest in protecting the ROC and subsequently brokered a settlement between PRC and ROC.[77] Relying on United States military assistance, however, was a double-edged sword. As Chiang Kai-shek had experienced during the civil war on the mainland, there was no guarantee that such geopolitical alliances would necessarily last. This vulnerability of the KMT regime was not lost on critics of one-party rule. The declining international standing of the ROC, which by the end of the 1970s could no longer claim to represent the entirety of mainland China and Taiwan, meant that the KMT had rapidly lost prestige, both at home and abroad. Among critics of the KMT party-state "this evoked fears of a sellout of Taiwan ... [where] the KMT could turn to the Chinese Communist Party ... in a premature bid for unification".[78]

Taiwan's democratisation as a means to preserve hegemonic KMT rule?

The KMT politically survived the difficult decade of the 1970s, but not without ceding ground both ideologically and organisationally. The KMT's evolution in the early 1980s was highly contradictory. On the one hand it imprisoned a large group of militant *dangwai* opposition politicians following a human rights rally in Kaohsiung (*Gaoxiong*) in 1979. The mother and twin daughters of one of the imprisoned *dangwai* politicians, Lin Yi-hsiung, were stabbed to death despite being under constant police surveillance at the time. The KMT party-state also ordered one of Taiwan's triads, the United Bamboo Gang (*zhulianbang*), to assassinate Chiang Ching-kuo critic Henry Liu (*Chiang Nan*), a naturalised American citizen of Taiwan descent in the United States in 1984. These developments tarnished the ROC's reputation of supposedly representing a "free China" as opposed to the PRC, which in the early 1980s was widely perceived to be opening up after the horrors of the Cultural Revolution.

Yet on the other hand, it is widely being acknowledged that the KMT did transform itself.[79] As a consequence of Chiang Ching-kuo's Taiwanisation approach, some of the early recruits swiftly rose to the party ranks. Maguire has rightly pointed out that initially, "the majority of the Taiwanese who were recruited to the KMT held positions of little real power but in due course they rose through the ranks and held positions of increasing power".[80] The political career of Lee Teng-hui is a case in point. He first became minister without portfolio in the 1970s, was appointed mayor of Taipei in 1978, and became governor of the now defunct Province of Taiwan in 1981. In 1984 Chiang Ching-kuo nominated him as vice-premier. In 1996, Lee became the first democratically elected president. Jacques deLisle has argued that the KMT's transformation in the 1980s was the result of international pressures and domestic pushback. DeLisle has specified that

> the roots of these external factors in spurring Taiwanese democratization date back to the President Chiang Ching-kuo's apprehension that US derecognition of his government mean that his regime would have to open the door wider to democratic reforms. During the 1980s, particularly in the wake of the Kaoshiung and Henry Liu incidents, Washington increased pressure on Chiang to democratize. US initiatives were

dovetailed with developments in Taiwan, including the rise of the dang-wai opposition, which began largely as a prodemocracy and government reform movement and had begun to enjoy limited success in the highly constrained elections that the KMT regime had begun to permit.[81]

This view is supported by Nathan and Ho who argue that Chiang Ching-kuo's "subsequent decision to resume and accelerate political reform may be interpreted as an attempt to strengthen the KMT's ability to survive in Taiwan after derecognition".[82] This development underscores that during liberalisation and democratisation processes, the "orientations to action" among members of the pro-establishment camp can and do change. Whereas in the early 1950s becoming part of the KMT nomenclature required aspiring members to simply accept Chiang Kai-shek's unchecked power, under the rule of his far more open-minded son and successor Chiang Ching-kuo pro-establishment KMT politicians had far greater leeway to reform the party's ideology and approach to governance. Such findings are highly relevant for our understanding of the potential for future political reform in the PRC, as it underscores that under certain conditions the pro-establishment camp can become a strategic ally of democracy movements, as discussed in greater detail in Chapter 3.

Such findings also raise questions about the nature of Taiwan's democratisation process. Leng Tze-Kang has argued that "Taiwan's democratization under Chiang Ching-kuo was a top-down transition or 'transformation' type of political change, according to Samuel Huntington's classification".[83] Croissant and Merkel have similarly suggested that Taiwan should be considered a case of a political transformation orchestrated and led by the KMT regime.[84] Copper has questioned narratives of seeing Taiwan's democratisation merely as a metamorphosis of the KMT: "Whether it was 'democracy from the bottom up', as some observers said, is difficult to judge; it came from both the bottom and the top".[85] Lo Shiu Hing has furthermore pointed out that for "the ruling class, democratization serves as a legitimizing tool to prolong its political dominance".[86] With the benefit of hindsight it becomes clear that Chiang's decision to Taiwanise the KMT in the early 1970s extended the life span of the KMT for another 45 years.

Ethnic conflict and the question of national identity

Cheng Tun-jen and Tien Hung-mao have emphasised that the "democracy movement in Taiwan has been, one way or another, entangled with the issue of sub-ethnic divisions and national identity".[87] In the democratisation literature, the politicisation of ethnicity is generally being frowned upon. Diamond and Plattner have suggested that countries "with extreme ethnic complexity experience high levels of deadly political violence, which severely strains the fabric of their democratic orders"[88] and that once "deep ethnic divisions are mobilized into electoral and party politics … they tend to produce suspicion rather than trust, acrimony rather than civility, polarization rather than accommodation and victimization rather than toleration".[89]

In the case of Taiwan it should come to nobody's surprise that the opposition used "available material in the domestic debate to recall darker chapters in the history of the ruling KMT".[90] From an oppositional view, the KMT's decade-long pretence that it "was still the government on the mainland"[91] was seen as "a cynical attempt by a small minority to run the island for their own benefit".[92] Maguire has observed that "the DPP's style of campaigning has often tended to focus on Taiwan pre-1987 rather than where Taiwan is going in the 21st century".[93] In this book I argue that the *dangwai* movement in the 1970s and the DPP after its establishment in 1986 had every right to highlight the historical errors of the KMT. In Chapter 4 I outlined Saul Alinsky's TOPC. Alinsky argued that *particular ends* justify *particular means*.

Murray Rubinstein has put the tendency to weaponise historical grievances in the opposition's struggle against a highly corporatist KMT party-state in perspective:

> Taiwanization and the acceptance of Taiwan as home as well as the obvious economic growth that had created a prosperous society for all its citizens—muddied the differences and reduced the tension between mainlander and Taiwanese, but only to a degree. The ethnic identity card was too valuable for many to give it up. Many politicians in the Democratic Progressive Party … who had bitter memories in their conflicts with the state felt there was much to lose by forgiving and forgetting … Thus even as the real differences were fading, and as the government was opening the system up and allowing more Taiwanese and Hakka dialects to be heard and was allowing Taiwanese culture and history to be studied and to be taught, the divisions between ethnic groups seemed to remain and become the subtext of sometimes poisonous public discourse.[94]

Instead of engaging in means-ends moralising, academics interested in the topic of Taiwan's democratisation should acknowledge the very real hardships and extreme suffering which members of the democracy movement had to endure at the hands of the KMT's secret police.

The KMT's cruel treatment of Taiwanese elites arguably laid the foundation for the island's independence movement. As I have argued before, the resulting national identity conflict is one that has been fought between Chinese and Taiwanese nationalists since the incorporatisation of Taiwan into the ROC after 1945. It should be seen as a political conflict "couched in rhetoric that stresses constructed ethnic differences among two social groups, the waishengren and benshengren. This conflict has evolved around the problems of (a) the authoritative allocation of resources and (b) by whom and how the Taiwanese people should be represented."[95] I will discuss the simmering ethnic conflict between *waishengren* and *benshengren* by the Taiwanese democracy movement and the strategic exploitation by Hong Kong independence advocates of the national identity crisis in greater detail in Chapter 8.

In this chapter I provided an overview of the rise and demise of the KMT party-state in Taiwan from 1945 until 2016. From the early 1950s until the mid-1980s the KMT's essentially neocolonial approach to governance relied on hard and soft authoritarian means. Liberalisation and democratisation occurred from the 1970s onwards. In hindsight we can see that Chiang Ching-kuo's strategy of Taiwanisation expanded the life span of the KMT party-state for another 45 years until it was effectively stripped of its party assets in 2016. My critique of authoritarian KMT one-party rule in Taiwan forms the backdrop for the episodes 5 to 8 in Chapter 8. I will illuminate the trajectory of Taiwan's democracy movement in greater detail, including how the oppositional *dangwai* movement evolved from the mid-1970s and culminated in the establishment of Taiwan's DPP in 1986; how increasingly free and fair elections and the two-party competition between the DPP and KMT between 1987 and 2000 accelerated Taiwan's liberalisation and democratisation; I will dissect the controversies surrounding Chen Shui-bian presidency (DPP) from 2000 to 2008; and critically assess the equally contentious Ma Ying-jeou presidency (KMT) from 2008 to 2016.

Notes

1 *Taipei Times* (2014), KMT Is Again "World's Richest Party". Available online: www.taipeitimes.com/News/taiwan/archives/2014/07/24/2003595820 (accessed 5 November 2018).
2 *Economist* (2016), From Riches to Rags: Taiwan's Kuomintang Party Is Broke and Adrift. Available online: www.economist.com/asia/2016/12/15/taiwans-kuomintang-party-is-broke-and-adrift (accessed 5 November 2018).
3 Ibid.
4 Fulda, Andreas (2002), Reevaluating the Taiwanese Democracy Movement: A Comparative Analysis of Opposition Organizations under Japanese and KMT Rule, *Critical Asian Studies*, 34(3), 365–9.
5 Cheng, Tun-Jen (2006), Strategizing Party Adaptation: The Case of the Kuomintang, *Party Politics*, 12(3), 368–9.
6 Wu, Jaushieh Joseph (1995), *Taiwan's Democratization: Forces Behind the New Momentum*, Oxford University Press, Oxford, 11.
7 Wilson Centre (2018), November 26, 1943 The Cairo Declaration; Available online: https://digitalarchive.wilsoncenter.org/document/122101.pdf?v=d41d8cd98f00b204e9800998ecf8427e (accessed 5 November 2018).
8 Phillips, Steven (1999), Between Assimilation and Independence: Taiwanese Political Aspirations under Nationalist Chinese Rule, 1945–1948, in: Murray A. Rubinstein (Ed.), *Taiwan: A New History*, M.E. Sharpe, Armonk, NY, 278.
9 Roy, Denny (2003), *Taiwan: A Political History*, Cornell University Press, Ithaca, NY, 61–2.
10 Ibid., 64.
11 Fell, Dafydd (2012), *Government and Politics in Taiwan*, Routledge, Oxon, 13–14.
12 Maguire, Keith (1998), *The Rise of Modern Taiwan*, Ashgate, Farnham, 104.

13 Phillips, Steven (1999), Between Assimilation and Independence: Taiwanese Political Aspirations under Nationalist Chinese Rule, 1945–1948, in: Murray A. Rubinstein (Ed.), *Taiwan: A New History*, M.E. Sharpe, Armonk, NY, 295.
14 Ibid.
15 Ibid.
16 Chen, Ketty (2008), Disciplining Taiwan: The Kuomintang's Methods of Control during the White Terror Era (1947–1987), *Taiwan International Studies Quarterly*, 4(4), 192.
17 SCMP (2017), 70 Years after Taiwan's "White Terror", Relatives of Victims Still Seeking Justice. Available online: www.scmp.com/news/china/policies-politics/a rticle/2074156/70-years-after-taiwans-white-terror-relatives-victims (accessed 6 November 2018).
18 Ibid.
19 Maguire, Keith (1998), *The Rise of Modern Taiwan*, Ashgate, Farnham, 101.
20 Rigger, Shelley (1999), *Politics in Taiwan: Voting for Democracy*, Routledge, London, 56.
21 Kosack, Stephen (2012), *The Education of Nations: How the Political Organization of the Poor, Not Democracy, Led Government to Invest in Mass Education*, Oxford University Press, Oxford, 100.
22 Long, Simon (1991), *Taiwan: China's Last Frontier*, Macmillan, Houndmills, 62.
23 Jacobs, Bruce (2014), Taiwan's Colonial Experiences and the Development of Ethnic
    Identities: Some Hypotheses, *Taiwan in Comparative Perspective*, 5(July), 48.
24 Ibid.
25 Chen, Ketty (2008), Disciplining Taiwan: The Kuomintang's Methods of Control during the White Terror Era (1947–1987), *Taiwan International Studies Quarterly*, 4(4), 198.
26 Ching, Leo (2001), *Becoming "Japanese"*, University of California Press, Berkeley, CA, 37.
27 *Taipei Times* (1999), Review. Available online: www.taipeitimes.com/News/front/a rchives/1999/12/31/0000017803/2 (accessed 5 November 2018).
28 Ibid.
29 Phillips, Steven (1999), Between Assimilation and Independence: Taiwanese Political Aspirations under Nationalist Chinese Rule, 1945–1948, in: Murray A. Rubinstein (Ed.), *Taiwan: A New History*, M.E. Sharpe, Armonk, NY, 276.
30 Fulda, Andreas (2002), Reevaluating the Taiwanese Democracy Movement: A Comparative Analysis of Opposition Organizations under Japanese and KMT Rule, *Critical Asian Studies*, 34(3), 357–94.
31 Heylen, Ann (2005), The Legacy of Literacy Practices in Colonial Taiwan: Japanese–Taiwanese– Chinese: Language Interaction and Identity Formation, *Journal of Multilingual and Multicultural Development*, 26(6), 505.
32 Ibid., 506–7.
33 Wachman, Alan (1994), *Taiwan: National Identity and Democratization*, M.E. Sharpe, New York, 85.
34 Rigger, Shelley (1999), Competing Conceptions of Taiwan's Identity: The Irresolvable Conflict in Cross-Strait Relations, in: Suisheng Zhao (Ed.), *Across the Taiwan Strait: Mainland China, Taiwan and the 1995–1996 Crisis*, Routledge, London, 233.
35 Long, Simon (1991), *Taiwan: China's Last Frontier*, Macmillan, Houndmills, 35.
36 Chen, Han-Seng (1948), Agrarian Reform in China, *Far Eastern Survey*, 17(4, 25 February), 42.
37 Walker, Richard (1959), Taiwan's Development as Free China, *Annals of the American Academy of Political and Social Science*, 321(January), 129.
38 Chen, Ketty (2008), Disciplining Taiwan: The Kuomintang's Methods of Control during the White Terror Era (1947–1987), *Taiwan International Studies Quarterly*, 4(4), 200.

39 Ibid., 199.
40 Chen, Ketty (2008), Disciplining Taiwan: The Kuomintang's Methods of Control during the White Terror Era (1947–1987), *Taiwan International Studies Quarterly*, 4(4), 199.
41 Dickson, Bruce (1997), *Democratization in China and Taiwan: The Adaptability of Leninist Parties*, Oxford University Press, Oxford, 45.
42 McGregor, Richard (2011), *The Party. The Secret World of China's Communist Rulers*, Penguin, London, 123.
43 Dickson, Bruce (1997), *Democratization in China and Taiwan: The Adaptability of Leninist Parties*, Oxford University Press, Oxford, 45–6.
44 Ibid., 51–2.
45 Tien, Hung-mao (1989), *The Great Transition: Political and Social Change in the Republic of China*, SMC Publishing, Taipei, 12–13.
46 Ibid., 5.
47 Weller, Robert (1999), *Alternate Civilities: Democracy and Culture in China and Taiwan*, Westview: Oxford, 45.
48 Hsiao, Michael (1990), Emerging Social Movements and the Rise of a Demanding Civil Society in Taiwan, *Australian Journal of Chinese Affairs*, 24(July), 164.
49 Kuo, Cheng-tian (2008), *Religion and Democracy in Taiwan*, State University of New York Press, New York, 10.
50 Ibid.
51 Read, Benjamin (2012), *Roots of the State: Neighbourhood Organization and Social Networks in Beijing and Taipei*, Stanford University Press, Stanford, CA, 6.
52 Cheng, Tun-Jen (2006), Strategizing Party Adaptation: The Case of the Kuomintang, *Party Politics*, 12(3), 370.
53 Rigger, Shelley (1999), *Politics in Taiwan: Voting for Democracy*, Routledge, London, 85.
54 Fell, Dafydd (2012), Government and Politics in Taiwan, Routledge, Oxon, 116.
55 Fell, Dafydd (2005), Political and Media Liberalization and Political Corruption in Taiwan, *China Quarterly*, 184, 879.
56 Cheng, Tun-jen and Lin, Gang (2008), Competitive Elections, in: Bruce Gilley and Larry Diamond (Eds), *Political Change in China: Comparisons with Taiwan*, Lynne Rienner, Boulder, CO, 165.
57 Cheng, Tun-jen and Chou, T.C. (2000), Informal Politics in Taiwan, in: Dittmer, Lowell, Fukui, Haruhiro and Lee, Peter N.S. (Eds), *Informal Politics in East Asia*, Cambridge University Press, Cambridge, 48.
58 Ibid.
59 Dickson, Bruce (2000), Cooptation and Corporatism in China: The Logic of Party Adaptation, *Political Science Quarterly*, 115(4, Winter), 529.
60 Ibid.
61 Dickson, Bruce (1997), *Democratization in China and Taiwan: The Adaptability of Leninist Parties*, Oxford University Press, Oxford.
62 Gold, Thomas (1986), *State and Society in the Taiwan Miracle*, M.E. Sharpe, New York, 4–5.
63 Ibid., 5.
64 Clough, Ralph (1996), The Enduring Influence of the Republic of China on Taiwan Today, *China Quarterly*, 148(December), 1063.
65 Schubert, Gunter (1994), *Taiwan. Die demokratische Alternative. Demokratisierung in einem ostasiatischen Schwellenland (1986–1993)*, Mitteilungen des Instituts für Asienkunde, 316–20. In Chapter 8 I will explain how this new middle class differed from the traditional middle class, which supported the Taiwanese opposition movement.
66 Cheng, Tun-Jen (1989), Democratizing the Quasi-Leninist Regime in Taiwan, *World Politics*, 41(4, July), 484.
67 Jacobs, Bruce (2012), *Democratizing Taiwan*, Brill, Leiden, 11.

68 Cao, Liqun, Huang, Lanying and Sun, Ivan Y. (2014), *Policing in Taiwan: From Authoritarianism to Democracy*, Routledge, London, 140.
69 Chen, Ketty (2008), Disciplining Taiwan: The Kuomintang's Methods of Control during the White Terror Era (1947–1987), *Taiwan International Studies Quarterly*, 4(4), 195.
70 Ibid., 193.
71 Ibid., 196.
72 Wu, Timmy (2017), Dictatorship and Secret Police in Taiwan and the Philippines. Available online: http://bwog.com/2017/04/27/dictatorship-and-secret-police-in-ta iwan-and-the-philippines/ (accessed 8 November 2018).
73 Greitens, Sheena Chestnut (2016), *Dictators and Their Secret Police: Coercive Institutions and State Violence*, Cambridge University Press, Cambridge, 181.
74 Schubert, Gunter (1994), *Taiwan. Die demokratische Alternative. Demokratisierung in einem ostasiatischen Schwellenland (1986–1993)*, Mitteilungen des Instituts für Asienkunde, 319.
75 Lee, Bernice (1999), *The Security Implications of the New Taiwan*, Oxford University Press, Oxford, 19.
76 Ibid., 16–17.
77 Ibid., 18.
78 Fulda, Andreas (2002), Reevaluating the Taiwanese Democracy Movement: A Comparative Analysis of Opposition Organizations under Japanese and KMT Rule, *Critical Asian Studies*, 34(3), 379.
79 Maguire, Keith (1998), *The Rise of Modern Taiwan*, Ashgate, Farnham, 112.
80 Ibid.
81 DeLisle, Jacques (2008), International Pressures and Domestic Pushback, in: Bruce Gilley and Larry Diamond (Eds), *Political Change in China: Comparisons with Taiwan*, Lynne Rienner, Boulder, CO, 191.
82 Nathan, Andrew and Ho, Helena (1993), Chiang Ching-kuo's Decision for Political Reform, in: Leng, Shao-chuan (Ed.), *Chiang Ching-kuo's Leadership in the Development of the Republic of China on Taiwan*, University Press of America, London, 37.
83 Leng, Tze-kang (1996), *The Taiwan–China Connection: Democracy and Development across the Taiwan Straits*, SMC Publishing, Taipei, 21.
84 Croissant, Aurel and Merkel, Wolfgang (1999), Die Demokratisierung in Ost- und Südostasien, in: W. Merkel (Ed.), *Die Demokratisierung in Ost- und Südostasien*, VS Verlag für Sozialwissenschaften, Wiesbaden, 323–4.
85 Copper, John (1999), *Taiwan: Nation-State or Province?*, Westview Press, Boulder, CO, 43.
86 Lo, Shiu Hing (1997), Liberalization and Democratization in Taiwan: A Class and Functional Perspective, in: Laothamatas, Anek (Ed.), *Democratization in Southeast and East Asia*, St Martin's Press, New York, 221.
87 Cheng, Tun-jen and Tien, Hung-mao (1999), Crafting Democratic Institutions, in: Steve Tsang and Hung-mao Tien (Eds), *Democratization in Taiwan: Implications for China*, Hong Kong University Press, Hong Kong, 25.
88 Diamond, Larry and Plattner, Marc (1994), Introduction, in: Larry Diamond and Marc Plattner (Eds), *Nationalism, Ethnic Conflict, and Democracy*, Johns Hopkins University Press, Baltimore, CO, xix.
89 Ibid.
90 Sachsenröder, Wolfgang (1998), Party Politics and Democratic Development in East and Southeast Asia: A Comparative View, in: Wolfgang Sachsenröder and Ulrike Frings (Eds), Friedrich-Naumann-Stiftung, Aldershot, 8.
91 Maguire, Keith (1998), *The Rise of Modern Taiwan*, Ashgate, Farnham, 115.
92 Ibid.
93 Ibid., 117. For an excellent discussion on why different historical views exist both within Taiwan and between Taiwan and mainland China, see Rigger, Shelley

(1999), The Origins of Conflict across the Taiwan Strait: The Problem of Differences in Perceptions, in: Suisheng Zhao (Ed.), *Across the Taiwan Strait: Mainland China, Taiwan, and the 1995–1996 Crisis*, Routledge, New York, 41–74.

94 Rubinstein, Murray (1999), Taiwan's Socioeconomic Modernization, 1971–1996, in: Murray Rubinstein (Ed.), *Taiwan: A New History*, M.E. Sharpe, New York, 391.

95 See footnote 159 in Fulda, Andreas (2002), Reevaluating the Taiwanese Democracy Movement: A Comparative Analysis of Opposition Organizations under Japanese and KMT Rule, *Critical Asian Studies*, 34(3), 393.

8

TAIWAN'S ELECTION-DRIVEN DEMOCRATISATION

In Chapter 7 I outlined how the lessons of the civil war and conflicting elements of the KMT's party ideology led to cracks in the authoritarian edifice. In this chapter I will examine how the Taiwanese democracy movement has exploited the inherent weaknesses of the KMT party-state. The case of Taiwan differs from the experience of the mainland Chinese democracy movement insofar as from 1969 onwards the door to electoral contestation on the national level was opened. Prior to 1969, opposition to the KMT regime was highly individualised and sporadic. The attempt by mainland Chinese intellectual Lei Zhen to form an opposition party in the late 1950s ended in political suppression and a ten-year jail sentence for Lei. Another call for an end to KMT one-party rule and the establishment of constitutional democracy by Taiwanese professor Peng Ming-min in 1964 resulted in an eight-year jail sentence for Peng.[1]

In this chapter I examine how opposition to the KMT party-state became more systematic and strategic in the early 1970s and 1980s. This book's fifth episode analyses Taiwan's "outside the Nationalist party" (*dangwai*) movement between 1969 and 1986, the year the DPP was founded. The sixth episode discusses the DPP's contributions to liberalisation and democratisation throughout the late 1980s and 1990s. This chapter will show that while the door to more emancipatory politics was opened after 1986/7, the consolidation of Taiwan's young democracy remains an ongoing task. At the heart of the seventh episode is a critical review of the controversial DPP presidency of Chen Shui-bian from 2000 until 2008. The eighth episode in equal measure critiques the KMT presidency of Ma Ying-jeou between 2008 and 2016. The case of Taiwan highlights the challenge of ethnic polarisation and the danger of authoritarian backsliding in newly established democracies. Echoing the leading questions for the case studies in Chapter 6 I will once again highlight antecedents and political opportunities which informed the struggle for democracy at the given time. I will also discern which reform camp initiated the specific struggle for democracy, which strategic reform approach was taken and what were the key lessons learned.

Episode 5: Taiwan's *dangwai* movement, 1969–86: street protests or elections?

Antecedents and political opportunities

In Chapter 7 I outlined how Chiang Ching-kuo attempted to rejuvenate the KMT party-state by co-opting younger Taiwan-born politicians from the early 1970s onwards. As the KMT continued to cling to its party ideology of representing all of China, however, up until 1969

> most of the seats in the Legislative Yuan are still occupied by legislators representing constituencies on the Communist-controlled Chinese mainland. This unique representational arrangement is a consequence of the Nationalist regime's insistence on maintaining on Taiwan the national-level political institutions established in the constitution of the ROC adopted in Nanking in 1946. The preservation of that constitutional structure is, of course, central to the continued legitimacy of the Nationalist regime and its territorial claims.[2]

This particular feature of Taiwan's political system under KMT party-state rule created rather unflattering optics, even for the Legislative Yuan as a primarily rubber-stamp parliament for President Chiang Kai-shek's policies. Images of grey-haired and seriously ill legislators being wheeled into parliament for important elections created a public image of a KMT which lacked vitality.

In order to mitigate the problem of its ageing legislators in "1969 the ROC government expanded the limited electoral process by introducing a supplementary quota of elected representatives to serve in the National Assembly, the Legislative Yuan or Parliament, and the Control Yuan of the central government".[3] Supplementary elections thus helped to replace legislators who were either unfit for service or had passed away. Shelley Rigger has summarised that "Taiwanization, supplementary elections and party reform together constituted a tacit admission that change was needed. By conceding the need for reform, the regime gave the opposition legitimacy. Repressing the KMT's opponents became more difficult, since calls for reform now were coming from within the ruling party itself."[4] As a consequence of Chiang's Taiwanisation strategy aimed at shoring up pro-establishment support two major factions began to struggle for dominance over the party apparatus: more hardline and older KMT members organised in the United Caucus

Clique were pitted against more reform-minded politicians of both mainland Chinese and Taiwanese descent in the CC Clique.[5] The KMT, however, did not succeed in co-opting all aspiring politicians into its ranks. As I have argued before young

> KMT cadres like Xu Xinliang and social scientist Zhang Junhong defected from the KMT and joined forces with other intellectuals and independent political activists like Kang Ning-hsiang, Wu Nairen, and Wu Naide. While the modernizers in the KMT used the democractization and modernization of the state and party as a tool to improve their influence in the government, the highly fragmented dangwai opposition was divided over the choice of means and its ultimate goals.[6]

Key actors

The Taiwanese lawyer Yao Chia-wen has described the *dangwai* movement as a broad coalition of opponents to KMT rule without an organisational structure or party. The *dangwai* movement consisted of four groups: both mainland Chinese and Taiwanese opponents to continued KMT one-party rule; proponents of a comprehensive Taiwanisation of state and society; religious activists with an interest in protecting individual human rights, primarily belonging to Taiwan's Presbyterian church; and young and well-educated reformers both within and outside the KMT party-state, who were critical of traditional notions of Chinese authoritarianism.[7] Yet despite the wide range of supporting actors and interests, the *dangwai did* succeed in finding common ground. By 1978 the *dangwai* promulgated three key principles for their work: election assistance for *dangwai* candidates in order to compete with the KMT; isolating "false" independent candidates who are seen as stooges of the KMT; and to cooperate with liberals within the KMT to rebuild Taiwan.[8]

More importantly, the *dangwai* issued a "12-point plan", which can be considered a "grand strategy", as discussed in Gene Sharp's TOPC in Chapter 4. From 1978 onwards the *dangwai* demanded a strict adherence to the ROC constitution; a complete election of all representatives from the National Assembly and Legislative Yuan; direct elections for provincial governors and mayors; the nationalisation of the armed forces; an independent judiciary; making courts answerable to Taiwan's Judicial Yuan; abolishment of the police law; academic freedom; an end to party control of schools; freedom of speech and freedom of the press; change to press laws; allowing the publication of newspapers and magazines; and freedom to travel abroad. The *dangwai* also called for an end to martial law; the protection of individual rights; the abolition of unlawful detention and torture, inviolability of the home; and protection of the private sphere from state surveillance.[9]

Due to the KMT's ban on political opposition parties the *dangwai* movement "was sustained by a series of magazines that began with the Taiwan Political Review".[10] According to Berman the "use of political opinion journals as a base for opposition political activities follows a tradition that began in 1895 with Liang Ch'i-ch'ao's Peking-based Chinese and Foreign News".[11] He further outlines that "the political conditions in Taiwan under the KMT until the late 1980s made magazines the only mass medium available for transmitting opposition viewpoints".[12] The KMT tolerated such magazines, since their limited circulation and readership was not seen as a direct threat to regime survival.[13] Gary Rawnsley has emphasised that "the opposition press performed many of the same functions of traditional political parties: they provided the movement with ideological direction, opportunities for patronage, the aggregation of interests, and the recruitment and training of leaders".[14]

Strategic reform approach

Joseph Wu has argued that the "most important source of factional division within the opposition in Taiwan has been ideological and philosophical differences concerning how democracy is to be achieved. A second source was the leadership style of individual opposition politicians."[15] Wu describes the highly polarised Taiwan's political arena, which, as in mainland China, consists of competing reform camps: "Opposition politicians gradually formed themselves into two ideological camps, one which sought to 'reform the system' (*gaige tizhi*), led by Huang Hsin-chieh, and one which was content with 'reform within the system' (*tizhinei gaige*), led by Kang Ning-hsiang".[16] Wu's description mirrors the pro-establishment and anti-establishment reform camps I outlined in Chapter 3. Whereas Huang's faction organised around the journal *Formosa* and emphasised the importance of street protests—a distinctively anti-establishment reform approach—Kang's faction members coalesced around the more policy-oriented journal *The Eighties* and advocated electoral democratisation instead—thus opting for a trojan horse reform strategy.[17]

Differences within the *dangwai* movement were not only confined to the question of strategy. Each camp also relied on vastly differing constituencies. Sutter has suggested that Huang's activist and grassroots-oriented Writers and Editors Association (*bianlianhui*) was seeking an "alliance with the working class rather than with the opposition's traditional base of support in the Taiwanese middle class".[18] The more moderate *dangwai* factions, on the other hand, relied on Taiwan's "traditional" middle class[19]—as opposed to the new middle class' support for the KMT regime, discussed in Chapter 7. This constituency included relatively deprived members of Taiwanese society: the children of Taiwanese elites who had been socialised under Japanese colonial rule; victims of the KMT's land-reform policies; and workers.[20]

The militancy of the more activist support base of the Writers and Editors Association became evident when supporters of Xu Xinliang, a former KMT-turned-*dangwai* politician, suspected that an election fraud in Taoyuan county may jeopardise his victory. His supporters consequently burned down a police station, an event in Taiwan's political history which has come to be known as the Chung-li incident in 1977.[21] In the wake of this street violence Xu Xinliang sought refuge in the United States and established the overseas Taiwan Revolutionary Party. Linda Chao and Ramon Myers reveal that during his exile in the United States Xu became increasingly radical. He advocated urban guerrilla warfare as a means to overthrow the KMT party-state.[22] In 1979, Formosa activists furthermore engaged in a human rights rally in the southern port city of Kaoshiung (*Gaoxiong*), which soon spiralled out of control and ended in street violence. Its eight leading faction members were subsequently arrested and received long prison sentences.[23] Whereas Rigger has called the Kaoshiung (*Gaoxiong*) march "the most famous event in the history of Taiwan's democratization",[24] the subsequent trial was perhaps far more consequential for the future development of the *dangwai* movement, as by the early 1980s the defending lawyers, including Chen Shui-Bian and Xie Changting, became leading *dangwai* politicians in their own right.[25]

When re-evaluating Taiwan's democracy movement from 1914 until 1986 I argued that the

> dangwai's uniting force was opposition to hegemonic rule, but apart from this its members shared few political ideas in common. The opposition was divided over the choice of strategy (reform within the system vs. reform of the system) the distribution of resources (office-holders vs. social activists), and its main ideology (support for self-determination of the ROC vs. advocacy of Taiwan Independence).[26]

In marked contrast, Cheng Tun-Jen has argued that democratisation scholars have perhaps overemphasised strategic disagreements within Taiwan's *dangwai* movement in the late 1970s and early 1980s. Whereas Rigger has underlined the importance of activists who followed radical democrat Huang Hsin-chieh[27] and I have highlighted the contributions of moderates around Kang Ning-hsiang,[28] Cheng probably is right in pointing out that by the mid-1980s the *dangwai* as a whole started to skilfully mix both an anti-establishment with a trojan horse strategy. According to Cheng the *dangwai* operated in "four bargaining spheres: the streets, the Legislative Yuan, the third-party mediated dialogue, and overseas arenas (notably the U.S. Congress)".[29] According to Cheng, the radical wing of the *dangwai* initially made a strategic error in relying too much on street protest. This coincides with Gene Sharp's critique of the over-reliance of political activists on one mode of action, as described in his TOPC in Chapter 4. Cheng points out that after 1979 the more moderate members of the *dangwai* rather skilfully expanded the scope of the domestic debate by proposing a "German solution" to the issue of unification between ROC and PRC. This trust-building manoeuvre gained Kang Ning-hsiang currency among Chiang Ching-kuo and the reformist wing within the KMT.[30] Nathan and Ho have suggested that by "1980, CCK and the more moderate TW [*dangwai*] leaders understood one another well and were moving, with or without conscious coordination, in a way as to outflank together both the KMT conservatives and the TW-radicals".[31] This tacit alliance of the early 1980s can be considered an informal "elite settlement", as understood in Burton and Higley's terms.[32]

Kang Ning-hsiang managed to simultaneously engage with the *dangwai*'s activist base as well as with the reformist wing of the KMT. He organised the defence team for the rival Formosa faction members while simultaneously leading the *dangwai* movement back to a parliamentary line, a distinctively trojan horse approach to reforming the party-state from within the circumscribed electoral arena. Doing so drew the ire of more anti-establishment *dangwai* activists, who were opposed to any cooperative approach towards the KMT regime and started a campaign to criticise Kang (*pi kang*).[33] Such disunity within the *dangwai* movement led to temporary set-backs such as the disappointing showing during the 1983 supplementary elections for the Legislative Yuan.[34] Unfazed, Kang continued to reach across the political aisle. Bruce Jacobs has pointed out that Kang engaged in repeated direct communications with Chiang Ching-kuo.[35] While the exact content of their talks is not known, through these talks Kang must have gained the trust of Chiang. This is evident from Chiang's tacit approval for Kang to internationalise the *dangwai* movement. Kang led the first *dangwai* delegation to the United States in 1982.[36] Cheng has explained the significance of this development:

> [this] trip broadened the horizon of opposition members and transformed the social ties between them and overseas Taiwanese into a political nexus. The opposition thereby made a quantum jump in its own foreign relations. Previously the FMG [Formosa Magazine Group] had only maintained loose contacts with private human rights organizations, such as Amnesty International, which have little bargaining power vis-à-vis the government. Now the opposition had found an arena in the United States (as a security provider) through which the KMT regime (as a security consumer) might be indirectly influenced.[37]

The United States visit by *dangwai* politicians internationalised the issue of Taiwan's democratisation and enlisted American lawmakers as allies of the *dangwai* movement.

Lessons learned

It is worth pointing out that without the continuous muck raking by the Formosa faction and its successor Writers and Editors Association and

Progress factions, Kang's more intellectual Mainstream faction could not have claimed the mantle of middle-of-the-road opposition politics. To put it more succinctly: if the more activist Formosa faction had not absorbed the first hit of KMT party-state retaliation in the late 1970s, Kang's Mainstream faction most likely would have been the alternative casualty. We must not forget that even by the mid-1980s the KMT did *not* shift from hard to soft authoritarianism, as Edwin Winkler has suggested.[38] Instead, it upheld its hard authoritarianism until the end of martial law in 1987. The *dangwai* movement under Kang's leadership employed a combination of anti-establishment and trojan horse strategies. In Cheng's words, the

> DPP leaders also changed arenas, deemphasising the bargaining table and instead working in a coordinated fashion in the three other arenas: the Legislative Yuan, the streets, and overseas. By playing the game in the Legislative Yuan, they obtained information and secured a hand in rewriting the rules. They used street demonstrations to amplify their voices, but did not resort to violence—the younger and more restive supporters being restrained by reminders of the debacle of the FMG [Formosa Magazine Group]. Thus, despite some strained relations between prime and lesser leaders, mass movement in the streets and opposition in the Legislative Yuan were skilfully coordinated.[39]

The fifth episode of the *dangwai* reveals that Taiwan's democracy movement of the late 1970s and early 1980s can be considered a broad church. It included individuals, groups and more organised factions which held onto vastly differing world-views and ideologies. Despite these differences, however, the centrist Kang faction and the more activist Formosa faction managed to agree on a set of key principles when opposing the KMT party-state during supplementary elections. This process of strategic alignment was not conflict-free. Kang Ning-hsiang simultaneously engaged with the radical members in the *dangwai* as well as with the moderates in the KMT, thus revealing a preference for trans-establishment politics. Gaining the trust of Chiang Ching-kuo allowed Kang to internationalise the *dangwai* movement. By combining both anti-establishment and trojan horse reform strategies Kang managed to hold a fractious *dangwai* movement together.

Episode 6: Taiwan's DPP: democratising or nation building?

Antecedents and political opportunities

The year 1986 marked a turning point in the development of Taiwan's democracy movement. Following the successful ousting of Philippine dictator Ferdinand Marcos Kang's Mainstream faction started establishing sub-branches across the island. As this move contravened policies prohibiting opposition organisations a dialogue between the KMT and the *dangwai* ensued. When these talks proved futile, *dangwai* leaders realised that the time had come to challenge the party-state head on. What was supposed to be a candidate selection meeting at the Taipei Grand Hotel on 28 September 1986 became the moment the DPP was founded. Instead of cracking down on the DPP, Chiang Ching-kuo used an interview with the *Washington Post* to announce the lifting of martial law in 1987. In this interview he simultaneously put pressure on the new opposition party to respect the ROC constitution, uphold the KMT's policy of anti-communism and stay clear of public calls for Taiwan's self-determination.[40]

Key actors

Only two months after its inauguration the newly formed DPP held its first meeting to discuss its organisational structure. It's new party platform advocated a political order based on democracy and freedom. More specifically, the DPP issued nine suggestions. Its platform called for greater respect of human dignity and basic human rights; a parliament which represents the wish and will of the people; checks and balances between different branches of government; freedom, equality and democracy for all political parties; freedom of assembly and acceptance of political and social movements; freedom of the press; constitutional rule of law free from political interference; a neutral administrative system; and limits to the KMT's emergency decrees.[41] While the DPP's platform called for respect for the principle of self-determination, in 1986 there were no references to be found which called for de jure Taiwan independence.

In terms of the new opposition party's organisational structure, Sutter has pointed out that

> the DPP created a structure almost identical to that of the KMT: a 31-member Central Executive Committee was elected for two years with powers to appoint a eleven-member Central Standing Committee and a chairman, both for one-year terms. Unlike the KMT, however, the DPP granted little control to the chairman, and the party is carefully designed to prevent over-centralization of power.[42]

Such formal party structures, however, did not reveal the real centre of power in the new opposition party. Rigger has pointed out that all leading *dangwai* factions—apart from the Formosa faction, whose leaders were still in jail—were part of the new opposition party. An important founding member of the DPP was the New Tide faction (henceforth NT faction), which succeeded the activist Writers and Editors Association. Throughout the 1980s and 1990s the NT faction began to compete with the radical-turned-moderate Formosa faction.[43]

Strategic reform approach

Rigger explains that from

> the beginning, a division of labor existed within the party between the moderate factions, which included a large number of elected officials, and the New Tide Faction, which was more interested in leading social movements than in winning elected offices. The moderates (first the Kang Group and other centrists, and later the Formosa Faction) dominated the party's decision-making apparatus (the party chair and the Central Standing Committee), while New Tide activists obtained a disproportionate share of posts in the party bureaucracy.[44]

Such intra-party coalitions between centrist party leaders who rely on tacit support from a radical NT faction-dominated party bureaucracy, thus has been a defining feature of the DPP since its foundation in 1986. Alexander Ya-li Lu has aptly described the hybrid nature of the DPP:

> The DPP is essentially a party movement. On the one hand, it functions as a normal party by participating in elections, engaging in legislative work, and even running a few county and city governments. On the other hand, it considers itself as a mass movement, the principle mission of which is to mobilize the people to exert pressure upon the ruling KMT and government to democratize the political structure as well as to carry out other reforms.[45]

According to Alfred Stepan, under authoritarian conditions an opposition party is supposed to perform five key functions: "resisting integration into the regime; guarding zones of autonomy against the regime; disputing its legitimacy; raising the costs of authoritarian rule; creating a credible democratic alternative".[46] Stephan Grauwels has pointed out that the "Democratic Progressive Party has been at the vanguard for democratic change in Taiwan".[47] Grauwels suggests that "the party has led the clamour for constitutional change on a variety of issues, such as the lifting of martial law, the retirement of mainland-elected representatives, the abolishing of the Temporary Provisions, the lifting of the taboos on the February 28 Incident and Taiwan Independence, and direct elections for the president".[48] He further outlines that "the DPP mobilize against the National Security Law and Article 100 of the Criminal Law in order to defend the right to free speech".[49] In parliamentary elections throughout the 1980s and 1990s the DPP achieved respectable results. Despite losing to the much better resourced KMT, the DPP nevertheless managed to gain between 25 percent of the votes in the 1986 Legislative Yuan election and around 30 percent during the subsequent elections in 1992, 1995 and 1998.[50]

In 1991 the DPP evolved from a party movement into a nation-building party. Since the early beginnings of the *dangwai* movement, the Taiwanese opposition camp included ardent Taiwanese nationalists who clamoured for Taiwan independence. Advocating Taiwan independence, however, was akin to crossing a red line of the unification-minded KMT. Grauwel recalls that the "passing of a clause approving a referendum on a 'Republic of Taiwan' triggered threats of a ban on the DPP, causing one of the most severe domestic political crisis since the DPP's founding in 1986".[51] I have argued that while

> it led to elite settlement within the party its external implications were disastrous: it provoked the enmity of the DPP amongst hardliners in the KMT as well as the PRC's Chinese Communist Party ... By settling its internal elite conflict the DPP started a much bigger ideological dispute, which severely limited the DPP's options in engaging its political opponents.[52]

I have extensively discussed the problems of faction politics which led to this outcome. One of the key problems with the DPP's party factions is that they have never been institutionalised.[53] DPP party factions "do not openly name their followers, and the faction composition of main party branches ... does not depend on the factions' size but on inter-factional horse trading".[54] To complicate matters even more, "factionalism within the DPP encompasses all administrative levels and penetrates all party institutions".[55] While all DPP factions were supposed to dissolve by 2006, due to their nature as informal "dyadic patron-client networks" they continue to exist until the present day.[56]

Lessons learned

How did Taiwan independence become a salient issue for the DPP in the late 1980s? Rigger argues that the DPP was a victim of its early democratising successes:

> Between 1986 and 1991, the DPP's internal debate over the independence issue intensified. Key political reforms were enacted in this period, including lifting martial law, increasing the number of locally-elected national legislators, easing restrictions on the mass media and legalising opposition parties. Ironically, in winning the fight for such reforms, the DPP was deprived of its most appealing demands. As a result, it increased its emphasis on ethnic justice and self-determination. In addition, the DPP successfully persuaded the KMT to allow exiled dissidents—including many independence activists—to return to Taiwan. Meanwhile, enforcement of the law banning independence advocacy grew

lax. Together, these trends tilted the balance within the party towards the independence cause.[57]

The incorporation of the Taiwan independence clause into the DPP's party platform was a direct consequence of lobbying by the NT faction. According to Cheng and Hsu, the "DPP was not born as a nation-building party, but was turned into one via the shrewd manipulation by the New Tide faction on the issue of Taiwan independence".[58] In order to soften the impact of such a controversial move, Chen Shui-bian

> offered an amendment to soften the proposal. Instead of advocating independence directly, Chen suggested that the party seek a referendum on the issue. The DPP's moderate Formosa Faction found itself in a weak position vis-à-vis the pro-independence New Tide faction and the returned exiles, and accepted Chen's compromise in exchange for a larger share of leadership positions.[59]

The DPP's Taiwan independence position, however, became a liability during Taiwan's elections in the early 1990s. The most obvious set-back was the first free and fair presidential election in 1996, where the openly pro-independence DPP presidential candidate Peng Ming-min only garnered 21 percent of the overall vote and lost to incumbent KMT president Lee Teng-hui. It also tarnished the DPP's image abroad, in particular among Taiwan's allies in Washington, DC, where foreign policy makers worried about the reaction from mainland China perceived by the Taiwanese opposition as unnecessarily reckless and provocative.

The DPP in opposition thus played a rather contradictory role. In the late 1980s and as a party movement it successfully heaped pressure on the ruling KMT party-state to liberalise and democratise. Yet by morphing into a nation-building party in 1991 it also limited its electoral appeal and suffered during subsequent national-level elections. It's presidential candidate Peng Ming-min lost the first presidential election by a big margin. In terms of its party caucus in the Legislative Yuan, the DPP also did not manage to go beyond the vote of 33 percent during the 1995 parliamentary election. As the seventh case study of the two-term Chen Shui-bian presidency will show, the DPP only managed to come into power due to a split in the so-called pan-blue camp of unification-minded parties in the run-up to the 2000 presidential election.

Episode 7: Chen Shui-bian's two-term presidency (2000–8): a missed historical opportunity?

Antecedents and political opportunities

Chen Shui-bian's election as the first DPP president in 2000 was the result of two factors. First and foremost, throughout the 1990s the DPP engaged in tactical moderation and started to downplay its Taiwan independence party platform. In 1999 the DPP also adopted a more conciliatory policy towards mainland China which was widely seen as a way to win over centrist voters. This allowed Chen to portray himself as a middle-of-the-road reformer comparable to the United Kingdom's then prime minister Tony Blair.[60] Chen had entered the political arena as a lawyer for the "Kaohsiung Eight". He gained his first experiences as a member of the Taipei City Council. In 1985 his wife Wu Shu-chen was the victim of a politically motivated attack, which left her paralysed from the waist down. As Taipei mayor from 1994 until 1998 he had shown his credentials as a pragmatic city administrator who could get things done.[61] These credentials propelled him onto the national stage.

The second factor that won the DPP the presidency was the lack of unity in the so-called pan-blue camp. For decades the KMT had shown a remarkable unity and an ability to attract and integrate new political talent. By the late 1990s, the KMT started splintering. In 1993 the New Party was founded by disgruntled hardcore unificationists who profoundly disliked the Taiwanisation of the KMT under Chiang Ching-kuo and later Lee Teng-hui. Yet the New Party only attracted a small following and soon became a footnote in Taiwan's political history. Far more consequential was the emergence of the People's First Party by the former governor of Taiwan province, James Soong. After Taiwan province was abolished as a consequence of constitutional reform in the 1990s, this left Soong as a heavyweight KMT politician without a portfolio. KMT chairmen Lien Chan and James Soong, however, did not get along. Lien and Soong competed not only against the DPP's Chen Shui-bian but also against one another, thus splitting the vote of the so-called blue camp of unification-minded political parties in Taiwan.[62] This meant that with a vote share of 39.3 percent Chen did not win the presidential election decisively, but in fact benefited from a split in the pan-blue camp.[63]

Key actors

Fell has aptly summarised how after a short honeymoon the Chen presidency quickly deteriorated into bitter acrimony between the DPP administration and the KMT and People's First Party opposition:

> The attempt by the opposition parties to recall the DPP's president Chen Shui-bian over his handling of the Fourth Nuclear Power Station construction project represents the first in a series of unprecedented political crises during the DPP era. These include the island's worst economic recession, record levels of unemployment, high levels of political violence, a series of corruption scandals involving high-ranking DPP politicians including Chen and his close relatives, huge demonstrations calling on the president to step down over corruption allegations and three votes in parliament to recall the president.[64]

Chen Shui-bian has also been criticised for his rather lacklustre efforts to reform the judiciary, a necessary precondition to effectively combat the phenomenon of black gold in Taiwan politics.[65] From the outset, Chen Shui-bian had made a number of fundamental mistakes: he had overestimated his authority in the ROC's constitution, where the president has to share power with the premier who is accountable to parliament.[66] Diamond and Plattner have argued that in ethnically polarised societies it is of paramount importance for politicians "to avoid the indefinite and complete exclusion from political power of particular groups, whether majority or minority. All groups must be given some stake in the system."[67] Yet Chen only half-heartedly reached out to the defeated KMT and/or People's First Party. While appointing a KMT politician, Tang Fei, as his first premier, he did so without consulting the KMT first. Chen's reluctance to enter a formal coalition with the KMT was in great part the result of his over-reliance on the radical NT faction. While the NT faction has traditionally been open to intra-party coalitions between DPP factions, it has steadfastly opposed formal coalitions with political parties which pursue the goal of unification with mainland China.[68] The NT faction's opposition to coalition governments thus can be explained by their unwillingness to compromise on the issue of Taiwan independence. Chen Shui-bian also bowed to the Taiwan independence faction when unilaterally scuppering the nuclear power plan project in the first year of his presidency, thus setting himself on a collision course against the pan-blue-dominated parliament.[69]

To complicate matters further, the KMT and People's First Party—unaccustomed to its fall from power—started playing the role of a disloyal opposition.[70] This was most evident by both opposition parties bypassing the DPP government and unilaterally reaching out to the CCP and forming in all but name a third united front.[71] The CCP leadership interpreted such overtures as a profound sign of weakness of the new DPP-led administration and subsequently refused to engage with President Chen unless he accepted the "One China" principle and abandoned the party's Taiwan independence platform. Such concessions, however, would have cost Chen the support of the DPP's powerful NT faction, which had played the role of king maker when selecting Chen as the DPP's presidential candidate in 1999. Chen Shui-bian's over-reliance on the support of the NT faction not only derailed his first term in office but also explains why during his second term in office "Chen pursued his 'deliberate nation building effort', enacting aggressive programmes of symbolic Taiwanization and de-Sinification".[72]

Strategic reform approach

Neither the Legislative Yuan elections of 2001 nor 2004 provided the DPP with a majority in parliament. This meant that throughout his two terms in office, Chen Shui-bian was essentially a lame duck president, who had to rely heavily on symbolic politics to leave his mark. As president, his political reform options were fairly limited. Anti-establishment approaches were out of the question given that the DPP was now holding on to the presidency. As outlined above, Chen was also neither willing nor able to engage in trans-establishment politics. This left him only with the option of employing trojan horse strategies and tactics along the line of Saul Alinsky's TOPC. A case in point is the 2-28 Hand-in-Hand rally which was staged to secure his re-election in 2004. Stefan Fleischauer provides an excellent account of the DPP's mass mobilisation for electoral gain:

> On 28 February 2004, on the eve of the presidential elections to be held on 20 March, an estimated two million people took part in the biggest ever mass rally held in Taiwan, forming a human chain of more than 300 km that spanned the entire length of the island. This mass rally, which was organized by the Taiwan Solidarity Union ... and the DPP (the 'pan-green camp'), was announced as a defensive move in the face of mainland China, which was accused of constantly developing military capabilities for an eventual invasion of the island. The memory of the 2-28 Incident was thereby reactivated for the purpose of drawing a dividing line—this time, however, it was a boundary that was to set Taiwan apart from the People's Republic of China.[73]

In 2004 Chen Shui-bian narrowly secured a second term in office, but only after an assassination attempt at him and vice-president Annette Lu during an election rally in southern Gaoxiong, which was widely suspected to be stage managed to get sympathy votes. Chen secured 50.11 percent of the vote share against KMT opponent Lien Chan, who received 49.89 percent. The razor-thin majority again did not provide Chen with a convincing mandate to govern. Throughout his two-term presidency Chen exploited nationalist sentiment for political gain. Copper has argued that

> Chen's fallback strategy was to play on ethnic tensions. Advancing the use of the Taiwanese language, which many Mainland Chinese did not speak, but neither did the aborigines or Hakka (Taiwan's other two ethnic groups); favoring Fukien Taiwanese (the early-arrival Chinese from Fukien Province and the DPP's base) in hiring; and adopting other policies of ethnic bias worked. But it did not work well enough; many in Chen's ethnic group stayed loyal to the KMT.[74]

Lessons learned

Chen's actions were not merely a case of political opportunism but exemplary of long and deeply held political convictions. For those readers who are familiar with contemporary British politics, the following analogy may prove useful. While Chen Shui-bian likened himself to the pragmatist prime minister Tony Blair, the other side of his personality can be compared with hard Brexiter Jacob Rees-Mogg. We should not forget that in an interview with Alan Wachman in 1993 Chen Shui-bian stated that "[D]emocracy is the process and independence is the goal".[75] His long-standing commitment to the goal of Taiwan independence stood him in good stead with the NT faction, which according to Yang Yizhou has articulated the belief that "Taiwan Independence is the precondition for democracy, and democracy is the development of Taiwan Independence".[76] Ngeow has pointed out that "it should not surprise anyone that the internal factions of the DPP consisted of camps emphasizing contrasting nationalist discourses (radical ethnic nationalists versus moderate civic nationalists), whereas the party mainstream converged around a discourse that could be described as non-ethnocentric yet emphasizing Taiwanese identity, the 'Taiwanness' of Taiwan".[77]

While it would be an overgeneralisation to describe the latter as a hotbed of ethnic and cultural nationalists, there can be no doubt that the NT faction has long specialised in harnessing the power of Taiwanese nationalist sentiments and social movements.[78] As part of the treasure trove of United States State Department cables published by Wikileaks, a wide range of reports by American diplomats working for the American Institute Taiwan (AIT), the unofficial embassy of the United States in Taipei, are now in the public domain. One of the cables by AIT director Douglas Paal was written in 2005, the first year of the second term of the Chen presidency. Paal reported to Washington, DC that the NT faction "is the best organized, best financed, and most united faction in exercising its influence in the DPP, and it has an established core of theorists, strategists, and organizers. Its influence continues to expand, with many of its leaders now serving in important government, legislative, and party positions."[79] Just like David Cameron's inability to confront Eurosceptics in his own party led to the highly divisive Brexit referendum, Chen Shui-bian's strategic alignment with the NT faction limited his political choices, both vis-à-vis the pan-blue camp as well as in terms of cross-strait relations. The disastrous eight years of Chen's presidency "left a record that led to the KMT landslide victories in both the legislative and the presidential elections of January and March 2008".[80]

Episode 8: Ma Ying-jeou's two-term presidency (2008–16): a KMT-led political restoration?

Antecedents and political opportunities

In 2009 and only a year after the end of Chen Shui-bian's "unfortunate presidency",[81] the former DPP president and his wife Wu Shu-chen were indicted on charges of accepting bribes and engaging in money laundering. They were given life sentences,[82] which were later reduced to 20 years. Chen was released on medical parole in 2015 after serving six years in prison.[83] Chen's fall from grace led to a decisive election of KMT president Ma Ying-jeou in January 2008. The Taiwanese electorate, frustrated after eight years of political grid-lock, also provided the KMT with clear parliamentary majority two months later. The two elections provided Ma with an unprecedented opportunity to reset both the domestic political agenda and improve relations across the Taiwan Straits.[84] As this eighth episode will show, however, Ma squandered this opportunity during his two-term presidency. From the start, his adminis-tration was let down by inadequate crisis management. The KMT's return to power coincided with the global financial crisis. As a highly export-dependent economy, Taiwan was affected particularly hard.[85] Also, during the first year of his presidency, Ma mismanaged the rescue efforts following Typhoon Morakot, which devastated large parts of the island and led to more than 500 casualties in August 2009.[86] In more ways than one the rocky start of the new KMT administration echoed the birth pains of the DPP presidency in 2000–1.

Key actors

While enjoying a much more decisive public mandate for change, Ma, just like Chen Shui-bian before him, engaged in executive over-reach. To a certain extent, the KMT under Ma Ying-jeou was a victim of its own success. Hold-ing on to the presidency and enjoying a parliamentary majority meant that there was no need to accommodate the opposition, which after the fiasco of the Chen presidency was in almost complete disarray. In another United States State Department cable published by Wikileaks, "DPP New Tide fac-tion elder Wu Nai-jen told us he expects it will take some time for the DPP to recover from its back-to-back election defeats earlier this year. The party must first confront the reasons for the losses: corruption, excessive ethnic identity politics, and economic conditions."[87] This meant that Ma, just like Chen, saw no value in creating "multiethnic political coalitions that will bring multiple groups into political power and keep them mutually dependent on one another".[88]

The renewed domination of all three branches of government by the KMT, however, raised the spectre of a return to party-state authoritarianism. As we will see from the following discussion, Ma's authoritarian approach to gov-erning the island led to a rise in social movement activism, not dissimilar to the tumultuous years of street protests during the 1970s and 1980s. When discussing the 17 social movements which took place between 1980 and 1988, Michael Hsiao observed that "most of the emerging social movements have taken a rather depoliticized strategy by avoiding any obvious connection with the political opposition"[89] and that "the most significant collective sentiment expressed in most of the emerging social movements has been a feeling of 'victim consciousness', the 'feeling of being ignored and excluded".[90] In his collection of news articles in the edited volume *Black Island: Two Years of*

Activism in Taiwan, Canadian journalist and scholar Michael Cole has argued that "the real rebirth [of pugnacious civic activism] ... began in 2012".[91] In response to "government-sanctioned expropriations, abuse in the military, theft of Aboriginal land, police violence, and restrictions of press freedoms",[92] Cole describes "the emergence of charismatic leaders, the refinement of techniques, the snowballing effect, and above all the cross-pollination and coming together of various sectors of civil society to include students, NGOs, university professors, artists, and ordinary citizens in response to government intransigence".[93]

Strategic reform approach

Ma's reform approach was distinctively pro-establishment and can be seen as an attempt to resurrect the "old" KMT party-state. Following the disaster of the Chen presidency Chuang Ya-chung discerned a "rise to political nostalgia. The two decades of democracy is seen by the returned Kuomintang as a lost time—a deviation from its reign of prosperity before the end of the 1980s."[94] Without an effective opposition, Ma enjoyed considerable license to implement a wide range of domestic policies, almost all of which turned out to be highly controversial. In the following I will concentrate on the three policy arenas of tourism, education and cross-strait trade and investment to elucidate the KMT's elitist approach to governing a democratic Taiwan.

During his first term Ma opened the island to group tourism from mainland China. While helping Taiwan's tourism industry to flourish,[95] the economic benefits were soon offset by the widely felt negative perceptions by Taiwanese of unruly mainland Chinese tourists.[96] Rather than simply a transient phenomenon of a mainland Chinese tourist industry in its infancy, Ian Rowen has argued that

> the recent rise in leisure tourism from the PRC to Taiwan is producing multiple, overlapping, and contradictory sensations of stateness, state territory, and national identity within Taiwan. These effects are produced in part by the highly regimented structure of group tourism as managed by industry actors from Taiwan, the PRC, and Hong Kong, which reproduces a tourist experience sufficiently similar to that of the PRC. Subtle and inconsistent linguistic performances of national identity take place throughout tours, both reproducing and undermining the effect of state territory.[97]

Rowen finds that

> tourism is producing a contradiction between PRC tourists' admiration and identification with their Taiwanese hosts, and Taiwanese hosts' alienation from their guests. PRC tourists praise Taiwanese for their manners

and kindness, attributing such charms to an idealized Chinese essence projected onto the people of Taiwan. Meanwhile, Taiwanese people avoid PRC tourists and decreasingly identify themselves as Chinese.[98]

The KMT's calculus to use tourism as a bridge to foster closer cross-straits ties therefore backfired. The double-edged sword of mainland Chinese inbound tourism was but one example of the unintended consequences of policies pursued by the new KMT administration.

In the field of education the new KMT administration opened up another frontline. Whereas the former DPP administration had tasked the Ministry of Education to make textbooks more Taiwan-centric,[99] under Ma the KMT attempted to reverse this trend and re-emphasise Taiwan's historical links to the mainland.[100] This attempt to rewrite history, however, did not go unchallenged. Ketty Chen describes how in 2014:

> university professors, high school teachers, historians, students and social organizations took to the streets and congregated at the Ministry of Education to voice their concerns and discontent. Opponents of the revisions lambasted the Ministry of Education of "de-Taiwanizing (去臺化)", "sinicization" and for "brainwashing" the students by manipulating history in order to spread the "Greater China Awareness (大中國意識)".[101]

Just as Alan Wachman had observed throughout the 1990s, "what the KMT did not anticipate is that by promoting Chinese identity as exclusive and trivializing or denying the validity of sentiments Taiwanese had for their own subcultural forms, the KMT ended up emphasizing, rather than muting, the differences between its view of culture and that of the Taiwanese".[102] Chen has argued that during the Ma presidency the old KMT party-state re-emerged through education. An alternative explanation is that previous DPP-led efforts to disentangle the island's education and cultural sector from the KMT party-state had met continuous resistance from the pan-blue camp. Taiwan, not too dissimilar to the political polarisation in the United States, has seen its own brand of culture wars since the early 1990s. Sebastian Hsien-Hao Liao reminds us that

> toward the end of the eighties, cultural criticism was gradually radicalized and divided into two: pro-Taiwanese nationalism, on the one hand, and the criticism of all totalizing discourses, including nationalism, on the other. Accordingly, the Taiwanese public sphere was more or less divided into two, with each side dominated by one for cultural criticism and hostile to the other.[103]

Instead of attempting to bridge this long-standing cultural divide, the Ma administration arguably fanned the flames of Taiwanese nationalism by doubling down on its own China-centric view of history and culture.

The third example of the unintended consequences of KMT policies is the field of cross-strait trade and investment. Similar to the TTIP negotiations between the United States and Europe, the KMT engaged in secret talks with the CCP about a so-called "Economic Cooperation Framework Agreement" (ECFA). Matsuda has pointed out that since "the negotiations were kept secret, there were concerns about the ECFA not only among the members of the DPP but also across many industries and societal organizations".[104] One item on the ECFA agenda, a proposed Cross-Strait Service Trade Agreement (CSSTA), proved controversial. Young people in particular were concerned that ever closer integration into the mainland Chinese economic orbit may undermine Taiwan's de facto political independence. The CSSTA controversy proved one step too far for critics of a Ma-led administration. Michael Cole has succinctly summarised the public discontent with the

> Ma Ying-jeou administration, which has oftentimes smothered internal dissent, intervened in the judiciary, and for the most part ignored input from civil society—including input on the agreement at the heart of the current crisis, the Cross-Strait Services Trade Agreement ... For all intents and purposes, the Taiwanese government has drifted towards what Diamond terms a competitive authoritarian regime, little more than an empty shell.[105]

Enraged by the intransparent and unaccountable pursuit of the CSSTA by the Ma administration, student protesters occupied the Legislative Yuan from 18 March until 10 April 2014. When activists started decorating the parliament with sunflowers this protest came to be known as the Sunflower movement. On 30 March 2014 Taiwan's Sunflower movement culminated in a large street demonstration in Taipei which attracted more than 100,000 protesters. Its poignant symbolism and ability to mobilise the masses helped the movement to stall the KMT's CSSTA.

The Sunflower movement not only undermined the authority of the KMT government but subsequently also helped pave the way for the DPP's victories in the 2016 presidential and parliamentary election. While the DPP was a direct beneficiary, Jean-Pierre Cabestan has pointed out that contrary

> to what the CCP propaganda indicates, the DPP was not behind-the-curtain conductor of the movement. Though it later helped the [Legislative Yuan] occupiers, it reacted slowly and hesitantly to the movement's demands ... As the KMT, the DPP is an ageing party that has had difficulties keeping up with Taiwan's new generation of political activists and social movements.[106]

While critical of the student activists' anti-establishment tactics, Cabestan suggests that the Sunflower movement highlighted a number of structural weaknesses of the KMT government: its overly close and intransparent relationship with the CCP and big business as well as its revival of "an old-fashioned Chinese nationalism—a kind of *dahanzhuyi* (Great Han chauvinism) to recycle a term used by Mao Zedong—that is totally disconnected by the islanders' mainstream Taiwanese identity".[107]

Lessons learned

It is widely acknowledged that the Sunflower movement had strong nationalist overtones. Cole has suggested that the movement signifies a shift from ethnic and cultural Taiwan nationalism to a more civic form of nationalism.[108] Drawing on personal observations when covering social movements between 2012 and 2014 he convincingly argues that the multiethnic composition of the various protest groups and networks heralds a new age where to "be Taiwanese meant to be a participant in the democratic experiment that is Taiwan, regardless of one's ethnic background, language, social status or voting tendencies".[109] He suggests that "Taiwan has … developed a kind of nationalism that is defined by civic values and the democratic system that, though imperfect, has been embraced by the majority of people in Taiwan".[110] This echoes Christopher Hughes' argument that Taiwan can develop its own brand of civic nationalism "that has emerged as the foundation of the Western liberal-democratic state. In principle, this is participatory and inclusive, because it is based more on legal and territorial definitions and subjective loyalty than it is on predetermined culture, blood line or origins."[111]

One of the persistent problems of such interpretations, however, remains that civic, cultural and ethnic nationalism cannot be neatly separated. Drawing on the examples of European and American nationalisms, Bernhard Yack encourages us to be

> skeptical about this familiar contrast between civic and ethnic nationalism. It all seems a little too good to be true, a little too close to what we would like to believe about the world … Designed to protect us from the dangers of ethnocentric politics, the civic/ethnic distinction itself reflects a considerable dose of ethnocentrism, as if the political identities French and American were not also culturally inherited artifacts, no matter how much they develop and change as they pass from generation to generation.[112]

Anson Au, on the other hand, has suggested that the Sunflower movement in fact married an organic bottom-up civic nationalism with the more exclusive ethnic and cultural nationalism advocated by the DPP's hardcore Taiwan independence supporters.[113] For many decades, DPP nationalists have argued that a person's ethnic origin does not necessarily amount to membership in a state; that a distinct Taiwanese political identity is not inconsistent with a historical connection to the mainland; that there is a fundamental difference between political identity and cultural identity; and that a shared history with mainland China should not be seen as Taiwan's destiny.[114]

Commenting on the rise of nativism under former president Chen Shui-bian, Jean-Pierre Cabestan is particularly critical of DPP politicians who have "made this nativist nationalism the main theme of their politics, ostracising, in order to marginalise them, those mainlanders who, although they are Tai-wanised, have remained influential within the army, academia and the opposition parties".[115] It is rather unfortunate that one of the side effects of Taiwan's democratisation has been a rise of a political Japanophilia among hardcore Taiwan independence supporters, where the island's colonial past is being instrumentalised to highlight the supposed distinctiveness of the island's population vis-à-vis mainland China.[116] Cabestan has aptly suggested that

> in order to consolidate this nationalism, it will have to cultivate, not so much its ambiguity, as its plural character, its belonging both to the Chinese cultural world and to a sovereign Taiwanese nation called the Republic of China. It will have to exclude its most nativist manifestations if it wants to maintain on the island the political consensus necessary for the spirit of defence of a state which is not only called into question, but threatened by a People's Republic of China whose power increases daily.[117]

In Chapter 9 I will discuss the development trajectory of Hong Kong's political system. Following my analysis of continuity and change of political control before and after the handover of the former British crown colony to mainland Chinese sovereignty in 1997 I will discuss the evolution of the struggle for democracy in Hong Kong in Chapter 10. Episodes 9 to 12 will show that while Hong Kong's democracy movement started from a struggle which initially aimed for political liberalisation and democratisation under the "One Country, Two Systems" formula, it now also includes individuals, groups and political parties who either make the case for Hong Kong's right of self-determination or alternatively openly advocate Hong Kong independence. Against the backdrop of my critique of the entanglement of Taiwan's democratisation process with the objective of nation building since 1991 this should be considered a rather ominous sign.

Notes

1   Reinhardt, Monika (1989), *Politische Opposition in Taiwan, 1947–1988. Demokratische Fortschrittspartei*, Brockmeyer, Bochum, 15–26.
2   Engstrom, Richard L. and Chu, Chi-hung (1984), The Impact of the 1980 Supplementary Election on Nationalist China's Legislative Yuan, *Asian Survey*, 24(4, April), 447–8.

3   Chao, Linda and Myers, Ramon H. (2000), How Elections Promoted Democracy in Taiwan under Martial Law, *China Quarterly*, 162, 388.
4   Rigger, Shelley (1999), *Politics in Taiwan*, Routledge, London, 112–13.
5   Cheng, Tun-jen and Chou, T.C. (2000), Informal Politics in Taiwan, in: Peter Chow (Ed.), *Taiwan's Modernization in Global Perspective*, Praeger, Westport, CT, 47.
6   Fulda, Andreas (2002), *Reevaluating the Taiwanese Democracy Movement*, Routledge, London, 374.
7   As cited by Halbeisen, Hermann (1982), Tangwai: Entwicklung und Gegenwärtige Lage der Opposition in Taiwan, *Zeitschrift für Politik*, 29(2), 209.
8   Ibid., 2012.
9   Ibid., 2013.
10 Berman, Daniel (1992), *Words Like Colored Glass: The Role of the Press in Taiwan's Democratization Process*, Westview Press, Boulder, CO, 170.
11 Ibid.
12 Ibid., 171.
13 Ibid., 172.
14 Rawnsley, Gary D. (2000), The Media and Popular Protest in Pre-Democratic Taiwan, *Historical Journal of Film, Radio and Television*, 20(4), 567.
15 Wu, Jaushieh Joseph (1995), *Taiwan's Democratization: Forces behind the New Momentum*, Oxford University Press, Oxford, 90.
16 Ibid.
17 Ibid.
18 Sutter, Robert (1988), *Taiwan: Entering the 21st Century*, University Press of America, Lanham, MD, 47.
19 Lo, Shiu Hing (1997), Liberalization and Democratization in Taiwan: A Class and Functional Perspective, in: Anek Laothamatas (Ed.), *Democratization in Southeast and East Asia*, Institute of Southeast Asian Studies, Singapore, 227.
20 Domes, Jürgen (1980), *T'aiwan im Wandel. Politische Differenzierung und Opposition, 1978–1980*, Peter Lang Verlag, Frankfurt am Main, 111.
21 Rigger, Shelley (2001), *From Opposition to Power: Taiwan's Democratic Progressive Party*, Lynne Rienner, Boulder, CO, 19.
22 Myers, Ramon (1998), *The First Chinese Democracy: Political Life in the Republic of China on Taiwan*, Johns Hopkins University Press, Baltimore, MD, 2.
23 Rigger, Shelley (2001), *From Opposition to Power: Taiwan's Democratic Progressive Party*, Lynne Rienner, Boulder, CO, 21.
24 Ibid.
25 Ibid.
26 Fulda, Andreas (2002), *Reevaluating the Taiwanese Democracy Movement*, Routledge, London, 374.
27 Rigger, Shelley (1999), *Politics in Taiwan*, Routledge, London, 103–30; Rigger, Shelley (2001), *From Opposition to Power: Taiwan's Democratic Progressive Party*, Lynne Rienner, Boulder, CO, 15–36.
28 Fulda, Andreas (2002), *Reevaluating the Taiwanese Democracy Movement*, Routledge, London, 374–80.
29 Cheng, Tun-Jen (1989), Democratizing the Quasi-Leninist Regime in Taiwan, *World Politics*, 41(4, July), 491.
30 Ibid., 493.
31 Nathan, Andrew and Ho, Helena (1993), Chiang Ching-kuo's Decision for Political Reform, in: Shao-chuan Leng (Ed.), *Chiang Ching-kuo's Leadership in the Development of the Republic of China on Taiwan*, University Press of American, Lanham, MD, 43.
32 Burton, Michael G. and Higley, John (1987), Elite Settlements, *American Sociological Review*, 52(3, June), 304.

33 Ferhat-Dana, Samia (1998), *Le Dangwai et la démocratie à Taïwan*, L'Harmattan, Paris, 365.
34 Rigger, Shelley (2001), *From Opposition to Power: Taiwan's Democratic Progressive Party*, Lynne Rienner, Boulder, CO, 21–3.
35 Jacobs, Bruce (2012), *Democratizing Taiwan*, Brill, Leiden, 62.
36 Reinhardt, Monika (1989), *Politische Opposition in Taiwan, 1947–1988. Demokratische Fortschrittspartei*, Brockmeyer, Bochum, 52.
37 Cheng, Tun-Jen (1989), Democratizing the Quasi-Leninist Regime in Taiwan, *World Politics*, 41(4, July), 487–8.
38 As quoted by Rigger, Shelley (1999), *Politics in Taiwan*, Routledge, London, 112.
39 Cheng, Tun-Jen (1989), Democratizing the Quasi-Leninist Regime in Taiwan, *World Politics*, 41(4, July), 493.
40 *Washington Post* (1986), Taiwan President to Propose End to Island's Martial Law; Action Would Mean the Lifting of Restrictions after 37 Years. Available online: www.washingtonpost.com/wp-dyn/content/article/2010/05/14/ AR2010051403509.html (accessed 13 November 2018).
41 Political Platform of the Democratic Progressive Party (1993), *World Affairs*, 155 (3), 135–8.
42 Sutter, Robert (1988), *Taiwan: Entering the 21st Century*, University Press of America, Lanham, MD, 46.
43 Wu, Jaushieh Joseph (1995), *Taiwan's Democratization: Forces behind the New Momentum*, Oxford University Press, Oxford, 94.
44 Rigger, Shelley (2001), *From Opposition to Power: Taiwan's Democratic Progressive Party*, Lynne Rienner, Boulder, CO, 25.
45 Lu, Alexander Ya-li Lu (1992), Political Opposition in Taiwan: The Development of the Democratic Progressive Party, in: Tun-Jen Cheng and Stephen Haggard (Eds), *Political Change in Taiwan*, Lynne Rienner, Boulder, CO, 129.
46 As quoted by Rodan, Garry (1996), Theorising Political Opposition in East and Southeast Asia, in: Garry Rodan (Ed.), *Political Opposition in Industrialising Asia*, Routledge, London, 12.
47 Grauwels, Stephan (1996), The Democratic Progressive Party at a Turning-Point: From Radical Opposition to a Potential Coalition Partner, in: Gunter Schubert and Axel Schneider (Eds), *Taiwan and der Schwelle zum 21. Jahrhundert. Gesellschaftlicher Wandel, Probleme und Perspektiven eines asiatischen Schwellenlandes*, Mitteilungen des Instituts für Asienkunde, Hamburg, 85.
48 Ibid.
49 Ibid.
50 Rigger, Shelley (2014), Political Parties and Identity Politics in Taiwan, in: Larry Diamond and Gi-Wook Shin (Eds), *New Challenges for Maturing Democracies in Korea and Taiwan*, Stanford University Press, Stanford, CA, 108.
51 Grauwels, Stephan (1996), The Democratic Progressive Party at a Turning-Point: From Radical Opposition to a Potential Coalition Partner, in: Gunter Schubert and Axel Schneider (Eds), *Taiwan and der Schwelle zum 21. Jahrhundert. Gesellschaftlicher Wandel, Probleme und Perspektiven eines asiatischen Schwellenlandes*, Mitteilungen des Instituts für Asienkunde, Hamburg, 88.
52 Fulda, Andreas (2002), The Politics of Factionalism in Taiwan's Democratic Progressive Party, *Internationales Asienforum*, 33(3–4), 327.
53 Wu, Jaushieh Joseph (1995), *Taiwan's Democratization: Forces behind the New Momentum*, Oxford University Press, Oxford, 96.
54 Fulda, Andreas (2002), The Politics of Factionalism in Taiwan's Democratic Progressive Party, *Internationales Asienforum*, 33(3–4), 324.
55 Ibid.
56 Ibid.

57 Rigger, Shelley (2001), The Democratic Progressive Party in 2000: Obstacles and Opportunities, *China Quarterly*, 168, 952.
58 Cheng, Tun-Jen and Hsu, Yung-ming (1996), Issue Structure, the DPP's Factionalism and Party Realignment, in: Tien, Hung-mao (Ed.), *Taiwan's Electoral Politics and Democratic Transition: Riding the Third Wave*, M.E. Sharpe, Oxon, 139.
59 Ibid., 953.
60 Chen, Shui-bian (2000), *The Son of Taiwan: The Life of Chen Shui-bian and His Dreams for Taiwan*, Taiwan Publishing, Taipei, 120–37.
61 *Washington Post* (1998), Taipei's Ambitious Mayor. Available online: www.washingtonpost.com/archive/politics/1998/02/06/taipeis-ambitious-mayor/7f004c41-06bf-499d-a54a-9a8d8b63a76a/?utm_term=.bea585744039 (accessed 14 November 2018).
62 BBC News (2000), James Soong: KMT Rebel, Available online: http://news.bbc.co.uk/1/hi/in_depth/asia_pacific/2000/taiwan_election/661119.stm (accessed 19 November 2018).
63 Copper, John F. (2000), Taiwan's 2000 Presidential and Vice Presidential Election: Consolidating Democracy and Creating a New Era of Politics, *Maryland Series in Contemporary Asian Studies*, 2(1), 53.
64 Fell, Dafydd (2011), The Polarization of Taiwan's Party Competition in the DPP Era, in: Robert Ash, John W. Garver and Penelope Prime (Eds), *Taiwan's Democracy: Economic and Political Challenges*, Routledge, London, 75.
65 Copper, John (Ed.) (2002), *Taiwan in Troubled Times: Essays on the Chen Shui-bian Presidency*, World Scientific Publishing, River Edge, NJ, 32.
66 Fulda, Andreas (2002), The Politics of Factionalism in Taiwan's Democratic Progressive Party, *Internationales Asienforum*, 33(3–4), 340.
67 Diamond, Larry and Plattner, Marc (1994), Introduction, in: Larry Diamond and Marc Plattner (Eds), *Nationalism, Ethnic Conflict and Democracy*, Johns Hopkins University Press, Baltimore, MD, xxiii.
68 Chao, Chien-min (2002), The Democratic Progressive Party's Factional Politics and Taiwan Independence, in: John Copper (Ed.), *Taiwan in Troubled Times: Essays on the Chen Shui-bian Presidency*, World Scientific Publishing, River Edge, NJ, 111.
69 *Guardian* (2001), Taiwanese Government in Crisis over Nuclear Plant. Available online: www.theguardian.com/world/2001/jan/31/china.johngittings (accessed 19 November 2018).
70 For a discussion on what constitutes a loyal or disloyal opposition see Rodan, Garry (1996), Theorising Political Opposition in East and Southeast Asia, in: Garry Rodan (Ed.), *Political Opposition in Industrialising Asia*, Routledge, London, 9.
71 Fulda, Andreas (2002), The Politics of Factionalism in Taiwan's Democratic Progressive Party, *Internationales Asienforum*, 33(3–4), 334.
72 Sullivan, Jonathan and Lowe, Will (2010), Chen Shui-bian: On Independence, *China Quarterly*, 203, 624.
73 Fleischauer, Stefan (2007), The 228 Incident and the Taiwan Independence Movement's Construction of a Taiwanese Identity, *China Information*, 21(3), 389.
74 Copper, John F. (2008), Taiwan's Failed President, *Asian Affairs: An American Review*, 34(4), 181.
75 Wachman, Alan (1994), *Taiwan: National Identity and Democratization*, M.E. Sharpe, Armonk, NY, 162.
76 Yang, Yizhou (2004), *Minjindang zuzhi paixi yanjiu*, Jiuzhou chubanshe, Beijing, 62.
77 Ngeow, Chow Bing (2010), Strategic Ambiguity and Differentiation: Ethnic and

Civic Nationalist Discourses in Taiwan from 1945 to the 1990s, *Ethnopolitics*, 9(2), 160.

78 Ai, Linda (1998), *Jitang! Taiwan fandui yundong zong pipan*, Qianwei chubanshe, Taibei, 192.

79 Wikileaks (2018), Factions in Taiwan's Ruling DPP: An Overview. Available online: https://wikileaks.org/plusd/cables/05TAIPEI3580_a.html (accessed 14 November 2018).

80 Jacobs, Bruce (2012), *Democratizing Taiwan*, Brill, Leiden, 228.

81 Copper, John F. (2008), Taiwan's Failed President, *Asian Affairs: An American Review*, 34(4), 189.

82 *Guardian* (2009), Taiwan Court Jails Former President for Corruption. Available online: www.theguardian.com/world/2009/sep/11/taiwan-jails-former-president-corruption (accessed 20 November 2018).

83 ABC News (2015), Former Taiwan President Chen Shui-bian Released from Jail on Medical Parole. Available online: www.abc.net.au/news/2015-01-06/former-taiwan-president-chen-shui-bian-on-medical-parole/6002650 (accessed 20 November 2018).

84 *South China Morning Post* (2010), Dancing to the Same Tune: There Has Never Been a Better Time for Both Sides to Reach an Agreement on Taiwan's Right to Self-Rule, Writes Steve Tsang, 18 September.

85 Woodrow Wilson International Center for Scholars (2009), Taiwan and the Global Economic Storm. Available online: www.wilsoncenter.org/sites/default/files/Asia_143.pdf (accessed 20 November 2018).

86 Asia News (2009), Typhoon Morakot Hits Ma Ying-jeou's Government. Available online: www.asianews.it/news-en/Typhoon-Morakot-hits-Ma-Ying-jeou's-government-16087.html (accessed 20 November 2018).

87 Wikileaks (2018), New Tide Faction Elder Wu Nai-jen on DPP Politics. Available online: https://wikileaks.org/plusd/cables/08TAIPEI509_a.html (accessed 20 November 2018).

88 Diamond, Larry and Plattner, Marc (1994), Introduction, in: Larry Diamond and Marc Plattner (Eds), *Nationalism, Ethnic Conflict and Democracy*, Johns Hopkins University Press, Baltimore, MD, xxiii.

89 Hsiao, Michael Hsin-Huang (1990), Emerging Social Movements and the Rise of a Demanding Civil Society in Taiwan, *Australian Journal of Chinese Affairs*, 24, 178.

90 Ibid.

91 Cole, J Michael (2015), *Black Island: Two Years of Activism in Taiwan*, CreateSpace, 9.

92 Ibid.

93 Ibid.

94 Chuang, Ya-chung (2013), *Democracy on Trial: Social Movements and Cultural Politics in Postauthoritarian Taiwan*, Chinese University Press, Hong Kong, 13.

95 BBC News (2011), Chinese Tourists Go It Alone in Taiwan. Available online: www.bbc.co.uk/news/world-radio-and-tv-15173456 (accessed 20 November 2018).

96 Phneah, Jeraldine (2018), 5 Reasons Why Chinese Tourists Are So Rude. Available online: www.jeraldinephneah.com/5-reasons-why-chinese-tourists-are-so-rude/ (accessed 20 November 2018).

97 Rowen, Ian (2014), Tourism as a Territorial Strategy: The Case of China and Taiwan, *Annals of Tourism Research*, 46, 63.

98 Ibid., 73.

99 Jacobs, Bruce (2012), *Democratizing Taiwan*, Brill, Leiden, 219–26.

100 Chen, Ketty (2014), Party-State Reemerges through Education in Taiwan. Available online: http://theasiadialogue.com/2014/02/23/party-state-reemerges-through-education-in-taiwan/ (accessed 20 November 2018).

101 Ibid.
102 Wachman, Alan (1994), *Taiwan: National Identity and Democratization*, M.E. Sharpe, Armonk, NY, 85.
103 Liao, Sebastian Hsien-Hao (2000), Becoming Cyborgian: Postmodernism and Nationalism in Contemporary Taiwan, in: Arif Dirlik and Xudong Zhang (Eds), *Postmodernism and China*, Duke University Press, Durham, NC, 185–6.
104 Matsuda, Yasuhiro (2015) Cross-Strait Relations under the Ma Ying-jeou Administration: From Economic to Political Dependence?, *Journal of Contemporary East Asia Studies*, 4(2), 12.
105 Cole, Michael (2014), In Defense of the Sunflower Movement. Available online: http://theasiadialogue.com/2014/04/09/in-defense-of-the-sunflower-movement/ (accessed 22 November 2018).
106 Asia Dialogue (2014), Sunflower Movement and the Future of Democracy in Taiwan … and Hong Kong. Available online: http://theasiadialogue.com/2014/09/25/sunflower-movement-and-the-future-of-democracy-in-taiwan-and-hong-kong/ (accessed 20 November 2018).
107 Ibid.
108 Cole, J. Michael (2017), *Convergence or Conflict in the Taiwan Strait: The Illusion of Peace?*, Routledge, Oxon, 126–34.
109 Ibid., 130–1.
110 Ibid., 132.
111 Hughes, Christopher (2011), Negotiating National Identity in Taiwan: Between Nativization and De-Sinicization, in: Robert Ash, John W. Garver and Penelope Prime (Eds), *Taiwan's Democracy: Economic and Political Challenges*, Routledge, London, 71.
112 Yack, Bernhard (1999), The Myth of the Civic Nation, in: Ronald Beiner (Ed.), *Theorizing Nationalism,* State University of New York, New York, 105.
113 Au, Anson (2017), The Sunflower Movement and the Taiwanese National Identity: Building an Anti-Sinoist Civic Nationalism. Available online: http://berkeleyjournal.org/2017/04/the-sunflower-movement-and-the-taiwanese-national-identity-building-an-anti-sinoist-civic-nationalism/ (accessed 20 November 2018).
114 Rigger, Shelley (1999), Competing Conceptions of Taiwan's Identity: The Irresolvable Conflict in Cross-Straits Relations, in: Suisheng Zhao (Ed.), *Across the Taiwan Strait: Mainland China, Taiwan, and the 1995–1996 Crisis*, Routledge, New York, 229–40.
115 Ibid., 9.
116 Foreign Affairs (1996), Taiwan's New Nationalists: Democracy with Taiwanese Characteristics. Available online: www.foreignaffairs.com/articles/asia/1996-07-01/taiwans-new-nationalists-democracy-taiwanese-characteristics (accessed 22 November 2018); and Fulda, Andreas (2002), *Reevaluating the Taiwanese Democracy Movement*, Routledge, London, 382–5.
117 Cabestan, Jean-Pierre (2005), Specificities and Limits of Taiwanese Nationalism, *China Perspectives*, 62(November–December), 12.

9

ORIGINS OF HONG KONG'S
SEMI-DEMOCRATIC STATUS

So far our discussion has primarily focused on the struggle for democracy in mainland China and Taiwan. In the following two chapters I will examine the case of Hong Kong, which shares a number of intriguing commonalities with Taiwan. The first is its geographic proximity to the PRC, although there is an important caveat: whereas Hong Kong has a land border, the island of Taiwan is separated from mainland China by sea. In both regions, southern Chinese languages have traditionally dominated the everyday life of its people: Cantonese in Hong Kong, and Minan and Hakka dialects in Taiwan. The other major commonality is that both regions were previously colonised: Whereas from 1895 until 1945 Taiwan was a colony of Japan's, the crown colony of Hong Kong was part of the British Empire from 1843 until 1997. During World War II and from 1941 until 1945 the city was briefly occupied by the Japanese.[1] Last but not least, in the case of both Taiwan and Hong Kong, modernising colonial regimes harnessed the entrepreneurial spirit of the colonised subjects. In the pursuit of their respective imperial ambitions, Japanese and British colonial administrators laid the foundation for rapid economic development.

The political trajectories of both regions, however, show marked differences. In the first part of this chapter I argue that the British colonial administration's decision against democratisation in the early 1950s and the belated political liberalisation of its colonial regime in the early 1980s left a rather weak democratic legacy following the return under PRC sovereignty in 1997. Hong Kong's democracy movement, described in greater detail in Chapter 10, developed as a consequence of top-down liberalisation initiated by the last British governor Chris Patten. A highly circumscribed electoral democratisation during the 1990s provided Hong Kong's democracy activists only with limited means to slow down the city's subsequent slide into authoritarianism after 1997. Political reforms under the Patten administration were too little, too late, lacked the support from the Chinese party-state and thus were unable to prevent the gradual hollowing out of nascent liberal democratic institutions and procedures in Hong Kong following the handover.

In the second part of the chapter I will show that since the Chinese party-state agreed with the British government in 1984 to maintain Hong Kong's capitalist system for the next 50 years, it could not engage in a wholesale dismantling of the city's British colonial institutions following 1997.[2] Yet it would also not allow Hong Kong to democratise, as a successful democratisation would have raised aspirations for greater political liberties among mainland Chinese citizens. Instead the CCP opted to play a long game. Using its united front approach to advance a selective decolonisation of Hong Kong former beneficiaries of British colonial rule such as the Catholic Church and other Christian denominations were increasingly disenfranchised. Other sectors of Hong Kong's society, most notably the local business community, continued to benefit from party-state patronage. Hong Kong's Special Administrative Region (HKSAR) government has also started to work closely with the CCP-controlled Liaison Office and implemented policies which are predominately in the Chinese party-state's interest.[3]

More ominously, the HKSAR government's ill-tempered response to Occupy Central with the Love and Peace (OCLP)/Umbrella movement (UM) in 2014 has shown that it has started to use the Hong Kong police as a tool of political oppression. The OCLP/UM, which I will discuss in greater detail in Chapter 10, was a civil disobedience campaign aimed at securing a free and fair election of the HKSAR's chief executive in 2017. Even more concerning is the HKSAR government's turning of a blind eye to the emergence of "thugs for hire" during the OCLP/UM. While political decay in Hong Kong has greatly accelerated since 2014,[4] Hong Kong's overall political trajectory during the 1990s and early 2000s raises doubts over the CPP's willingness to honour the Sino-British Joint Declaration of 1984 and its own "One Country, Two Systems" formula. I will substantiate this argument by comparing British colonial rule with the subsequent approach to governance by the successive HKSAR governments in the eight areas of trade and commerce, the role of local business elites, rule of law, policing, language policy, education system, press censorship and political institutional design. Rather than offering a strictly chronological account, I will hone in on defining features of the different approaches to governing Hong Kong. As I will show, post-1997 the CCP has started a process of firmly integrating Hong Kong into the mainland Chinese economic and political orbit.

Hong Kong under British colonial rule

Hong Kong became part of the empire following the British victory in the first Opium War. Steve Tsang has argued that with its "deep-water natural harbour by its north shore and good quality fresh water supplies",[5] Hong

Kong was a coveted prize for the British Empire. A key concern for successive British colonial administrators was the promotion of trade and commerce. In this process, the British co-opted Chinese merchants, which they provided with "privileges such as land grants and offering important lucrative monopolies".[6] Carroll has shown that colonial "expansion in Hong Kong was made possible with Chinese co-operation throughout the early history of the colony".[7]

A functioning rule of law served the purpose of advancing the economic interests of the British Empire: "By the nineteenth century, the British had already developed and adopted, however imperfectly, the concept of the rule of law based on the due process, the presumption of innocence, trial by jury and the testing of evidences through adversarial discourse in a court of law".[8] In the early decades of British colonial rule, however, the rule of law was applied rather selectively. Christopher Munn has argued that by

> the 1890s, 99.5 per cent of all criminal cases were being decided in the Magistracy, not so much by a system of justice, but by what amounted to a peremptory regime of discipline and punishment. Richer, more "respectable" Chinese received exemption from some of the system's harsher provisions ... For the great majority of the Chinese population, however, English justice in Hong Kong meant intrusive policing, racial and class discrimination, and periodic campaigns of repression.[9]

Colonial policing, on the other hand, was not static. Kam Wong has shown that "colonial policing was not all like everywhere, nor did it remain unchanged over time".[10] By the late 1960s "colonial policing improvised, adjusted, mutated and morphed to suit colonial missions and/or soothe liberal conscience".[11] Wong has summarised colonial policing as "neither British nor Chinese, but a hybrid, with concepts from the British, such as legal justice, and practices from the Chinese, such as street justice".[12] According to Wong,

> Chinese elites and powers-to-be used colonial policing to their own personal advantages (political) and for the benefit of the group. For them, to be successful in improving Hong Kong–Chinese interests, it was best to embrace and deploy British colonial policing, in the image and to the liking of the Chinese, rather than to resent and dismiss it outright.[13]

Steve Tsang has similarly emphasised the tendency of Hong Kong's colonial police to exercise restraint, rather than implementing colonial laws and regulations with brute force. He recounts how anti-riot training throughout the 1960s allowed the Hong Kong police to deal with the Star Ferry Riots in 1966 as well as street violence of Maoists in 1967 in fairly measured ways aimed at de-escalating the situation.[14]

Driven by "commercial considerations"[15] and as "an outpost of empire, Hong Kong was certainly not founded with any 'civilising' mission in mind on the part of the British government".[16] The British reluctance to engage in large-scale attempts to socially re-engineer its colonial subjects is best exemplified by the colonial government's attitude towards language. Chi Kuen Lau highlights that the British

> did not force every Chinese in Hong Kong to learn English. However, there was a compulsion in a more subtle form. As the English language was part and parcel of the British administrative, commercial, and judicial systems that came with colonial domination, it paid for the colonized to learn it. Although a minority of Hong Kong Chinese, for nationalistic reasons, refused to push themselves to learn the language of their colonial master, realism prevailed for the majority.[17]

While primarily serving the interests of the expatriate community, the colonial government also "looked after the Chinese community paternalistically".[18] British colonial administrators devoted considerable time and energy to prevent the building up of public resentment against colonial rule. As part of a wider corporatist strategy, the British co-opted the Catholic Church and licensed it to run the education sector. John McCarthy, David Britt and Mark Wolfson have called the subordinate role of the church "institutional channeling".[19] Ng and Fulda have argued that

> the colonial government used the church as a political tool to curb the infiltration of communists, British colonial administrators were convinced that only Christianity could resist the subversive elements of Communism, whereas non-religious or secular primary education would produce an atheistic proletariat. The colonial government thus favored Christian churches as agents that might curb the activities of communist and resist communist infiltration by having the Roman Catholic Church enlarge its schoolwork ... [this] indirect approach took the form of a contractual system.[20]

This arrangement granted Catholic and Anglican churches license to provide education and social services. It is worth pointing out that by the mid-1990s, half of Hong Kong's primary and secondary schools were operated by Christian churches.[21] This also explains Governor Patten's observation that "at the heart of the life of this very Chinese city, the Catholic Church—missionaries and locals, with so many Chinese priests and nuns today—contributes to public life and social service out of all proportion to its numbers".[22]

Throughout the British colonial period the press was relatively free to report, yet the colonial government also imposed limits on certain types of journalism. Chi Kuen Lau explains that whenever "the nationalistic spirit of the Chinese population was whipped up, it could threaten British control of Hong Kong and other British settlements in China. Both for reasons of appeasing China and maintaining its grip over the colony, the Hong Kong government considered it necessary to keep a lid on anti-Chinese activities."[23] This led to a successive introduction of censorship instructions aimed at halting Chinese-language print publications, which either could be considered to exacerbate the lingering conflict between the CCP on the mainland or the KMT on Taiwan or alternatively which questioned the political legitimacy of British colonial rule. When Hong Kong "became a battleground for two brands of Chinese patriotism" following the end of World War II, the colonial government issued wide-ranging ordinances which allowed the governor in council to "deal with an emergency, including the censorship, control and suppression of publications and other means of communication".[24] While in practice such press censorship was seldom applied, it meant that from the 1960s onwards "press freedom in Hong Kong is better understood as allowing the press great latitude to comment on Chinese politics, but not on the legitimacy of British rule".[25]

In terms of political institutional design, the British colonial government can be described as authoritarian and ethnically exclusive. Political power was concentrated in the hands of the British governor of Hong Kong, who presided both over the executive and legislative branches, acted as the commander in chief and had the power to appoint judges and government officials.[26] Such sweeping powers were only limited insofar as the governor "required the approval of the British Secretary of State for Foreign and Commonwealth Affairs before taking any action. He was also required to take public opinion into consideration (mainly from the British merchants and Chinese elite) so as to avoid enquiries by the British government on public discontent."[27] When Hong Kong citizens were appointed to the colonial government, they could only play subordinate and consultative roles.[28] In political practical terms, however, the governor's sweeping powers were constrained by the norm that he should consult both the Executive Council as well as the Legislative Council (LegCo).[29]

In 1946 Governor Mark Young (1941–7)

> carefully tested public opinion and vigorously pushed for the introduction of what in effect was a "super municipal council", with "a degree of administrative and financial autonomy unknown in other British municipal councils" (Tsang, Democracy Shelved, 183–4) of the time so that it could, if the political environment should permit, gradually replace the existing colonial government and give the local Chinese greater self-government.[30]

Young was mindful that opening the door to electoral democratisation may lead to an infusion of:

the two warring factions in the Chinese Civil War, the ruling Kuomintang and the Chinese Communist Party, and normal democratization at the colonial legislature might lead to it being turned into a political cockpit of the two Chinese parties. Hence, his proposals for a "super municipal council" by which the electoral elements could be introduced and gradually expanded and, if the elected members should prove politically responsible, its scope of government expanded without allowing Chinese politics to dominate its proceedings.[31]

While initially receiving support for his reform ideas from London, the succeeding conservative governor of Hong Kong Alexander Grantham (1947–57) put an end to Young's reform plan, which Grantham considered both difficult and dangerous.[32]

Political change in Hong Kong in the post-World War II era was incremental at best and mostly limited to administrative reforms aimed at enhancing the performance of the colonial government. Steve Tsang has argued that the colonial cadet system produced administrative officers who

made a huge difference to the quality of governance in Hong Kong. Individually, while most of them might not have been intellectually brilliant, they were mostly highly able and dedicated public servants. Collectively, they added up to more than the sum of their individual efforts and abilities. Team work and a strong esprit de corps enabled them to work together for the general interest of the Hong Kong community (the meaning of which changed in the "official mind" over time) and, though opportunities for graft existed aplenty, by and large they resisted the temptation of corruption.[33]

When political reforms finally arrived in the early 1980s, they were prompted less by a sudden revelation about the downsides of paternalistic colonial rule and more by the very real prospect of a looming handover from British colonial rule to PRC sovereignty in 1997.

In 1984 the British colonial government admitted that Hong Kong would come under PRC control under the "One Country, Two Systems" formula, according to which "the territory would be allowed to maintain its capitalistic way of life for 50 years after returning to the embrace of the socialist motherland".[34] It subsequently promulgated its *Green Paper: The Further Development of Representative Government in Hong Kong*. Mirroring the approach suggested by Governor Mark Young in 1946 the consultation paper suggested "to develop progressively a system of government the authority for which is firmly rooted in Hong Kong, which is able to represent authoritatively the views of the people of Hong Kong, and which is more directly accountable to the people of Hong Kong".[35] During the colonial period, the British appointed members of the LegCo,[36] which only played an advisory role.[37] The green paper paved the way to an expansion of the LegCo, which by 1985 still consisted exclusively of 57 unelected members. Far more consequential was the public reaction to the consultation paper, as it raised expectations for a fully fledged electoral democratisation of Hong Kong's political system. Due to strong opposition from the PRC, however, in a subsequent white paper in 1988 the colonial government back-peddled and "the emphasis was changed from promoting greater democracy to maintaining continuity beyond 1997".[38] Following the 1989 crackdown on mainland China's anti-corruption and pro-democracy movement, a select committee of the Westminster House of Commons recommended "that 50 per cent of the legislators be directly elected in 1991; the chief executive be selected by a grand electoral college six months before the transfer of sovereignty; and the second chief executive be directly elected by universal suffrage".[39] Subsequent reforms to election reform in 1993–4 by Governor Patten "were introduced unilaterally and implemented without Beijing's approval, but were advertised at the time as modest variations on Basic Law themes".[40]

In the run-up to the 1997 handover, increasing numbers of LegCo members thus were directly elected. The first direct elections of LegCo members took place in 1991, just two years after the crackdown on mainland China's anti-corruption and pro-democracy movement in 1989, and led to a resounding victory of the pro-democracy camp. In the last LegCo election before the handover in 1995, the pro-Beijing establishment was similarly defeated by the pro-democracy camp.[41] Such election successes, however, proved to be rather transient and, more importantly from Beijing's view, reversible. Following the suppression of the 1989 anti-corruption and pro-democracy movement, the "PRC excluded from the [Hong Kong Basic Law] drafting committee Martin Lee and Szeto Wah, the two most vocal advocates of democratization on the committee and the founders of the Hong Kong Alliance in Support of the Patriotic Democratic Movement in China".[42] This was a working group under the auspices of the PRC's rubber stamp parliament, the National People's Congress, which was tasked with the formulation of the Basic Law, Hong Kong's mini-constitution. Angered by the direct election of all 60 seats of the LegCo members in 1995, the HKSAR also decided to replace the LegCo with the Provisional Legislative Council from 1997–8.[43] In Chapter 10 I will show how these fundamental disagreements between Governor Patten and the Chinese party-state about Hong Kong's political institutional design after the handover politically neutered the LegCo and from the outset hamstrung the Basic Law as the HKSAR's future mini-constitution.

In an interview with the *Guardian* Patten suggested that he and his administration should have done more to democratise Hong Kong's political institutions.[44] His self-critical retrospective view, however, does not do justice to the rather wide-ranging political reforms he helped implement as Hong Kong's last governor. While Patten creatively interpreted a vaguely worded Sino-British Joint Declaration of 1984[45] to justify far-reaching constitutional reforms, the debate about the content and language of the to-be-established Basic Law showed that the international treaty between the United Kingdom and the PRC could also be viewed as a call for political tutelage, where genuine democratic reforms could be postponed for quite some time.[46] Commenting on his advocacy of political liberalisation and democratisation in an interview with the *South China Morning Post* in 2014, Patten told reporters that the "Chinese were very much against this moving to greater democracy ... because they thought it might lead people in Hong Kong to think they will eventually be independent like, say, Singapore".[47] Lau Siu-kai has summarised the CCP's long-standing attitude towards Hong Kong as follows: "Beijing's view is that Hong Kong's political development must serve the purpose of the 'one country, two systems' policy, which is ... to protect investors' interest and the capitalist system and avoid welfarism and populism".[48]

One of the persistent challenges for the Patten administration were repeated and unambiguous threats by the CCP that following the 1997 handover the newly established HKSAR government would roll-back any measures that it deemed not to be in its interest. As Ming K. Chan's account of Hong Kong's political transition post-1997 reveals, such threats weren't empty words. The HKSAR

> ushered in several deliberate measures of drastic institutional change such as the December 1999 abolition of the Urban Council (which had the longest history of local elected representation) and Regional Council, and the reintroduction of appointed members to the previously all-elected District Boards (renamed District Councils). From July 1997 through April 1998, the SAR was also burdened with an unelected and extra-constitutional (as it was not provided for in the Basic Law) "provisional legislature" which replaced the all-elected Legislative Council ... formed in 1995 under British auspices. This provisional legislature of dubious legitimacy and low public esteem, after repealing a host of prehandover era liberal laws and labor protection and civil rights, enacted a set of regressive electoral rules for the creation of future HKSAR legislature.[49]

Chan has argued that pre-1997 the British-led political reforms "opened up the electoral arena for grassroots political participation and gave birth to party politics".[50] After 1989 the fear of an increasingly authoritarian mainland China galvanised the public's support for greater political representation. But while Patten's electoral reforms of the early 1990s "directly benefited the democratic camp in 1992–97 [the PRC's stern stance in the Sino-British discords] derailed the 'through-train' institutional and personnel continuity transcending the 1997 handover".[51] In Chapter 4 I outlined Paulo Freire's TOPC. Freire's TOPC raised questions about the wisdom of elites bestowing democracy as a gift to its people. This, however, was in essence Patten's approach to political reform. While his intention was to develop more democratic institutions in tandem with Hong Kong's democracy movement, neither he nor Hong Kong's democracy activists enjoyed sufficient leverage over the CCP. Patten is certainly right in stating that at "least Hong Kong had experienced a free and fair election, knew what it was like, had self-confidently enjoyed its liberties"[52] but they reckoned without Hong Kong's host post-1997. While Westminster had been warned by Scottish National Party leader Jim Sillars that the 1984 Sino-British Joint Declaration would be unenforceable, then prime minister Margaret Thatcher failed to heed such warnings, primarily since she did not want to grant all 3.25 million British nationals in Hong Kong the right to abode in the United Kingdom.[53]

Hong Kong under PRC sovereignty: continuity and change

In the following I will compare and contrast the successive pro-Beijing HKSAR administrations' post-transition approach to governance with British colonial rule in the eight areas of trade and commerce, the role of local business elites, rule of law, policing, language policy, education system, press censorship and political institutional design. The comparison will reveal that while change did not happen overnight and the CCP exercised remarkable restraint in the first decade after Hong Kong's reversion to China, seen from a longitudinal perspective the cumulative effect of CCP-directed reform measures can be considered a clear breach of the 1984 Sino-British Joint Declaration as well as the "One Country, Two Systems" formula.

Hon-Chak Lam has made the case that mainland Chinese economic policies, which are often sold to the Hong Kong public as a preferential policy treatment, should in fact be seen as long-term measures which are "designed to build closer economic ties and partnership with China will lead to economic over-reliance on China".[54] Lam cites the Closer Economic Partnership Arrangement, a free trade agreement which benefited mainland Chinese state-owned enterprises more than Hong Kong-based business, led to deindustrialisation rather than reindustrialisation and caused a brain drain of Hong Kong talent.[55] He also points out that the introduction of the Individual Visit Scheme has led to an over-reliance on mainland Chinese visitors in Hong Kong's tourism sector.[56] Last but not least, the CCP's efforts to establish a Greater Bay Area (GBA)

> is part of the grand national strategy to prop up domestic demand by building 19 city clusters across China. The extra demand created by these city clusters is supposed to offset the negative impact from the ongoing trade war. Apart from its economic mission to provide a cushion to growth, the GBA has the underlying political goal to integrate Hong Kong and Macau with China further.[57]

Last but not least, Lam considers the Guangzhou–Hong Kong Express Rail Link (XRL) as another highly symbolic measure to further integrate Hong Kong into mainland China's economy.[58] Ma has pointed out that since "it was both unfeasible and not within the CCP's plans to use Hong Kong's CCP apparatus to run Hong Kong after 1997, the Chinese government had to look elsewhere. The business sector became a convenient coalition partner."[59] Following the handover, Hong Kong tycoons proved to be highly flexible: instead of supporting British colonial rule, they have now become supportive of mainland China's crony-capitalist system. Lim and Ping have pointed out that Hong Kong "tycoons also represent an unwritten social contract between Beijing's elites and Hong Kong society—that the tycoons will be rewarded economically or left alone to conduct their business activities if they remain compatible with Beijing's policy directions (or at least remain neutral in contentious issues) and facilitate policy implementation if necessary".[60] Both in terms of trade and commerce and the role of local business elites, therefore, we can thus identify considerable continuity between the colonial and the post-colonial political regime.

In the following six areas—rule of law, policing, language policy, education system, press censorship and political institutional design—rather marked differences and departures from British colonial rule can be observed. According to Jacques deLisle and Kevin Plane, there are now fundamental differences between "what the 'rule of law' means, how it is linked to prosperity, and what maintaining it will require. How uncompromising and substantially broad must legality be in order to secure the territory's material success? Is narrowly economic legality possible without a rule of law that extends to more 'political matters'?"[61] Lieberthal has rightly pointed out that

> Hong Kong has long been a society that practices the rule *of* law, while China after the Cultural Revolution has evolved increasingly from rule *without* law toward rule *by* law ... currently the mainland remains overwhelmingly a system in which political power bends the law to its needs, rather than one in which the law serves as an absolute constraint on the exercise of political power. On this crucial issue, Hong Kong has long operated in a diametrically opposite fashion ... Unfortunately, very few Chinese on the mainland understand the dynamics of a society characterized by the rule of law.[62]

Benny Tai has argued that the Chinese party-state

> adopts a very thin conception of the rule of law and promote[s] it to be the official discourse of the rule of law in Hong Kong. Under a narrow understanding of this well-accepted constitutional principle, the power-holder needs only to conform to some general procedural requirements and implement decisions through among other things independent courts

following some vaguely drafted legal rules. Any substantive legal provisions do not constrain the powerholder as all laws including the constitution can be given any meaning or even be changed as the powerholder likes. There is also no government institution including the court [that] can impose a real constraint on the powerholder as all government institutions are subject to the highest legal authority of the powerholder. This understanding of the rule of law can also be referred to as the authoritarian rule of law.[63]

Commenting on the use of tear gas and pepper spray following the OCLP/UM in Autumn 2014, Steve Tsang has argued that

Hong Kong is heading towards a crisis. And it is not the making of students and the Occupy Central movement who were protesting over the weekend. It is the result of the unnecessary over-reactions by the authorities in Hong Kong, who have decided to use the police and a carefully calibrated escalation in the use of force to end the peaceful demonstrations.[64]

During OCLP/UM the social worker and Occupy activist Ken Tsang was also severely kicked and beaten by seven police members, an incident that was captured by TV crews.[65] More ominously, the Hong Kong police turned a blind eye to triads attacking peaceful protesters in Mong Kok on 3 October 2014.[66] The use of triads to intimidate a restless Hong Kong society resembles the phenomenon of "thugs for hire" on the mainland, described in detail in Chapter 5. It echoes Japanese practices during the occupation of Hong Kong during World War II, where local triads retained public order in return for the tacit toleration of their illegal casinos.[67] It also resembles the co-optation of gangsters by local KMT governments since the early 1950s, a practice which led to the black gold (*heijin*) phenomenon in Taiwan politics. The political instrumentalisation of underworld groups since 2014 thus can be considered a particularly nefarious feature of the HKSAR's increasingly authoritarian approach to governance.

Another point of departure from pre-handover practices can be seen in the field of language policy. Whereas the British colonial government contracted the management of primary and secondary schools to the Catholic Church and other Christian denominations to run them in a semi-autonomous way, the PRC's approach to language acquisition has been far more prescriptive. Jacob Mey and Hans Ladegaard have highlighted that after 1997

new language policies were adopted, including a controversial medium of instruction policy, which stipulated that at least 75% of secondary schools in the territory should be Chinese-medium schools. Subsequently, 307 secondary schools were forced to give up English as their medium of instruction and adopt Chinese; a controversial move which left many parents frustrated not only about the lack of choice but also with the prospect of seeing their children lose out on university education which is still largely English medium-of-instruction.[68]

To overcome the binary choice between English or Chinese as a main language of instruction at Hong Kong schools, Chao Fen Sun has argued that "in the process of developing a language policy that is fair to all, the government should vigorously engage in building up a bilingual system for secondary schools and universities, whereby students will not face additional linguistic barriers or be placed in socially disadvantaged positions by the educational system".[69] Such sensible solutions, however, would require a co-creative approach to legislating the education sector. The HKSAR government has primarily pursued a policy of selective decolonisation, primarily directed against Church-controlled Hong Kong schools. Ng and Fulda have highlighted that "Christian civil society actors started to feel the pinch of decolonization after the handover in 1997. The introduction of the Education (Amendment) Ordinance by the HKSAR government in 2004 required all schools to establish an Incorporated Management Committee ... with 40 percent of the board members from a non-sponsoring body, by 2010."[70] While the new institution of the Incorporated Management Committee was sold to the public as a means to widen participation, enhance professionalism and evaluate effectiveness,[71] it was in fact a thinly disguised attempt to break the monopoly of Christian denominations over Hong Kong's primary and secondary education sector.

Another area of concern has been the evolution of press freedom in the former colony. While Hong Kong's press was subject to various censorship ordinances under the British, the CCP has used both intimidation tactics and commercial pressure to bring Hong Kong's freewheeling press under control. Tuen-yu Lau and Yiu-ming To have described the Hong Kong media landscape after 1997 as "sandwiched between the Beijing and HKSAR leaders, while also facing economic tough times and gradual staff layoffs".[72] While Lau and To have argued that "economic pressure is much stronger than political forces in shaping media developments in posthandover Hong Kong",[73] in recent years the situation has changed rather significantly. Following the firebombing of offices and the home of media tycoon Jimmy Lai, a Beijing critic and OCLP/UM supporter,[74] Lai sold his flagship *Next Magazine* to a local businessman. Under Lai's editorial *Next Magazine* was "well known for its in-depth investigative reports about Chinese and local politics, as well as gossipy articles about the city's social elite, triads and entertainers".[75] Lai was also a major donor of Hong Kong's Democratic Party and had provided financial support to OCLP/UM.[76] In another controversial development, in 2016 Hong Kong's flagship English-language newspaper *South China Morning Post* was acquired by Jack Ma,[77] a mainland Chinese entrepreneur and CCP party member.[78] In the early 2000s Heike Holbig lauded the *South China Morning Post* for playing "a crucial role in stimulating and leading a critical public discourse on relevant subjects"[79] and suggested that the fact that "the paper enjoys a high international reputation and is read widely outside Hong Kong is also a factor in safeguarding press freedom in the SAR".[80] In 2018 long-term *South China Morning Post* columnist Stephen Vines accused the new editorial under Ma's leadership of peddling CCP propaganda, as evident from the extensive and uncritical *South China Morning Post* coverage of a forced confession of the abducted Swedish national and Hong Kong bookseller Gui Minhai.[81] There are credible allegations that Gui Minhai was abducted by Chinese security forces from his residence in Pattaya, Thailand in October 2015. He reappeared in mainland China in January 2016, claiming that he had voluntarily travelled to the PRC. He was one of five co-workers of Causeway Bay Books who had caused the ire of the CCP leadership by publishing bestsellers critical of the mainland Chinese party-state. Carolyne Cartier has warned about:

> the unusual extension of non-transparent forms of governance and control over individuals' rights and protections from unwarranted search and seizure, as well as about freedoms of the press and publication in the Hong Kong SAR. Any potential for mainland security agents to detain Hong Kong citizens in Hong Kong and then to transport them to the mainland undermines the Basic Law and poses complex questions about territorial governance.[82]

The fact that for both commercial and political reasons the future of two flagship publications in Hong Kong, the Chinese-language *Next Magazine* and the English-language *South China Morning Post*, hang in the balance is concerning.

Last but not least, under the leadership of pro-Beijing chief executives Tung Chee-hwa (1996–2002), Donald Tsang (2005–7), Leung Chun-ying (2012–17) and Carrie Lam (2017–), the SAR's rather weak democratic institutions have been steadily hollowed out. One of the persistent problems with Hong Kong's Basic Law is that it "intentionally leaves a wide scope of discretion for some parties. Under the Basic Law, the Central Government has a much wider scope than the LegCo."[83] Benny Tai has criticised the undermining of the "One Country, Two Systems" formula by prioritising the PRC's party constitution over the Basic Law, thus undermining the concept of local self-government. He is particularly critical of the fact that Hong Kong's Basic Law is being unilaterally interpreted by the Standing Committee of mainland China's rubber-stamp parliament, the National People's Congress. In Tai's words, the

> Basic Law is the constitutional foundation of the system of law in Hong Kong. Through the power to interpret the Basic Law enjoyed by the [National People's Congress], the [Chinese Communist Regime] can give

any meaning to the Basic Law whatever and whenever it desires, even if the meaning is something which the language of the legal instrument cannot bear, and such additional meanings are applied retrospectively.[84]

This institutional set-up makes the chief executives beholden to National People's Congress judgments and thus undermines the autonomy of the HKSAR government.

A rather intriguing feature of Hong Kong's parliament has been the distinction between functional constituencies and geographic constituencies. While after 1997 the HKSAR government made procedural changes to the functional constituencies, which currently make up 30 of the 70 seats of Hong Kong's parliament, it never considered abolishing this relic of British colonial rule. Former under secretary for the environment in C.Y. Leung's HKSAR administration, Christine Loh, has pointed out that "for the 2004 LegCo election, there were some 3.207 million registered voters in the [geographic constituencies] and 199,539 registered functional constituency voters for the 28 functional constituencies. Beijing's declared belief that the functional constituencies provide 'balanced participation' leading to 'stability and prosperity' needs to be critically examined."[85] Loh has issued a scathing critique of functional constituencies:

> For a city as sophisticated as Hong Kong, to be discussing the merits of indirect elections and functional constituencies as an alternative to universal suffrage seems absurd. No other community as prosperous and pluralistic as Hong Kong in today's world is burdened with such a relic of 19th century imperialism as a substitute for a directly elected legislature. For Hong Kong's post-colonial government to engage at Beijing's behest in public consultations on reforming rather than abolishing [functional constituencies] has all the intellectual attractions of a discussion of the merits of the abacus over the computer in modern banking.[86]

As functional constituencies are industry-based and since Hong Kong's business community is largely pro-Beijing, this creates a structural disadvantage for the pro-democratic camp in each and every LegCo election.

While the democratic camp has to a certain extent been successful in monitoring the HKSAR government, following the "Oathgate" debacle in 2016, to be discussed in Chapter 10, it lost its veto power to censure bills from the pro-Beijing political camp.[87] And while electoral reforms of the 1990s have certainly helped to broaden political representation, elected LegCo members in fact only enjoy limited scope to introduce their own legislation, e. g. in the form of private member bills. Prior to 1997, private member bills were effectively used by the pro-democracy camp to disrupt "the government's legislative agenda and [challenge] the executive's dominance on policy initiation and making".[88] Since 1997, however, the procedural hurdles for introducing private member bills have become extremely high: "Article 74 of the Basic Law prohibits legislators from putting forward bills that affect public expenditure, political structure, or government operations unless the chief executive has given his or her written consent to the introduction of the bills."[89] The chief executive's wide-ranging veto power over oppositional bills led prominent democracy activist Christine Loh to "stand down in July 2000 when her Legco term ended, citing legislative impotence as her reason".[90] In Chapter 10 I will discuss how the gradual closing of the route of electoral democratisation has led to a surge in street protests since 2003.

In Hong Kong's post-OCLP/UM period, however, freedom of association can no longer be taken for granted. Chan Kin-man highlights the difficulties of OCLP to register an organisation prior to OCLP/UM. He also points out the difficulties Joshua Wong's new party Demosistō had in registering. Last but not least he questions the shutting down of the Hong Kong National Party.[91] Chan argues that freedom of assembly in Hong Kong has also been greatly reduced. According to Chan, the

> freedom of assembly and demonstrations in Hong Kong is constrained by the Public Order Ordinance, inherited from the colonial period. The Ordinance stipulates that the organisers of any protest over 30 people, or assemblies of over 50 participants, have to apply for a "letter of no objection" (LONO) from the police. Public assemblies without LONO is liable to prosecution as "unauthorised" or "unlawful assembly" depending on whether the social order has been disturbed.[92]

Following OCLP/UM and taking "advantage of the restrictive Public Ordinance and other Common Law charges, the authorities have been prosecuting more protestors with more severe offences in these years".[93] In tandem, the HKSAR has stated:

> [the] tactic to suppress freedom of assembly is to harass participants or disrupt the proceeding of the political assembly through social groups or individuals indirectly funded by the authorities. Studies show that China's "united front work" in Hong Kong, mainly through CLO, has used different tactics including integration of pro-Beijing groups, co-optation of or collaboration with more independent outsiders, containment or denunciation of oppositional groups … Participants were also found receiving cash from organisers of events supporting the government or opposing the democracy movement such as the march against Occupying Central.[94]

In this chapter I have traced the evolution from British colonial rule prior to Hong Kong handover to the increasing deterioration of governance under successive HKSAR governments from 1997 onwards. Working in concert with the CCP HKSAR governments have greatly reduced the available space for political contestation. The previous discussion about continuity and change in the eight areas of trade and commerce, the role of local business elites, rule of law, policing, language policy, education system, press censorship and political institutional design has shown that Hong Kong's semi-democratic political system has come under considerable strain. Benny Tai has critiqued the political status quo by stating that "Hong Kong no longer is what it was, nor what it is supposed to be".[95] The incremental closing of available political space for contestation is now severely limiting the strategic choices of Hong Kong's democracy movement. In Chapter 10 I will show that following the 1997 handover Hong Kong's pan-democratic camp has to a certain extent benefited from the organisational prowess of the Catholic Church and other Christian denominations. This religious influence arguably had a moderating effect, which in recent years appears to be waning. Hong Kong's democracy movement consequently has become increasingly nativist and started to advocate Hong Kong independence, or in its less radical form, called for the right of self-determination of the Hong Kong people. I will argue that the securitisation of Hong Kong should be considered a deliberate strategy by the CCP to turn Hong Kong into a regular mainland Chinese city. This ongoing development is likely to further radicalise Hong Kong's democracy movement, making ever harsher crackdowns on political dissent increasingly likely in the not too distant future.

Notes

1 Snow, Philip (2003), *The Fall of Hong Kong: Britain, China and the Japanese Occupation*, Yale University Press, New Haven CT.
2 Lau, Chi Kuen (1997), *Hong Kong's Colonial Legacy*, Chinese University Press, Hong Kong.
3 Loh, Christine (2010), *Underground Front: The Chinese Communist Party in Hong Kong*, Hong Kong University Press, Hong Kong, 232.
4 Tai, Benny Yiu-ting (Ed.) (2018), China's Sharp Power in Hong Kong, Civil Hub, Hong Kong. Available online: https://drive.google.com/file/d/1G2kb4jBC9q81qO DUyvFTAwjI-EMSVLRw/view (accessed 21 November 2018).
5 Tsang, Steve (2006), *A Modern History of Hong Kong*, Hong Kong University Press, Hong Kong, 16.
6 Carroll, John (1999), Chinese Collaboration in British Hong Kong, in: Ngo, Tak-Wing (Ed.), *Hong Kong's History: State and Society under Colonial Rule*, Routledge, London, 15.
7 Ibid., 24.
8 Tsang, Steve (2006), *A Modern History of Hong Kong*, Hong Kong University Press, Hong Kong, 8.
9 Munn, Christopher (1999), The Criminal Trial under Early Colonial Rule, in: Ngo, Tak-Wing (Ed.), *Hong Kong's History: State and Society under Colonial Rule*, Routledge, London, 66.
10 Wong, Kam C. (2015), *Policing in Hong Kong: History and Reform*, Taylor and Francis, Boca Raton, FL, 47.
11 Ibid.

12 Ibid., 76.
13 Ibid.
14 Tsang, Steve (2006), *A Modern History of Hong Kong*, Hong Kong University Press, Hong Kong, 188.
15 Ibid., 21.
16 Ibid., 23.
17 Lau, Chi Kuen (1997), *Hong Kong's Colonial Legacy*, Chinese University Press, Hong Kong, 102.
18 Ibid., 25.
19 McCarthy, John, Britt, David and Wolfson, Mark (1991), The Institutional Channeling of Social Movements by the State in the United States, *Research in Social Movements, Conflict and Change*, 14, 45–76.
20 Ng, Nancy and Fulda, Andreas (2018), The Religious Dimension of Hong Kong's Umbrella Movement, *Journal of Church and State*, Oxford University Press, Oxford, 383.
21 Goossaert, Vincent and Palmer, David (2011), *The Religious Question in Modern China*, University of Chicago Press, Chicago, 350.
22 Patten, Christopher (1998), *East and West: China, Power, and the Future of Asia*, Random House, New York, 136.
23 Lau, Chi Kuen (1997), *Hong Kong's Colonial Legacy*, Chinese University Press, Hong Kong, 155.
24 Ibid., 156.
25 Ibid., 158–9.
26 Liu, Shuyong (1997), Hong Kong: A Survey of Its Political and Economic Development over the Past 150 Years, *China Quarterly*, 151, 583.
27 Ibid., 584.
28 Tsang, Steve (2006), *A Modern History of Hong Kong*, Hong Kong University Press, Hong Kong, 26–8.
29 I am grateful to Steve Tsang for bringing this to my attention.
30 Tsang, Steve (2008), Young, Sir Mark Aitchison (1886–1974). Available online: www.oxforddnb.com.ezproxy.nottingham.ac.uk/view/10.1093/ref:odnb/9780198614128.001.0001/odnb-9780198614128-e-51588 (accessed 23 November 2018).
31 Ibid.
32 Pepper, Suzanne (2002), Hong Kong and the Reconstruction of China's Political Order, in: Ming Chan and Alvin So (Eds), *Crisis and Transformation in China's Hong Kong*, M.E. Sharpe, Armonk, NY, 27.
33 Tsang, Steve (2007), *Governing Hong Kong: Administrative Officers from the Nineteenth Century to the Handover to China, 1862–1997*, I.B. Tauris, London, ix.
34 Lau, Chi Kuen (1997), *Hong Kong's Colonial Legacy*, Chinese University Press, Hong Kong, 34.
35 Tsang, Steve (Ed.) (1995), *Government and Politics: A Documentary History of Hong Kong*, Hong Kong University Press, Hong Kong, 94.
36 Tsang, Steve (2006), *A Modern History of Hong Kong*, Hong Kong University Press, Hong Kong, 28.
37 Ibid., 19.
38 Ibid., 95.
39 Chang, David Wen-wei and Chuang, Richard (1999), *The Politics of Hong Kong's Reversion to China*, Macmillan Press, Houndmills, 50.
40 Pepper, Suzanne (2002), Hong Kong and the Reconstruction of China's Political Order, in: Ming Chan and Alvin So (Eds), *Crisis and Transformation in China's Hong Kong*, M.E. Sharpe, Armonk, NY, 33.
41 Chang, David Wen-wei and Chuang, Richard (1999), *The Politics of Hong Kong's Reversion to China*, Macmillan Press, Houndmills, 86.

42 John M. Carroll (2007), *A Concise History of Hong Kong*, Rowman and Littlefield, Lanham, MD.

43 Legislative Council of the Hong Kong Special Administrative Region of the PRC (2018), History of the Legislative Council. Available online: www.legco.gov.hk/yr98-99/english/intro/hist_lc.htm (accessed 27 November 2018).

44 *Guardian* (2017), "I Should Have Done More": Chris Patten on Leaving Hong Kong without Democracy. Available online: www.theguardian.com/world/2017/jun/28/i-should-have-done-more-chris-patten-leaving-hong-kong-without-democracy-china (accessed 23 November 2018).

45 Constitutional and Mainland Affairs Bureau (2018), Joint Declaration of the Government of the United Kingdom of Great Britain and Northern Ireland and the Government of the People's Republic of China on the Question of Hong Kong. Available online: www.cmab.gov.hk/en/issues/jd2.htm (accessed 23 November 2018).

46 Lau, Chi Kuen (1997), *Hong Kong's Colonial Legacy*, Chinese University Press, Hong Kong, 35–8.

47 *South China Morning Post* (2014), China Was Very Much against Democracy in Hong Kong Even before Handover, Says Chris Patten. Available online: www.scmp.com/news/hong-kong/article/1645156/china-was-very-much-against-democracy-hong-kong-even-handover-says (accessed 23 November 2018).

48 *South China Morning Post* (2015), Beijing Will Combine Functional Constituencies with One Man, One Vote, Mainland Professor Says. Available online: www.scmp.com/news/hong-kong/article/1703801/beijing-will-combine-functional-constituencies-one-man-one-vote (accessed 23 November 2018).

49 Chan, Ming (2002), Introduction: The Hong Kong SAR in Flux, in: Ming Chan and Alvin So (Eds), *Crisis and Transformation in China's Hong Kong*, M.E. Sharpe, Armonk, NY, 8.

50 Chan, Ming (2002), Realpolitik Realignment of the Democratic Camp in the Hong Kong SAR, in: Ming Chan and Alvin So (Eds), *Crisis and Transformation in China's Hong Kong*, M.E. Sharpe, Armonk, NY, 68.

51 Ibid., 69.

52 Patten, Christopher (1998), *East and West: China, Power, and the Future of Asia*, Times Books, New York, 69.

53 *Hong Kong Free Press* (2017), Declassified Files: UK Warned in 1989 It Would Be "Impotent" if Hong Kong Deal Breached after Handover. Available online: www.hongkongfp.com/2017/07/22/declassified-files-uk-warned-1989-impotent-hong-kong-deal-breached-handover/ (accessed 28 November 2018).

54 Lam, Hon-Chak (2018), Chinese Sharp Power in Hong Kong: An Economic Perspective, in: Benny Tai (Ed.), *China's Sharp Power in Hong Kong*, Hong Kong Civil Hub, Hong Kong, 92.

55 Ibid., 93–4.

56 Ibid., 94–5.

57 Ibid., 96.

58 Ibid., 98.

59 Ma, Ngok (2007), *Political Development in Hong Kong: State, Political Society and Civil Society*, Hong Kong University Press, Hong Kong, 36.

60 Lim, Tai Wei and Ping, Xiaojuan (2016), *Tycoons in Hong Kong: Between Occupy Central and Beijing*, Imperial College Press, London, 1.

61 deLisle, Jacques and Plane, Kevin (1997), Cooking the Rice without Cooking the Goose: The Rule of Law, the Battle over Business, and the Quest for Prosperity in Hong Kong after 1997, in: Warren Cohen and Li Zhao (Eds), *Hong Kong under Chinese Rule: The Economic and Political Implications of Reversion*, Cambridge University Press, Cambridge, 31.

62 Lieberthal, Kenneth (1997), Post-July 1997 Challenges, in: Warren Cohen and Li Zhao (Eds), *Hong Kong under Chinese Rule: The Economic and Political Implications of Reversion*, Cambridge University Press, Cambridge, 241–2.

63 Tai, Benny (2018), Authoritarian Rule of Law in Hong Kong, in: Benny Tai (Ed.), *China's Sharp Power in Hong Kong*, Hong Kong Civil Hub, Hong Kong, 19.
64 Tsang, Steve (2014), How Not to Make a Crisis out of Hong Kong, Forbes. Available online: www.forbes.com/sites/forbesasia/2014/09/30/how-not-to-make-a-crisis-out-of-hong-kong/ (accessed 5 December 2016).
65 *South China Morning Post* (2017), Seven Hong Kong Police Guilty of Beating Occupy Activist Ken Tsang. Available online: www.scmp.com/video/hong-kong/2070748/seven-hong-kong-police-guilty-beating-occupy-activist-ken-tsang (accessed 27 November 2018).
66 *Guardian* (2014), Hong Kong Protesters Beaten and Bloodied as Thugs Attack Sit-In. Available online: www.theguardian.com/world/2014/oct/03/hong-kong-protesters-democracy-occupy (accessed 27 November 2018).
67 Snow, Philip (2003), *The Fall of Hong Kong: Britain, China and the Japanese Occupation*, Yale University Press, New Haven CT, 254.
68 Mey, Jacob and Ladegaard, Hans (2015), Discourse, Democracy and Diplomacy: A Pragmatic Analysis of the Occupy Central Movement in Hong Kong, *WORD*, 61(4), 320.
69 Sun, Chao Fen (2002), Hong Kong's Language Policy in the Postcolonial Age, in: Ming Chan and Alvin So (Eds), *Crisis and Transformation in China's Hong Kong*, M.E. Sharpe, Armonk, NY, 304.
70 Ng, Nancy and Fulda, Andreas (2018), The Religious Dimension of Hong Kong's Umbrella Movement, *Journal of Church and State*, Oxford University Press, Oxford, 387.
71 Education Bureau HKSAR (2018), School-Based Management and School-Based Management Governance Framework, Available online: www.edb.gov.hk/en/sch-admin/sbm/gov-framework/index.html (accessed 27 November 2018).
72 Lau, Tuen-yu and To, Yiu-ming (2002), Walking a Tight Rope: Hong Kong's Media Facing Political and Economic Challenges since Sovereignty Transfer, in: Ming Chan and Alvin So (Eds), *Crisis and Transformation in China's Hong Kong*, M.E. Sharpe, Armonk, NY, 323.
73 Ibid.
74 BBC (2015), Hong Kong Media Tycoon Jimmy Lai Targeted by Firebombs. Available online: www.bbc.co.uk/news/world-asia-china-30776405 (accessed 27 November 2018).
75 Reuters (2017), Jimmy Lai Magazine Sale Stokes Concern over HK Media Landscape. Available online: www.reuters.com/article/us-hongkong-media/jimmy-lai-magazine-sale-stokes-concern-over-hk-media-landscape-idUSKBN1A20MB (accessed 27 November 2018).
76 *New York Times* (2015), For Jimmy Lai, Hong Kong's Rebellious Tycoon, Next Battle May Be in Court. Available online: www.nytimes.com/2015/01/12/business/media/for-jimmy-lai-hong-kongs-rebellious-tycoon-next-battle-may-be-in-court.html (accessed 27 November 2018).
77 *South China Morning Post* (2016), Alibaba's Jack Ma Reveals Why He Bought the South China Morning Post and What He Wants to Do with It. Available online: www.scmp.com/news/china/society/article/1937256/alibabas-jack-ma-reveals-why-he-bought-south-china-morning-post (accessed 27 November 2018).
78 Reuters (2018), Alibaba's Jack Ma Is a Communist Party Member, China State Paper Reveals. Available online: www.reuters.com/article/us-alibaba-jack-ma/alibabas-jack-ma-is-a-communist-party-member-china-state-paper-reveals-idUSKCN1NW073 (accessed 27 November 2018).
79 Holbig, Heike (2003), Hong Kong Press Freedom in Transition, in: Robert Ash, Peter Ferdinand, Brian Hook and Robin Porter (Eds), *Hong Kong in Transition: One Country, Two Systems*, RoutledgeCurzon, London, 208.
80 Ibid.

81 *Hong Kong Free Press* (2018), Why I Will No Longer Write for the South China Morning Post. Available online: www.hongkongfp.com/2018/11/13/i-will-no-longer-write-south-china-morning-post/ (accessed 27 November 2018).

82 Cartier, Carolyn (2017), Policing the Borders: Hong Kong Conundrums, in: Jane Golley, Linda Jaivin and Luigi Tomba (Eds), *Control: China Story Yearbook 2016*, Australian National University Press, Acton, 245.

83 Tai, Benny (2002), Chapter 1 of Hong Kong's New Constitution: Constitutional Positioning an Repositioning, in: Ming Chan and Alvin So (Eds), *Crisis and Transformation in China's Hong Kong*, M.E. Sharpe, Armonk, NY, 210.

84 Ibid., 18.

85 Loh, Christine (2006), *Functional Constituencies: A Unique Feature of the Hong Kong Legislative Council*, Hong Kong University Press, Hong Kong. Available online: www.oapen.org/search?identifier=420804;keyword=china (accessed 20 February 2015).

86 Ibid.

87 CNN (2016), Hong Kong Moves to Disqualify More Pro-Democracy Lawmakers. Available online: https://edition.cnn.com/2016/12/02/asia/hong-kong-lawmakers-oathgate/index.html (accessed 26 November 2018).

88 Ma, Ngok (2007), *Political Development in Hong Kong: State, Political Society and Civil Society*, Hong Kong University Press, Hong Kong, 109.

89 Lui, Percy Luen-tim (2007), The Legislature, in: Wai-man Lam, Percy Luen-tim Lui, Wilson Wong and Ian Holliday (Eds), *Contemporary Hong Kong Politics: Governance in the Post-1997 Era*, Hong Kong University Press, Hong Kong, 45.

90 Chan, Ming (2002), Realpolitik Realignment of the Democratic Camp in the Hong Kong SAR, in: Ming Chan and Alvin So (Eds), *Crisis and Transformation in China's Hong Kong*, M.E. Sharpe, Armonk, NY, 92.

91 Chan, Kin-man (2018), Contraction of Civil Society under China's Sharp Power, in: Benny Tai (Ed.), *China's Sharp Power in Hong Kong*, Hong Kong Civil Hub, Hong Kong, 32–3.

92 Ibid., 33.

93 Ibid.

94 Ibid., 34–5.

95 *New York Times* (2018), Benny Tai Yiu-ting: Hong Kong Isn't What It Was, Nor What It's Supposed to Be Available online: www.nytimes.com/2018/11/18/opinion/china-hong-kong-benny-tai-umbrella-movement-trial.html (accessed 28 November 2018).

10

HONG KONG'S DEMOCRACY MOVEMENT

A canary in the coal mine?

In this chapter I trace the evolution of Hong Kong's democracy movement from the late years of British colonial rule until late 2018. A key focus is on two distinctive and yet inter-related arenas: the realm of LegCo politics and the politics of grassroots-level social movements. Following the structure of Chapters 6 and 8 I once again address the four leading questions about antecedents and political opportunities of the respective struggles for democracy; the question as to which reform camp initiated the specific struggle; which strategic reform approach was taken; and what the key lessons learned were.

I will show that Hong Kong's democracy movement should be considered the proverbial canary in the coal mine. Operating under the conditions of a semi-democratic political system, Hong Kong's democrats have not only struggled to defy an increasingly authoritarian HKSAR government but have also struggled to maintain unity. In episode 9 I will highlight the various challenges Hong Kong legislators have faced when working within the confines of a politically neutered LegCo. In episode 10 I will discuss how in 2003 a broad coalition of political actors and CSOs joined the movement against the enactment of Article 23 of the Basic Law. Episode 11 will highlight the diversification of social movements in the subsequent years and hone in on the rise of youth-led activism in the wake of the 2012 movement against the new Moral and National Education Policy. In the twelfth and final episode I will trace the development from Hong Kong's OCLP/UM to Hong Kong's independence movement. My discussion will show that while Hong Kong democrats have successfully engaged in various defensive actions against illiberal encroachments by the HKSAR government, Hong Kong's democracy movement so far has also failed to significantly liberalise and democratise the region's key political institutions. I will argue that while Hong Kong's democrats have been impeded by the HKSAR's imperfect political institutions, they have also time and again made their own unforced strategic and tactical errors. I will end this chapter by questioning the wisdom of the nativist turn in Hong Kong politics, which not only weakens the struggle for democracy in Hong Kong but also in mainland China.

Episode 9: Working within the confines of a politically neutered LegCo

Antecedents and political opportunities

In Chapter 9 I outlined how from 1984 onwards the British colonial government adopted top-down political reforms aimed at making Hong Kong's LegCo more representative. After 1991, the number of directly elected LegCo members increased successively, from 18 in 1991, 20 in 1995 and 1998, to 24 in 2000 and 30 in 2004.[1] Such incremental progress, however, was overshadowed by a lack of consensus between the British colonial administration and the CCP about Hong Kong's political future. Patten's vision of an emancipatory LegCo, which one day should evolve into a fully fledged Westminster-style parliament, was not shared by his mainland Chinese counterparts. Fundamentally different interpretations of Hong Kong's ambiguously worded mini-constitution, the Basic Law, also meant that constitutional democracy in the former colony remained an aspiration, not a reality. Michael Davis provides an apt summary of the dilemma at hand:

> The Basic Law faithfully incorporates most of the requirements of the [Sino-British] Joint Declaration, but in three key areas the Basic Law sometimes comes up short, either in its text or in its interpretation. Malleability of existing institutions has put a high premium on democratic development to afford the highest level of public oversight. Disputes over Basic Law interpretations were evident in a variety of crises Hong Kong faced in the first ten years. Full direct election of the LegCo is promised but not provided. Liberal human rights guarantees are adequately provided but are put at risk by national security and public order provisions elsewhere in the Basic Law. Constitutional judicial review was long in doubt from the lack of explicit reference in the text. Although that doubt has been resolved favorably by judicial decisions, Beijing and pro-Beijing politicians at critical moments have sought to challenge such resolution. Actions of the government to overturn decisions of Hong Kong's courts as well as the various [Standing Committee of the National People's Congress] interpretations have especially put the health of the judicial institution at risk.[2]

While Hong Kong's democracy movement managed to take advantage of the political opportunities offered by the late British colonial government prior to the handover, post-1997 it came up against the institutional bottlenecks of incomplete LegCo reforms and a rather ambiguously worded Basic Law.

Key actors

While the British colonial government sowed the seeds of liberalisation and short-term democratisation, political developments in mainland China in the late 1980s facilitated the emergence of political parties in Hong Kong. The CCP's crackdown on mainland China's anti-corruption and pro-democracy movement in 1989

> captured the imagination of the people in Hong Kong, who showed an unprecedented degree of responsibility and maturity in the demonstrations and marches in support of the Beijing demonstrations. As the Tiananmen Incident unfolded and subsided, earlier doubts about the political readiness of the Hong Kong people for participatory politics dissipated ... This provided the climate for the founding, in April 1990, of the first true political party in Hong Kong, the United Democrats of Hong Kong ... by activists who had been advocating a faster pace for developing democracy in Hong Kong.[3]

When faced with an anti-establishment United Democrats of Hong Kong (UDHK), Hong Kong's pro-establishment camp soon followed suit and, in 1992, established the Democratic Alliance for Betterment of Hong Kong. This quickly gained a reputation of being very close to the Chinese government.[4] Another party, the Liberal Party of Hong Kong, was established in 1993, occupying the space "somewhere in between the UDHK and the [Democratic Alliance for Betterment of Hong Kong], and is the party which advocates building on the previous laissez-faire approach of Hong Kong as closely as possible".[5] In 1994, the UDHK merged with Meeting Point, "which was originally formed as a pressure group with a predominantly middle class intellectual membership in 1982"[6] and formed what is now known as the Democratic Party (DP).

In the years that followed, the pro-democracy camp splintered and much smaller parties have emerged: the Citizens Party (from 1997 until 2008), Democratic Alliance (since 2001), Civic Party (since 2006), League of Social Democrats (also since 2006), Neo Democrats (since 2010), Labour Party (since 2011), People Power (also since 2011), Civic Passion (since 2012), Youngspiration (since 2015), Third Side (also since 2015), Demosistō (since 2016) and the Hong Kong National Party (also since 2016). I concur with Mathew Wong who has pointed out that with "more parties competing for the same group of supporters, the level of intra-camp competition has intensified".[7] The ongoing fragmentation of Hong Kong's pro-democracy camp and later split between pan-democrats and nativists/localists can also be directly attributed to the DP's inability post-1997 to integrate new political talent and be explained by the DP leadership's aversion to adopting a multitude of strategies and tactics in the struggle for democracy.

Strategic reform approach

The arrival of political parties since the 1991 elections brought "social and political cleavages into the open, manifesting in the legislative politics in the years that followed".[8] Ngok Ma has suggested that "in 1995–97 political parties can be largely positioned along two axes: pro-China versus pro-democracy/pro-Hong Kong and pro-grassroots versus pro-business".[9] Following the defeat of OCLP/ UM in 2014 and since the 2016 LegCo elections, a third cleavage has emerged between supporters of the "One Country, Two Systems" formula versus advocates of Hong Kong self-determination and/or Hong Kong independence.[10] Strategies of the pro-democracy camp also continuously evolved after the 1997 handover. In the following I will focus on three important turning points which highlight the rather convoluted search for an appropriate democratisation strategy: the immediate years after the 1997 transition, the DP's constitutional reform debacle in 2010 and the post-OCLP/UM radicalisation since 2014. I will argue that early successes in defending Hong Kong's young democratic institutions have given way to mounting failures of the pan-democratic camp. As I will show, the latter set-backs can be directly attributed to the use of one-sided and often ineffective strategies and tactics.

In response to the dismantling of the 1995 LegCo and the establishment of the Provisional Legislative Council (PLC), "the full array of democrat camp LegCo members firmly opposed the PLC as an illegitimate, extraconstitutional organ not provided for in the Basic Law".[11] Boycotting the PLC was a rare moment of unity within the pro-democracy camp, where "a majority of these ex-Legco members took advantage of their 'outside the establishment' status to sharpen their public image as the principled and even martyred opposition against antidemocratic regression".[12] Ming Chan has argued that following the 1997 transition, the DP repositioned itself and "adopted a 'walking-on-two-legs' strategy with a double track approach—democracy and socioeconomic justice".[13] Rather than opposing PRC sovereignty over Hong Kong, the DP accepted the premise of the "One Country, Two Systems" formula and lobbied for greater local democracy and social justice.[14] Such moderation paid off in the 1998 LegCo election, where the democratic camp—despite electoral changes by the first HKSAR government under chief executive Tung which benefited the pro-Beijing camp—managed to garner 19 seats.

Following the 1998 LegCo elections the pan-democratic camp struggled to cope with the reformed proportional representative election system, which increased intra-party rivalries. To complicate matters even more, at the turn of the millennium a struggle about strategies and tactics threatened to tear Hong Kong's DP apart. Similar to the divisions in the *dangwai* movement in Taiwan in the early 1980s, a group of grassroots activists who felt "politically disempowered or even legislatively crippled"[15] proposed bottom-up grassroots activism as an alternative to the more top-down and elite-driven parliamentary route. While DP founder Martin Lee managed to placate grassroots activists by paying lip service to their grassroots approach, the conflict laid bare the fundamental tension that has always existed within the DP. Ming Chan has pointed out that the

> mixed membership backgrounds of the DP was formed by the amalgamation of several groups in 1994 were a root cause of this internal polarization on socioeconomic policies and targeted social bases. DP chair Martin Lee has been a champion for the party fulfilling middleclass aspirations for democracy through electoral campaigns and parliamentary participation. The more populist DP elements, some with rich mass movement repertoire, preferred more militant direct collective actions in the economic crisis when rising unemployment endangered grassroots livelihood.[16]

Justifying the pursuit of a parliamentary line, however, has become increasingly difficult post-1997. Ming Chan has bemoaned that the "pro-democracy opposition saw their policy influence drastically reduced, at least if compared to 1995–1997, as they became a minority opposition in a weakened legislature under the executive-dominant system".[17]

Martin Lee's reluctance to augment his parliamentary line with grassroots activism was also due to a persistent structural weakness of Hong Kong's DP, which lies in its contentious relationship with the CCP and the resulting lack of a party base. Since the DP was established in response to the 1989 crackdown on the mainland, the CCP has blacklisted DP party members and prevented them from visiting the mainland. Christine Chung, Hong Kong-based resident country director for China for the National Democratic Institute for International Affairs from 2002 until 2006, has pointed out that this decision meant that with "DP leaders effectively banned from traveling to the mainland, many members and supporters regard affiliation with it to be a potential professional liability, and for years its membership has hovered around 600".[18] This ban was only overturned on 30 November 2016, when "the People's Republic's Hong Kong and Macau Affairs Office announced that the central government was lifting the ban on travel by pan-democrats to the mainland".[19]

Chung argues that political parties in Hong Kong generally suffer from both political institutional impediments as well as internal organisational weaknesses. Chung elucidates that various factors handicap the development of political parties in this system: 1) no explicit legal recognition of political parties exists although the SAR's constitution, the Basic Law, does allude to them; 2) the balance of executive-legislative relations that endows most power to the executive branch though the chief executive is expressly forbidden from maintaining any party affiliation, thus cutting off parties from access to political power; 3) policy decisions have undermined party development, including the 1999 elimination of the Municipal Councils that had provided a training ground for aspiring politicians, Chief Executive Tung Chee-hwa's decision to resume appointment of District Council members in 2002 and the failure to give the councils additional power as promised when the Municipal Councils were eliminated; 4) a unique legislative system which has half of the members directly-elected by geographical constituencies and the other half by extremely restricted functional constituencies, which means that votes on motions and certain bills essentially require a majority of both groups; 5) a change from a more appropriate first-past-the-post to proportional representation system for the directly-elected half of the legislature; and 6) an election campaign subsidy regime that does not encourage party membership but rather provides incentives to independents.[20]

In the following I argue that the DP's inability to become a party movement, similar to the DPP in Taiwan in the late 1980s, should be considered the Achilles heel of the pan-democratic camp. Instead of positioning the DP as a broad church, which is able to accommodate different generations of political activists serving different constituents, post-1997 the DP under Martin Lee stuck to an accommodating middle-of-the-road strategy of engagement with the HKSAR government. Under Lee's leadership the DP adopted a buffering strategy aimed at shielding the party from social movement co-optation.[21] A leaked United States State Department cable written by American diplomat Cunningham reported on the resulting internal dissent within the DP, whereby

> 'reformist' members of the Hong Kong Democratic Party ... recently sent an internal memorandum to the party's leaders, expressing deep concern over the party's poor showing in the November 18 [2008] district council election ... as well as its overall strategic and policy direction ... and [calling] for a thorough review of "inadequacies" in the party, the group offered eight recommendations for recruiting young political talent, improving the organization of the party, and directly linking funds to community-oriented programs.[22]

The DP's inability to pursue a two-pronged approach which marries the parliamentary route with street action would cost the party dearly. In 2004, the HKSAR government proposed a limited constitutional reform package, which was roundly defeated by the pro-democratic camp on the grounds that it did not go far enough: neither did the government's proposal provide a roadmap to a free and fair election of Hong Kong's chief executive nor did it abolish Hong Kong's controversial functional constituencies. When the HKSAR government repeated this exercise in 2010, however, the DP was won over by a last-minute concession. Albert Chan has outlined the in-built limitations of a democratisation strategy which limits the DP's struggle for democracy to the parliamentary route:

> the paradox of the constitutional dynamics of Hong Kong's democratization is that the pan-democrats have the voting power to defeat any government proposal for democratization which they consider to be not democratic enough and thus unsatisfactory, even though the pan-democrats do not themselves have the power to initiate any democratic reform or to secure its passage in LegCo.[23]

This institutional bottleneck also soured the relationship between political parties in the pan-democratic camp. Edmund Cheng has observed that

> the pan-democrats were barely able to claw back their leadership position. In fact, in the 2010 civil referendum only two-thirds of their traditional supporters were mobilized to vote, causing an internal split. When the opposition's inability to rally its supporters was exposed, it lost its mandate to perform backroom deals and its members began to function as delegates rather than as representatives.[24]

In a United States State Department cable from 2010 an American diplomat describes the level of discontent among the pan-democratic camp by suggesting that the "coming months may see the end of the pan-democratic coalition as it exists now, which one DPHK observer suggested is perhaps the only way Hong Kong's currently ossified pro-democracy/pro-Beijing bipolarity might evolve into a more productive political environment".[25] While the pan-democratic camp did not collapse as anticipated, in the subsequent 2012 and 2016 LegCo elections the DP paid a heavy price for its compromise on constitutional reform with the HKSAR government. In 2012 it only gained four out of 18 seats allocated by geographic constituencies. In 2016, the DP's share of the seats won by pan-democrats only marginally increased to 5 out of 13 seats.

Lessons learned

Observing the fragmentation of the pan-democratic camp Ming Chan made the case for a "class-based middle-class/grassroots ad hoc alliance on the socio-economic front [which] will fundamentally reshape HK politics. This type of coalition in LegCo, based on livelihood issues, is likely to further fragment the already unstable pro-Beijing bloc of leftist mass organs and conservative tycoons."[26] This shift from an elite-driven DP towards a party movement co-chaired by career politicians and social movement leaders, however, did not materialise. Instead, the HKSAR government succeeded to divide and rule the pan-democratic camp in the 2010 constitutional reform vote. Christine Loh has argued that "perhaps this is what the CCP would most like to see—politics that keep a technically competent executive slightly more on its toes in the HKSAR, but under the leadership of the party in fact if not in name".[27] There can be no doubt that with the help of a politically neutered LegCo the HKSAR government has been able to implement its own policies regardless of public opinion and opposition from the pro-democracy camp.

This institutional set-up, however, has serious shortcomings, which arguably neither benefit the pro-democracy nor the pro-Beijing camp. Chi Kuen Lau has rightly pointed out that it has failed to

> produce political leadership. On the one hand, elections have brought representatives of interest groups into the legislature, but they have not produced political leadership because the majority party in the legislature does not form the government. On the other hand, power is concentrated in the hands of the Chief Executive who is not returned by popular election. The result of separating elections from political leadership is that while the people's representatives (legislators) have no power, those who have power (the Chief Executive and the senior civil servants) do not have a mandate from the people. This is not the kind of legacy the British wanted to leave behind.[28]

Ming Chan has further highlighted that "with the dwarfing of the legislature in the policy-making process, and with the SAR government content with using majority Legco support as a legitimacy tool, the post-colonial state lost one of the most important institutions which could have bridged the gap between state and society".[29] As the final three case studies will show, Chan's words would prove prophetic. Following the relatively calm years after the 1997 handover state–society relations deteriorated markedly, as evident from the anti-Article 23 protests of 2003. The next episode serves as a textbook example of the advantages of mobilising the anti-establishment, pro-establishment and trans-establishment in a concerted effort to defeat the HKSAR's imposition of national security legislation.

Episode 10: 2003 movement against the enactment of Article 23 of the Basic Law

Antecedents and political opportunities

The discussion thus far has primarily focused on what could be termed Hong Kong's political society, a realm of politics which is primarily occupied by government officials, legislators and their respective political parties. In the following I will outline how civil society actors have joined Hong Kong's struggle for democracy through social movements. It should be noted that there can be some overlap between political and civil society, e.g. in the form of civil society practitioners transitioning from NGO work into political parties and government or vice versa. An example would be Christine Loh, who initially worked as a pan-democrat in the LegCo and later joined chief executive C.Y. Leung's administration as under secretary for the environment in the government. Such political careers underline the points I made in Chapter 3 about the porousness of the boundaries between anti-establishment, pro-establishment and trans-establishment and the reversibility of ascribed membership in one of the three reform camps.

At the heart of the tenth episode is the movement against the enactment of Article 23 in 2002–3. The significance of this particular struggle for democracy becomes clearer when we briefly pause and contemplate how civil society-led social movements differ from party-led political movements. The previous discussion has primarily focused on DP attempts to liberalise Hong Kong's political system by working within the confines of the region's semi-democratic institution, a distinctively trojan horse strategy. Unburdened by such institutional constraints, civil society-led social movements in Hong Kong on the other hand have had more license to pursue distinctively anti-establishment strategies. The Taiwanese experience during the crucial decade of liberalisation throughout the 1980s is instructive here. Joseph Wu has argued that social protest movements tend to highlight the "deficiencies of laws and governmental institutions which no longer meet the needs of an increasingly complex society".[30] In the case of Taiwan, Michael Hsiao has outlined that all 17 social movements from the 1980 consumer movement to the 1998 Hakka Rights movement demanded reforms by the ruling KMT state; they all made claims against the state; and in order to avoid state reprisals kept a distance from the *dangwai* movement; expressed a sentiment of relative deprivation; became increasingly institutionalised; and built bridges across other single-issue social movements.[31] As we will learn from the tenth, eleventh and twelfth episodes, the trajectory of Hong Kong's social movements since the early 2000s differs from its counterparts during Taiwan's period of liberalisation and democratisation throughout the 1980s. Whereas in 2003 political and civil society succeeded in forming an ad hoc coalition against the HKSAR government, in subsequent years Hong Kong's civil society-led social movements have become increasingly anti-establishment, militant and, following the failure of OCLP/UM, nativist and nationalistic.

Key actors

Hong Kong's broad-based movement against the enactment of Article 23 of the Basic Law has been called a "miracle" by DP politicians.[32] According to Ma Ngok the

> struggle against Article 23 in 2002–03 was a case of civil society in self-defence against perceived encroachment by the state. It marked a rare occasion after 1997 in which CSOs of different natures joined together in a territory-wide, loosely organised counter united front, the Civil Human Rights Front (CHRF). The movement saw better cooperation between the CSOs and the political society, culminating in the largest indigenous social movement in Hong Kong history.[33]

At the heart of contention was Article 23 of the Basic Law, which stipulates that the HKSAR

> shall enact laws on its own to prohibit any act of treason, secession, sedition [or] subversion against the [central government], or theft of state secrets, to prohibit foreign political organisations or bodies from conducting political activities in [Hong Kong], and to prohibit political organisations or bodies of [Hong Kong] from establishing ties with foreign political organisations or bodies.[34]

Resistance against the enactment of Article 23 was in part driven by the concern among Hong Kong's pan-democratic camp who "viewed the proposed national security law as a threat to civil liberties. There was intense debate over the potential impact on human rights and freedom of expression and assembly."[35] In response to Beijing's calls for the HKSAR government to enact Article 23 the CHRF built a wide coalition of 44 civil society actors, which included "human rights groups (four of the 44), political groups/parties (ten), professional unions (three), religious groups (six), labour groups (four), student groups (three), feminist, gay and lesbian groups (seven)".[36] And while the CHRF "only had one full-time paid staffer throughout the campaign against Article 23, and all its activities were manned by volunteers of the member groups",[37] the coalition in fact benefited from the organisational support of Hong Kong's Catholic Church and Baptist Church.[38] Cardinal Zen and Reverend Chu Yiu Ming held a historical ecumenical prayer meeting "prior to the historic demonstration of 500,000 people against the National Security (Legislative Provisions) Bill based on Article 23 of the Basic Law on July 1, 2003", thereby signalling to Hong Kong's Christian population that participating in the protest was acceptable.[39] Such support by Christian denominations was crucial for mass mobilisation.

Strategic reform approach

Nancy Ng and I have argued that the role of religion in Hong Kong's social movements remains a largely under-researched and overlooked phenomenon. Prior to the landmark 2003 demonstrations the "Franciscan Justice and Peace Group and the Union of Hong Kong Catholic Organizations in Support of the Patriotic and Democratic Movement in China"[40] had helped to co-organise annual candlelight vigils in commemoration of 4 June 1989. Such large-scale commemorative events drew between 35,000 participants in 1995 and more than 180,000 in 2014.[41] Beatrice Leung and Shun-hing Chan have emphasised the Catholic "Church's involvement and support for the pro-democratic movement in China".[42] The two authors describe how major rallies in support of the 1989 anti-corruption and pro-democracy movement in mainland China were organised by Catholics.[43] During the campaign opposing Article 23, "the Justice and Peace Commission of the Hong Kong Catholic Diocese … the Catholic body responsible for campaigns for social justice and a CHRF member, organized discussions on Article 23 in individual churches".[44] In addition, Jimmy Lai's pro-democracy news outlets "*Apple Daily* and *Next Magazine* led the opinion battle against Article 23. Both were relentless in attacking the government and openly called on the public to join the July 1 demonstration."[45] While playing a supporting rather than coordinating role, the "DP managed to collect phone numbers of about 40,000 supporters, and their volunteers and staff called them up one by one to ask them to join the July 1 demonstration".[46] The CHRF's combined efforts paid off. Following the highly symbolic 1 July 2003 protest rally, which drew more than 500,000 protesters from all walks of life, the HKSAR shelved its plan to enact Article 23.

Lessons learned

While the CHRF had won a major victory, it subsequently did not manage to translate this act of collective self-defence into an institutionalised force for Hong Kong's democratisation. Due to differences in visions and mandates among CHRF members it remained an ad hoc organisation where the participation of varying civil society actors "was bound to be more sporadic, spontaneous, more dependent on the initiative of individual participants, while at the same time making it difficult to effect institutional changes".[47] The unity of Hong Kong's pan-democratic political society and the pro-democratisation civil society thus was a fleeting phenomenon. The HKSAR, overwhelmed by the public backlash and heavily criticised by mainland China's central government, drew different lessons from its defeat. In Chapter 5 I described how the CCP governs mainland China by combining "rule by bribary" with "rule by fear".

When the CCP leadership realised that it could not (yet) autocratically impose its national security legislation on the Hong Kong population, it resorted to more indirect means to manipulate the Hong Kong public. Christine Loh outlines that after 2003 the CCP stepped up its united front activities in Hong Kong. It engaged in fact-finding missions, publicly propped up the badly undermined chief executive Tung Chee Hwa, and offered economic concessions to the HKSAR.[48] It also formed a Central Leading Group under Standing Committee of the CCP member and vice president Zheng Qinghong.[49] After replacing the hapless chief executive Tung with Donald Tsang, the CCP, through its Hong Kong Liaison Office, started to prop up the left-leaning Democratic Alliance for Betterment of Hong Kong, which by 2008 had 11,000 members as opposed to the approximately 600 members of the DP.[50] In addition to such activities aimed at the pro-Beijing-leaning members of Hong Kong's political society, after

> the 2003 rally, communal and kinship organizations such as unions of societies (*shetuan* 社团) and native associations (*tongxianghui* 同乡会) were revived, first as agencies of the grassroots machine to contest the pan-democrats and then as sponsors of the counter-movement to contain the social activists. By 2010, pro-regime "civil" organizations had begun to emerge, most notably Caring Hong Kong Power and the Silent Majority for Hong Kong, which claimed to represent the silent majority who treasure order and business, liberty and peace, and to love the city as much as the activists.[51]

Such efforts to Lebanise[52] Hong Kong's civil society, however, backfired. Yishai has remarked that inclusion "is detrimental for democracy when the state is overactive in its inclusionary role, namely, suffocating civic initiative and autonomy. Absorption of opposition groups into the political system may end with the loss of discursive democratic vitality."[53] Cheng has shown that CCP-led countermobilisation "increased regime control and reduced political opportunities failed to demobilize collective action and instead provoked radicalization".[54]

Episode 11: 2012 movement against the new Moral and National Education Policy

Antecedents and political opportunities

After the successful 2003 rally against the enactment of Article 23 of the Basic Law, social movements in Hong Kong underwent significant change. Edmund Cheng explains that young activists in Hong Kong were growing increasingly dissatisfied with staged political rallies by Hong Kong politicians, which they considered an "absorption of street protests into electoral politics, in which organized elites articulate and express public interests through contentious yet controlled means. This inevitably makes protests contrived or calculated, contradicting the impression that they should be genuine or spontaneous."[55] They were increasingly sceptical about the utility of the annual 1 July rallies, which they considered as "ritualistic and impotent".[56] Young social movement participants also realised that following the 2003 victory against the enactment of Article 23 of the Basic Law, the HKSAR was effectively disempowered by an increasingly overbearing central government in Beijing. In combination with the inability of an increasingly ossified pan-democratic camp to counter the CCP's influence on the HKSAR government, this trend of centralisation triggered "a series of critical events synchronizing pro-heritage, anti-hegemonic and anti-integration claims [which] both expounded and defied the legitimacy of the regime".[57]

Cheng outlines that between

> 2006 and mid-2014, a total of six critical events occurred that met the aforementioned criteria. They included actions to preserve the Star Ferry Pier in 2006 and preserve the Queen's Pier in 2007 (pro-piers), to oppose the Guangzhou–Hong Kong express railway link in 2009–2010 (anti-railway), to oppose the national education curriculum in 2012 (anti-curriculum), to protest the North-East New Territories Development Plan in 2012–2014 (anti-development), and to call for the re-issue of free-to-air television licences in 2013 (pro-licence).[58]

These bottom-up movements saw increasing levels of public participation (from 450 participants in the pro-pier demonstrations to 120,000 protesters joining the anti-curriculum events); were often organised in short periods of time and with the help of social media; involved strategies of occupation and encirclement of buildings; and lasted on average for 67 days.[59] Furthermore, often very young activists started to command the stage. Stephan Ortmann has highlighted that "the young generation are not only opposed to conservative pro-establishment organizations, but they have also become suspicious of pan-democratic parties and organizations, which are viewed as overly hierarchical and centralized around a political leader".[60]

Key actors

Hong Kong's anti-national education curriculum movement merits further investigation, as it is indicative of how young social activists have started to protect their interests and values in unconventional ways. Chitat Chan has emphasised that the "alliance behind the movement consisted of students, parents and teachers. One of the core organisations in the alliance, Scholarism (Xueminsichao), was founded by secondary school students; its leader, Joshua Wong (JW), was only 15 (Ting, 2012; Yuwen, 2012)."[61] Chan has described the latter as a "social activist network, which is largely enhanced nowadays by social media, [and] functions as a 'learning community' which provides a trajectory of civic identity".[62] Alliance members were incensed by "guidelines in a booklet distributed by the government's National Education Services Centre to schools".[63] The latter included "provocative statements, including that China's ruling party is 'progressive, selfless and united'. It also criticized multi-party systems as bringing disaster to countries such as the United States. The booklet also makes no mention of major events that many view as integral to China's history, such as the 1989 Tiananmen Square massacre."[64]

Against the background of the Hong Kong Education Bureau's proposed national education curriculum the booklet was seen as an attempt to brainwash young people into loving the mainland Chinese party-state. Tensions were exacerbated by provocative statements of "Jiang Yudui of the pro-Beijing China Civic Education Promotion Association of Hong Kong [who suggested that] '[a] brain needs washing if there is a problem, just as clothes need washing if they're dirty, and a kidney needs washing if it's sick'".[65] In the preamble of "The Moral and National Education Curriculum Guide (Primary 1 to Secondary 6)" the Education Bureau also did not pull any punches by stating that "promoting national education and enhancing students' understanding of their country and national identity have become a common goal of primary and secondary schools".[66] If the curriculum guide had been accepted this would have reversed belated experiments with pro-democratic civic education which only started in 1996, a year prior to the handover.[67] CCP-led national education would have transformed Hong Kong's formally semi-autonomous education sector into an arena of political indoctrination "aimed at containing the influence of critical and democratic discourses prevalent in Hong Kong society since the early 1990s".[68]

Strategic reform approach

The anti-national education curriculum movement can be considered the first large-scale protest which skilfully combined online agitation with the offline strategy of occupying physical space. When investigating the Twitter account of the student group Scholarism Chitat Chan learned that Scholarism founder Joshua Wong was the most popular member of the online community. At the same time other opinion leaders included more mature and "well-known Chinese dissidents and critics"[69] such as Wen Yunchao, Hu Jia and Yu Jie. Other influential members of the Twitter community included "local teachers, critics and activists".[70] With the help of Twitter and other social media outlets the student group Scholarism shared information among like-minded activists and reached out to a wider public. Such online platforms helped Scholarism members to prepare their highly consequential offline activities. Activists saw occupation as a key tactic to "disrupt the established order by disrupting traffic, work patterns and the very idea of ordinariness".[71] In order to bring pressure on the HKSAR government, protesters led by Scholarism laid siege to government headquarters for ten days. Members of the Parents Concern Group supported the students by going on a hunger strike.[72] On 9 September 2012, chief executive C.Y. Leung conceded defeat and announced that during the remainder of his five-year term he would no longer attempt to implement the controversial national education policy and would allow "schools to introduce the new subject voluntarily".[73]

Lessons learned

The defeat of the HKSAR's flagship education policy under C.Y. Leung was a remarkable show of strength of Hong Kong's newly invigorated civil society. Encouraged by mainland Chinese dissidents and supported by their Hong Kong parents and educators very young activists—many of whom were still secondary school students—exercised leadership. Senior pan-democratic legislators followed the young protesters' lead and subsequently threatened to "introduce a private bill aimed at barring implementation of the subject".[74] The 2012 movement against the new Moral and National Education Policy therefore is indicative of how a civil society-led social movement provided a much needed shot in the arm for political society to stand up to an increasingly authoritarian HKSAR government. Matthew Torne, a British filmmaker who documented the secondary student-led campaign, has furthermore suggested that perhaps "Scholarism's greatest effect has been to radicalise the university students". The *Economist* noted that in "2012 just a handful of them marched to the central government Liaison Office, a frequent target of protesters' ire, after the annual vigil on June 4th for victims of the 1989 Tiananmen Square crackdown ... In 2014 they led the way."[75]

Episode 12: From OCLP/UM to Hong Kong's independence movement

Antecedents and political opportunities

Edmund Cheng has called the 2012 movement against the new Moral and National Education Policy a rehearsal for the subsequent UM in 2014.[76] While there are indeed many parallels between the two civil society-led movements, the upswell of public discontent in autumn 2014 in fact had two organisational sources. Frustrated with the slow pace of constitutional reform in Hong Kong, university professor Benny Tai penned an op-ed in January 2013 in which he made a case for a civil disobedience campaign, which he branded as "Occupy Central with Love and Peace".[77] He called on members of the public to occupy Hong Kong's financial district during the three-day public holiday in October 2014. Such an act of defiance was supposed to send a strong signal for the public's craving for a free and fair election of Hong Kong's next chief executive in 2017. Ng and Fulda have outlined that

> Tai's original plan was thwarted when Joshua Wong ... led 1,200 students to join a rally on September 26, 2014, and to occupy the Hong Kong's LegCo compound. This was the Hong Kong's students way to protest the August 31, 2014, ruling by the Chinese government's National People's Congress Standing Committee to allow only candidates with pro-Beijing views to stand for the 2017 election of the chief executive.[78]

The harsh response by the HKSAR government subsequently escalated the situation: TV footage of students forcibly removed from the LegCo compound led to an upswell in public support. When Hong Kong police started to use tear gas to disperse crowds, protesters used umbrellas to defend themselves. When images of peaceful demonstrators defending themselves with umbrellas were broadcast around the world, commentators coined the term Umbrella movement for Hong Kong's latest iteration of civic protest.

Key actors

Edmund Cheng and Wai-yin Chan have critiqued OCLP as a "staged, temporary civil disobedience action [which] was substituted by a spontaneous, resilient occupation".[79] They go so far as to critique OCLP as a "pro-democracy civil disobedience campaign lacking a social base".[80] This characterisation, however, overlooks that in the case of OCLP and the UM, an "old" and a "new" type of social movement overlapped. Benny Tai, the spiritual father of OCLP, had engaged in painstaking groundwork prior to the civil disobedience campaign. He not only organised a series of meetings for civic groups and political parties to consider his proposals, but also facilitated the subsequent civil referendum about the best ways to select Hong Kong's chief executive. Last but not least, he visited more than 100 churches "to explain the principles and practices of a civil disobedience movement to leaders, pastors, and laity".[81]

Supporters of the UM, which upstaged the carefully planned OCLP with their occupation of the LegCo compound in late September 2014, on the other hand, comprised Joshua Wong's Scholarism group as well as the Hong Kong Students' Federation. This coalition of secondary and university students convinced more than 13,000 pupils to boycott classes in response to the Standing Committee of the National People's Congress' decision to only allow the election of pro-Beijing candidates for chief executive.[82] Ortmann has argued that while "students were not in control of the movement, they were still regarded as the main protagonists".[83] In an interview with a report, Benny Tai himself supported this view when asked about the question of leadership:

> The students have organized the largest occupying act in Hong Kong history. We share the same goals, we share the same method. The Occupy Central movement has no choice: we must come out and stand behind the students and join hands with the students to fight for the democracy and fight for the demands put forward by the students.[84]

The complementary nature of OCLP and the UM becomes clearer when observing how each movement mobilised their respective constituencies: While OCLP gave license to practising Christians in Hong Kong to join the UM, the latter helped mobilise Hong Kong's youth.

Strategic reform approach

The following occupation of central and other parts of Hong Kong lasted for 79 days. During the UM attempts

> to start negotiations, which failed repeatedly, always involved the student leadership. Eventually, there was a televised 90 minute dialogue on 21 October between five leaders of the Hong Kong Federation of Students and five government officials which only highlighted the huge gulf between the two sides but did not lead to any substantive change. As the government made clear there was no room for any discussion about the electoral reform decision, the best they could offer was to send a letter to the Chinese government, which the students rejected as insufficient. Despite promises that this would be the first discussion, no other forums took place.[85]

When student demands for concessions on universal suffrage fell on deaf ears, movement participants demanded that C.Y. Leung step down. Hong Kong's chief executive, however, weathered the political storm by heeding CCP instructions[86] to play the long game and allow the movement to fizzle out on its own.

Whereas the ten-day student-led siege of 2012 had forced the HKSAR to make a U-turn on its controversial patriotic education policy, in 2014 mass mobilisation by OCLP and the UM in and of itself was insufficient to force a democratic breakthrough. I would argue that while OCLP/UM used all available means to draw public support for a democratic election of the chief executive, Hong Kong student leaders, just like their forbearers in mainland China in 1989, shared a rather unfounded optimism in the utility of dialogue. In Chapter 6 I argued that student leaders in 1989 erred in their assumption that political dialogue with the CCP could bring about political change. Hong Kong student leaders should have understood that the HKSAR government would not be able to make political concessions against the wishes and will of the CCP's top leadership. Furthermore, the occupation lasted too long to lead to any kind of conclusive "end game". The long duration gave the HKSAR government time to countermobilise pro-Beijing united front groups. Using blue ribbons as opposed to the yellow ribbons of OCLP/UM protesters, this led to confrontational scenes between opposing civic groups. The occupation of Mongkok also back-fired, as it allowed the HKSAR government to turn a blind eye to violent triad attacks on occupying protesters in a traditionally mafia-controlled part of Hong Kong.

Lessons learned

OCLP/UM failed to secure a free and fair election of Hong Kong's chief executive in 2017. This underlies that social movements in Hong Kong can be effective in the defence against authoritarian encroachments, as the 2003 movement against the enactment of Article 23 of the Basic Law as well as the 2012 movement against the new Moral and National Education Policy have shown, but they lack the capability to instigate future-oriented democratic institutional change. For this to happen, street protests would need to be combined with a parliamentary route. Yet, as my discussion of the difficulties of working within the confines of a politically neutered LegCo has shown, a parliamentary route on its own also does not offer a remedy.

In the wake of this failure to force a democratic breakthrough with a sustained civil disobedience campaign and in response to Xi Jinping's increasingly hard authoritarian and inflexible approach to Hong Kong since 2012, the pan-democratic camp has seen the rise of nativist parties such as Civil Passion, Youngspiration and the now outlawed Hong Kong National Party. This development mirrors the development of the DPP in Taiwan in the late 1980s, which led to the incorporation of the controversial Taiwan independence platform in 1991. Just like in Taiwan in the late 1980s and early 1990s, Hong Kong has witnessed the emergence of a new political cleavage which pits supporters of the "One Country, Two Systems" formula against adherents of Hong Kong self-determination or Hong Kong independence. While the latter two positions overlap they offer different remedies in the struggle against indirect CCP rule in Hong Kong.

Elaine Chan and Joseph Chan have argued that support "for self-determination paved the ground for an even more radical but small movement of political independence".[87] Chan and Chan have argued that there

> are, however, nuanced differences behind the ideologies of the groups involved. The socio-political stance of the self-determinists is close to social liberalism in the Western sense. They uphold social equality and care about the interests of the grassroots and marginal groups, while opposing the domination of business conglomerates. They support local economy to resist the tide of globalization; thus, they promote buying local produce, back farmers and farming, and support environmental and

cultural conservation. The sense of localism is social and economic rather than ethnic and cultural.[88]

They juxtapose supporters of self-determination with Hong Kong independence advocates, which

> regard Hong Kong as a separate nation from the Mainland, thus deserving its own political independence. Following this train of thought, this group underscores the distinctions between Hongkonger and Mainlander identities. They are unafraid of using militant and confrontational styles of expression. Seeing crowds of grey goods traders that flocked towns close to the border, they organised a series of protests to recover the towns. Using the pretext that these grey goods traders were a nuisance to the local communities, protestors shouted insults and, in some cases, used force to drive them away. Riding on the sentiments of the Umbrella Movement, a series of protests took place at the beginning of 2015 to recover Tun Mun, Yeun Long, Sheung Shui, Shatin, and Mongkok. Such protests heightened the tension between Hongkongers and Mainlanders, and reinforced the definition of mainlanders as others who are different from we the Hongkongers.[89]

In order to combine street protest with the parliamentary route, a number of localist politicians stood for LegCo elections in 2016. When six candidates were elected this not only further fragmented the pan-democratic camp, but also culminated in the publicity stunt which has come to be known as "Oathgate". To show their distinctiveness from mainland China, anti-establishment localist legislators literally disqualified themselves by misreading the obligatory oath which forces them to pledge allegiance to the PRC.[90] Such antics resulted in the disqualification of numerous lawmakers and stripped the pan-democratic camp of its veto power vis-à-vis the HKSAR government.[91] Such ineptitude has raised suspicions that localist parties in Hong Kong are in fact red-flag operations orchestrated by the CCP. More likely, however, young localist lawmakers were politically naive and did not appreciate the extent of their new responsibilities.

"Oathgate" revealed a general lack of political maturity in Hong Kong's democracy movement, which can be traced back to the late British colonial period. When Patten introduced political reforms, he was gifting electoral democracy to the Hong Kong people. Seen from the perspective of Paulo Freire's TOPC such acts of political leaders bestowing liberation as a gift to their people are problematic, since the latter may not be sufficiently involved in such essentially top-down political reform processes to learn that the development of a liberal democratic political system requires not only muck raking and issuing public demands for reform, but also entails the difficult search for common ground and compromise with political adversaries.

Instead, Hong Kong's democracy camp, which developed during a period of a British colonial government which was highly responsive to public demand for reform, seems to have learned the wrong lessons: assuming that it was sufficient to simply protest in order to get their way rather than developing member-based political parties. It is fair to say that many Hong Kong democrats do not seem to have fully understood and appreciated that a political party can only gain power by being able to amalgamate and accommodate diverse interests, and that democratic politics involves constant compromise between striving for the ideals and for getting as wide as possible a coalition to hold together to advance collective objectives.[92]

This lack of political leadership has resulted in a proliferation of ever increasing numbers of pan-democratic political parties, which very often resemble NGO start-ups without a clearly defined constituency. This fragmentation has fundamentally weakened the pan-democratic camp, which requires a single party to take on the pro-Beijing establishment. The need for greater unity is also apparent in the wake of the rise of hard authoritarianism under Xi Jinping. In Chapter 9 I showed that the securatisation of mainland Chinese politics under Xi is already undermining Hong Kong's political process. The increasing polarisation of mainland Chinese politics arguably requires Hong Kong democrats to reconsider their repertoire of reform strategies, which will require a new mix of anti-establishment, trojan horse and trans-establishment approaches. After all, the basic rule of democratic politics is the art of the possible. In her co-authored book *No Third Person: Rewriting the Hong Kong Story*, Christine Loh has made a case for a new reform approach which focuses on trust building with Beijing.[93] Yet it remains doubtful whether her advocacy of political moderation will find much resonance in the highly polarised political climate in present-day Hong Kong.

Instead, we are witnessing a certain extent of pathological learning. In an interview with Stephen Colbert Michelle Obama has argued that "it is so easy and lazy to lead by fear. It is much harder to lead by hope."[94] While localist politicians in Hong Kong skilfully exploited anti-mainland sentiment during the 2016 LegCo election, they did not succeed in channelling this public discontent into a constructive legislative agenda which would advance Hong Kong's democratic self-government. This underscores my initial observation of a lack of political leadership in Hong Kong's LegCo, as discussed in episode 9. Steven Hung is certainly right that "Hong Kong's dilemma is difficult to solve—too much radicalism may alienate moderate democratic supporters. Quite obviously, politicization did not emerge at first because of the social mobilization of democrats, since it was aroused generally by the authorities' actions to stifle the democratic development with authoritarian social control or the suppression of liberties."[95] I am, however, deeply sceptical about the rise of localism in Hong Kong. Throughout this book I have argued that the survival of Taiwan's democracy and Hong Kong's semi-democracy to a large extent will depend on a successful liberalisation and democratisation of mainland China. To give up hope for mainland China's democrats to overcome authoritarianism means to settle for the political status quo. The political status quo, however, does not work in either Taiwan's or Hong Kong's favour, as the CCP continues to use united front tactics to undermine and undo liberal democratic thought and practice in both regions.

Notes

1 Ma, Ngok (2007), *Political Development in Hong Kong: State, Political Society and Civil Society*, Hong Kong University Press, Hong Kong, 98.
2 Davis, Michael (2008), Interpreting Constitutionalism and Democratization in Hong Kong, in: Hualing Fu, Lison Harris and Simon Young (Eds), *Interpreting Hong Kong's Basic Law: The Struggle for Coherence*, Palgrave Macmillan, New York, 84–5.
3 Tsang, Steve (Ed.) (1995), *Government and Politics: A Documentary History of Hong Kong*, Hong Kong University Press, Hong Kong, 227.
4 Ibid., 229.
5 Ibid., 231.
6 Ibid., 232.
7 Wong, Mathew (2017), *Comparative Hong Kong Politics: A Guidebook for Students and Researchers*, Palgrave Macmillan, Singapore, 48.
8 Ma, Ngok (2007), *Political Development in Hong Kong: State, Political Society and Civil Society*, Hong Kong University Press, Hong Kong, 104.
9 Ibid., 107.
10 Lim, Tai Wei (2017), The Future of Hong Kong Governance: The Pro-independence Legislators' Election Fallout and Beijing's Political Voice in Hong Kong, *Asia and the Pacific Policy Studies*, 4(2), 343–53.
11 Chan, Ming (2002), Realpolitik Realignment of the Democratic Camp in the Hong Kong SAR, in: Ming Chan and Alvin So (Eds), *Crisis and Transformation in China's Hong Kong*, M.E. Sharpe, Armonk, NY, 71.
12 Ibid.
13 Ibid., 72.
14 Ibid., 73.
15 Ibid., 81.
16 Ibid., 83.
17 Ibid., 121.
18 *Hong Kong Journal* (n.d.), Political Party Development in Hong Kong. Available online: http://carnegieendowment.org/hkjournal/PDF/2006_fall/chung.pdf (accessed 28 November 2018).
19 Cartier, Carolyn (2017), Policing the Borders: Hong Kong Conundrums, in: Jane Golley, Linda Jaivin and Luigi Tomba (Eds), *Control: China Story Yearbook 2016*, Australian National University Press, Acton, 250.
20 Ibid.
21 For a discussion about the boundary problems between political parties and social movements, see Schwartz, Mildred (1996), Boundary Problems in Political Organizations, *Journal of Organizational Change Management*, 9(4), 51.
22 Wikileaks (2018), Internal Dissent Hampers Hong Kong Democratic Party. Available online: https://wikileaks.org/plusd/cables/08HONGKONG53_a.html (accessed 3 December 2018).
23 Chen, Albert (2014), The Law and Politics of Constitutional Reform and Democratization in Hong Kong. Available online: http://hub.hku.hk/bitstream/10722/201515/1/Content.pdf?accept=1 (accessed 29 November 2018).

24 Cheng, Edmund (2016), Street Politics in a Hybrid Regime: The Diffusion of Political Activism in Post-colonial Hong Kong, *China Quarterly*, 226(June), 398.
25 Wikileaks (2018), Third Force? Democratic Party Seeks Moderate Coalition. Available online: https://wikileaks.org/plusd/cables/10HONGKONG16_a.html (accessed 3 December 2018).
26 Chan, Ming (2003), The Dynamics of Compensatory Politics in Hong Kong, in: Robert Ash, Peter Ferdinand, Brian Hook and Robin Porter (Eds), *Hong Kong in Transition: One Country, Two Systems*, 106–7.
27 Loh, Christine (2010), *Underground Front. The Chinese Communist Party in Hong Kong*, RoutledgeCurzon, London, 233.
28 Lau, Chi Kuen (1997), *Hong Kong's Colonial Legacy*, Chinese University Press, Hong Kong, 54.
29 Chan, Ming (2002), Realpolitik Realignment of the Democratic Camp in the Hong Kong SAR, in: Ming Chan and Alvin So (Eds), *Crisis and Transformation in China's Hong Kong*, M.E. Sharpe, Armonk, NY, 132–3.
30 Wu, Jaushieh Joseph (1995), *Taiwan's Democratization: Forces behind the New Momentum*, Oxford University Press, Oxford, 62.
31 Hsiao, Michael (1990), Emerging Social Movements and the Rise of a Demanding Civil Society in Taiwan, *Australian Journal of Chinese Affairs*, 24(July), 177–8.
32 Wikileaks (2018), Internal dissent hampers Hong Kong Democratic Party. Available online: https://wikileaks.org/plusd/cables/08HONGKONG53_a.html (accessed 3 December 2018).
33 Ma, Ngok (2007), *Political Development in Hong Kong: State, Political Society and Civil Society*, Hong Kong University Press, Hong Kong, 210.
34 *South China Morning Post* (2017), Fear and Loathing: Which Way Forward for Article 23 National Security Law in Face of Stiff Opposition in Hong Kong? Available online: www.scmp.com/news/hong-kong/politics/article/2121035/fear-and-loathing-which-way-forward-article-23-national (accessed 30 November 2018).
35 Ibid.
36 Ma, Ngok (2007), *Political Development in Hong Kong: State, Political Society and Civil Society*, Hong Kong University Press, Hong Kong, 212.
37 Ibid.
38 Chan, Shun-hing (2015), The Protestant Community and the Umbrella Movement in Hong Kong, *Inter-Asia Cultural Studies*, 16(3).
39 Ng, Nancy and Fulda, Andreas (2018), The Religious Dimension of Hong Kong's Umbrella Movement, *Journal of Church and State*, Oxford University Press, Oxford, 388.
40 AsiaNews.it (2017), Christians Pray for Democracy in China, Dedicate Pentecost to the Victims of Tiananmen. Available online: www.asianews.it/news-en/-Christians-pray-for-democracy-in-China,-dedicate-Pentecost-to-the-victims-of-Tiananmen-40945.html (accessed 30 November 2018).
41 Wikipedia (2018), Memorials for the 1989 Tiananmen Square Protests. Available online: https://en.wikipedia.org/wiki/Memorials_for_the_1989_Tiananmen_Square_protests (accessed 3 December 2018).
42 Leung, Beatrice and Chan, Shun-hing (2003), *Changing Church and State Relations in Hong Kong, 1950–2000*, Hong Kong University Press, Hong Kong, 81.
43 Ibid.
44 Ma, Ngok (2007), *Political Development in Hong Kong: State, Political Society and Civil Society*, Hong Kong University Press, Hong Kong, 214.
45 Ibid.
46 Ibid., 215.
47 Ibid., 219.
48 Loh, Christine (2010), *Underground Front: The Chinese Communist Party in Hong Kong*, Hong Kong University Press, Hong Kong, 221.
49 Ibid., 222.

50 Ibid., 233.
51 Cheng, Edmund (2016), Street Politics in a Hybrid Regime: The Diffusion of Political Activism in Post-colonial Hong Kong, *China Quarterly*, 226, 400.
52 A reference to the particularly ferocious civil war in Lebanon.
53 Yishai, Yael (1998), Civil Society in Transition: Interest Politics in Israel, *Annals of the American Academy of Political and Social Science*, 555, Israel in Transition, 148.
54 Cheng, Edmund (2016), Street Politics in a Hybrid Regime: The Diffusion of Political Activism in Post-colonial Hong Kong, *China Quarterly*, 226(June), 401.
55 Ibid., 388.
56 Ibid., 396.
57 Ibid., 392.
58 Ibid.
59 Ibid., 392–4.
60 Ortmann, Stephan (2015), The Umbrella Movement and Hong Kong's Protracted Democratization Process, *Asian Affairs*, 46(1), 44.
61 Chan, Chitat (2013), Young Activists and the Anti-Patriotic Education Movement in Post-Colonial Hong Kong: Some Insights from Twitter, Citizenship, *Social and Economics Education*, 12(3), 149.
62 Ibid., 150.
63 CNN (2012), "National Education" Raises Furor in Hong Kong. Available online: https://edition.cnn.com/2012/07/30/world/asia/hong-kong-national-education-con troversy/index.html (accessed 3 December 2018).
64 Ibid.
65 *New York Times* (2012), Thousands Protest China's Plans for Hong Kong Schools. Available online: www.nytimes.com/2012/07/30/world/asia/thousands-p rotest-chinas-curriculum-plans-for-hong-kong-schools.html (accessed 4 December 2018).
66 Hong Kong Education Bureau (2012), The Moral and National Education Curriculum Guide (Primary 1 to Secondary 6). Available online: www.edb.gov.hk/atta chment/en/curriculum-development/moral-national-edu/MNE%20Guide%20 (ENG)%20Final_remark_09102012.pdf (accessed 3 December 2018).
67 Man, Kit (2013), Citizenship Education in Post-1997 Hong Kong: Civic Education or Nationalistic Education? Master's thesis, Lingnan University, Hong Kong. Available online: http://commons.ln.edu.hk/cgi/viewcontent.cgi?article=1031&con text=soc_etd (accessed 4 December 2018), 23.
68 Lam, Wai-man and Tong, Irene (2007), Civil Society and NGOs, in: Wai-man Lam, Percy Luen-tim Lui, Wilson Wong and Ian Holliday (Eds), *Contemporary Hong Kong Politics: Governance in the Post-1997 Era*, Hong Kong University Press, Hong Kong, 148.
69 Ibid., 155.
70 Ibid., 156.
71 Cheng, Edmund (2016), Street Politics in a Hybrid Regime: The Diffusion of Political Activism in Post-colonial Hong Kong, *China Quarterly*, 226(June), 394.
72 *South China Morning Post* (2012), Protest against National Education to End after Government Climbdown. Available online: www.scmp.com/news/hong-kong/a rticle/1032535/protest-against-national-education-end-after-government-climbdown (accessed 4 December 2018).
73 Ortmann, Stephan (2015), The Umbrella Movement and Hong Kong's Protracted Democratization Process, *Asian Affairs*, 46(1), 44.
74 *South China Morning Post* (2012), Pan-Democrats to Boycott Leung's Luncheon over National Education. Available online: www.scmp.com/news/hong-kong/a rticle/1037091/pan-democrats-boycott-leungs-luncheon-over-national-education (accessed 4 December 2018).

75 *Economist* (2014), Lessons in Dissent. Available online: http://ezproxy.notting ham.ac.uk/login?url=https://search-proquest-com.ezproxy.nottingham.ac.uk/doc view/1543236293?accountid=8018 (accessed 3 December 2018).

76 Ibid., 402.

77 Tai, Benny (2013), 公民抗命的最大殺傷力武器 (The Most Destructive Weapon of Civil Disobedience): Occupy Central with Love and Peace, *Hong Kong Economic Journal*, 16 January. Available online: www 1.hkej.com//dailynews/article/id/ 654855/公民抗命的最大殺傷力武器.

78 Ng, Nancy and Fulda, Andreas (2018), The Religious Dimension of Hong Kong's Umbrella Movement, *Journal of Church and State*, Oxford University Press, Oxford, 378.

79 Cheng, Edmund W. and Chan, Wai-Yin (2016), Explaining Spontaneous Occupation: Antecedents, Contingencies and Spaces in the Umbrella Movement, *Social Movement Studies*, 10 November, 224.

80 Ibid., 222.

81 Ng, Nancy and Fulda, Andreas (2018), The Religious Dimension of Hong Kong's Umbrella Movement, *Journal of Church and State*, Oxford University Press, Oxford, 393.

82 Ibid., 394.

83 Ortmann, Stephan (2015), The Umbrella Movement and Hong Kong's Protracted Democratization Process, *Asian Affairs*, 46(1), 46.

84 INT News Channel (2014), 2014.09.28: "Occupy Central" (13:24) Dr. Benny TAI: I Don't Mind the Students to Take the Lead. Available online: www.youtube.com/ watch?v=O5R5D1LYhDY (accessed 4 December 2018).

85 Ortmann, Stephan (2015), The Umbrella Movement and Hong Kong's Protracted Democratization Process, *Asian Affairs*, 46(1), 46.

86 *New York Times* (2014), Beijing Is Directing Hong Kong Strategy, Government Insiders Say. Available online: www.nytimes.com/2014/10/18/world/asia/china -is-directing-response-to-hong-kong-protests.html (accessed 4 December 2018).

87 Chan, Elaine and Chan, Joseph (2017), Hong Kong 2007–2017: A Backlash in Civil Society, *Asia Pacific Journal of Public Administration*, 39(2), 147.

88 Ibid., 147–8.

89 Ibid., 148.

90 *Al Jazeera* (2016), Oathgate Will Hurt Hong Kong Democracy. Available online: www.aljazeera.com/indepth/opinion/2016/11/oathgate-hurt-hong-kong-democra cy-161120085542934.html (accessed 4 December 2018).

91 Reuters (2018), Hong Kong Democrats Hope to Regain Veto Powers in Crucial By-Election. Available online: https://uk.reuters.com/article/uk-hongkong-politics/ hong-kong-democrats-hope-to-regain-veto-powers-in-crucial-by-e lection-idUKKCN1NU00P (accessed 4 December 2018).

92 I am once again grateful to Steve Tsang for pointing this out to me.

93 *Diplomat* (2018), How to "Rewrite the Hong Kong Story". Available online: http s://thediplomat.com/2018/11/how-to-rewrite-the-hong-kong-story/ (accessed 12 January 2019).

94 The Late Show with Stephen Colbert (2018), Full Interview: Michelle Obama Talks to Stephen Colbert. Available online: www.youtube.com/watch?v=jXwa QXquA7E (accessed 4 December 2018).

95 Hung, Chung Fun Steven (2017), Political Radicalization and Fragmentation of the Democratic Blocs and the Legislative Council Elections in the Hong Kong Special Administrative Region, *Asian Education and Development Studies*, 6(4), 372–84.

11

SHARP POWER AND ITS DISCONTENTS

In this book I have argued that the CCP's sharp power approach should be considered an extension of its united front method, a conceptualisation of the political process as a zero-sum game and a world-view which distinguishes between friends and enemies. Since its founding in 1921 the CCP has invested considerable resources to isolate its perceived enemies and has lobbied waverers to support them. In Chapter 5 I described the resulting party-state's governing approach as a two-pronged process of simultaneous co-optation and coercion, where proverbial carrots and sticks are applied to suppress any political opposition to party-state rule. In the case of CCP rule in mainland China, the party-state has tried to win over waverers by adopting a "rule by bribery" approach. Those unwilling to align themselves with the party-state have been at the receiving end of a "rule by fear" approach. In Chapter 7 I showed that the Nationalist Party in Taiwan, the KMT, adopted a very similar approach of corporatism and co-optation from 1945 until the beginning of the island's liberalisation and democratisation in the early 1980s. In Chapter 9 I explored the case of Hong Kong, where the CCP maintained pre-handover British colonial institutions (when they suited its united front approach, such as the use of functional constituencies in elections) and engaged in selective decolonisation of other institutions (when they were seen as a threat to its monopoly of power, for example, by breaking up the Catholic Church and other Christian denominations' monopoly on Hong Kong's education sector).

The problem with the CCP's "winner-takes-all" conception of politics is that it has resulted in a highly elitist and exclusive political system. Børge Bakken is on point when arguing that what "we might see in China is not so much an exemplary elite serving the people, but rather the strengthening of a lawless elite, looting China in the interest of its members".[1] In Chapter 2 I outlined how the party-state since 1989 has started to erratically move back and forth between the role of a developmental and predatory state. Drawing on He Qinglian's scholarship I argued that the party-state was effectively captured by rent-seeking elites from 1999 onwards. This is best reflected by the Politburo Standing Committee morphing from a party-state institution into a cabal of business empires, where CCP leaders defend their respective monopolies over vast industries. The resulting crony-capitalist system, understood in Minxin Pei's terms, is marked by endemic and systemic corruption and collusion. The continuous plundering of state assets has also led to very low levels of public expenditure for crucial public services such as health and education. One of the unintended consequences of low levels of public investment has been the rise of rent seeking in sectors ranging from the food-processing industry, the health and education sectors, to China's media. This means that corruption is no longer limited to individuals and organs under the control of the party-state, but is now a defining feature in every industry and sector in mainland China's business and society.

In Chapter 5 I showed that in order to protect its monopoly on power, the CCP has gone to great lengths to suppress any potential challenges to its continued rule. It has not only invested more money on domestic stability preservation than on national defence, but has also continued to use highly draconian means to intimidate and silence opponents of one-party rule. Among the repertoire of political control instruments are the highly invasive personal file system, the continued use of labour camps and re-education camps, the use of mainland China's psychiatric system to lock up dissidents and the rise of alliances between local governments and organised crime forming local mafia states and the resulting phenomenon of "thugs for hire". It is highly concerning that at mainland China's periphery, the CCP appears to have approved the "rent-a-mob" tactic to disrupt the democratic political process in Hong Kong and Taiwan, too. During the pro-democracy OCLP/ UM in 2014, the police under control of the pro-Beijing HKSAR government turned a blind eye to local triads beating up protesters. In Taiwan, the notorious gangster Chang An-le, also known as White Wolf, led a mob to roughen up students during the Sunflower movement in the same year.[2]

Michael Cole has recently reported about a major weapons find in the northern Taiwanese city of Keelong (*Jilong*). According to Cole,

> the [China Unification Promotion Party] and Bamboo Union, as well as other pro-Beijing triads, such as the Four Seas Gang, have access to fire-arms and other weapons, which they may attempt to bring into Taiwan and provide to a "civil society" bent on escalation. A large cache of fire-arms—the largest in a decade—was seized at the weekend originating in the Philippines and transiting via Hong Kong before arriving in Taiwan. A total of 109 firearms, including Bushmaster XM15-E25s, Spike's Tactical ST-15s and a Striker-12 shotgun, as well as 12,378 rounds of ammunition were seized in Keelung. One officer said of the arms cache,

"You could set up an army with those!" Minister of the Interior Yeh Jiunn-rong said that if the guns had flown into the market, "the consequences would have been disastrous". The individuals arrested in the case were from the Bamboo Union (some of them fled to Singapore but were sent back to Taiwan).[3]

Cole has warned that Chang An-le's China Unification Promotion Party's

> principal aim is to foster instability, with hopes that physical violence will spark a commensurate response by society. In some fundamental ways, these are akin to the *Sturmabteilung*, or Brown Shirts, in late 1920s and early 1930s Germany, which unleashed violence upon society and blamed the Weimar Republic—a democracy much reviled by the Nazis and other extreme-right political parties—for the social chaos.[4]

The fact that war weapons aimed for Taiwan's mafia organisations have been smuggled into the island in 2018 is alarming and raises the spectre of a Lebanisation of Taiwan's civil society during times of political crisis. While Trey Menefee has questioned to what extent one "can extrapolate many foreign policy implications from how the CCP works in HK and Taiwan. There's some overlap in U[nited] F[ront] behavior, but examples like hiring out triads are sui generis to those contexts",[5] I would argue that both Hong Kong and Taiwan should be seen as a testing ground for increasingly militant united front methods and tactics. While it is of course true that the political instrumentalisation of triads in Hong Kong and Taiwan indeed has a long history, something I pointed out in Chapters 7 and 9, it is alarming that at the beginning of the 21st century pro-Beijing triads and gangsters have started to disrupt pro-democracy social movements in both regions.

Long-term trends and developments

In this book I addressed the research puzzle to what extent political activists in mainland China, Taiwan and Hong Kong have made progress in their quest to liberalise and democratise their respective polities. In the empirical part of the book I answered the research question about the kind of lessons which democracy activists in all three regions have drawn from their struggles for democracy. In Chapters 6, 8 and 10 I analysed 12 cycles of democracy movements in mainland China, Taiwan and Hong Kong between 1969 and 2018. My longitudinal study of democracy movements has made previously overlooked long-term trends and developments visible. The 12 episodes revealed examples of lessons learned among democracy activists which have arguably advanced their political causes *as well as* cases of pathological learning.

In the case of mainland China episodes 1 to 4 revealed that it took the promulgation of Charter 08 in 2008 for the democracy movement to fully embrace a firmly anti-establishment position. Previous challenges to one-party rule were marked by a lack of a unified strategy. In 1989, workers subscribed to an anti-establishment strategy whereas students effectively pursued a trojan horse approach. The 12 writers and scholars who tried to mediate between movement leaders and the Chinese party-state, on the other hand, subscribed to a trans-establishment tactic. In their attempt to remedy the shortcomings of 1989, democracy activists attempted to register the CDP in 1998. This attempt also failed: While Wang Youcai pursued an anti-establishment objective, he opted for a trojan horse strategy of working within the system, which had no chance of succeeding. Only in 2008, mainland China's democracy movement thus managed to develop its "grand strategy" in the form of Charter 08. This was the first time that an end to one-party rule was made its declared goal.

The slow progress towards an explicit formulation of this ultimate goal of ending one-party rule in mainland China underlines Paulo Freire's observation that oppression is indeed domesticating. It clearly takes a long time for oppressed people to gain the confidence to address the root causes of their lack of liberty. I argued that with the emergence of mainland China's NCM a process of bottom-up self-liberation is now well under way. The way Xu Zhiyong has conceptualised the NCM promises a linked-up approach of anti-establishment, trojan horse and trans-establishment strategies. Admittedly, under the conditions of Xi Jinping's hard authoritarianism, trojan horse reform approaches are currently very difficult to implement. Many bargaining spheres such as China's nascent civil society sector or China's reforming legal sector, which provided venues for non-state actor participation during the eras of Jiang Zemin (1989–2002) and Hu Jintao (2002–12), are rapidly closing. Yet Xu Zhiyong's vision for the NCM nevertheless remains highly relevant, since it opens up the possibility for *future* elite settlements between mainland Chinese democracy movement leaders and members of the pro-establishment CCP nomenklatura. In his seminal study Xu argued that the "most ideal reform model for China is to develop constructive political opposition groups outside the existing political system that can negotiate with progressive forces within the system to enact a new constitution and, together, complete a transition to constitutional democracy".[6]

While in early 2019 Xu's scenario may seem far-fetched or even utopian, from a recent in-depth discussion which I had with a high-ranking party official I learned that Xi Jinping's illiberal political agenda has already greatly antagonised many pro-establishment figures in mainland China. While it is impossible to gauge how widespread this sentiment is felt among rank-and-file CCP members, it is entirely possible that increasing members of the pro-establishment are only paying lip service to Xi's rule whilst secretly harbouring hopes for greater liberalisation in the not too distant future. The emergence of the party discourse about so-called "two-faced" officials,[7] which are suspected to be corrupt or opposed to continued one-party rule, suggests that this is not only a theoretical possibility but in fact an acute concern for the CCP's top brass.

Furthermore, given the decentralised nature of the NCM it will be hard for the CCP to suppress it. At the same time, Xu Zhiyong and his supporters are arguably playing a very long game. Bottom-up democratisation strategies are hard to implement, not only due to the size of the country and number of people they will need to reach and convince. Such bottom-up attempts to enlighten the population are being countered by top-down united front efforts aimed at co-opting or coercing Chinese citizens to support one-party rule. As I argued in Chapter 1 the endemic and systemic corruption in mainland China is not just a problem of the party-state but has already spilled over into Chinese business and society. This is why it is particularly noteworthy that the NCM has a strong anti-corruption element aimed at restoring axiomatic moral and ethical principles.

One of the persistent challenges for mainland China's democracy movement is that so far it is mostly led by Han Chinese protagonists. As the current extra-legal internment of Uyghurs and Kazakhs in Xinjiang has shown, the Chinese party-state is also guilty of suppressing ethnic minorities on an industrial scale. The mainland Chinese democracy movement has yet to develop ideas and strategies to simultaneously liberalise and democratise the party-state, whilst preventing that during such a necessarily fractious and open-ended political transition process inter-ethnic and intra-ethnic conflicts as well as religious fault lines will not derail mainland China's liberalisation and democratisation. Charter 08's 19th demand of "truth in reconciliation" could be one way to prevent the flaring up of political violence during a period of liberalisation and democratisation. It is also heartening that the NCM is already addressing the issue of social justice and inequality, which will be central to any kind of political programme aimed at upholding domestic peace.

Episodes 5 to 8 have shown that it is possible to overcome Leninist forms of governance. But the case of Taiwan has also shown that it can take up to half a century for activists to achieve a democratic breakthrough. Episode 5 showed that in this protracted democratisation process, continuous muck raking but also strategic interaction with the party-state was instrumental to pressure the KMT to liberalise and democratise throughout the early 1980s. I highlighted the central role of Kang Ning-hsiang, a trans-establishment politician, who held the fractious *dangwai* movement together by marrying the street protests approach of the Formosa faction with the parliamentary route of his more policy-oriented Mainstream faction. This reform strategy was in part made possible by the changing nature of the KMT pro-establishment. Under the leadership of Chiang Ching-kuo and throughout the 1970s more liberal-minded Taiwan-born politicians were co-opted into the party-state.

This opened up the possibility for more constructive forms of communication and tacit collaboration between the pro- and anti-establishment camps in the early 1980s. This episode is particularly relevant, since it highlights the importance of distributed leadership which transcends ideological and political organisational boundaries.[8] I also showed that once the road to electoral democratisation was opened in the early 1990s, the DPP made a major strategic error by evolving from a party movement into a nation-building party. While the incorporation of the Taiwan independence platform in 1991 marked a successful *internal* elite settlement about the future direction of the DPP, it also antagonised its political opponents in Taiwan and mainland China and prevented future elite settlements *between* the DPP and KMT. By overplaying the ethnic card in the subsequent phase of election-driven democratisation, the DPP contributed to the island's political polarisation, as evident from the disastrous Chen Shui-bian presidency (2000–8) and the equally controversial Ma Ying-jeou presidency (2008–16).

In Chapter 10 I analysed Hong Kong's democracy movement in episodes 9 to 12. While on the surface Hong Kong's democracy movement appears to have been more assertive than mainland China's, due to its one-sided strategic approaches and tactical errors—first and foremost the unwillingness of the DP to forge a pact with social movements, second the DP's unwise support for extremely limited constitutional reform in 2010 and third the Localists' "Oathgate" in 2016—Hong Kong's pan-democrats have been underperforming since the 1997 handover.

The example of Hong Kong is instructive of the uneasy relationship between political parties, social movements and CSOs. While Hong Kong's political and civil society managed to come together to defeat the implementation of the controversial Article 23 of the Basic Law in 2003, such cross-sectoral alliances have been few and far between. To a certain extent it can be argued that in democratisation processes political parties are caught between a rock and a hard place. Whereas in Taiwan the DPP institutionalised its two-pronged approach of combining street protests with the parliamentary route, the price of this elite settlement on the issue of self-determination and Taiwan independence was the continued dominance of the party apparatus by the hardline NT faction, a highly nationalist group of ardent Taiwan independence supporters. The DPP consequently became what Yael Yishai has called an "interest party", which is now beholden to one particular political faction. In order to avoid the co-optation of Hong Kong's DP by social movement leaders, Martin Lee always kept social movements at arms length. This strategic decision, however, meant that the DP was limited to its parliamentary route and thus lacked a credible threat of street action whenever the HKSAR government balked at its legislative and constitutional reform proposals. Such a one-sided insistence on the parliamentary route has effectively weakened the entire pan-democratic camp, as the DP's inflexibility led to splintering into ever smaller pro-democracy parties. The rise of localist and pro-Hong Kong independence parties in present-day Hong Kong should also be seen as a direct consequence of the inability of the DP to reform itself.

I wrote this book with the ambition to not only engage in post facto rationalisations of episodes of struggles for democracy in mainland China, Taiwan and Hong Kong. Another ambition of this project was to develop the three TOPC as heuristic devices, which can be used to enhance practitioner reflexivity. When comparing the democracy movements in all three regions with the help of the three TOPC it becomes apparent to me that democracy activists stand the best chance to succeed when simultaneously embracing anti-establishment, trojan horse and trans-establishment strategies. This requires democracy activists to avoid the trap of binary thinking and to embrace holistic approaches to political reform. While it is of course important to fully embrace an anti-establishment position, without a complementary trojan horse approach and trans-establishment politics democracy activists are very likely to fail.

Three episodes stand out in terms of the involved activists' ability to forge the widest possible coalitions for democratic change. I have argued that in the case of mainland China, and despite the challenges of implementing a bottom-up approach to democratisation, Xu Zhiyong and his supporters of the NCM are already employing a combination of all three strategic approaches. In the case of Taiwan in the early 1980s Kang Ning-hsiang similarly managed to utilise all three TOPC by combining street protests with the parliamentary route, whilst keeping communication channels with Chiang Ching-kuo open. In the case of Hong Kong, political and civil society was most effective when combining forces during the anti-Article 23 movement in 2003. In more recent years, law professor Benny Tai and social movement leader Joshua Wong have been pursuing their respective anti-establishment approaches, but simultaneously have reached out to other societal actors such as Hong Kong's Catholic Church as well as other Christian churches. Joshua Wong's newly founded party Demosistō has also explored the parliamentary route and started aping Kang Ning-hsiang's strategy of internationalising Taiwan's *dangwai* movement. In December 2018 a delegation of Demosistō politicians visited the United States to drum up support for Hong Kong's democracy movement. One of the challenges in the case of Hong Kong, however, is that the PRC and HKSAR governments are not dependent on United States patronage as Taiwan under Chiang Ching-kuo was. This greatly reduces the leverage of the United States vis-à-vis the Chinese party-state. While neither Xu Zhiyong in mainland China nor Benny Tai or Joshua Wong in Hong Kong have been able to overcome the CCP's one-party rule, this is certainly not down to a lack of strategic awareness but due to the inherent power asymmetry between the pro-democracy camp in mainland China and Hong Kong vis-à-vis the CCP.

Implications for future research

In this book I also addressed the question as to what extent critical scholarship can advance our understanding of long-term democratisation processes whilst simultaneously enhancing practitioner reflexivity. Prior to writing this book I assumed that democracy activists, either consciously or not, would tend to act within the confines of one of the three TOPC. The 12 episodes have shown that in many cases individual and collective actors in struggles for democracy are indeed opting for one-sided strategies which tend to be confined to one bargaining area. Yet findings from the empirical analysis also suggest that democracy activists who creatively combine the three TOPC by Gene Sharp, Saul Alinsky and Paulo Freire enjoy the greatest leverage to pressure autocratic elites to agree to an elite settlement, understood along the lines of Burton, Gunther and Higley.[9]

One-sided strategies which are limited to one of the three TOPC are far less likely to succeed. This finding is particularly noteworthy as it suggests that a trojan horse approach of reforming the system from within—on its own—will not suffice to convince the top CCP leadership to reform mainland China's political system. The latter insight is also particularly relevant for scholars who concern themselves with the study of Chinese politics. In Chapter 1 I highlighted that one of the existing realities China scholars face is that under conditions of authoritarianism, the choice of research topics, research partners, as well as research approaches are all politically circumscribed. In this book I also critiqued the rather artificial distinction between theory and practice. Censorship and resulting self-censorship arguably undermine academic autonomy. Based on this insight I would argue that scholars of contemporary China, just like democracy activists in mainland China, Taiwan and Hong Kong, have to position themselves vis-à-vis the Chinese party-state. They can either align themselves with the pro-establishment, anti-establishment or trans-establishment.

In Chapter 1 I outlined that one of the challenges facing contemporary Chinese studies is the ongoing specialisation and fragmentation in ever growing academic sub-fields. This development towards what Alice Miller has termed "mountaintopism" undermines the ability among scholars interested in current Chinese affairs to have a productive dialogue across disciplinary boundaries. The increasing dominance of positivism in social and political science research in general and contemporary Chinese studies in particular also means that many scholars are very reluctant to reveal their political ideology and world-view due to the fear of upsetting the Chinese party-state. The German sinologist Heiner Roetz has argued that "Western sinology seems to be on the wrong side in the conflict between the government and its opponents. This does not necessarily mean that the sympathies of sinologists are with the dictatorial regime and not its victims. But they tend to treat the latter with a kind of benevolent incomprehension."[10] Roetz furthermore argues that many "Sinologists hold a protecting hand over 'Chinese culture', which the Chinese government is seen to somehow represent, and defend it against 'Western' criticism".[11] He has argued that "parts of Chinese Studies hesitate to openly take sides with the Chinese civil rights movement"[12] and that

> the reasons can be found above all in a syndrome of culturalistic, relativist, and exotic convictions according to which (a) the question of dissidence has to be posed as a question concerning the cultural identity of China and thus as a pre-political instead of a political question, (b) dissidence is something like a foreign body in Chinese culture, and (c) this is due to the absence of or, in contrast to the West, weak development of transcendence. Part of the syndrome is in many instances an understanding of the legitimacy of governance oriented not according to principles of participation, but, in a Hobbesian manner, to the preservation of stability. The image of a China that is opposed to dissent, a China that is addicted to harmony and devoted to order, is thereby created. This image is reminiscent of the World State in Aldous Huxley's *Brave New World* which likewise promotes "stability, identity and community" and is indeed at odds with a modern democratic culture of debate (*Streitkultur*). The consequence of this view is the direct or indirect, even if rarely ever outright, partisanship in favor of the authoritarian dictatorship of the People's Republic and a form of benign lack of understanding for its critics.[13]

I not only concur with Roetz but would also argue that it is about time that scholars with an interest in current Chinese affairs stop flirting with authoritarian rule in mainland China. Unless they develop a critical stance towards the excesses of CCP rule in mainland China and its periphery, contemporary Chinese studies as a whole runs the risk of becoming complicit in the CCP's united front work. This danger is not merely a theoretical possibility but based on experiential learning during China-related conferences in Europe during the last couple of years. In the following I would like to provide three examples of conferences where European participants have actively discouraged open and critical debates about the nature of CCP rule in mainland China. In 2011 I experienced how a European academic attempted to silence me and a colleague during a China-related conference in Brussels. Together with a fellow political scientist I had given a presentation describing four different strands in the mainland Chinese democracy discourse. During the subsequent Q&A session of our panel, a German conference participant attacked us and suggested that we should not study domestic views of China's democratisation, something he considered an act of cultural imperialism. We shot back by stating that we would not accept any form of censorship, be it from the party-state or from fellow European academics. It later transpired that the questioner had commercial interests in mainland China.

During another Brussels-based China conference in 2013 I provided the European External Action Service (EEAS) with policy recommendations regarding its China policy. During the Q&A session a young Brussels-based Chinese diplomat warned the EEAS against adopting any of my recommendations. When I spoke with him over the subsequent coffee break I started my conversation with him by saying that "in the UK I have learned that one can agree to disagree without being disagreeable". He immediately replied by admitting to me that in his official capacity "this is what I had to say". During the following 20 minutes we then had a very nuanced conversation in Chinese about EU–China relations and the importance of human rights protection. The Chinese diplomat ended our very amicable exchange of ideas by telling me that "if there were more people like you, we would have a better EU–China relationship". What he thus said in public and the things he told me in private were completely different. Ironically, and rather inexplicably, only days after the conference I received a sternly worded email from a fellow German colleague who had also attended the conference. She questioned my analytical distinction between anti-establishment, pro-establishment and trans-establishment. She even insinuated that I had somehow put Chinese democracy activists at risk by mentioning them in my presentation. I wrote to her a polite reply, pointing out that academics have every right to develop heuristic concepts whose utility of course can and should be openly debated and discussed. I also reminded her that my specific examples of anti-establishment, pro-establishment and trans-establishment figures in mainland China were all very well known and all of the information used could be found in the public domain, as the featured activists themselves had shared their ideas through their online publications and/or interviews with the media. I never heard back from her.

During a China-related conference in mainland Europe in 2018, I once again met a Chinese delegation, which included a high-ranking party official. Only two minutes into our first conversation he confided in me that he was highly critical of the hard authoritarian turn under Xi Jinping. What struck me again was that many other European conference participants were unable to pick up such overt signals from members of the Chinese official delegation. When during the conference proceedings I myself made comments critical of CCP rule in mainland China, overly cautious European conference participants later approached me and expressed their discomfort with my critique of authoritarianism.

My experiences with overly fearful Western scholars is not an isolated phenomenon. On 6 December 2018 Bernhard Bartsch tweeted about his experience of discussing the extra-legal internment camps in Xinjiang with Chinese delegations visiting Europe. He recounted: "I brought up #Xinjiang in discussions with half a dozen delegations from #China. None of them was upset by the issue. Who did get upset were some Europeans—who worried about the Chinese being upset. The powerful get so much empathy these days!"[14]

The above examples support Roetz's argument who has pointed out that the view that "China is not made for democracy has been the shared conviction of both Western colonialists and their heirs and Eastern anti-liberalists to this day".[15] Such repeat experiences with defenders of continued CCP rule also underlines that the real conflict line at the beginning of the 21st century does not lie between East and West, or mainland Chinese and non-Chinese citizens, but between individuals who are willing to accept the authority of the CCP on the one hand and more reform-minded individuals who believe in liberal-democratic values and practices and who would like to see democratic change aimed at protecting human rights in mainland China on the other hand. In this conflict, the ethnicity and nationality of discourse participants arguably is of secondary importance.

This is why I would also argue that China scholars need to embark on a "critical discovery that they and their oppressors are manifestations of dehumanization".[16] One of the persistent problems with self-censorship among China watchers is that whoever is willing to accept thought control is also likely to force others to follow suit. And by publicly rebuking non-Chinese speakers critical of CCP rule people may also be hoping for rewards from the Chinese party-state establishment, for example in the form of research access to China, speaker fees and consultancy opportunities. Christopher Balding has publicly critiqued Western scholars who are willing to compromise their values and ethics in exchange for money. He recently tweeted that if "you accept Party money and are featured in Chinese state media, you should ask yourself 'where did I as an intellectual go wrong?' Probably over envelopes of cash for speaking engagements."[17] And while scholars with an interest in contemporary China are of course at liberty to choose their respective research paradigm and research approach, as members of a global epistemic community of China watchers they should stop normalising the party-state. Another important task for China watchers should be to document and analyse mainland China's democracy movement in general and the NCM in particular. Greater international visibility is likely to open new bargaining arenas for mainland Chinese democracy activists, who are more likely to be invited to join study tours, international conferences and background briefings with diplomats, politicians and policy makers if they are globally known.

It is heartening that throughout the year 2018 two major developments occurred which suggest that the field of contemporary Chinese studies as a whole is already evolving in a more critical and constructive direction. Following the publication of her landmark research report, *Magic Weapons: China's Political Influence Activities under Xi Jinping*,[18] New Zealand's political scientist and China expert Ann-Marie Brady had her house burgled and laptop computers stolen. At the same time Dr Brady's mainland Chinese cooperation partners were interrogated about her China-related research.

Even more worryingly, "her car was found to have been tampered with in ways consistent with intentional sabotage".[19] In response to what has been considered a "harassment campaign [which] constitutes a response to her research on the CCP's influence, and an attempt to intimidate her into silence",[20] more than 295 signatories from 27 countries signed an open letter denouncing the intimidation of an independent scholar by the CCP. The list of signatories reads like a global "Who's Who" list of China experts, many of whom can be considered middle-of-the-road academics without particular anti-establishment leanings.

The trend towards a more assertive China watcher community is also evident from the thorny issue of minority rights. Following the publication of the edited book volume *Xinjiang: China's Muslim Borderland* in 2004 the Chinese party-state had retaliated by blacklisting 13 of the 16 book contributors.[21] While this move against critical scholars was widely noticed at the time, it did not lead to a public solidarity campaign. This has changed profoundly following the revelation about the mass incarceration of more than 1 million Uyghurs and Kazakhs in 2018. In response, Kevin Carrico made the suggestion that China scholars should sign what he termed the *Xinjiang Pledge*. In his contribution to a ChinaFile Conversation he explained the thinking behind this initiative:

> The idea is that people sign on to this pledge, and then at any public talk one does, regardless of where it is being held, one starts the talk by noting: "I would like to bring the audience's attention to the fact that hundreds of thousands of Uighurs are currently being arbitrarily held in political re-education camps in their homeland in Xinjiang. Facing a situation like this, the community of China scholars cannot remain silent." Such a public statement is an open disavowal of self-censorship, while also raising greater awareness of the situation in Xinjiang.[22]

By the end of November 2018, 269 signatories had publicly endorsed the Xinjiang Pledge, which is now called *The Xinjiang Initiative*. [23]

On 26 November 2018 606 scholars from 39 countries also signed the *Statement by Concerned Scholars on China's Mass Detention of Turkic Minorities*, highlighting their "concerns and ... [calls] the international community to action in relation to the mass human rights abuses and deliberate attacks on indigenous cultures presently taking place in China's XUAR [Xinjiang Uyghur Autonomous Region]".[24] Such public campaigns critical of hard authoritarian CCP rule as well as systemic and endemic human rights abuses at mainland China's periphery are indicative of an academic field in transition.

This means that China scholars are already developing a more critical stance toward the party-state. But just as is the case for democracy activists in mainland China, Taiwan and Hong Kong, I would argue that we need to tread a fine line between highlighting the deficiencies of authoritarian rule and wholesale condemnation of an entire people and culture. There is a need to distinguish between "official" and "unofficial China". Martin Thorley has rightly pointed out that observers

> of China need to be much more careful when discussing the influence tactics of the Chinese Party-state in order not to implicate vast swathes of people identified in various ways under the umbrella term "Chinese". We ought to pay greater attention to the difference between "official" China and "unofficial" China—that is, between the position of the state on the one hand and the often obscured lived experience of Chinese people in the private realm and in the diminishing space beyond officialdom's grasp.[25]

I concur with Martin Thorley and do think that there is indeed a danger of legitimate criticism of CCP sharp power operations, both at home and abroad, turning into a McCarthy-style campaign against mainland Chinese citizens. In this book I have raised doubts about the wisdom of the nativist turn in Taiwan's and Hong Kong's democracy movements. While this unfortunate political development is in part fuelled by a legitimate indignation about illegal CCP-led united front activities in both regions, Taiwan and Hong Kong nativists and nationalists have also been guilty of stereotyping and scapegoating mainland Chinese. As I have argued throughout this book, it is neither in Taiwan's, Hong Kong's or any other regions' enlightened interest to pigeonhole an entire people and hold them responsible for mainland China's authoritarian political system.

Policy implications

Aaron Friedberg is certainly right when pointing out that the

> strategy pursued by China's leaders ... was, and still is, motivated first and foremost by their commitment to preserving the Chinese Communist Party's monopoly on domestic political power. The CCP's use of militant nationalism, its cultivation of historic claims and grievances against foreign powers, and its rejection of the idea that there are, in fact, universal human values are essential pieces of its programme for mobilising popular support and bolstering regime legitimacy. It is impossible to make sense of the ambitions, fears, strategy and tactics of China's present regime without reference to its authoritarian, illiberal character and distinctive, Leninist roots.[26]

It is also true, as Samantha Hoffman has argued, that from the CCP's point of view, "each member of Chinese society has a responsibility to uphold the

Chinese Party-state's security. To understand this requires bearing in mind that China's state security strategy is fundamentally aimed at upholding the Communist Party of China's leadership."[27] While continued CCP-led corporatism and co-optation is indeed an impediment for mainland China's nascent civil society to emancipate and liberate itself from one-party rule, it is worth reiterating that Chinese democracy activists are already doing what they can to liberalise and democratise their polity.

This is why policy analysts should go beyond a one-sided China containment strategy, which would not only hurt "official China" but also "unofficial China". A more sensible China policy thus would be to cooperate with China where we can (e.g. in the fields of climate change mitigation, pandemic prevention, human trafficking, etc.) and critique China where we must (e.g. regarding the CCP's highly problematic ethnic policies, human rights violations and lack of transparency and accountability, etc.). Just like democracy activists need to be mindful not to fall into the trap of binary strategic thinking, critical scholars need to be aware that there are more roles to play than the proverbial "panda hugger" or "dragon slayer". Neither unconditional engagement nor reckless containment strategies will suffice when dealing with a formidable political opponent such as the Chinese party-state. As I have shown throughout this book, it is possible for us as independent and critical scholars to seek a third position where one does not align oneself with a political faction, be it the CCP in mainland China, the KMT or DPP in Taiwan or the DP or localist parties in Hong Kong.

In a recent Twitter debate about attitudes among non-Chinese China experts towards the Chinese party-state, Bernt Berger from the German Council on Foreign Relations made the point that "it is not my job as an independent scholar to enter the activist realm and go and try to change China. That is on the Chinese people."[28] I would argue that when non-Chinese scholars, as outsiders, critique authoritarianism in all three regions, this does not make them activists hell-bent on changing China against her will. Instead, in this book I have argued that any kind of socially and politically engaged scholarship should by default critique unaccountable, intransparent and arbitrary use of political power. In this book I also introduced the three categories of anti-establishment, pro-establishment and trans-establishment. This means that those China watchers who feel uncomfortable critiquing the CCP publicly can also choose to occupy a trans-establishment position, which in equal measure pays attention to what could be termed "official" (represented by the party-state) and "unofficial China" (which includes the civil rights movement and mainland China's nascent civil society).

Quo vadis?

In Chapter 2 I concurred with Godement's critique of naive beliefs in an "'the end of history': a benign Jurgen Habermas-Barack Obama project supported by a gaggle of economists"[29] and argued that history has returned. Rather than seeing the year 2018 as a turning point in mainland China's political development, I argued that the year 1989 was the key pivotal moment in mainland China's political development, which firmly set the country on its current development trajectory. In Chapter 3 I referred to the scholarship of German historian Reinhart Koselleck, who has argued that in order to interpret history scholars must familiarise themselves with their studied protagonists' "spaces of experience" as well as "horizons of expectation".[30] I critiqued the tendency in democratisation studies to exclusively look back and merely offer post facto rationalisations of concluded political development processes. I argued that democratisation studies need to overcome its theoretical stasis by linking theory and practice, by borrowing from the anthropological concept of *emic* and *etic* approaches, and by embracing the TOC discourse pioneered in the field of development studies. Based on this critique of conventional democratisation studies I offered three TOPC which can be useful both for *post facto* analysis of political history as well as for *ex ante* strategic planning in the struggle for democracy, in mainland China, Taiwan and Hong Kong, as well as in other parts of the world. The problem with the "horizons of expectation", however, is that only time will tell whose analysis or advocacy turned out to be prophetic.

I also argued that comparative scholarship about political development in the three regions is noticeably absent, and where attempts have been made to offer more poignant analysis they have often fallen short. In the following I would like to reflect on overly optimistic views of the regions' future which have proven to be wrong. In 1998, the Dutch journalist Willem van Kemenade published his highly thought-provoking book *China, Hong Kong, Taiwan, Inc.* In his afterword he speculated about future developments and argued that

> President Lee Teng-hui, reviled by Beijing, will have departed from the scene in the year 2000. A new leader, possibly from the DPP, will not necessarily be easier to tackle, but a new leaf can be turned and a new relationship with the Chinese leadership could emerge. These developments might coincide with the slow but irresistible trend towards liberalization on the mainland. A Chinese admission that any reunification deal should be acceptable to the people of democratic Taiwan could then pave the way for peaceful reunification in the distant future on the basis of a new formula, acceptable to both sides. In the meantime, the China–Hong Kong–Taiwan economic "triangle" will emerge as a more unified voice in the region in the near future.[31]

Ten years on, Larry Diamond came to similarly overoptimistic conclusions:

> China today is dramatically different from Taiwan, then and now. Its path and pace of regime transformation will not follow Taiwan's. But

many of the political and normative consequences of economic development will be the same. If new generations of Chinese political leaders,
technocrats, entrepreneurs, intellectuals, and artists can be vigorously and
yet respectfully engaged, the political outcome will, sooner or later, likely
be the same as in Taiwan: some form of genuine democracy.[32]

As I argued in Chapter 2, such assessments should be seen as grounded in
modernisation theory, which does not apply to the case of mainland China. The
short shelf life of such projections about the regions' political future should
caution any observer trying to look into the proverbial crystal ball.

Conscious of the fact that my following musings may turn out to be equally
incorrect, I will offer a far more pessimistic outlook for the region. What we
are witnessing, both on the global level and in the East Asian region, are
contradictory trends towards economic entanglement *and* political fragmentation. While modernisation theorists have long assumed that economic development would trigger political liberalisation and democratisation, the trajectory of
mainland China suggests that in its open-ended development processes an
increasing militarisation of state and society is equally possible. In this book I
have shown how in the case of both Taiwan and Hong Kong, their respective
democracy movements have become entangled in ethnic conflict and have given
birth to nativist and nationalist political parties advocating self-determination
and/or independence. The rise of Taiwanese and Hong Kong nationalism is evident from public opinion surveys conducted in both regions. They suggest that
nativist sentiment is clearly on the rise (see Figure 11.1). A longitudinal public
opinion survey conducted by Taiwan's National Chengchi University since 1992
highlights that by 2014 more than 60 percent of its respondents identified exclusively as Taiwanese (台湾人). Only a few respondents subscribed to being
exclusively Chinese (中国人) and also the support for seeing oneself as
both Taiwanese and Chinese (都是) dropped sharply.[33] Hong Kong University's Public Opinion Programme revealed a similar trend in the
HKSAR. In the years 2013 and 2014 increasing numbers of respondents
declared themselves as Hong Kongers (香港人), rather than as Chinese
citizens (中国人), Asians (亚洲人), members of the Chinese race (中华民族
一份子), citizens of PRC (中华人民共和国国民) or global citizens (世界公
民) (see Figure 11.2).[34]

As a post-positivist researcher I am fully aware of the shortcomings of
the design of such public opinion surveys. Yet from a longitudinal perspective I would concede that they do accurately trace changing public
sentiments in both regions. In Chapters 8 and 10 I critiqued the rise of
nativism and nationalism in Taiwan and Hong Kong. What I find worry-
ing is that we are now witnessing the emergence of three forms of
nationalism in all three regions: a CCP-led militant nationalism aimed at
preserving mainland China's crony-capitalist political regime; a Taiwanese
variant which has moved from ethnic, cultural to a more civic form of

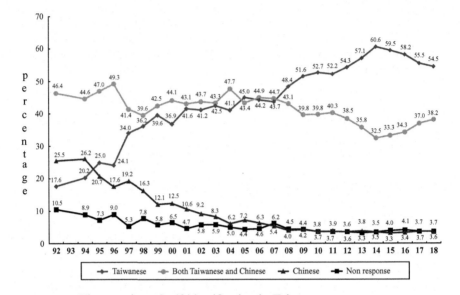

FIGURE 11.1 The question of self-identification in Taiwan
Source: Election Study Center, National Chengchi University (2019), Taiwanese/
Chinese Identity (June 1992–December 2018). Available online: https://esc.nccu.
edu.tw/course/news.php?Sn=166# (accessed 24 February 2019)

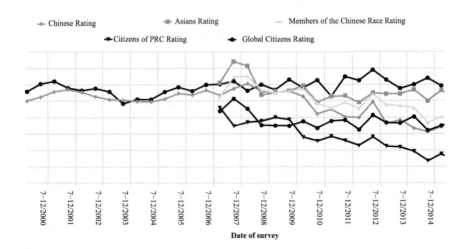

FIGURE 11.2 Changing self-identification in Hong Kong
Source: Public Opinion Programme, University of Hong Kong, Strength of Identity, Combined Charts (half-yearly average) (July–December 1997–July–December
2018). Available online: www.hkupop.hku.hk/english/popexpress/ethnic/overall/
halfyr/overall_halfyr_chart.html (accessed 24 February 2019)

nationalism; and a nascent Hong Kong nationalism which could either take on the form of an ethnic and cultural or civic nationalism.

My concern about this coming clash of nationalisms is that it appears to me that some democrats in Taiwan and Hong Kong seem to have concluded that they need to beat the CCP at its own game. This, however, is intellectually, ethically and politically short-sighted and could be self-defeating. Tong Lam has rightly pointed out that

> Chinese nationalism should not be seen as a totalizing ideology but as an agglomeration of interests, ideas, and practices that are appropriated by the state, business corporations, intellectuals and the middle class for different purposes. Yet despite the tension and incongruity between the official and popular forms of Chinese nationalism, the content underneath is strikingly homogeneous and monolithic. Expressions of Chinese nationalism, regardless whether they are spontaneous, state-sponsored, or commercially driven, are all articulated in terms of the simple East–West or China–U.S. binary opposition. Furthermore, the singularity and simplicity of this worldview tends to systematically overlook internal differences—for example, suppressing dissenting political voices and ignoring the rights of minorities and women, the interests of Tibet, the independent status of Taiwan, and the autonomy of Hong Kong.[35]

Taiwanese nationalists may argue that only by "consolidating" Taiwan's national identity the island state will be able to defend itself against an increasingly militaristic CCP. A survey conducted by the DPP-leaning Taiwan Foundation for Democracy found in spring 2018 that nearly "70 percent of Taiwanese are willing to go to war if China were to attempt to annex Taiwan by force".[36] Should a war between the PRC and ROC happen in the foreseeable future, and if Taiwan were able to defend itself, Taiwanese nationalists would be able to claim that there were no alternatives to their uncompromising stance and that, in Saul Alinsky's words, *particular* ends justify *particular* means. But having studied Taiwan's democratisation for the past 20 years, I am not convinced. Not only was the nationalist turn in Taiwan due to the manipulation of the DPP's NT faction. Within the DPP, there have also been middle-of-the-road reformers like former party chairman Xu Xinliang, who in the mid-1990s explored ways of peaceful co-existence between a civic form of Taiwanese nationalism and the CCP's militant nationalism. Unfortunately, his concept of Taiwanese citizens, as the "rising people" with "a restless always-on-the-move spirit with which the Taiwanese, being descendants of settlers, have been endowed and which underlies all past civilizations that reset the course of history" did not gain widespread political and popular support.[37] The problem is that when political leaders bank on nationalisms to solve interstate relations, the most likely solution will be war. Elizabeth Economy has rightly pointed out that "China's military expansionism in the

South China Sea and claim to sovereignty over Taiwan pose a significant threat to peace and stability in the Asia Pacific region".[38]

A war in the Taiwan Straits, however, would not only be catastrophic for both sides but would also have the potential to develop from a regional war into another world war. This is why I would argue that activists need to be more imaginative and find ways to build bridges between their respective democracy movements. It is important to bear in mind that not only in Taiwan but also in mainland China and Hong Kong there are voices calling for moderation. Liu Xiaobo and the signatories of Charter 08 have suggested that the conflict between the PRC and ROC could be solved peacefully by establishing a federated republic. The signatories argue that a

> democratic China should seek to act as a responsible major power contributing toward peace and development in the Asian Pacific region by approaching others in a spirit of equality and fairness. In Hong Kong and Macao, we should support the freedoms that already exist. With respect to Taiwan, we should declare our commitment to the principles of freedom and democracy and then, negotiating as equals, and ready to compromise, seek a formula for peaceful unification. We should approach disputes in the national-minority areas of China with an open mind, seeking ways to find a workable framework within which all ethnic and religious groups can flourish. We should aim ultimately at a federation of democratic communities of China.[39]

Benny Tai, the visionary behind Hong Kong's OCLP movement, has similarly argued "that following the end of 'dictatorship' in China, the country's various ethnic groups could exercise their right to self-determination and decide how they could link up with each other. 'We could consider going independent, being part of a federal system or a confederation system similar to that of the European Union', he said."[40] This suggests, that the "horizons of expectation" among mainland Chinese and Hong Kong democrats includes a vision of peaceful co-existence for all three regions.

In the coming years it will be the responsibility of activists and academics to find creative ways to overcome their differences and find common ground. Scholars and students of democratisation processes should continue to find ways to overcome the limitations of democratisation studies in general and modernisation theory in particular. This book can now also serve as a cognitive map for democracy activists in mainland China, Taiwan and Hong Kong and help them reflect on their respective reform strategies and tactics. It is my hope that with the help of this publication I will have made a small contribution to preserving peace, not only within mainland China, but also between mainland China, Taiwan and Hong Kong.

Notes

1 Bakken, Børge (2004), Norms, Values and Cynical Games with Party Ideology, in: Kjeld Erik Brødsgaard and Yongnian Zheng (Eds), *Bringing the Party Back In: How China Is Governed*, Eastern Universities Press, Singapore, 51.
2 *Sydney Morning Herald* (2014), Hungry Like the Wolf. Available online: www.smh.com.au/world/hungry-like-the-wolf-20140707-3bh7j.html
3 *Taiwan Sentinel* (2018), China Acting on "Lebanonization" Threat against Taiwan.
4 Ibid.
5 Menefee, Trey (2018), "I guess just agree to disagree that we can extrapolate many foreign policy implications from how the CCP works in HK and Taiwan. There's some overlap in UF behavior, but examples like hiring out triads are sui generis to those contexts." 12 December. Tweet. Available online: https://twitter.com/Comparativist/status/1072749611972849664 (accessed 12 December 2018).
6 Nathan, Andrew J. (2017), Introduction, in: Zhiyong Xu, *To Build a Free China: A Citizen's Journey*, translated by Joshua Rosenzweig and Yaxue Cao, Lynne Rienner, Boulder, CO, 11.
7 Ribao, Renmin (2018), Jianjue fandui zuo liangmian ren. Available online: http://paper.people.com.cn/rmrb/html/2018-07/02/nw.D110000renmrb_20180702_3-07.htm (accessed 11 January 2019).
8 Nunes, Rodrigo (2014), *Organisation of the Organisationless: Collective Action after Networks*, PML Books, Lueneburg, 41.
9 Burton, Michael G., Gunther, Richard and Higley, John (Eds) (1992), Introduction to *Elite Transformations and Democratic Regimes*, Cambridge University Press, Cambridge, 1–38.
10 Roetz, Heiner (2016), Who Is Engaged in the "Complicity of Power"? On the Difficulties Sinology Has with Dissent and Transcendence, in: Nahum Brown and William Franke (Eds), *Transcendence, Immanence, and Intercultural Philosophy*, Palgrave Macmillan, Cham, 284.
11 Ibid., 285.
12 Ibid., 307.
13 Ibid.
14 Bartsch, Bernhard (2018), "Lately I brought up #Xinjiang in discussions with half a dozen delegations from #China. None of them was upset by the issue. Who did get upset were some Europeans—who worried about the Chinese being upset. The powerful get so much empathy these days!" 6 December. Tweet. Available online: https://twitter.com/bernhardbartsch/status/1070946501415841794 (accessed 11 December 2018).
15 Roetz, Heiner (2016), Who Is Engaged in the "Complicity of Power"? On the Difficulties Sinology Has with Dissent and Transcendence, in: Nahum Brown and William Franke (Eds), *Transcendence, Immanence, and Intercultural Philosophy*, Palgrave Macmillan, Cham, 288.
16 Freire, Paulo (2014), *Pedagogy of the Oppressed*, Bloomsbury Academic, New York, 30.
17 Balding, Christopher (2018), "If you accept Party money and are featured in Chinese state media, you should ask yourself 'where did I as an intellectual go wrong?' Probably over envelopes of cash for speaking engagements." 10 December. Tweet.

Available online: https://twitter.com/BaldingsWorld/status/1072311944445612034 (accessed 12 December 2018).

18 Brady, Ann-Marie (2017), Magic Weapons: China's Political Influence Activities under Xi Jinping. Available online: www.wilsoncenter.org/sites/default/files/for_website_magicweaponsanne-mariesbradyseptember2017.pdf (accessed 12 December 2018).

19 Sinopsis (2018), Open Letter on Harassment Campaign against Anne-Marie Brady. Available online: https://sinopsis.cz/en/open-letter-on-harassment-campaign-against-anne-marie-brady-2/ (accessed 12 December 2018).

20 Ibid.

21 Chen, Yuwen (2012). "Xinjiang 13" Revisited, *Asian Ethnicity*, 13(1), 111.

22 ChinaFile (2018), How Should the World Respond to Intensifying Repression in Xinjiang? Available online: www.chinafile.com/conversation/how-should-world-respond-intensifying-repression-xinjiang (accessed 12 December 2018).

23 Xinjiang Initiative (2018). Available online: https://xinjianginitiative.wixsite.com/xjinitiative (accessed 12 December 2018).

24 Statement by Concerned Scholars on China's Mass Detention of Turkic Minorities (2018) Available online: https://concernedscholars.home.blog (accessed 12 December 2018).

25 ChinaFile (2018), We Need to Be Careful about How We Use the Word "Chinese". Available online: www.chinafile.com/reporting-opinion/viewpoint/we-need-be-careful-about-how-we-use-word-chinese (accessed 12 December 2018).

26 Friedberg, Aaron (2018), Competing with China, *Survival*, 60(3), 8.

27 Hoffman, Samantha (2016), "Dangerous Love": China's All-Encompassing Security Vision. Available online: https://nationalinterest.org/feature/dangerous-love-chinas-all-encompassing-security-vision-16239 (accessed 13 December 2018).

28 Berger, Bernt (2018), "It is a fact. But maybe less today than perhaps 10 years ago. But it is not my job as an independent scholar to enter the activist realm and go and try to change China. That is on the Chinese people. Remember: nation states are also our export." Tweet. Available online: https://twitter.com/bernt_berger/status/1075768991207968773 (accessed 12 January 2019).

29 Godement, Francois (2018), Xi's Rule for Life: What Does Our Anxiety Reveal?, European Council on Foreign Relations. Available online: www.ecfr.eu/article/commentary_xis_rule_for_life_what_does_our_anxiety_reveal (accessed 13 August 2018).

30 Koselleck, R. (2004), *Futures Past: On the Semantics of Historical Time*, translated by Keith Tribe, Columbia University Press, New York.

31 Van Kemenade, Willem (1998), *Hong Kong, Taiwan, Inc.*, Vintage Books, New York, 417–18.

32 Diamond, Larry (2008), Why China's Democratic Transition Will Differ from Taiwan's, in: Bruce Gilley and Larry Diamond (Eds), *Political Change in China: Comparisons with Taiwan*, Lynne Rienner, Boulder, CO, 256.

33 Election Center National Chengchi University (2018), Taiwanese/Chinese Identity (1992/06–2018/06). Available online: https://esc.nccu.edu.tw/app/news.php?Sn=166 (accessed 15 December 2018).

34 Menefee, Trey (2015), The Coming Storm of Hong Kong Nationalism. Available online: www.comparativist.org/?p=1665 (accessed 6 December 2016).

35 Lam, Tong (2000), Identity and Diversity: The Complexities and Contradictions of Chinese Nationalism, in: Weston, Timothy and Jensen, Lionel (Eds), *China beyond the Headlines*, Rowman and Littlefield, Lanham, MD, 164.

36 *Taipei Times* (2018), Taiwanese Willing to Fight China. Available online: www.taipeitimes.com/News/front/archives/2018/04/20/2003691661 (accessed 13 December 2018).

37 Liao, Sebastian Hsien-Hao (2000), Becoming Cyborgian: Postmodernism and Nationalism in Contemporary Taiwan, Duke University Press, Durham, NC, 191.
38 Economy, Elizabeth (2018), *The Third Revolution: Xi Jinping and the New Chinese State*, Oxford University Press, New York, 242.
39 Link, Perry (2009), China's Charter 08, *New York Review of Books*, 15 January. Available online: www.nybooks.com/articles/2009/01/15/chinas-charter-08/ (accessed 14 May 2019).
40 *South China Morning Post* (2018), Hong Kong Government "Shocked" by Occupy Leader Benny Tai's Independence Comments at Taiwan Seminar. Available online: www.scmp.com/news/hong-kong/politics/article/2139698/hong-kong-governm ent-shocked-occupy-leader-benny-tais (accessed 13 December 2018).

APPENDIX

TABLE A.1 Cycles of democracy movements in mainland China, Taiwan and Hong Kong, 1969–2018

PRC	1989	1998	2008	2009–
Cycle of democracy movement	Episode 1: Anti-corruption and pro-democracy movement	Episode 2: China Democracy Party	Episode 3: Charter 08	Episode 4: New Citizen movement
Antecedents and political opportunities	Hu Yaobang's death Corruption and collusion Disillusionment with CCP rule after Cultural Revolution	Bill Clinton and United Nations High Commissioner for Human Rights Mary Robinson visit to China in 1998; amendment of criminal law; signing of United Nations Covenant on Economic, Social and Cultural Rights; Release of Wei Jingsheng	Charter 77, anticipation of major political changes in 2009 due to 20th anniversary of 4 June crackdown, 50th anniversary of the exile of the Dalai Lama, 60th anniversary of the founding of the People's Republic of China, and 90th anniversary of 4 May movement	Charter 08; brief honeymoon between liberal and incoming Xi Jinping, who had signalled interest in constitutionalism
Key actors	Students Workers Intellectuals	Anti-establishment intellectuals, owners of small businesses, ordinary workers	Signatories from the anti-establishment, pro-establishment and trans-establishment reform camps	Political, social, cultural and peaceful progressive movement; loose network
Strategic reform approach	Anti-establishment (workers), trojan horse (students) and trans-establishment (intellectuals)	Trojan horse	Anti-establishment; Charter 08 offers an umbrella platform for all three reform camps	Anti-establishment, trojan horse and trans-establishment at the same time

(Continued)

TABLE A.1 (*Cont.*)

Taiwan	1969–86	1986–2000	2000–8	2008–16
Unfinished cycle of democracy movement	Episode 5: *Dangwai* (lit. outside the party) movement	Episode 6: Democratic Progressive Party	Episode 7: Chen Shui-bian presidency (DPP)	Episode 8: Ma Ying-jeou presidency (KMT)
Antecedents and political opportunities	Taiwanisation of KMT; supplementary parliamentary elections since 1969; inability to co-opt all aspiring politicians into KMT ranks	Successful founding of DPP in 1986; DPP party platform; adoption of Leninist party structure; rampant factionalism; from party movement to nation-building party; elite settlement within the DPP leads to ideological rift with KMT and CCP	Tactical DPP moderation throughout the 1990s; split pan-blue camp in 1999 leads to Chen's victory in 2000; DPP with minority in parliament	Chen Shui-bian's "unfortunate presidency" leads to 2008 election victories for KMT followed by indictment and imprisonment of Chen Shui-bian; KMT regains both presidency and parliamentary majority
Key actors	Critics of KMT one-party rule; Taiwanese nationalists; religious activists; young and well-educated reformers within and outside KMT; moderate and radical *dangwai* factions; social movements	Radical-turned-moderate Formosa faction vs militant New Tide faction; centrist DPP politicians who rely on tacit support of New Tide faction	Chen Shui-bian; New Tide faction; disloyal opposition (KMT, PFP) engaging in "third united front" with CCP	Ma Ying-jeou presidency and KMT majority in parliament; weakened DPP in opposition; re-emergence of social movements; Sunflower movement 2014
Strategic reform approach	Combination of anti-establishment and trojan horse, *dangwai* movement held together by trans-establishment politician Kang Ning-hsiang	Anti-establishment (DPP leadership) and trojan horse (New Tide faction)	Trojan horse (Chen Shui-bian in alliance with New Tide faction)	Trojan horse (Ma Ying-jeou in alliance with "old guard" of KMT)

(*Continued*)

PRC	1989	1998	2008	2009–
Hong Kong	*1984–97*	*2003*	*2012*	*2014–*
Unfinished cycle of democracy movement	Episode 9: Fragmentation of Hong Kong's pan-democratic camp	Episode 10: 2003 movement against the enactment of Article 23 of the Basic Law	Episode 11: 2012 movement against Moral and National Education Policy	Episode 12: From OCLP/ UM to Hong Kong independence movement
Antecedents and political opportunities	Green Paper 1984 White Paper 1988 Electoral reforms 1993–4	CCP's handling of SARS epidemic in mainland China, stalling of LegCo reforms	Moral and civic education since 2001, coming of age of first generation of young Hong Kong people after handover	Basic Law review of chief executive election procedures
Key actors	Governor Chris Patten, pan-democracy camp	Christian churches Pro-democracy camp	Scholarism, national education Parents' concern group, Civil Alliance against the National Education, Anonymous	Benny Tai, Christian churches, Scholarism and Hong Kong Federation of Students
Strategic reform approach	Trojan horse	Anti-establishment	Anti-establishment	Trans-establishment (OCLP), anti-establishment (UM), and trojan horse (localists)

INDEX

British Foreign and Commonwealth
Office xiv
British Governor Chris Patten 4, 168, see
Patten, Chris
Brown, Jeremy 77
Buckley, Chris 15, 24, 103
Burcu, Oana xv
Burton, Michael 51, 107, 147, 219
business 7, 21–22, 24, 26, 28, 30, 49, 85,
105, 109, 129, 131, 161, 169, 176–177,
179, 181, 183, 191, 199, 205, 213,
216, 229

Cabestan, Jean-Pierre xv
cables 11, 28, 56, 156, see Wikileaks
cadres 21–22, 25–26, 29, 31, 80, 84–85,
88, 91, 99, 108, 125, 144
campaign 11, 18, 43, 63, 76, 87, 99, 114,
129, 136, 147, 169–170, 192–193,
197–198, 202–203, 205, 223–224
capacity building xiii–xiv
capitalist modes of production 18–19
carcinogenic gutter oil 30
Carl von Ossietzky 110
Carothers, Thomas 16
carrots and sticks 84, 129, 212
causal relationship 16, see correlation
censorship 8–9, 40, 169, 172, 176–177,
179, 183, 219–220
Central Military Commission 17
centralism 4, 75, 129
Chai, Ling 42
Chang, Michael xi
Changchun 76
Charter 08 48, 98, 108–113, 115–116,
215–216, 230
Charter 77 108, 111
Cheek, Timothy 75
Chen, Dongdong 23
Chen, Jieren 28
Chen, Minglu 23
Chen, Shui-bian 51, 123, 137, 142, 146,
152–157, 217
Chen, Xi 86
Chen, Yun 28
Cheng, Edmund xv
Cheng, Tun-Jen 54, 123, 130–132, 135,
146
Chiang, Kai-shek 74, 124–127, 129–130,
132–133, 135, 143
child welfare xiv
China Association for NGO
Cooperation xiii
China Central Television 28
China Democracy Party 98, 104

China Social Sector Pioneer Program xiv
China: experts 15, 223, 225; observers of
224; official and unofficial 224; policy
221, 225; practitioners 7, 10, 45;
watchers 45, 222, 225
ChinaFile 45, 223
Chinese Academy of Social Sciences 29
Chinese Communist Party xii, 1, 72, 75,
78, 90, 134, 151, 173, 224
Chinese Communist Party, 1–7, 12,
15–25, 27, 29, 31–32, 42, 47–49, 51,
53–54, 72–92, 99, 103–108, 110, 113,
115–117, 124, 128–130, 154, 160–161,
169, 172, 175–177, 179–180, 183,
189–190, 192, 195, 198–201, 204–206,
208, 212–216, 218–225, 227, 229
Chinese Democracy and Justice
Party 106
Chinese People's Political Consultative
Conference 24, 83
Ci, Jiwei 30
citizens xv, 2, 6, 8, 11, 17–20, 23–25,
31–32, 47–48, 50–51, 79, 84, 86–87,
89, 92, 100, 109–115, 117, 131–132,
137, 158, 169, 172, 180, 190, 216, 222,
224, 227–229
civic groups 18, 54, 203, 205, see civil
society
civil society organisations 106
civil society: dialogues xiv; Lebanisation
of Taiwan's 214
Clarke, Donald 78
climate change xiv
Clinton, Bill 105
Clinton, Hillary 59
co-optation 24, 72, 84–85, 129–130, 178,
182, 193, 212, 217, 225
coercion 61, 68, 72, 84, 129, 212
cognitive map 111, 230
Coleman, James 16
collectivisation 78, 81, 128,
collusion 11, 21–22, 25, 30–31, 88, 99,
113–114, 213, see corruption and
anti-corruption
colonial: era 12; policing 170
Comintern 73–74, 76
communes 80–81
communication and collaboration
conference model xiv
community-based organisations 10
Confucianism 91, 127
constituency 112, 115, 145, 181, 207
constitutionalism 54, 90
contradictions 41, 64, 83, 87, 102,124
convergence 3, 16, 51

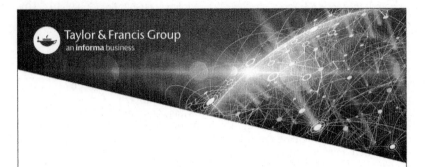